SOFTWARE ENGINEERING
FOR LARGE SOFTWARE SYSTEMS

Proceedings of the Centre for Software Reliability Conference entitled

Large Software Systems
held at The Watershed Media Centre, Bristol, UK
26–29 September 1989

Members of the Centre for Software Reliability

T. ANDERSON, Centre for Software Reliability, University of Newcastle upon Tyne, UK

K. BENNETT, School of Engineering and Applied Science, University of Durham, UK

R.E. BLOOMFIELD, Adelard, London, UK

R.J. COLE, Glasgow College, Glasgow, UK

C.J. DALE, CITI, Milton Keynes, UK

B. DE NEUMANN, Department of Mathematics, The City University, London, UK

J.E. DOBSON, Computing Laboratory, University of Newcastle upon Tyne, UK

N. FENTON, Centre for Software Reliability, The City University, London, UK

G.D. FREWIN, Standard Telecommunications Laboratories, Harlow, UK

M.A. HENNEL, Department of Statistics and Computational Mathematics, University of Liverpool, UK

D. INCE, Open University, Milton Keynes, UK

A.A. KAPOSI, South Bank Polytechnic, London, UK

B.A. KITCHENHAM, National Computing Centre, Manchester, UK

B. LITTLEWOOD, Centre for Software Reliability, The City University, London, UK

J. MCDERMID, Department of Computer Science, University of York, UK

R. MALCOLM, CAP Scientific, London, UK

P. MELLOR, Centre for Software Reliability, The City University, London, UK

M. MOULDING, Royal Military College of Science, Swindon, UK

M. OULD, PRAXIS, Bath, UK

P. ROOK, Marlow, UK

S. STOCKMAN, British Telecom Research Laboratories, Ipswich, UK

J.G. WALKER, STC Technology Ltd, Newcastle under Lyme, UK

A.A. WINGROVE, Farnborough, Hants, UK

R. WITTY, Software Engineering, Rutherford Laboratories, Didcot, UK

SOFTWARE ENGINEERING FOR LARGE SOFTWARE SYSTEMS

Edited by

B.A. KITCHENHAM

Software Metrics Consultant,
The National Computing Centre,
Manchester, UK

ELSEVIER APPLIED SCIENCE
LONDON and NEW YORK

ELSEVIER SCIENCE PUBLISHERS LTD
Crown House, Linton Road, Barking, Essex IG11 8JU, England

Sole Distributor in the USA and Canada
ELSEVIER SCIENCE PUBLISHING CO., INC.
655 Avenue of the Americas, New York, NY 10010, USA

WITH 46 ILLUSTRATIONS

British Library Cataloguing in Publication Data

Centre for Software Reliability, Conference (*6th; 1989;*
Watershed Media Centre)
Software engineering for large software systems.
1. Computer systems. Software. Development and maintenance.
Management
I. Title   II. Kitchenham, B.A.
005.1

Library of Congress CIP data applied for

ISBN-13: 978-94-010-6833-8   e-ISBN-13: 978-94-009-0771-3
DOI: 10.1007/978-94-009-0771-3

Softcover reprint of the hardcover 1st edition 1990

Preface

These proceedings include tutorials and papers presented at the Sixth CSR Conference on the topic of Large Software Systems. The aim of the Conference was to identify solutions to the problems of developing and maintaining large software systems, based on approaches which are currently being undertaken by software practitioners. These proceedings are intended to make these solutions more widely available to the software industry.

The papers from software practitioners describe:

- important working systems, highlighting their problems and successes;
- techniques for large system development and maintenance, including project management, quality management, incremental delivery, system security, independent V & V, and reverse engineering.

In addition, academic and industrial researchers discuss the practical impact of current research in formal methods, object-oriented design and advanced environments.

The keynote paper is provided by Professor Brian Warboys of ICL and the University of Manchester, who masterminded the development of the ICL VME Operating System, and the production of the first database-driven software engineering environment (CADES).

The proceedings commence with reports of the two tutorial sessions which preceded the conference:

- Professor Keith Bennett of the Centre for Software Maintenance at Durham University on Software Maintenance;
- Professor John McDermid of the University of York on Systems Engineering Environments for High Integrity Systems.

The remaining papers deal with reports on existing systems (starting with Professor Warboys' keynote paper), approaches to large systems development, methods for large systems maintenance and the expected impact of current research.

I should like to thank Professor Darrel Ince, Professor Bernard de Neumann and Mr John Walker for their help with the preparation of the conference programme, and Ms Carol Allen of the Centre for Software Reliability (City University) for organising the conference.

BARBARA KITCHENHAM

Contents

List of Contributors

K.H. BENNETT
Centre for Software Maintenance, University of Durham, Durham DH1 3LE, UK

B. CHATTERS
ICL Mainframe Systems, Wenlock Way, West Gorton, Manchester M12 5DR, UK

J. DOBSON
Computing Laboratory, University of Newcastle upon Tyne, Newcastle upon Tyne NE1 7RU, UK

D.R. GRAHAM
Grove Consultants, Grove House, 40 Ryles Park Road, Macclesfield SK11 8AH, UK

R.N. HALL
GEC Avionics Ltd, Airport Works, Rochester, Kent ME1 2XX, UK

S. LINKMAN
STC Technology Ltd, Copthall House, Nelson Place, Newcastle under Lyme, Staffordshire ST5 1EZ, UK

B. MALCOLM
Malcolm Associates Ltd, Savoy Hill House, Savoy Hill, London WC2, UK

J.A. McDERMID
Department of Computer Science, University of York, York YO1 5DD, UK

C. MINKOWITZ
STC Technology Ltd, Copthall House, Nelson Place, Newcastle under Lyme, Staffordshire ST5 1EZ, UK

T.A. PARKER

ICL Defence Systems, Eskdale Road, Winnersh, Wokingham, Berks RG11 5TT, UK

L. PICKARD

STC Technology Ltd, Copthall House, Nelson Place, Newcastle under Lyme, Staffordshire ST5 1EZ, UK

K.J. PULFORD

GEC–Marconi Software Systems, Elstree Way, Borehamwood, Herts WD6 1RX, UK

N. ROSS

STC Technology Ltd, Copthall House, Nelson Place, Newcastle under Lyme, Staffordshire ST5 1EZ, UK

I. SOMMERVILLE

Computing Department, Lancaster University, Lancaster LA1 4YR, UK

S.G. STOCKMAN

Systems and Software Engineering, Research Division, British Telecom Research Laboratories, Martlesham Heath, Suffolk, UK

B. WARBOYS

Department of Computer Science, University of Manchester, Oxford Road, Manchester M13 9PL, UK

R.H. WARDEN

K3 Group Ltd, Severn House, Prescott Drive, Worcester WR4 9NE, UK

P. WESTMACOTT

STC Technology Ltd, Copthall House, Nelson Place, Newcastle under Lyme, Staffordshire ST5 1EZ, UK

S.C. WILLMOTT

UK Civil Aviation Authority, CAA House, 45–59 Kingsway, London WC2B 6TE, UK

J.C.P. WOODCOCK

Oxford University Computing Laboratory, Programming Research Group, 8–11 Keble Road, Oxford OX1 3QD, UK

1

THE SOFTWARE MAINTENANCE OF LARGE SOFTWARE SYSTEMS:
MANAGEMENT, METHODS AND TOOLS

K H Bennett

Centre for Software Maintenance
University of Durham
Durham
England
DH1 3LE

Abstract

Software Maintenance is the general name given to the set of activities undertaken on a software system following its release for operational use. Surveys have shown that for many projects, software maintenance consumes the majority of the overall software lifecycle costs, and there are indications that the proportion is increasing. Our inability to cope with software maintenance can also result in a backlog of application modifications.

Sustaining the viability of a large software system over many years at an acceptable quality level is a major challenge. This paper discusses the management of the software maintenance process addressing both the organisational context and the implementation of the management plan in terms of the methods available and the tool support for those methods.

1 Introduction

The development of a software system is complete when the product is delivered to the customer or client, and the software installed and released for operational use. We shall use the term *software maintenance* to encompass the activities (technical and managerial) that are undertaken on the software subsequently. The term *software maintenance* has become well established in the computing profession, but in many ways it is an unfortunate choice of words, suggesting parallels or similarities with hardware maintenance. Hardware maintenance is required because of the progressive degradation or wearing out of physical materials whereas software is not subject to

1

such factors.

It is recognised that some organisations use terms such as *enhancement* or *system redevelopment* to express activities that we shall classify as software maintenance. Some professionals use software maintenance to refer only to bug-fixing. We justify the broader definition of the term because the management approach, the methods and the tool support are common, yet differ substantially from initial development.

We shall argue in section two that the major concern of software maintenance is with system *evolution*. There is hence a strong relationship between software maintenance and software reliability, since it is not sufficient simply to produce a reliable system in the first place: the reliability of that system must be sustained over a period of many years, in the face of staff turnover, changes in software technology , and new management methods. Military software in particular may have a lifetime of several decades. It is not sensible to argue that software should not change. It seems inevitable that the more successful a software system is, the more pressing will be the demands for it to evolve to meet new requirements.

Software maintenance has traditionally been regarded as of very low status within the computing community. Schneidewind (Schneidewind 1987) in his survey paper concludes that there is a general acknowledgement that the subject is an important area but at the same time that there is a substantial technical neglect in the study of it. In other engineering disciplines, maintenance is not a professional - track career (e.g. motor-car maintenance, lawnmower maintenance etc.) and this is another reason why the term software maintenance is not ideal. In the USA, there are attempts to change the name to *software management* to avoid the unwelcome connotations of maintenance. However in this paper we shall use conventional terminology.

There are a number of indications that the status of software maintenance is improving, and this welcome change is addressed in Section 5. The remainder of the paper is structured as follows. Section 2 defines four categories of software maintenance, and assesses their economic implications. Section 3 addresses the problem of maintaining existing code, which typically is poorly documented and has been developed without the benefit of modern software engineering technology. Section 4 considers the production of software which is easy to maintain. We shall define the ease with which software can be maintained as its *maintainability*.

Finally, Section 6 suggests a number of areas which need further research and development.

2   What is software maintenance?

2.1   Four types of maintenance activity

Software maintenance is required for three principal reasons (Lientz & Swanson 1980, Lientz, Tompkins & Swanson 1978, Swanson 1976). Firstly, there may be a *fault* in the software, so that its behaviour does not conform to its specification. This fault may contradict the specification, or it may demonstrate that the specification is incomplete (or possibly inconsistent), so that the user's assumed specification is not sustained. Typically, the fault will have manifested itself in the form of an error when the program has been run, and the fault must be removed. This is termed *corrective maintenance*, though colloquially it is often called *bug-fixing*. The computing profession abounds with anecdotes of emergency repairs *(patching)* - these can cause great difficulties for subsequent maintenance work.

Even if a software system is fault-free, the environment in which it operates will often be subject to change. The manufacturer may introduce new versions of the operating system, or remove support for existing facilities. The software may be ported to a new environment, or to different hardware. Modifications performed as a result of changes to the external environment are categorised as *adaptive maintenance*.

The third category of maintenance is called *perfective maintenance*. This is undertaken as a consequence of a change in user requirements of the software. For example, a payroll suite may need to be altered to reflect new taxation laws; a real-time power station control system may need upgrading to meet new safety standards. A "rule of thumb" often used in industry is that around 10% of a software system will change each year because of modifications to the user requirements.

Finally, preventative maintenance may be undertaken on a system in order to anticipate future problems and make subsequent maintenance easier. For example, a particular part of a large suite may have been found to require sustained corrective maintenance over a period of time. It could be sensible to re-implement this part, using modern software engineering technology, in the expectation that subsequent errors will be much reduced.

As noted in Section 1, not all organisations recognise adaptive and perfective maintenance as such, classifying them as 'redevelopment', 'evolution' or 'enhancement'. We argue that there is a key difference between software development and software maintenance as defined here. In the former, the project is undertaken within a timescale, and to a budget. An identifiable product, meeting the original customer requirement, is the deliverable. In contrast, software maintenance is usually open ended, continuing for many years, and this is seen as a revenue item. It is often the objective to extend the life of the software system for as long as economically possible.

2.2 Cost of software maintenance

It is generally recognised that software maintenance consumes a large part of the life-cycle costs of a software product, and hence the total cost of maintenance is huge. At a recent workshop on maintenance (Munro & Calliss 1987), it was informally reported that in the UK, £1 Billion is spent on software maintenance, while in the US, 2% of the GNP is consumed by software maintenance. These figures must be taken simply as guesses, but there is general agreement in the community that the magnitude is very large. Only one major survey has been undertaken to try to quantify the cost. This was carried by out by Lientz and Swanson (Lientz et al, 1980) in the late 1970's, and produced a number of results of interest. The mean distribution of effort expended on maintenance in 487 DP organisations was found to be:

Perfective	50%
Adaptive	25%
Corrective	21%
Preventive	4%

This suggests that "corrective maintenance" is a relatively small proportion of software maintenance. Clearly, preventive maintenance is not undertaken to any significant degree in the computing industry.

Lientz and Swanson also found that many organisations were spending 20%-70% of their computing (EDP) effort on maintenance. The proportion was influenced by the type of organisation; for example, consultancies spend only a small revenue on maintenance while EDP organisations spend a very substantial part of their budget. Results described by Ditri (Ditri, Shaw & Atkins 1971) and Hoskyns Ltd (Hoskyns 1973) provide support for these figures, though it is difficult directly to compare results as costs may be measured in different ways.

So far, attention has been directed at the direct costs of maintenance, but there are indirect costs which are more difficult to quantify. Many organisations rely on I.T. to maintain a competitive edge, and hence their software systems must be modified quickly and reliably. Unfortunately, serious delays are incurred because perfective maintenance cannot achieve these goals. The problem is known as the *applications backlog*, and delays of up to two years have been reported informally. One management approach divides modifications into *essential* and *desirable* to attempt to alleviate the backlog, but the basic difficulty remains. It is also a powerful stimulus for computing to be taken on by the end user, who finally runs out of patience with the EDP department for taking so long to make what is considered a simple change!

Much of the technological development in software engineering has been focussed on the early, development phases. This has been based on the assumption that high software quality is an end-product of the initial development. However, quality must be sustained, perhaps over many years, in an *evolving* system. While development is clearly of great importance, all surveys confirm the general result that it is software maintenance which is costly and lacks R & D input. This is the seven-eighths of the iceberg, which lurks out of sight of the development team, but may cause the organisational ship to founder unless the problems are anticipated, and solutions planned.

3   The maintenance of existing code

3.1   Characteristics of existing code

There is an enormous financial investment in existing software which has been produced through conventional or ad-hoc software engineering methods. Most of the software that is currently being written falls into this category. It is economically infeasible simply to discard this software and replace it by either off-the-shelf packages (if they exist), or by a rewritten system using modern engineering approaches. Much of this software will be required for many years yet. Furthermore, such software represents the accumulation of years of experience and refinement, and however imperfect, it is a valuable asset! Such software has been termed 'geriatric code', referring to the problem of sustaining the viability of code written many years ago and modified subsequently in an unmanaged way.

The major problems of maintaining old software (Schneiderman 1987) are:

1. most existing software is unstructured, and much was produced before the introduction of structured programming methods (Zvegintzov 1983). Source codes may be written in assembler or even machine code.

2. maintenance programmers have not been involved in the development of a product and find it difficult to map program actions to program source codes

3. the documentation of software is often non-existent, or incomplete, or out of date (Chapin 1985). Even if it is available, the documentation may not actually help the maintenance staff in an effective way

4. the ripple effect of changes to source codes are difficult to predict (Yau & Collofello 1985).

A major concern of maintenance programmers is the avoidance of introducing more problems than are solved by a modification. It was reported that in OS/360 (Brooks 1975), the number of known faults reached a steady state, despite a continuing programme of corrective maintenance to eliminate them.

We shall consider the maintenance of existing code under the following headings:

- maintenance management

- change control and configuration management

- program evolution and lifecycle model

- maintenance metrics

- program comprehension

- software reusability

- inverse engineering

- quality assurance

3.2   Maintenance management

Maintenance may be organised according to several models. Traditionally, software maintenance has been regarded as the final phase of the software lifecycle which can be managed quite separately from development. The most extreme example of this occurs when an organisation hands over its system to an external contractor who takes over all responsibility for maintenance following an initial investigatory period. A small number of companies specialize in offering this type of service. More commonly, the software is developed by an in-house team and then passed over to a maintenance group.

A different model, less common but gaining in popularity, is to retain the same team both to develop and maintain a product. There is a stronger incentive for such a team to anticipate and prepare for maintenance. This approach may gain further acceptance as the status of software maintenance improves.

It is also possible to hand over responsibility for maintenance to the end-users. Tools such as *Fourth Generation Languages* (4GLs) claim to enable the user to construct rapid prototypes and maintenance is achieved by a throw-away policy. This model has obvious drawbacks and needs to be used with care (the corporate database cannot be maintained in this manner!) but the move to expanding system functionality by code from user-produced application generators is growing rapidly in some sectors.

The human aspects area of maintenance management needs careful attention to reduce the problems of perceived low status and poor career structure, with consequent job mobility. Although this is not a well documented area, some additional information is given in (Munro et al, 1987a), (Boehm 1983) and (Parikh 1986).

The ability of management to plan, monitor and control software maintenance depends on establishing clear methods. There are currently no commonly accepted or "industry-standard" methods for software maintenance, as exist for software development (e.g. JSD, SSADM, Yourdon etc). As a consequence, tool support for methods is fragmented, with particular tools addressing one maintenance activity in isolation from a general approach.

Yau and Collofello (Yau 1979) have identified four basic steps in managing the maintenance phase:

1. understanding of the software;

2. determination of why a change is needed and what method will be used;

3. implementing the change;

4. validating the change.

3.3   Program evolution and lifecycle models

Traditionally, software maintenance has remained a final, independent phase on most lifecycle models, which concentrate on the development phase. This has led to a number of criticisms (e.g. McCracken & Jackson 1982, Gladden 1982). A view put forward by Lehman and Belady (Lehman 1980, Lehman 1984, Belady & Lehman 1976) is that large software systems evolve over time and reach a state of stability through a process of incremental enhancement. This suggests that perfective maintenance should be undertaken as a series of modest subprojects, each with a modest goal and a budget of perhaps a few person-years. The major issues here are the intervals at which new system versions are released (see section 3.4); program comprehension and understanding in order to be able to make alterations to the program; and tracing the changes and retesting the altered program.

A major topic in current software development research is the IPSE (Integrated Project Support Environment) which aims to support an integrated toolset to meet the needs of all parts of the software project lifecycle. This work is not addressing adequately the needs of maintenance. As an example, an important consideration in the development of a maintenance lifecycle model is the inclusion of change request handling (a change request is an input from a user or customer asking for a specific corrective, perfective or adaptive maintenance task to be performed). Change requests need to be logged, coordinated, and related to the corresponding requirements, specification and design changes. The QA procedures (e.g. test suite runs and results) also need recording. The argument that IPSEs are simply a framework for a toolset is insufficient. Most IPSEs implicitly or explicitly use some model of software development in their architecture. In recognition of the existence of large amounts of geriatric code, the approach we are taking at Durham is to develop an integrated maintenance support environment, which at least addresses the method and tool needs of the maintenance phase in a coherent way.

3.4   Version control and configuration management

A software manufacturer sells n copies of a program suite; in due course, a customer reports an error, and the manufacturer dispatches a fix to the complainant. Other customers report different bugs, which are fixed by different changes. The manufacturer also discovers and fixes errors. It is evident that soon the customer base is filled with slightly different *variants* of the same software. Not all fixes may be mutually compatible, and chaos soon reigns. Additionally, there will be requests for evolutionary changes to the software, so the manufacturer maintains many slightly different versions of the original product.

This problem was known well before software was invented, in other engineering fields. The solution is to use a version and configuration management system. Each revision of a component has an associated *version number*, which increases in time. In a simple system, a linear scheme is sufficient (version 1, version 2 ...). In due course, a consistent collection of (usually) latest versions is brought together as an operating, tested system. This is termed a *release*. Again, a simple linear scheme may be used. Often, a structured identifier is used e.g. Release 4.2 where the first integer refers to a major release incorporating significant changes, while the second integer denotes minor alterations only (perhaps small bug fixes or a variant). A structured identifier may also be used for versions e.g. 6.3.4.2 might refer to the second minor change to version 4 of a component in release 6.3.

Version management is basic to software maintenance and should be used in large and small projects (see (Buckle 1982), (Birsoff, Henderson and Seigel 1980), (Babich 1986) and (Bazelmans 1985)). It is one area where ample tool support exists e.g. DSEE (Leblang & Chase 1985), SCCS (Rochkind 1975) and (Tichy 1985).

Version management is a part of *configuration management*. A configuration of software modules refers to their interrelationship and structure which determines the overall structure of the system of which they form the components. A software module may be source code, but more generally will refer to any system component used in the production process eg test suites, documentation, requirements reports, PERT charts etc. Configuration management should support the following:

- the naming of configuration components
- an auditing process to check conformance to standards and to extract management summary information
- a detailed complete historical record of the project throughout its lifetime
- support of a control system for managing changes to components
- the availability of a library support system

This allows scope for automating the building of a release from its components.

The UNIX *make* tool (Feldman 1979) is a well known utility which enables the user to define component interdependencies, and then take associated actions should a component become out of date. This is a very useful, widely used tool, though it has some notable drawbacks e.g.

- the tools used to build the release from component versions cannot themselves be brought within the version control system. For example, it is often the case that a system must be generated using a particular version of a compiler etc.

- only time may be used to indicate a component needs regenerating. Other variables could include: QA status, version number, etc.

3.5 Metrics of maintenance

A *metric* is a quantitative measure representing some property of the software. It is a rule for assigning a number or identifier to a software object in order to characterize that object (Dunsmore 1984). A metric may be a *predictive* such that it is derived from an underlying theoretical analytical model; or it may be *phenomenological*, in that there appears to exist some correlation between the metric and the property but an explanation is lacking.

Maintenance metrics can be categorised as:

1. maintainability metrics: can we predict how easy a system will be to maintain at the design or even specification stage? This is considered in section 4.

2. maintenance metrics: how should we predict the cost of maintenance during the maintenance phase?

There is an extensive literature on software metrics, though the field can be characterised as lacking theoretical foundations. Most maintenance metrics are expressed in terms of source code; although it may be desirable to analyse design information and documentation, these are unlikely to be available.

Source code metrics may be applied at the microscopic level (source statement/module) and the system structure level. Probably the best known metrics are the complexity metrics proposed by Halstead (Halstead 1977) and by McCabe (McCabe 1976). Such

metrics try to give a measure to the understandability of a system, on the assumption
that a less complex program is easier to maintain. Also of importance is Yau and
Collofello's stability metrics (Yau et al. 1979) which measure the assumptions made by
the modules on the module under examination. This is relevant to the minimisation of
ripple effects caused by interaction between modules.

For metrics to be used with any confidence, they must be *validated*, that is, we must
establish the degree to which the metric actually represents the particular attribute or
property in which we are interested. In a subject with weak theoretical foundations,
this proves difficult, though it has stimulated a great deal of work over the last ten
years.

Work on metrics has prompted a number of tools to collect and analyse data. These
can be built into compilers, though this is rare. More recently, so-called "CASE" tools
employing graphics have been used to calculate and present metrics.

It can be seen that the topic of software metrics extends well beyond maintenance,
and we have identified the main themes of metric identification, validation and tool
support.

3.6 Program Comprehension and Understanding

At the heart of the software maintenance process is the maintenance programmers comprehension and understanding of programs. Many theories of program comprehension
have been proposed. A review is available in (Robson, Bennett, Cornelius & Munro
1988).

Shneiderman and Mayer (Schneiderman & Mayer 1979) argue that comprehension is
based on syntactic and semantic knowledge. Syntactic knowledge is the knowledge
of the format of various statements in the language concerned. Semantic knowledge
consists of more general concepts which are independent of the programming language.
The authors argue that comprehension involves applying the syntactic knowledge to
develop an internal semantic representation. This internal representation can then be
altered or translated into an alternative programming language.

Brooks (Brooks 1983) puts forward a theory of program comprehension which is based
on the hypothesis of a mapping between the problem domain and the programming

domain. He argues that the developer produces these mappings and the maintainer has to reconstruct them. He views this reconstruction as a bottom-up approach rather than the more usual top-down approach to design. He also argues that the reconstruction of the mappings is an iterative, progressive activity. Thus a maintainer might start with an initial hypothesis which is adapted as more knowledge of the program is gained. He suggests that the initial hypothesis might be formed from just the name of a particular activity. Brooks also argues that one of the differences between programmers and their ability to comprehend programs is their domain knowledge. Thus in order to make comprehension easier it is important not only to state the requirements, but also a history of the decisions that led to those requirements.

Letovsky (Letovsky 1986) describes an experiment in which maintenance programmers were given a program to modify and encouraged to think out aloud so that their thoughts could be recorded. From the recordings he focuses on two types of events, namely questions and conjectures and develops taxonomies of these events. His taxonomy of questions leads him to hypothesise that a mixture of top-down and bottom-up strategies are employed during comprehension, where the top layer is the specification and the bottom is the implementation. These two layers are connected through various intermediate levels to form the programmer's mental model of the program. This work has been extended by Letovsky and Soloway (Letovsky & Soloway 1986).

Several techniques and systems have been developed to automate code reading to facilitate program understanding. The techniques used can be categorised into either static or dynamic analysis strategies.

Static analysis is the analysis of a program without its execution and an overview of this topic is given by Fairley (Fairley 1978). With a static analyser it is possible to identify uninitialised variables, departures from coding standards, code which can never be executed, the frequency of use of statements and to obtain cross reference information. More recent work is described by Calliss and Cornelius (Calliss & Cornelius 1988).

Ryder (Ryder 1979, Ryder 1987) has applied static analysis techniques to develop call graphs of a system which have aided the maintenance programmer's understanding of a system.

Several tools based on this approach are now available commercially. Some are aimed specifically at COBOL sources, while others present a selection of source languages.

Systems which have been specifically developed to aid understanding have frequently been based on cross referencers. Munro and Robson (Munro & Robson 1987) have described a system which allows the user to submit queries to determine where a variable is used or where a particular procedure is called from. Unlike most simple cross referencers, the system is aware of the scope rules of the target language and can distinguish between different uses of the same name. A documentation system for recording the knowledge obtained from the source code with the cross reference information has also been developed (Foster & Munro 1987).

3.7   Software reusability

This is a research field in its own right (see for example the IEEE special issue (IEEE 1984)) but has strong links with software maintenance in the following way. In maintaining a system, we are trying to identify those parts that can remain unchanged (i.e. reused) and those parts which require replacement or modification. A "part" may refer not only to a component such as a module, but also to a design process, a specification etc. The main thrust of work on reuse is concerned with generic component libraries with some form of associated intelligent information retrieval. However, the recording of development histories and high level abstractions for components poses similar challenges to those found in program comprehension.

Tools such as 4GL's and parser writers represent reuse of design information. The maintenance of "programs" for these tools is not yet well understood. The claim has been made that software produced by 4GL's will not require maintenance - it will be discarded and replaced. This claim has to stand the test of time.

3.8   Inverse Engineering

Inverse engineering is defined as the process of recreating the requirements, specification and design of an applications system from the existing source code, and the creation of new code from the old.

The conversion of unstructured source code into structured code by means of some restructuring tool is a reasonably well understood problem (Bush 1985). We shall term this *reverse engineering*; the term re-engineering is also used in the USA. Several restructuring tools are available on the commercial market. Examples include RETROFIT from Peat Marwick (Miller, 1983), RECODER from Language Technology and SUPERSTRUCTURE from Group Operations Inc. These basically use compiler writing technology to parse the input, normalise it and output in well structured form. A key requirement is that the unstructured and restructured program should have identical behaviours under all valid inputs. Problems can occur when assumptions have been made by programmers about constructs where semantics are deliberately not defined by the language definition, or where the language allows access to machine dependent activities.

In a more recent approach, Ward (Ward 1988) has developed a novel transformational theory in which a construct in a given language can be provably transformed to an equivalent construct or constructs in the same language. A catalogue of such transformations has been developed, so that a programmer can convert a program by application of one or more transformations from (say) an unstructured form to a structured form, without being concerned with how to apply the transformations.

This approach can be extended to transform a program in one language into an equivalent program in another. Firstly, a "core language" with mathematically defined semantics is used. This is extended by definitional-transformations to an intermediate language, into which our source language is converted by conventional compiler-writing techniques. Each source language is extended by its own set of definitional transformations.

Transformations are performed on the intermediate representation, and finally the program is converted (again by compiling type techniques) into the destination code. In (Ward 1988) Ward demonstrates this, showing in steps how an initially highly unstructured program is converted into a structured program, uncovering a serious program error in the process.

In more recent work, a high level specification language is chosen as the destination language, so that we can move formally from unstructured code to a structured specification. This may be used as an aid to program understanding, or as a specification for reimplementation of the original code.

The key issue in this system (as in theorem-provers) is the selection of which transformation to apply next. Humans become very adept at this, and Ward is currently building an expert system to try to incorporate the expertise in order to produce an advisor for the maintenance programmer.

A serious criticism of this type of approach is that inverse engineering a large software system would be an enormous effort. However, Foster and Munro (Foster et al 1987) have shown that a viable strategy is to concentrate only on those parts of the system that require modification, leaving the remainder alone. This has an additional advantage that it is more motivating for the maintenance staff. Other related work includes Arango's TMM transformation system (Arango, Baxter, Freeman & Pidgeon 1986). The IBM Federal Systems Division has reported on a major effort to upgrade the 20 year old Federal Aviation Administration National Airspace System by modelling programs as either function abstractions or data abstractions (Britcher & Craig 1986). Sneed (Sneed 1984) describes a case study in which a large suite of PL/1 programs were renewed by redocumentation using an automatic static analyser. This was developed further in (Sneed & Jandrasics 1987); it represents an interesting approach, by trying to recapture design information.

The current best source of material on the state of the art of reverse engineering is in the IEEE Tutorial on Software Restructuring edited by Robert Arnold (Arnold 1986).

3.9 Quality assurance

The issue of quality assurance (QA) is very wide, so only points directly related to maintenance will be considered here.

The quality of software products seems likely to be a matter of greatly increasing importance in the 1990's. For software maintenance staff, the quality of the original product might not simply be sustained subsequently, but improved to meet rising expectations. For management, each incremental evolutionary step will need to be accompanied by thorough regression testing (Harman & Robson 1988). Currently, there are no standards in software maintenance procedures (by standards we mean both those defined by National Standards Organisations and what are called "industry standards"). This reflects the relative immaturity of the subject, but it is certain that increasing quality expectations will force both more productivity in the maintenance phase together with an increased emphasis and sophistication of testing, including automatic test suite generation. In contrast, most QA work is neglecting software maintenance.

16

3.10 Summary

Maintenance of existing, installed software is consuming very large resources. Good management of software maintenance is an achievable objective, but there is inadequate technical support from methods and tools. Standards in the field are completely lacking. Many tools in current use derive from the initial development phase, and are not well suited to the needs of maintainers.

In the USA a section of the General Service Administration (GSA), an office of the Federal Government called the Federal Software Management Center, has identified software maintenance as a major problem area and established a task force to assess, select and support software maintenance tools. It has identified eleven classes of maintenance tools and invited tool vendors to submit their existing tools as a candidate for inclusion in a Programmers Workbench aimed at providing tools for the maintenance of COBOL programs. The categories of tools identified by the GSA were *test coverage monitor, source compare, file compare, translator, reformatter, data standardisation tool, restructuring tool, code analyser, cross referencer, documentation and metric analyser, and a data manipulation tool.* The full structure of the Programmers Workbench has been described in Software Maintenance News (Zvegintzov 1986) and reported in (Munro et al 1987a).

Another US organisation, the National Bureau of Standards has been active in producing management guides which provide methods and procedures for conducting an effective maintenance programme (Martin & Osborne 1983, McCall, Herdon & Osborne 1985).

4 Software maintainability

4.1 Problems of maintainability

How do we avoid the mistakes of the past? How do we write software that is cheap, quick and easy to maintain?

There is a huge amount of literature in the annals of programming language development concerned with the relationship between program constructs and the associated ease of programming and maintenance. Topics to have been scrutinized in particular include comments, information hiding, data abstraction, variable names, and program layout.

In the early days of programming, machine resources were modest, and quality was equated to efficiency. Currently, maintainability is regarded as a prime indicator of program quality, despite the fact that maintainability is not well understood, certainly to the extent that we are not really sure how to measure it.

We argue that the strategic mistake made by the "programming language" school has been to regard the end program as being of central importance for a maintainable system. It is now widely accepted that the use of structured *design techniques* is important for maintainability, particularly if a record of design history can be retained. This is just one example however. What are the general principles behind maintainability?

Work on maintainability models has been undertaken by Boehm et al (Boehm, Brown, Kaspar, Lipow, MacLeod & Merrit 1978). Boehm regards maintainability as having three components: testability; modifiability and understandability. The two principal ideas running through this and other work are **system complexity** and **system modularity** (Harrison, Magel, Kluczng & DeKock 1982). Complexity may be regarded as having two components (Curtis & Sheppard 1979) : computational complexity and psychological complexity. According to Curtis and Sheppard, computational complexity is a property of the algorithm which makes proof of correctness hard. Psychological complexity is a property which makes human understanding difficult. However, these two concepts have a substantial amount in common.

Modularity is concerned with the way in which a software system is decomposed into smaller subproblems. The hypothesis is that a programme is more maintainable if the modules have minimum external *coupling* and maximum internal *cohesiveness* (Constantine, Stevens & Myers 1974).

While these ideas are important, they are not the complete picture. A large system is continually evolving in time - how does a maintenance programmer retain an up-to-date mental model of the system? How should requirement, specification and design information be represented to ease maintenance? The source codes represent the final design step, and ideally the maintenance staff should be acquiring the great majority of the knowledge of a system and performing changes to it at a much higher level of abstraction. Documentation produced during initial development may not be best suited for this.

4.2 What can be done now?

Section 4.1 has exposed some of the problems of producing maintainable systems, but it is desirable to produce current software which is as good as possible using current technology.

A key technique is to prepare for maintenance both during initial development and during subsequent evolution. In other words, preparation for maintenance starts right at the requirements capture stage. This implies full consistent documentation (with QA audits), change control procedures, version and release management, regression testing, internal standards and cost monitoring. It is difficult to see how any **large-scale** software project can succeed without strong management to implement these techniques. In small scale developments (and small scale enhancements to a large system) it is very tempting to take short cuts. The use of technology where available (such as data dictionaries, normal form data representation, use of metrics as a project control function) can make a substantial contribution. Modern design methods involving data hiding and abstraction should also be used.

Perry (Perry 1985) has identified five objectives in planning software maintenance:

1. a manager with clearly identified responsibility for software maintenance should be appointed;

2. objective for software maintenance should be clearly established;

3. the maintenance release mode method should be used;

4. the value added by software maintenance should be evaluated;

5. the maintenance tasks should be subject to full QA and control procedures.

5 The status of software maintenance

There are indications that software maintenance, for so long the "Cinderella" of software engineering, is on track to become a key issue in the 1990's. What are these signs?

1. Software maintenance has been explicitly included in the ESPRIT II workplan for IT research (ESPRIT is the name of the collaborative program of research

funded by the European Economic Community).

2. There is an increasing number of conferences and workshops on software maintenance. The first such event (Arnold, Schneidewind & Zvegintzov 1983) is claimed
   to be a maintenance workshop held at the Naval Postgraduate School, Monterey,
   California in 1983. The first UK Workshop was held at Durham University in
   1987. There are now several major annual conferences.

3. In 1989, a new journal "Software Maintenance: Research and Practice" will be
   launched, providing a forum for the publication of academic and practitioners in
   the field. Papers will be refereed.

4. The World's first research centre in software maintenance has been set up at the
   University of Durham.

5. Ph.D. work on maintenance is starting to appear, and final year courses on the
   subject are becoming available in undergraduate Computer Science courses.

6. In the USA, the *Software Maintenance Association* (SMA) has been established;
   it organises an annual conference and acts as a forum for practitioner topics. An
   independent publication that reports the activities of the SMA is the *Software
   Maintenance News*, published by N. Zvegintzov.

Most textbooks on software engineering still concentrate heavily on initial development.
Titles specifically concerned with maintenance include (Glass & Noiseux 1981), (Martin
& McClure 1983), (McClure 1981), (Parikh & Zvegintzov 1983) and (Parikh 1982).
Probably the most cited work in the field is that by Lientz and Swanson (Lientz et al
1980).

6   Research topics in Software Maintenance

A theme running through sections 3 and 4 is the need for technical development to
help us cope with existing installed software and with building new software that is
maintainable. There are many opportunities to be seized, once the prejudice is removed
that software maintenance is neither a challenging or interesting area in which to work.
Further information is provided in (Bennett, Cornelius, Munro & Robson 1988).

Some research topics are:

1. Theory of maintenance. No adequate theoretical insights to software maintenance exist. We need to develop models of the maintenance process, particularly to address maintainability and methods.

2. metrics and cost modelling.

3. inverse engineering of installed software, including redocumentation where none exists.

4. associated quality assurance mechanisms and policies.

5. support environments for maintenance.

6. maintenance for 4GL programs.

There is considerable research in the use of mathematical specifications (in notations such as VDM or Z) to derive rigorously software systems. These techniques are starting to be industrialised, yet the issue of maintenance and maintainability has not been addressed.

Similarly, expert systems are now becoming widely used in industry and commerce. The knowledge base is a valuable asset that will certainly require corrective and perfective maintenance.

Software maintenance is a field which would seem to warrant an interdisciplinary approach to research. Knowledge based techniques offer great potential in areas such as program comprehension and understanding. So too does cognitive science. The interaction of the maintenance support system with the programmer needs careful attention to the human-computer interface design.

Finally, we note that there is almost no up-to-date information on current software maintenance *practise*. The survey by Lientz and Swanson was undertaken around ten years ago i.e. before the microcomputer, 4GL's, relational databases etc. The Centre for Software Maintenance at Durham is planning to undertake a major survey in 1989 to address this.

Acknowledgements

The author acknowledges the substantial contributions made to this paper by other members of the Centre for Software Maintenance, particularly Barry Cornelius, Malcolm Munro and David Robson. The financial support of the UK Alvey Directorate (now the Information Engineering Directorate) and of British Telecom, K3 Software Services and AGS Information Services is acknowledged.

Biographical notes

Keith H. Bennett was educated at Manchester University, England, where he received the degree of Ph.D. for research in the compiling system of the MU5 computer. He then worked in industry for three years before taking up an appointment as Lecturer in the then newly-formed Computer Science Department at the University of Keele. He undertook research on distributed computer systems, with a particular emphasis on reliable distributed filestores.

In 1986 he was appointed to the first Chair of Computer Science in the School of Engineering and Applied Science at the University of Durham, UK. Along with colleagues Malcolm Munro, Barry Cornelius and David Robson, he formed the Centre for Software Maintenance at Easter 1987. He has acted as consultant to a number of organisations and has lectured internationally on his work in both distributed systems and software maintenance. He is a Fellow of the British Computer Society, a Fellow of the Institution of Electrical Engineers, and a Chartered Engineer.

7   References

Arnold, R.S., Schneidewind, N.F. and Zvegintzov, N., *A Software Maintenance Workshop*, Commun. ACM, 27, (11), 1983

Arnold R. S., *Tutorial: Software Restructuring*, IEEEComputer Society Press, April 1986

Arango, G., Baxter, I., Freeman, P. and Pidgeon, C., *TMM : Software Maintenance by Transformation*, IEEE Software, 3, (3), 1986 pp 27-39

Bazelmans R., *Software Configuration Management*, ACM Software Engineering Notes, 10, (5), 1985 pp 37-46

Babich W. A., *Evolution of Configuration Management*, Addison Wesley, 1986

Belady, L.A. and Lehman, M.M., *A Model of Large Program Development*, IBM Systems Journal, 15, (3), 1976 pp 225-252

Bennett K. H., Cornelius B. J., Munro M. & Robson D. J., *Software Maintenance: a New Area for Research*, University Computing, 10, (4), 1988   pp 184-188

Birsoff E. H., Henderson V. D. and Seigel S. G., *Software Configuration Management*, Prentice Hall, 1980

Boehm, B.W., Brown, J.R., Kaspar, H., Lipow, M., MacLeod, G.J. and Merritt, M.J., *Characteristics of Software Quality*, North-Holland Publishing Company, 1978

Boehm, B., *The economics of software maintenance*, Proc. Software Maintenance Workshop, IEEE, 1983

Britcher, R.N. and Craig, J.J., *Using Modern Design Practices to Upgrade Aging Software*, IEEE Software, 3, (3), 1986 pp 16-24

Brooks F. P., *The mythical man-month*, Addison Wesley, 1975

Brooks, R., *Towards a Theory of the Comprehension of Computer Programs*, Int. Journal of Man–Machine Studies, 18, 1983 pp 543-554

Buckle, J.K., *Software Configuration Management*, MacMillan, 1982

23

Bush, E., *The Automatic Restructuring of COBOL*, Proc. Conf. Software Maintenance, IEEE, 1985 pp 35-41

Calliss F. W. & Cornelius B. J., *Software Maintenance : A Different View*, Proc. 21st. Annual Hawaii Int. Conf. on System Sciences, 1988 Vol. 2, pp 518-523

Chapin, N., *Software Maintenance : A Different View*, AFIPS Conf. Proc. 54, National Computer Conference, 1985 pp 509-513

Constantine, L.L., Stevens, W.P. and Myers, G.J., *Structured Design*, IBM Systems Journal 2, 1974 pp 115-139

Curtis, B.and Sheppard, S.B., *Identification and Validation of Quantitative Measures of the Psychology Complexity of Software*, Software Management Research, 1979

Ditri, A.E., Shaw, J.C. and Atkins, W., *Managing the EDP function*, McGraw Hill, 1971

Dunsmore, H.E., *Software Metrics: An Overview of an Evolving Methodology*, Information Processing & Management, 1984 pp 183-192

Fairley, R., *Static Analysis and Dynamic Testing of Computer Software*, IEEE Computer, 11, (4), 1978 pp 14-23

Feldman, S.I., *Make - A program for maintaining computer programs*, Software Practice and Experience, 9, 1979

Foster, J.R. and Munro, M., *A Documentation Method Based on Cross Referencing*, Proc. Conf. on Software Maintenance, IEEE, 1987 pp 203-210

Gladden, G.R., *Stop the Life Cycle, I Want to Get Off*, ACM Software Engineering Notes, 7, (2), 1982 pp 35-39

Glass, R.L., Noiseux, R.A., *Software Maintenance Guidebook*, Prentice–Hall, 1981

Halstead M. H. , *Elements of Software Science*, Elsevier North-Holland, 1977

Harrison, W., Magel, K., Kluczny, R.. & DeKock, A., *Applying Software Complexity Mterics to Program Maintenance*, IEEE Computer, Vol. 15 September, 1982 pp 65 - 79

Harrison, W. and Magel, K.I., *A Complexity Measure Based on Nesting Level*, ACM SIGPLAN Notices, Vol. 16, no. 3 March 1981 pp 63-74

Hartmann, J. & Robson, D. J., *Approaches to Regression Testing*, Centre for Software Maintenance Report 88/7, University of Durham 1988

Hoskyns Ltd., *Implications of using modular programming*, Hoskyns Systems Research, 1973

IEEE, *Special issue on Software Reuse*, IEEE Trans. on Software Engineering, Vol. SE-10, no. 5 1984

Leblang, D. and Chase, R., *Configuration Management for Large Scale Software Development Efforts*, Workshop on Software Engineering Environments for Programming in the Large, Harwhichport, Massachussets, 1985

Lehman, M.M., *Programs, Life Cycles, and Laws of Software evolution*, Proc. IEEE, vol 68 (9), 1980 pp 1060-1076

Lehman, M.M, *Program Evolution*, Inform. Processing Management, 20, (1-2), 1984 pp 19-36

Lientz, B., and Swanson, E.B., *Software Maintenance Management*, Addison–Wesley, 1980

Lientz, B.P., Swanson, E.B. and Tomkins, G.E., *Characteristics of Application Software Maintenance*, CACM, Vol 21, (6), 1978 pp 466-471

Letovsky, S., *Cognitive Processes in Program Comprehension*, Proc. Conf. Empirical Studies of Programmers, pub. Ablex, Norword, New Jersey, 1986

Letovsky, S. and Soloway, E., *Delocalised Plans and Program Comprehension*, IEEE Software, 3, (3), 1986 pp 41-49

McCabe, T.J., *A complexity measure*, IEEE Trans. Soft. Eng., SE-2, 1976

McCall, J.A., Herdon, M.A., and Osborne, W.M., *Software Maintenance Management*, Nat. Bureau Standards, NBS Special Publ. 500-129, 1985

McClure, C.L., *Managing Software Development and Maintenance*, New York : Van Nostrand, 1981

McCracken, D.D. and Jackson, M.A., *Life Cycle Concepts Considered Harmful*, ACM Software Engineering Notes, 7, (2), 1982 pp 29-32

Martin, J. and McClure, C., *Software Maintenance : The Problems and its Solutions*, Prentice–Hall, 1983

Martin, R.J. and Osborne, W.M., *Guidance of Software Maintenance*, Nat. Bureau Standards, NBS Special Publ. 500-106, 1983

Miller J. C., *Structured Retrofit: in IEEE Tutorial on Software Maintenance*, Computer Soc. Press, 1983 pp 235-236

Munro, M. and Calliss, F.W., *Notes of the First Software Maintenance Workshop*, Centre for Software Maintenance, Durham, England, 1987

Munro, M. and Robson, D.J., *An Interactive Cross Reference Tool for use in Software Maintenance*, Proc. 20th Hawaii Int. Conf. on System Sciences, 1987 pp 64-70

Parikh, G., *Techniques of Program and System Maintenance*, Winthrop Publishers, 1982

Parikh, G. and Zvegintzov, N., *Tutorial on Software Maintenance*, IEEE Computer Society, 1983

Parikh, G., *Handbook of Software Maintenance*, Van Nostrand Reinhold, 1986

Perry W. , *A plan of action for software maintenance*, Data Management, 23 (3), 1985

Robson D.J., Bennett K. H. , Cornelius B. J. & Munro M., *Program Comprehension*, Centre for Software Maintenance Report 88/8, University of Durham, UK, 1988

Rochkind M. J., *The Source Code Control System*, IEEE Trans. Software Engineering, December 1975

Ryder, B.G., *Constructing the Call Graph of a Program*, IEEE Trans. on Software Engineering, 5, (3), 1979 pp 216-225

Ryder, B.G., *An Application of Static Program Analysis to Software Maintenance*, Proc. 20th Hawaii Int. Conf. on System Sciences, 1987 pp 82-91

Schneidewind, N.F., *The State of Software Maintenance*, IEEE Transactions on Software Engineering, 13, (3), 1987 pp 303-310

Shneiderman, B. and Mayer, R., *Syntactic/Semantic Interactions in Programming Behaviour*, Int. Journal of Computer and Information Science, 8, (3), 1979 pp 219-238

Schneiderman, B., *Designing the user interface: strategies for effective human computer interaction*, Addison Wesley, 1987

Sneed, H., *Software Renewal : A Case Study*, IEEE Software, 1, (3), 1984 pp 56-63

Sneed, H. and Jandrasics, J., *Software Recycling*, Proc. Conf. on Software Maintenance, IEEE, 1987 pp 82-90

Swanson, E.B., *The Dimension of Maintenance*, Proc. of Conference of Software Engineering, IEE, 1976 pp 492-497

Tichy, W.F., *RCS - a system for version control*, Software-Practice and Experience, 15(7), 1985 pp 637-654

Ward M., *Transforming a Program into a Specification*, Centre for Software Maintenance Report 88/1, University of Durham 1988

Yau S. S. & Collofello J. S., *Design Stability Measures for Software Maintenance*, IEEE Trans. Software Eng. SE-11, September 1985

Yau, S.S., and Collofello, J.S., *Some Stability Measures for Software Maintenance*, IEEE Transactions on Software Engineering, 6, (6), 1979 pp 545-552

Zvegintzov, N., *Nanotrends*, Datamation, 1983 pp 106-116

Zvegintzov N. (Ed.), *GSA Launches the PWB*, Software Maintenance News, Sept. 86 and others 1986

2

INTEGRATED PROJECT SUPPORT ENVIRONMENTS: GENERAL PRINCIPLES
and
ISSUES IN THE DEVELOPMENT OF HIGH INTEGRITY SYSTEMS

John A McDermid

Professor of Software Engineering
Department of Computer Science, University of York
and
Director, York Software Engineering Limited

Part I: Introduction

There have been many advances in software development technology and in software engineering methods and tools since the introduction of computers in the late 1940's and early 1950's. Perhaps the most significant advance in software quality and *individual* programmer productivity has arisen from the development, and evolution, of the high level programming language. A significant effect on software development productivity, if not always quality, has also arisen from the dramatic increase in the performance/price ratio of computer hardware, particularly from the advent of the workstation.

These developments, particularly in hardware, have also (at least partially) contributed to increased expectations about what can be achieved with computers. These expectations have led to the undertaking of many large, and all too often unsuccessful, software development projects. Brooks in his article "No Silver Bullet" [Brooks1987] articulates some of the problems underlying large software developments and casts doubts on the possibility of general solutions to these problems. Brooks, and many other authors, make it clear that the problem of managing the interactions and communication within large development *teams* is one of the key difficulties facing the software industry.

Intellectual solutions are required to the problems of organising and managing large team projects. However the issues of scale make it clear that such solutions will only be practical if they are given adequate machine support. Unfortunately, until recently, there was little in the way of support for team working. Integrated Project Support Environments (IPSEs) are intended to address these problems - the objective being to provide a "complete" development facility for a project team. The primary means of doing this is by providing an infrastructure and a set of tools to:

* facilitate communication within the team;

* support all (or most) of the technical and managerial activities in the software development and maintenance processes; and

* control access to data shared by members of the team in order to prevent inconsistent modification to the software under development.

In practice IPSEs often fall far short of these objectives, e.g. by supporting only a limited number of activities in the development process. We will expand on these basic requirements for IPSEs, and illustrate the capability of current environments, later in this chapter.

A further trend in the defence sector, industry and commerce is to use computers and software in increasingly large numbers of increasingly critical applications. Example classes of critical applications include:

- safety critical - where deaths or injury may be caused by computer or software malfunction, eg fly by wire aircraft, and active suspension for cars;

- military security critical - where loss or disclosure of sensitive information may be highly damaging to the nation, eg a command and control system providing information on troop disposition to military commanders;

- enterprise critical - where malfunction of a computer leading to incorrect operation or loss of information could bankrupt of otherwise critically damage some business or enterprise, eg programmed trading systems on the stock market.

We will use the term high integrity as a generic name for the classes of applications illustrated above to indicate that integrity (trustworthiness; freedom from impairment or corruption) is required for the software in those applications.

As the above classes of application require high integrity software there are demands on the integrity of the development processes, tools and the IPSE (if any) used to produce the application programs. Consequently there are additional integrity requirements on IPSEs intended for use in support of the development and maintenance of high integrity applications, by comparison with IPSEs intended for less stringent applications. We will address the basic requirements of IPSEs for developing high integrity systems later in this chapter, and we will also present a fuller treatment of the concept of integrity.

We are now in a position to outline the aim and contents of the chapter. The aim is to explicate the principles and concepts of IPSEs; to indicate how effective current IPSEs are when judged against these principles; and to consider what additional requirements are placed on IPSEs by the need to support the development of high integrity systems. Due to limitations of space we can only briefly address these issues and we have to gloss over a number of issues altogether, eg implementation strategies for IPSEs.

Part II thus sets out the basic concepts and principles of IPSEs, focusing on the term integration. It analyses five different forms, or types, of integration that (we believe) are required in order that IPSEs can satisfy their basic objectives.

Part III considers the evolution of computer based support tools from simple, single user, tools to the current concepts of IPSE architecture. It also reviews the capabilities of three, very different, current examples of IPSEs.

Part IV discusses the high integrity issues. The treatment is in terms of likely requirements for high integrity development - we must stress the term "likely" as this is still an active area of research. The focus is on integrity in the IPSE itself.

Part V considers trends and presents some general conclusions.

Part II: General Principles

The basic concepts underlying IPSEs were first expounded about a decade ago, and the Stoneman document produced by John Buxton and Vic Stenning for the DoD [DoD1980] is generally accepted as being the seminal reference on IPSEs, although it was explicitly aimed at APSEs - Ada Programming Support Environments. We will discuss the Stoneman view of IPSEs in more detail later in this chapter but, for now, we are only concerned with two key aspects of the Stoneman ideas. First, there is a *kernel* of an APSE (or IPSE) which is charged with storing the project data, managing the user interface, and managing other interfaces, eg to target computers in a host-target development. Second, a set of tools are provided, exploiting the kernel facilities, to facilitate specific development capabilities, eg compiling high level languages, or drawing structured analysis (SA) diagrams [DeMarco1978]. Thus the kernel provides generic capabilities which are required by the range of tools to be supported by the environment.

It perhaps seems inappropriate to deal with principles and concepts in terms of (possible) implementation structures. However the Stoneman ideas have influenced most IPSE developments so many of the concepts used in descriptions of IPSEs reflect these notions. Further many development projects have been concerned with producing kernels rather than full IPSEs and many of the basic principles apply to the kernel, or infrastructure, so it seems helpful to employ this architectural information in discussing principles and concepts.

A key factor influencing the development of IPSEs has been the concept of integration. Integration is a many-faceted concept. In our discussion we will be concerned with integration in five different senses: between related tools; within a team; throughout the stages of the development process; between technical development and management; and in terms of user interaction with the tools in the IPSE. We shall refer to these as tool integration; team integration; method integration; management integration; and interaction integration. These facets of integration are the main concern of section II.1.

The set of tools provided by, or supported by, an IPSE reflects the development strategy and methods selected for the project. Typically the tools will cover the use of diagrammatic methods of software development, testing, documentation, compilation, linking and loading. Less typically they will cover project planning, cost estimation, and the use of formal methods. The issues of populating an IPSE with tools are addressed in section II.2.

II.1   IPSE INFRASTRUCTURE AND INTEGRATION

We use the term infrastructure to refer to the kernel in Stoneman terminology. As should be clear from the above this includes the database (or possible simply the set of files) used to hold information shared by a number of tools, or which simply needs to be preserved over some period of time. It also encompasses other basic tool support mechanisms, e.g. program invocation and communication primitives, and a user interface facility. All these facilities are made available (accessible) through a public tools interface, or PTI (see the figure on p24). This is essentially the tool implementors' interface to the infrastructure facilities and is strongly analogous to the supervisor call interface in an operating system such as UNIX. Some PTIs have a narrower range of facilities than those described above, for example they might not include a user interface component.

However, for the purposes of our discussion, we assume this broad definition of the scope of a PTI.

An open environment is one that does not have a fixed set of tools and which facilitates the introduction of new tools via provision of a PTI. We identified five different forms of integration above. With an open environment the infrastructure can contribute to four aspects of integration:

- interaction integration - through the user interface management component;
- tool integration - through the PTI in general and the database in particular;
- management integration - through the database;
- team integration - again through the database.

We discuss each topic at some length, but at an abstract level, as the details of the approaches to each of these topics depends on the particular environment chosen. Technical integration is covered when we discuss populating an IPSE in section II.2.

II.1.1   Interface Integration

One of the keys to making an IPSE easy to use is to achieve consistent interaction styles with all the tools in the environment. Provision of a consistent style makes it easier to learn to use new tools and to move between tools without making mistakes. These characteristics contribute, in turn, to human productivity in the use of the IPSE. Clearly there is a limit to the degree of consistency that can be achieved between tools as they will by definition have different functionality, however common commands should be invoked in the same way and the style (or styles) of interaction, e.g. via pull-down menus, should be consistent unless there are very good reasons to diverge from a standard approach. This idea can perhaps be clarified by considering two commonly used systems.

One of the biggest difficulties about using UNIX is the very great divergence in interface styles (and the unhelpful interface styles) of its many tools. By way of contrast, the Macintosh is probably the epitome of interface consistency. In the case of the Macintosh consistency is achieved by publishing guidelines on interface design and, in general, developers of programs for the Macintosh follow these guidelines quite faithfully. Thus there is a fairly common experience that it is possible to use a new Macintosh program - at least at an elementary level - simply by running it, without having to read the documentation. Note that some of this ease of learning relates to the quality of the interface, not just the consistency between tools.

Most PTI definitions also include an OTI - an Open Tool Interface - which is a means for invoking tools which run on the underlying operating system. For the reasons outlined above the OTI clearly won't give interface consistency unless the tools invoked happen to have been developed to use the same interface style. Whilst this may seem a rather trivial point it is significant as the OTI is often sold as a "cheap route to integration" yet, in reality, it can only be of limited utility. At least from the interface point of view a set of tools brought in to an IPSE via an OTI will be no more integrated than they are in the host operating system. In addition, OTIs only provide limited help in respect of the other facets of integration - they must be regarded as a form of "fool's gold" at least from the point of view of providing a simple means of integration.

There is a further important aspect of interface integration, which also relates to the tool functionality. This concerns the ability to "do anything from anywhere", ie the ability, whilst carrying out one function, to invoke another function and transferring some data between the two functions in the process. A concrete example might be the ability to invoke a mail program from the context of a compiler error message display to send an example of a program which exposes a "bug" in the compiler to the compiler writer. Again this ease of moving between programs, carrying some context, increases productivity and reduces opportunities for error.

There are essentially two ways in which the current weaknesses in IPSE interface integration can be reduced or alleviated. One is via the improvement of the interface support mechanisms provided by the operating system. Note that this is then available via the OTI as well as the PTI. The second is via provision of a user interface management system (UIMS) within the infrastructure. Each has its advantages and disadvantages. We will summarise the advantages and disadvantages below, but first we consider the trends in interface facilities provided by operating systems - in particular UNIX as this is the most widely used operating system on workstations supporting bit-mapped graphic displays, and these are now being widely used in support of software engineering.

The situation with UNIX interfaces is evolving quite rapidly as it is becoming the prevalent operating system on workstations supporting bit-mapped displays, and a key issue for such an OS is the management of sub-parts of the complete display. These sub-parts are usually known as windows, and each window can be read from or written to "simultaneously". Typically the operating system will support a process connected to each window, and a windowing system to support management of the screen, e.g. for dealing with windows when they overlap. There are windowing standards emerging, e.g. X-windows, and although these don't define the "look and feel" (i.e. interaction style) of the interfaces they do standardise on basic screen manipulations. In addition individual computer manufacturers, e.g. SUN with OpenLook, are defining their own interaction styles. Also there are groupings of computer manufacturers defining particular "flavours" of UNIX and associated utilities, including an interface manager which defines a particular "look and feel". For instance OSF, the Open Software Foundation, has defined MOTIF which is layered on top of X-windows and provides a Macintosh-like "look and feel". The trend towards definition of these standard interfaces should facilitate the provision of well-integrated toolsets on UNIX.

A primary advantage of relying on the operating system for interface integration is that it should enable consistency to be provided between tools developed on the PTI and those simply invoked through the OTI. On the other hand the need to provide generality in an operating system may limit interface functionality, and it may be rather hard to provide the "do anything from anywhere" capability without being restrictive about the sort of data that can be passed between tools.

For tools developed directly using the PTI then the situation seems potentially much better, as the IPSE designer can build a UIMS with facilities much more closely geared to software development. The Alvey research programme set up in the UK in the mid 1980's, and funded in part by the UK government, gave considerable emphasis to IPSEs. The Alvey funded ECLIPSE project defined a user interface management component for the IPSE tools [England1987]. This gives a set of primitives which enable, for example, tools supporting graphically based methods such as Structured Analysis to be built quickly and in a consistent way. The Alvey ASPECT project has also worked on an interface component, known as the Presenter [Took1986]. Presenter has many technical strengths, including the ability to pass on to the user the ability to interactively tailor the interaction style to individual preference. However this level of capability is not yet available in commercial products.

The big disadvantage of a UIMS approach is that integration between the OTI and PTI is not possible. Additionally it may not be possible to provide very much "software engineering oriented" functionality through the UIMS as an IPSE is also a very general purpose system.

Interface integration is often neglected, and most IPSEs are rather weak from this point of view. However there are encouraging signs that operating system and IPSE designers are taking this facet of their work more seriously so IPSEs should begin to improve, in this respect. It is also reasonable to expect IPSEs to change from having fixed functionality interfaces to providing facilities for building and customising interfaces.

II.1.2   Tool Integration and PTIs

From a technical point of view the main facilities, other than user interfaces, provided by the infrastructure of an IPSE are for tool integration through the database and via tool to tool communication (or invocation). In general the facilities are unremarkable, being largely extensions and generalisations of standard database and operating system facilities. Many IPSEs use entity-relationship models, extended with the ability to store large, unstructured, objects, e.g. text files. It is also common to give database support for versions and variants of software in the database, thus supplanting mechanisms in tools such as SCCS (see section III.1.2).

In general, one of the most significant aspects of the infrastructure of an IPSE is the database management system. This is true from the point of view of the implementation of the IPSE, but much more importantly it is true in terms of the potential for integration. Information is necessary in order to achieve project control, and the database, if suitably designed, can contain most of the essential information about a project, the relationships between the sources, specifications and other data shared between the tools, and so on. A practical example of this would be storing relationships between module specifications, programs, test specifications and test results. This gives the basis for integrating tools concerned with specification analysis and testing to calculate, for example, test coverage metrics. Further it would then be possible to constrain the testing process to ensure that certain levels of coverage were achieved. Thus the database forms a (logically) centralised repository for all the key project information, and provides the basis for integration and control.

The extensions of the tool communication and invocation facilities can be relatively simple additions to the operating system facilities. Often the primary change is to record (certain aspects of) the behaviour, or use, of the tools in the IPSE database. This might be to capture information for automatically producing "make files" ie files which describe how to build particular items of software or documentation (see section III.1.2), or to provide an audit trail of how certain items were constructed.

However these facilities really provide tool "aggregation" not integration. Unless the tools are designed together from the point of view of their technical characteristics, internal data structures, and interaction styles they will not be truly integrated. It is quite common to build "shells" around particular tools in order to include them in an environment, and to improve their degree of "integration" with the other tools, e.g. by modifying they way they interact with the user, but usually such approaches are of limited success due to fundamental limitations imposed by the decisions made by the tool designers. The author has observed such problems trying to put a graphical interface on a textually based theorem proving system, and similar interfacing problems have been cited by others in trying to extend UNIX tools [Thimbleby1986].

There is considerable interest in developing PTIs, much of it aimed at providing a good basis for tool integration (see section V.1 for a brief overview of some of the current PTI definitions). Indeed production of a PTI often seems to be the "holy grail" of the IPSE/infrastructure developer, rather than development of an effective working environment. It is clear that PTIs are potentially generally, and genuinely, useful eg for providing tool portability and as a basis for integration. However it should be remembered that they are part of one possible architectural solution for IPSE development - not the only one - and our main aim is to provide effective IPSEs not PTIs.

Following this general observation we should stress two points. First, PTIs give the opportunity for achieving tool integration - they don't guarantee it. Second, there are many who believe that standardisation on PTI definitions is premature. There is almost no experience of using IPSEs based on PTIs (indeed there is relatively little experience of using IPSEs at all) and it is far from clear that we yet know what are necessary and sufficient facilities to provide in such an interface. In the absence of such information standardisation is a risky process. Thus PTIs should be an important development in IPSE technology - but this does not mean that the current batch of interface definitions will prove effective and long-lasting (see part V for a discussion on this point).

11.1.3   Management Integration

In an IPSE, management integration is achieved primarily through linking the management and technical information in the database. For example the specifications of modules of software should be linked, through a work breakdown structure, to activity descriptions and perhaps estimates of cost and duration for the activities. This is a further important facet of the use of the database to link various activities and data. In practice a key to management integration will be the establishment of project plans in the database and the linking of technical information to the activity descriptions.

It is now becoming comparatively common to use (parametric) software cost estimation models, for estimating the cost and duration of software projects. The term parametric refers to parameters given to the models to define properties, or attributes, of the software development, e.g. how difficult the job is thought to be, how experienced the development team is, etc. One of the difficulties of applying estimation models such as COCOMO which are based on historical cost figures is in obtaining the data with which to calibrate the models [Boehm1981], including providing the model parameters. IPSEs offer the opportunity to collect this historical cost data, and offer a relatively stable basis for development which should improve the reliability of the estimates. Such data collection can be achieved by placing monitoring code in the IPSE infrastructure, although it is not always possible to make the data collection entirely unobtrusive.

Information collected in an IPSE can also be used as the basis of pragmatic management decisions. For example, modules which have atypically high error rates in testing may have been badly designed (or may just be very complex and error prone). Conversely modules with very low error rates may not have been properly tested (or may just be very simple). However measurement can provide indications of possible trouble spots which, coupled with intelligent assessment of the sources of the anomalous data, can be an aid to focusing management attention on critical areas of a project. Both the calibration and pragmatic aspects of measurement in IPSEs are discussed by Kitchenham and McDermid [Kitchenham1986].

Perhaps the key pragmatic point to make about management and IPSEs is that IPSEs can, in principle, greatly facilitate project management. In essence this arises in two related ways: first an IPSE helps to make development information visible to the project manager; second it ensures that the information the manager receives relates to the actual development status, not the imaginings or wishes of the development staff. However, apart from the example cited in section III.2.3 there is little evidence of this benefit being realised in practice.

Finally the use of an IPSE makes it possible for management support to become active not passive. For example, if deliverables are not produced on time, a "Daemon" (periodically executed monitor process) programmed to check on progress can send a message to the project manager, alerting him to the situation. This is of benefit in a number of ways including the fact that it reduces the need for a manager to delve in to the mass of detailed technical information held in an IPSE. However at present few IPSEs are capable of operating in an active manner.

II.1.4   Team Integration

There are two primary facets of team integration: control over sharing of data (program source, etc.) between members of the team, and communication within the team. Both facets of team integration are important, but most emphasis is usually put on controlled sharing as this is perhaps the most difficult issue, and because it can most readily be supported by the infrastructure (given our current stage of understanding of infrastructure design and implementation). In this section we use the term "data item" to refer to any of a wide class of objects which may be stored by the IPSE infrastructure.

A major aim in project management is to ensure that work is allocated (based on a work breakdown structure) such that there is as clean and clear as possible a division of work between individual members of a project team. Pragmatically this means that specific individuals will have complete responsibility for developing some specification or item of code. In general, therefore, in a well-run (ideal) project there will be no need for individual software engineers to have modify access to the same data items held by the infrastructure (eg programs or specifications). However they will need to share data, eg so that one software engineer can develop his module, using a module produced by another member of the team. Thus it is still necessary to provide a limited form of sharing - and such facilities can be provided by an IPSE infrastructure.

Two of the requirements on the IPSE infrastructure are particularly relevant to team integration. First, it is necessary to ensure that no item which is depended upon by one member of the team, although it was produced by another team member, can be deleted whilst it is still needed (depended upon). Second, it is necessary to ensure that the creator of an item has control over which versions of it are used by others in the team so that, for example, versions of modules are not used until they have been adequately tested by the originator. There are several ways of implementing mechanisms to support this requirement. Perhaps the simplest uses private and shared domains, where a domain is simply a set of files or a part of the IPSE database which is disjoint from any other. In addition this solution uses a form of "handshake protocol" for moving items between private and shared domains.

In such an approach each member of the team would have their own private domain which contains all the data items which he or she is developing. Private means that only the originator of the information has the capability to read and write the data items. When one item is believed to be in a state suitable for use by other members of the team it can be moved ("promoted") into the shared domain. The data item can now be used by other members of the team. This stops untried versions of data items being used, but doesn't stop them being deleted whilst being used. This problem can be addressed by requiring users of shared items to "reserve" the item before use, and then to "release" it once they have finished with the item. The originator may only delete the item from the shared domain once all users of the item have released it. This satisfies the basic requirements identified above.

In practice, however, more complex requirements may need to be satisfied. For example one member of the team may have multiple roles, eg module developer and module specifier, and it may be appropriate for him to have one domain for each role. Similarly it may be appropriate to have more than one shared domain, perhaps relating to a subsystem of the system under construction or a stage of the development process. These facilities cope well with the straightforward development of a system which goes through multiple versions - the ideal case outlined above - but they do not deal with the development of multiple parallel variants of a system.

For many projects it is necessary to work on multiple variants of the system at once. In other words there are similar, but not identical, sets of modules making up different variants of a system. Reasons for this might be implementation of the system on different machines, or carrying out "bug-fixing" on released software whilst carrying on development (adding new features) to the system. In these cases it might be necessary for multiple individuals to have write access to the same data item (albeit different versions thereof). Normally this is handled by making copies of the data item, but this leads to problems when the variants of the item need to be merged, eg in retrofitting "bug fixes" from the released version of the system to the development system. In general the domain concept can be used for controlled access, but there is relatively little automated aid for merging (this is not surprising as it depends on the semantics of the changes).

Viewed more generally the control aspects of the requirements for team integration can be thought of as those of version and configuration mangement, plus the issues of sharing illustrated above. In many instances these control issues are also extended to issues such as release management, but treatment of such issues is outside the scope of this chapter. We note however that one can imagine a "release domain" into which the complete software system is deposited, once it is deemed ready for release. These broader access control and release management issues are also important where more than one project shares common data items, eg by re-using existing modules or libraries.

The communication aspect of team integration is often overlooked. This is perhaps because managers worry about the tangible problems which can be caused by accidentally deleting source, or integrating the wrong set of configuration units, but don't see the costs of poor communication between team members as these may be much more subtle. Indeed problems of poor communications may simply manifest themselves as morale problems, rather than in any overt technical sense. At the simplest level electronic mail is a necessary form of machine supported communication for team integration. Elementary mail services are helpful, but more elaborate systems are likely to be of more use.

There is value in setting up mail systems with group distribution and mailing lists so that, for example, a programmer can communicate easily with everyone else working on his subsystem, or can ask a group of experts in database design how to solve some particular data structuring problem. Thus setting up distribution lists relevant to the project as a whole, can aid communication. However this can be taken further in two ways.

First, one can get the infrastructure to originate mail messages. For example, in the case of the shared domains, it would be possible for the infrastructure to send a mail message to all users of a particular data item if a later version is placed into the shared domain. This reduces the likelihood of team members unwittingly using an out of date module or specification.

Second, there is the whole area of computer supported cooperative work, or CSCW. In the paper world (and on whiteboards) software engineers interact in developing designs, carrying out reviews, etc. In many ways the machine support of an IPSE can be seen as stultifying to the normal social processes involved in less automated software development. Clearly an ideal IPSE would provide for this interactive and cooperative working by embracing and supporting the ideas of CSCW. Indeed one could see this as a primary objective for IPSEs - to support all the cooperative tasks in software development except those which rely on group psychology, such as reviews. This certainly is beyond the state of the art in IPSE design, and it is perhaps over-optimistic to believe that such functionality can be provided in the near future, although it remains a valid long-term goal.

II.1.5   Commentary

We have set out some basic IPSE integration requirements, based on the premise that the requirements can be implemented by an appropriate infrastructure. This is true in part - but to a varying degree for the different requirements. For example controlled sharing is almost entirely an infrastructure matter, but interface integration is also heavily dependent on tools. Specifically the IPSE can provide the means for integration - but it cannot enforce it if the individual tool designers choose to use the facilities available to them in incompatible ways. Also some of the functions which we have ascribed to the infrastructure, eg configuration management, can also be achieved by tools.

Thus the infrastructure is very important in achieving integration, and this tends to lead to IPSE developers focusing on infrastructure issues. However, perhaps one of the worse failings of many current IPSE projects is that they have developed sophisticated infrastructures without the supporting tools - they have provided the means to the end, but not the end itself. It is thus appropriate now to consider the population of an IPSE infrastructure with tools.

II.2   POPULATING AN IPSE

The basic aim in populating an IPSE (infrastructure) is to provide support for all the major (automatable) activities in software development. Thus we require one or a number of tools to support each major technical or managerial activity, plus query (and other) mechanisms for accessing the data held in the IPSE infrastructure database. Clearly all these tools and related facilities have to be suitably integrated. Populating an IPSE is not so simple, in practice, eg due to the potential overlap between tools for essentially different tasks. Thus any attempt to expand on the above description runs the risk of turning into the production of a "shopping list" which gives no real insight into the underlying technical and managerial issues. So, as an alternative, we consider some of the basic issues in method integration in support of technical development. In other words we are dealing with the fifth aspect of integration identified above. This aspect of integration is treated separately because it is primarily a methodological and tool issue, rather than an infrastructure issue.

In principle it would be possible to talk about the general requirements for such integrated toolsets but, in order to make the discussion more concrete, we refer to a number of extant "coherent method and tool sets". The examples cited below are somewhat incomplete, but they are typical of what can be (has been) achieved with current methods. Many developers of methods and method sets (often incorrectly referred to as methodologies) claim to have "complete" methods in the sense that they cover the whole software life cycle. These claims are not, in general, well founded and most method sets are limited in life cycle coverage, scope, or both. The shortcomings of a method set can usually be discerned quickly by considering how the set would deal with the latest project with which you found difficulties! The limitations are usually that there are stages of the life cycle, or important issues such as interface design, which the method doesn't address - not that the method does badly what it is intended to do. In other words most of the limitations arise from omissions, rather than from flaws in the techniques used.

II.2.1   Basic Requirements for Method Integration

The basic requirement for method integration is that the set of methods should be coherent, and non-conflicting. Informally we would probably say that they are complementary. This means that there should be techniques and notations for dealing with all activities in the software development (and maintenance) process, including management issues, and that there should be no conflicting techniques or notations. This does not mean that there should never be more than one way of carrying out some activity. Instead when there are multiple possibilities it should always be clear (by considering the characteristics of the system under development) which technique to choose, and the complete set of methods should still be complementary no matter which option is adopted. A practical example might be the availability of more than one technique for database design.

The requirement for the methods to be complementary sounds obvious and unarguable, but it is surprising how few method sets meet this basic criterion. Worse, however, there is a much more subtle test of method integration, which is even less often satisfied. This relates to the "conceptual integrity" of the methods employed. In order to achieve conceptual integrity the methods used should be based on a compatible set of concepts, or perhaps more importantly a compatible system model. This, rather obscure, definition can be clarified by considering separately the conceptual integrity of process and product, and by giving examples and counter-examples. We will consider coherence of the product first.

Consider two different classes of method for describing a system, one class based on asynchronous processes with a flat process structure (i.e. no processes have sub-processes), and the other class based on a hierarchy of synchronous processes. By synchronous we mean that data can be thought of as leaving the sender and arriving at the recipient at the same time, ie the sender and receiver are synchronised (executing together) at the time of communication. This means that if the sender is not ready to produce some data then the receiver has to wait, and *vice versa*. This may be thought of as a form of "procedure call" between two processes, such as is exhibited by the Ada rendezvous mechanism. With asynchronous communication the sender and receiver processes are more loosely coupled, and one can continue operating without waiting for the other. The most obvious example of asynchrony is communication via message passing although it is also possible to communicate asynchronously using shared store.

We could use two methods from the same class, at different stages of the life cycle, to describe the same system. For example an asynchronous model of the system might be used at requirements and architecture, and it should be relatively easy to demonstrate that the architecture corresponded to the requirements (by comparison with conceptually different methods). However it is also possible to use conceptually different methods at different stages, if they can be related in an appropriate way. For example it would be quite reasonable to use "conventional" methods of functional decomposition to design and develop the individual processes of a system, once these processes had been identified in the architecture. The significant distinction between these two cases is the need to verify consistency between the whole of one description and part of another, as opposed to the consistency of the whole of two descriptions.

It would be hard to use methods based on divergent views of process structure and communication, eg synchronous and asynchronous, to describe a system at two adjacent levels of abstraction where it is necessary to verify the consistency of the two complete descriptions. That is not to say that they couldn't be used to describe the same system, rather that it would be difficult to do so and that it is likely that there would always be doubts about the equivalence of specifications produced using the two notations. Thus, for example, Hoare's Communicating Sequential Processes [Hoare1985] which is based on a synchronous model of communication and MASCOT would not fit together well. By contrast the CORE method for requirements specification [Mullery1979], and the MASCOT design notation [Jackson1986] are based on models of asynchronous processes, are coherent, and have been successfully used together.

Similarly methods need to have compatible view of the process. Thus a method based on the notion of stepwise refinement, and another which took a monolithic view of specifications, e.g. viewing them as contracts, would be incompatible, especially when it came to managing changes. This can perhaps best be seen by considering the verification processes. With stepwise refinement verification may be carried out incrementally on what are (in some senses) incomplete and inconsistent specifications. This would be difficult to reconcile with a method that insisted on complete and internally consistent specifications before carrying out a "big bang" verification. Again this is not to say that such techniques could not be used in conjunction - merely that the conjunction of the techniques could cause both technical and management difficulties. Pragmatically the process compatibility problems are probably the easiest to resolve, unless key facets of the process are rigidly implemented in method support tools (or the IPSE infrastructure).

Perhaps more significantly than either of these two points is their combination. It must be possible to verify consistency between the descriptions of a system produced by two methods. Thus they must have compatible semantics *and* a set of rules for checking the consistency of descriptions written in the two notations. Thus there is intellectual work to be done, often of a subtle nature, when trying to link two methods, and possibly software development work in terms of the production of further support tools (for the additional verification activities).

It must be pointed out that method coherence does not simply mean compatible and consistent notations (this is another popular misconception). Further it does not even mean consistently using formal (mathematical) or structured (graphical) notations. For example the view of systems taken by structured methods such as MASCOT and formal methods such as CCS [Milner1980] are essentially asynchronous concurrency, and it would be quite possible to use them in conjunction. Indeed it is now becoming quite popular to "underpin" structured methods with formal descriptions to try to gain the benefits of both styles of development method, and to try to obtain the benefits of both classes of technique. Current work includes investigation of links between SSADM and Z.

II.2.2   Examples of Method Integration

One good example of a coherent method set and environment developed for use on a real project, is Safra [Cronshaw1986]. Safra was developed by British Aerospace (BAe) for the Experimental Aircraft Programme (EAP). A flyable demonstrator fighter aircraft was produced in a very short time and the software development timescales were compressed to about one third of those normally achieved in the aerospace industry (i.e. they were brought down to about two and a half years). Perhaps unsurprisingly very high gains in productivity, by comparison with earlier projects, were observed.

Safra was developed to support the complete software development process including requirements analysis, design, production and testing of the software in the EAP. The method was based on CORE and MASCOT and the underlying environment was Perspective produced by Systems Designers (now SD-Scicon). Although some problems with the method and environment were cited by BAe they acknowledge that it would not have been possible to carry out the development in the time without the method and environment support. More information on this project is given in section III.2.3 and in the above reference.

Examples of other possible method sets are given in a study of Ada life-cycles by McDermid and Ripken [McDermid1984]. One of these examples is backed up with experimental evidence of its use and the book gives some indication of the characteristics (expected) of complete method sets. There is a lot of dogmatism surrounding the choice of methods and method sets, and many proponents of particular methods claim "universality" for their approach. However there are few, if any, universally applicable methods and in widely applicable methods generality is often achieved at the expense of "power" or effectiveness. In many cases, eg compiler design, it is more helpful to use an application specific method as the power of the method in guiding the software development will far outweigh any disadvantages accruing from lack of generality.

In practice, selecting a method sets for a project is a matter for some judgement. We discuss this issue in detail elsewhere [McDermid1989a] but the basic principle is to identify the critical factors relating to a project - reliability, performance, security, algorithmic complexity, data(base) complexity etc. and to select methods which deal well with the most critical factors. In other words methods should be chosen to suit the technical characteristics of the project. It is then usually necessary to "adapt" the chosen methods, e.g. by borrowing techniques from other methods, to deal with other aspects of the system. Thus it is usually necessary to *design or develop* a method set for a particular application.

As might be expected it is also necessary to design the development process, ie one should consider the process required for developing the system under consideration in order to provide an effective way of managing the risks attendant to the development. This is an important topic, but outside the scope of our paper; the interested reader is referred to [McDermid1990]. for an introduction to the concepts of software process design. This need for process design is one of the strongest arguments in favour of having open environments which can be tailored to support different tools and techniques. Indeed this realisation has fostered a lot of research on "software process models" - indeed there is now an annual workshop on the subject. We will briefly return to this point in section V although it should perhaps be noted that excessive flexibility in process selection or design can result in management problems.

II.2.3   Constraints on Establishing a Coherent Method Set

As indicated above space does not permit a full account of the issues in establishing a coherent method set - but it is worthwhile making some observations on constraints especially as some of them relate to issues of integration and the design of the IPSE infrastructure. We consider two "managerial" constraints, two technical constraints and one technico-managerial issue.

In general one can't simply select the best methods for a project without considering the available personnel, and their training. Training is expensive and, the smaller the project, the greater the cost of training as a proportion of the overall budget. In many cases it will be better to use a non-ideal, but satisfactory and familiar, method set than an ideal but unfamiliar method set. In practice it is probably a good idea for an organisation to have a number of "standard" method sets available suited to its range of applications.

In some cases the developers may have no choice over the method set - this might be dictated by the customer. For example this might happen in a safety critical application where some particular standard or set of tools is mandated by the procurement agency. In this case it is only to be hoped that the imposed method has the desired characteristics.

It is not very satisfactory to be able to link methods if one can't link the support tools. Thus one may be constrained to use methods whose support tools can be run on the same PTI or, more strongly, have been designed so that they make available the necessary information to achieve integration. This indicates that, for example, it would be helpful to do work on canonical representations of different classes of specifications, eg graphcal notations [Black 1987], and that these representations should be supported by the IPSE infrastructure.

Methods used in development also should be used (and usable) in maintenance. Thus the method set chosen for the development should also take into account the different technical activities undertaken in maintenance. Thus the chosen method set may have to be a compromise between the "ideal" for development and the "ideal" for maintenance. Again training is an issue because maintenance staff cannot be expected to be familiar with an enormous panoply of methods.

In some very risky projects it is only possible to decide what methods to use as the project proceeds and the range of issues to be addressed becomes clear. This suggests that the IPSE should be able to support the incremental definition of the tool set, and perhaps modifications to the tool set, as the project proceeds. This has ramifications for the way in which the data and database schema is managed. Indeed it might imply that we need to be able to keep the database schema and tool set under version control - which causes some interesting technical problems!

II.3   Commentary

Although we have presented an extensive discussion of IPSE requirements we have still only scratched the surface of the subject. For example it is possible to make the infrastructure "active", eg to include daemon processes which volunteer information to the users, to include inference mechanisms, and so on. Thus the reader should view the discussion as being representative of IPSE requirements, but far from complete.

However we have stressed requirements oriented towards integration. This is appropriate as it is the integration which is the main extra capability offered by IPSEs over and above what one gains by running a set of tools on an operating system. Hence we believe that we have focussed on the main IPSE issue. To put it another way if IPSEs don't facilitate integration to a significant degree then they are likely to prove nugatory.

It is also worth commenting more generally about IPSE requirements. The requirements are potentially immensely complex - in principle the requirements are to support all possible development processes for all possible software development projects in a cost-effective, reliable, etc. way! Clearly providing a detailed exposition of even a representative subset of such requirements would be rather time-consuming, and it is (arguably) of little value as the main difficulties of IPSE design and development seem to be in dealing with the central issues such as integration rather than the minutiae of particular development methods and processes.

The above perhaps suggests that work on requirements is not worthwhile. This is not so and some interesting and valuable work has been done on IPSE requirements. The difficulty is in identifying key requirements without being swamped in the detail of particular development methods or projects. Perhaps the most pertinent work on IPSE requirements is by a group of major European Aerospace companies in a project known as AIMS. The intention here is to specify requirements for, and then build, an IPSE supporting development of avionics software by the Aerospace companies and their subcontractors in the context of multi-national collaborative projects. The work is particularly interesting as it is one of the few really detailed studies of IPSE requirements by **users** of IPSEs, rather than would-be IPSE purveyors.

Part III: Current IPSEs

We have given an overview of the basic requirements for IPSEs, focusing on the general issue of integration. Realisation that these are appropriate requirements (if indeed history shows that they are appropriate) has not come about quickly, and has certainly not come about purely by intensive study of the way in which software is, or should be developed. Instead the requirements have effectively evolved and emerged from experience with available tools and IPSEs, and assessments of the shortcomings of current tools and environments.

Consequently it is useful to discuss both the historical evolution of software development tools, and to give an overview of some current IPSEs. This discussion should help clarify and elucidate the requirements presented earlier, and indicate the shortcomings which IPSEs are intended to overcome. It should also make clear what are the capabilities of current tools and environments and hopefully enable the reader to see to what extent available tools and IPSEs can support their development activities.

We start by discussing IPSEs from a historical perspective. The aim is to give a flavour of the major developments that have occurred in support tools and IPSEs, rather than to give an accurate historical account of the development of the subject, so we make extensive use of examples. This is followed by a relatively detailed account of the capabilities of three IPSEs which are currently commercially available, or which are in use in the industry. We conclude with a discussion of some current work on PTIs.

III.1   HISTORICAL PERSPECTIVE

The following overview represents a "rational reconstruction" of the evolution of IPSEs. It is not completely accurate chronologically, but it reflects the logical progression of the ideas of environments for programming and project support. We should perhaps stress here the emphasis only shifted from programming support to project support in the mid 1980s, so many of the issues discussed in part II are quite new ideas.

The major value of the historical perspective is that it enables us to identify most of the significant technical threads which underly the design and development of current IPSEs. Taken in conjunction with the survey of current IPSEs this enables us to see, to some extent, what are the primary research issues.

We consider five stages in this rational reconstruction:
*   Individual Tools
*   Groups of Tools
*   Early Integrated Environments
*   The Influence of Ada
*   CASE Tools

It should be clear, however, that the early stages aren't "finished" and that there are still important issues to be addressed in the design and development of individual tools, eg to support the use of formal methods.

Arguably work on individual programming tools is (almost) as old as computers themselves although the perception of what tools are required has changed almost beyond recognition. Work in the 1950s was primarily on tools such as compilers, assemblers, linkers, and debuggers which provided fairly direct programming support. Initially all program preparation occurred "off-line" although, of course, basic utilities such as editors became important software development tools as soon as computers advanced to the state where it was possible to develop programs "on-line".

Work on tools supporting activities other than program development and testing really started about fifteen to twenty years ago, i.e. in the late 1960's and early 1970's, and was soon followed by work on related groups of tools. One could perhaps characterise the 1980s as being concerned with support for graphically based methods, especially on personal computers and workstations. Much work has already been carried out on tools to support formal (mathematically based) methods but it seems fair to say that these techniques are still immature. Consequently one might expect formal method support tools to be one of the main areas of activity in the domain of individual support tools in the 1990s.

Work on early integrated environments commenced in the early to mid 1970's although it didn't really come to fruition until nearer the end of the decade. Some of the early environments (eg CADES, see below) are still in use today. This is true of both the "mainstream" work on environments which are really the precursor to the present day IPSEs and more innovative approaches, eg those based on AI and object oriented techniques. Logically and temporally the Ada influence comes after the early environments because it tries to draw out general principles for developing environments based on practical experience with environments. However, at least partly because of the timescales required for developing IPSEs, some of the work overlapped. Arguably the Ada-related work was the most important in the evolution of IPSEs as it essentially "set the agenda" for future IPSE developments.

Computer Aided Software Engineering, or CASE, tools developed independently of of the "mainstream" IPSE work. They have evolved based largely on the growth in popularity of structured methods (often incorrectly called methodologies) in commercial application areas. In many cases the tools have been produced by database vendors (eg ORACLE) and have aided directly in the development of database applications. The distinction between IPSEs and CASE tools is now becoming blurred as CASE developers are becoming concerned with providing team support, and the IPSE (infrastructure) developers are providing support for particular methods. However there still are differences of emphasis and, to a first approximation, the CASE tools are commercially oriented, and IPSEs are geared more towards technical applications.

The trend to open environments, essentially reflects current designs and aspirations for IPSEs. The requirements for the provision of open environments is based on the realisation (often through major problems on projects) that it is very difficult to ensure that an adequate set of tools is available in an IPSE, and a satisfactory tool set can only be provided if companies other than the original infrastructure developer can provide tools. Thus the discussion on closed and open environments reflects the live issues of the second half of the 1980s, and probably of the first half of the 1990's (or possibly beyond as there are still major problems to be overcome).

III.1.1 Individual Tools

For many years software developers have produced individual tools to support particular activities in software development, e.g. compilers, loaders and symbolic debugging tools. Here the term individual implies both that the tool "stands alone" and is intended for use by a single individual. Whilst these tools sometimes shared data structures, e.g. symbol tables and store maps, they were rarely, if ever, truly integrated. In other words they did not share interface styles or interaction styles, were not callable from each other, and so on. Lack of integration led to problems including constraints on programmer productivity, eg caused by the need to leave one tool in order to invoke another, and unnecessarily high error rates, eg caused by confusion between interface styles. Although there are improvements in individual tools the main advances are to be found in modern tool sets, or groups of tools, and these are discussed in section III.1.2 below.

Most of these early tools were geared for use by an individual programmer. This characteristic is still true of commercially available individual tools, in the sense of stand-alone tools to do one function. IPSEs give support for teams, but each tool is still used on an individual basis. More recently work has been carried out on computer supported cooperative work which genuinely has more than one individual using a tool (working on a specific task) at once. CSCW can perhaps most readily be thought of as the electronic equivalent of working together on a whiteboard. There are many research problems to be addressed in producing such a tool, but if the problems can be overcome, then the results should be very useful.

A further limitation of the early individual tools was that they usually only supported the idea of the "current version" of a piece of software. However with large systems it is often necessary to have different variants of the same program, e.g. compilers for different target computers, and to have many versions of a program (representing it's change history). Tracking versions is important not only so that it is possible to revert to an earlier state if errors in development are discovered, but also to understand the reasons for changes to the software. Typically the early tools left management of variants and versions of programs to the individual or (if he was lucky) to the operating system. Some later tools did give support for versions. Ironically such tools are difficult to integrate into IPSEs as the view of versions held by the tool and IPSE may not be compatible. Nowadays we would view version management as being a job for the IPSE infrastructure, operating system, or a specialised tool, rather than being the province of each individual tool.

Whilst we have stressed issues to do with the infrastructure of IPSEs it must be remembered that it is the tools which actually "do things", ie provide the functionality necessary for carrying out software development in a semi-automated way. As such the individual tools are a very important aspect of an IPSE. We would now expect many software development activities to be carried out by groups of tools, but there are some classes of tools which may still "stand alone". Examples might be:

- Cost Estimation - eg to support COCOMO [Boehm1981];
- Performance Analysis - eg based on queuing models of system behaviour;
- Language independent debugger.

Of course such tools may still share data via an IPSE infrastructure.

III.1.2   Groups of Tools

A natural extension of the idea of simple programming tools is a group of tools which are designed and conceived not only to carry out individual tasks, but to work closely together to support some larger task (this is a form of tool integration). An obvious example might be a suite of tools intended to establish the test coverage (number of paths executed) by executing a program with some test data. Here one tool may instrument the program source to be tested with calls to a journalling tool. The journalling tool would keep a log of program execution, detailing all the branches executed during testing. A third program would then calculate test coverage from the journal and information provided about the program structure by the instrumentor. Whilst each tool carries out a specific job, the group carries out a much more major task which is clearly only possible because they share data and are designed to common data formats, etc.

Many organisations, systems and projects have helped foster the development of groups of tools. However it is perhaps UNIX which has done most to foster this notion. One example should illustrate the point. UNIX supports a set of tools, known as the Programmer's Work Bench (PWB), which facilitates version and configuration management. These tools achieve close integration by using shared file formats, and provide facilities for the management of versions and the building of software systems.

We can further illustrate the idea of groups of tools by means of an example of the use of the PWB. The UNIX PWB includes the much-imitated Source Code Control System (SCCS) [Rochkind1975] which provides efficient storage of, and access to, multiple versions of source modules. Instead of recording a complete copy of each version of a file SCCS maintains one (or a small number of) complete copies of the file and "deltas" which represent the changes (edits made) in proceeding from one version to the next. Clearly it is possible to recreate any version by applying the appropriate set of deltas to one of the complete files. There are now many systems available based on this principle. Typically they can store twenty versions of a file in the space that would be needed for two complete versions. Thus SCCS is useful in itself, but much more so in conjunction with Make.

Make [Feldman1979] uses stored representations of the commands (scripts) necessary for constructing an item of software from its constituent parts, e.g. a set of modules. Make will then build an item of software (or another item such as a document), by invoking the necessary programs on the appropriate files, minimising the amount of work carried out. (An example of the use of Make is shown overleaf.) If the program or document is always "made" from the latest version of the sources then SCCS is of little value except as a way of saving space. If, however, the program is to be made from a mixture of the latest versions and specific named versions of items, eg items for a particular target machine, then SCCS and Make can be used together very effectively to retrieve and use the necessary versions of the items. Make and SCCS facilitate the production and maintenance of multiple variants of the same system quite effectively - so long as only one individual is working on the project.

SCCS and Make are efficient both in human time and machine time (assuming that the scripts are designed correctly). In general this is the aim of most software engineering tools - to remove or reduce clerical tasks to allow the software engineer to focus on the primary intellectual tasks, rather than the clerical and administrative detail of the development process.

MAKE EXAMPLE - SYSTEM STRUCTURE

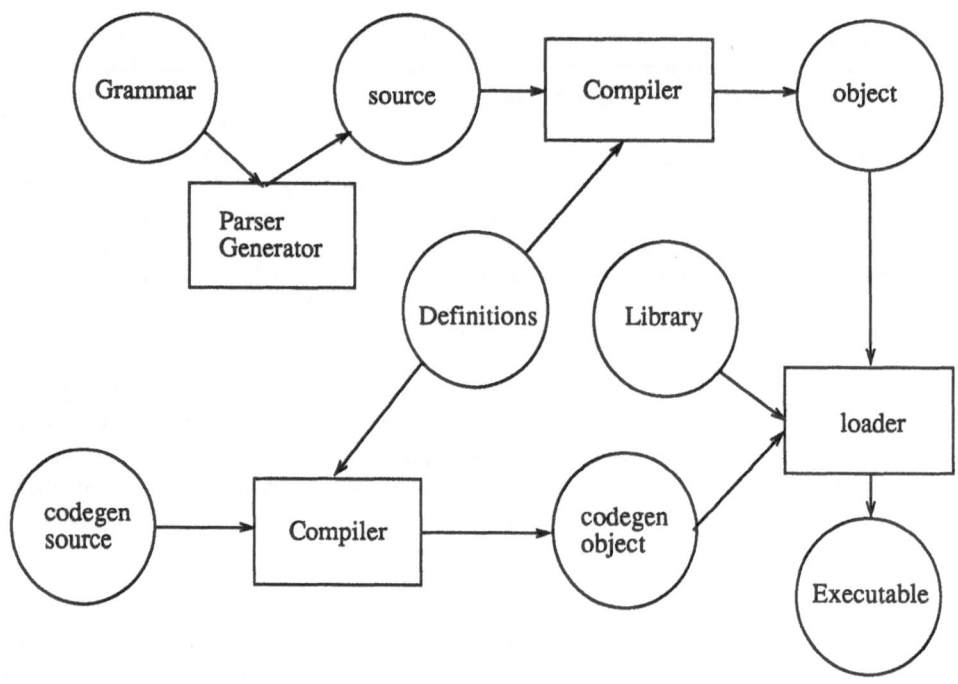

MAKE EXAMPLE - SCRIPT

Executable: codegen.object object Library
         load codegen.object Library object

codegen.object: codegen.source Definitions
         compile codegen.source

object: source Definitions
         compile source

source: Grammar
         parse Grammar

The example shows the structure of a system (some form of compiler) which is part produced by a parser generator, and part produced by compilation and loading. The circles represent data objects (typically files) and the rectangles represent programs. The script shows the file that would be used by make to reconstruct the Executable. For each pair of lines the first line indicates that the item before the colon is dependent on the items after the colon. The second line says what needs to be done (eg recompilation) afterf any of the items which are depended upon change. The changes "ripple through", so a change in Grammar would result in "parse Grammar" being executed, resulting in a new source, resulting in "compile source" and so on until the Executable is reconstructed. Although the example is simple it shows the principle on which Make works quite clearly.

Make is useful, but it has a number of limitations. Most seriously the user has to define the dependencies between the modules correctly otherwise the program (or whatever) will be built incorrectly. In addition there is no automated checking of the consistency of the Make scripts. This is primarily because Make views the file as the basic unit to be managed, and it does not look at the internal structure of files. (This is an illustration of the point made earlier: in order to be general the tool is weak in the sense of generating or checking the build information.) Thus, even with a programming language such as Ada where module dependencies are explicit, Make files have to be generated manually. In principle one could write a program to produce a Make script in each specific case, eg Ada programs, and some such tools have been produced. Nonetheless Make could be more effective in eliminating clerical work and errors in building programs and documents.

Make doesn't deal particularly well with teams. There is a useful extension to Make, known as Build, [Erickson1984] which goes some way towards team integration. This allows different programmers to share a Make script, but to use their own local versions of some of the files. Thus individuals can work on parts of the system independently whilst sharing those parts of the system sources which are stable. This is a tool-based mechanism for achieving the style of controlled sharing via "domains" illustrated in section II.1.4.

Reflecting our concern with mechanisms for achieving integration, it is interesting to consider the tool integration facilities available in UNIX for producing co-operative groups of tools, especially as UNIX is often cited as being one of the most effective operating systems, in this respect. UNIX allows groups of tools to interact via sequential byte streams known as pipes. As well as allowing tools to interoperate, pipes also make possible an incremental approach to developing tools, the re-use of code, and the adoption of standard approaches to standard problems. This basic principle was seen as fundamental even in the early development of UNIX [Ritchie 1978]. In some senses UNIX provided an early example of a PTI (see section II.1.2) although the term PTI wasn't coined until much later.

However, although UNIX offers some opportunity for integration, including the production of groups of tools, it does not do so entirely satisfactorily. Some of the problems are simply issues of usage. Although tools can be integrated via pipes there are some technical limitations. Pipes are unidirectional communication channels, and the standard way of connecting programs (via the UNIX shell) makes it impractical to construct feedback paths between the tools. Experience with software engineering tools, eg with a literate programming tool known as CWEB [Thimbleby1986], has shown that this lack of feedback paths leads to complications in tool design, and the replication of code in different tools (because information has to be worked out in more than one place as it can't be fed back down the series of pipes). Thus although UNIX, and other operating systems, offer some integration capabilities they are not adequate to support integration in the full sense of the term. This can lead to inefficiencies in use of the UNIX tools. For example, when producing documents using the troff toolset (a set of text and diagram formatting programs) diagrams are produced by one tool, and the text is actually laid out by another. Diagrams are processed before text. Consequently a change in point size by the text formatter can't be reported to the diagram formatter for it to change the size of boxes to include text. The necessary changes can only be effected by the user iteratively making changes to the box size. Tool integration in an IPSE would aim to eliminate these problems by facilitating bidirectional communication.

III.1.3   Early Integrated Environments

In many respects CADES represents a milestone in IPSE development and arguably was the first "true IPSE" [McGuffin1979] (although the term IPSE post-dates CADES by many years). CADES was initially developed by ICL in the mid 1970's for the development of the VME operating system. It is still used for ongoing support and maintenance of VME which is a now very large-scale (several million line) suite of programs which exists in many variants (eg a High Security Option - VME HSO). CADES provides "planes" which are essentially consistent (in the sense of update state) views of the complete software development. A programmer works in one plane, and changes which he makes are propagated only to those planes where they are relevant. This is another style of solution to the controlled sharing/domain problem identified above and was a major innovation at the time (indeed many more recent systems solve this controlled sharing problem less well).

CADES also pioneered the use of (commercial) database technology for the IPSE infrastructure. Whilst there are still arguments about the best form for an IPSE database it is now becoming common, if not standard, practice to develop IPSEs on top of a commercial database. Thus CADES was innovative in its implementation technology, as well as in its solution to the team sharing and version management problems.

At about the same time as the initial work on CADES there were a number of interesting tool developments in the Artificial Intelligence (AI) community. Most of these developments could be categorised as tool integration, where the tools have intimate knowledge of each other's data structures, although a lot of work was also done on interface integration. For example, in AI environments, it is common to link compilers and editors so that only those lines of a program which have been changed are submitted for recompilation. The minimal amount of recompilation is then carried out, based on an analysis of the ramifications of the changes. This is often referred to as incremental compilation, and it yields a very fast edit-compile-execute cycle thus facilitating high productivity in program development (although arguably it leads to "hacking"and the production of low quality programs, and wasted development efffort). Examples of such environments are the AI/Lisp machines such as the Symbolics, and toolsets such as POPLOG [Sloman1983].

The main distinction between the AI and "conventional" IPSEs is that the AI environments focus on productivity, and the conventional ones focus on control over software development. A secondary distinction is between the stress on support for teams with conventional IPSEs, and the stress on individual productivity in the AI environments. There are similar (perhaps concomitant) differences in technology. The conventional IPSEs use databases whereas the AI environments share in-store data structures. Note that this latter facility overcomes the problems of the unidirectional communication via pipes found in UNIX - but at the cost of hiding the interface between the tools and making it difficult to extend the toolset. The aim, or hope, with current IPSE trends is to get the benefits of secure, typed, data storage gained from using database technology in the infrastructure with the fast and efficient inter-tool communication achieved by the AI environments.

The early Object-Oriented programming environments, typified by Smalltalk [Goldberg1983], were (and perhaps still are) noteworthy for the high degree of integration achieved. Again the integration was largely oriented towards achieving productivity for single users, rather than control over teams. From the point of view of what they tell us about tool integration these systems are perhaps little different from the AI environments. However the object-oriented technology is now beginning to effect mainstream IPSE development, so it is instructive to consider the topic in a little more detail.

The essence of object-oriented systems is that they encapsulate data with the procedures which operate on the data, and that access to data is only allowed through these procedures. In many object-oriented systems invokation of the procedures (usually known as methods) is via message passing, and there are often inheritance mechanisms which enable the functionality of one object to be (partly) derived from that of another. There are considerable variations between different object-oriented systems, so the above simple description does not accurately characterise all such systems. However despite these variations, it appears that object-oriented approaches aid software development (and arguably they represent a form of integration). There is now a significant trend in IPSE design towards so-called object-oriented environments. Stress is being laid on the production of object-oriented databases for the IPSE infrastructure, although the production of such databases, and demonstration that they are effective for IPSEs, is still an open research question. However this serves to illustrate ways in which the early work on integrated programming environments is now affecting current IPSE research and development.

III.1.4   The Influence of Ada

All major procurers of software systems have observed the rising cost of defence software development and maintenance during the 1970s and 1980s. The US DoD tried to reverse this trend, which was believed to be at least partly caused by diversity in programming languages used on their projects, by sponsoring the development of a new programming language and an associated support environment. The language was called Ada and the environment was called an Ada Programming Support Environment (APSE). The language evolved after a series of competitive design studies, and it is now an accepted international standard; there are also many production quality compilers for the language.

The DoD embarked on a similar programme for the development of APSEs - but with significantly less success. However they sponsored the production of a requirements definition for an APSE which has been extremely influential. The results of the study, known as Stoneman [DoD1980], identified what has for some time been accepted as the basic architecture for an APSE (or IPSE). The Stoneman architecture identified a set of layers, or rings, as illustrated overleaf. We have already referred to most of the components of the Stoneman architecture, but it is worthwhile briefly reviewing the architecture, as it was conceived.

The architecture assumes that a kernel environment is implemented on top of an operating system, providing the common facilities on which all the tools depend, and through which they communicate. In other words this is the basic infrastructure for integration and it is produced by extending the operating facilities to provide capabilities more appropriate to software development, and perhaps hiding some operating system facilities which could compromise the APSE integrity.

STONEMAN ARCHITECTURE

Public Tools Interface

Tools

Kernel

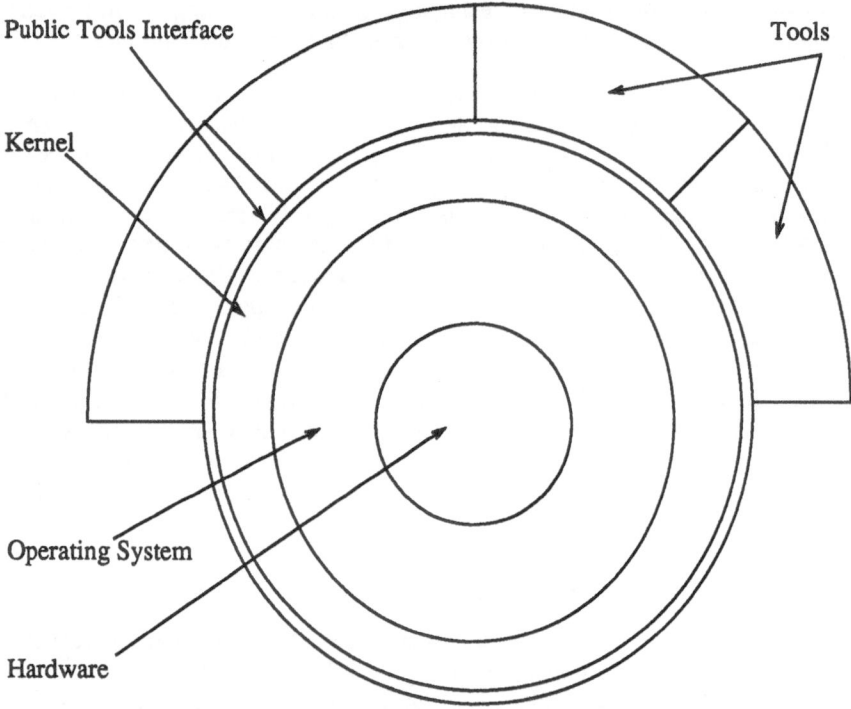

Operating System

Hardware

It was assumed that a database would be used within the kernel to provide a repository for the project data. As should be clear from earlier discussions, the kernel was also intended to provide mechanisms for tool invocation and control over team working, e.g. controlled sharing of sources. The PTI is the interface between the tools and the kernel; this interface would be used by tool developers instead of (in preference to) the operating system facilities. It is referred to as "public" as the intention was that the interface definition would be made widely available to facilitate a "tools industry". These ideas have been very influential - as should be clear by comparing them with the discussion on integration in part II. There are, however, some intersting observations which we can make about method support as conceived at the time.

Stoneman identified the concept of a Minimal APSE (MAPSE) which was the kernel plus the minimum set of tools needed to give "useful" project support. Stoneman wasn't very specific about the set of tools that should be provided, but it was clear about the scope of the tools. The authors of Stoneman believed that it was not possible to develop an APSE including management integration, in the sense described in part II, within the "state of the art". The advent of the term IPSE (which interesting initially stood for Integrated Programming Support Environment and was only subsequently changed to use the term Project) saw the broadening of the idea of a support environment to cover management and other non-programming activities. Given the relative lack of success in producing IPSEs it appears that Stoneman's authors correctly assessed the situation, and that the "acronym engineering" producing the term Integrated Project Support Environment was perhaps ill-judged.

At least partly because of the (apparently unwise) limits placed on the set of tools to be provided in the MAPSE the Commission of the European Communities (CEC) commissioned a study to consider more fully the issues of support of software development throughout its entire life cycle. The study produced several suggestions for coherent sets of methods to cover the life cycle [McDermid1984]. The discussion of method integration in part II reflects this initial study, and the evolution of the basic ideas of method coherence in the subsequent years.

This study also considered the links between the technical and management activities. Particular issues which were addressed included establishment of links between the architecture, especially the module (work) breakdown structure, and the project plans. The study also considered how other managerial issues, eg software cost estimation, could be related to (derived from) the technical information produced in software development. It remains one of the few detailed studies of management integration. From the point of view of clarifying long-term requirements this was a useful and instructive study. However, if it has contributed to over-ambition on the part of IPSE developers, then it may also have done some harm to the cause of IPSE development.

Interestingly the authors of the CEC study report did not consider that PTIs, and open IPSEs, were feasible - again this was an issue of lack of maturity in the technology, and in understanding of the detailed technical requirements. We will discuss current IPSEs in section III.2 and PTI developments in section IV.1 to try to assess whether such views were sound, or over-conservative.

III.1.5 CASE Tools

In commercial data processing there has been, for some time, emphasis on the use of Computer Aided Software Engineering (CASE) tools. Typically these tools support one of the well-known structured techniques for software development and are based on personal computers. These tools have really only become widely available and used with the availability of cheap personal computers, which is almost synonymous with the availability of the IBM PC range.

The methods supported are, without exception, graphically based and include Structured Analysis [DeMarco 1978] and JSD [Suttcliffe1988]. It is common for these tools to support single users, but this is changing as the database vendors, eg ORACLE, make use of their own database technology to improve their CASE products. Many of these tools are quite well integrated, from the technical point of view, as they support related technical activities at different stages of the development process. One limitation is that they often only support a small part of the life cycle, eg code generation from a fourth generation language (4GL). These tools are often also well integrated from the interfacing point of view, by comparison with, say, UNIX tools. This is both because they were conceived as a logical whole, and because the size of the market makes it possible (and perhaps necessary) to make the investment in interface design.

A recent press report indicated that there 67 varieties of CASE tool available in the UK. Most support the better known methods such as Jackson System Development (JSD) and Structured Analysis (SA). The "varieties" are defined by having a unique combination of vendor, hardware platform, and method supported. In practice there are much fewer (perhaps less than 20) methods supported by such tools. A recent survey of (some) tools available in the United Kingdom, categorised by the stage of the life cycle which they support, can be found in the STARTS Guide [DTI1987].

CASE tools and IPSEs are currently evolving so that their distinctions are becoming less marked. IPSEs are tending to become better populated with method support tools, and CASE tools are beginning to address the issues of multi-user support, configuration management, and so on. Arguably those CASE vendors who are also database suppliers have a very strong market position. Not only do they have access to the database technology to produce effective tools but they can, if necessary, adapt the database technology to achieve good performance and functionality in the CASE tools. There is some evidence that this is happening, and it is likely that companies such as ORACLE will become market leaders in this area.

Historically IPSEs have been used more in technical applications, eg avionics, and CASE have been used more in commercial applications. This meant that different classes of methods were supported by CASE tools and IPSEs. The technical characteristics of these application domains are becoming less distinct, eg banks now not only have centralised databases, but also distributed, fault-tolerant systems of ATMs, so there will need to be a merging of the methods employed. Thus it seems probable that the distinctions between CASE tools and IPSEs will be eliminated, in due course. Given the observations above the database and CASE vendors may have the edge over the IPSE suppliers in terms of market penetration and long-term viability.

III.1.6   Current IPSEs

We will discuss some current IPSEs in detail below, but it is worth briefly summarising the nature of current IPSEs and IPSE infrastructure. More or less without exception, amongst companies who are concerned with producing IPSEs as a business proposition, there has been an adoption of the idea of an infrastructure and a "PTI". This is true even where the PTI is not published, as having a clean interface helps the IPSE implementors. Much of the work that has been undertaken with public funding (and most companies in the IPSE business have received some measure of public support) has been aimed at producing a common or standard PTI, and implementations of infrastructures supporting that interface. In Europe the CEC has been a major influence on this work through the definition the Portable Common Tools Environment (PCTE). However, at the time of writing, several very major projects are producing tools to populate PCTE so this balance in effort is shifting.

Projects within companies, intended to produce environments in support of their own development work, rather than to become products, have been rather more pragmatic. Typically these have been aimed towards producing usable integrated toolsets, without being concerned too much about elegant infrastructure interfaces, etc. Whilst many of the concepts set out in part II are evident in these IPSEs, pragmatism has tended to mean that certain requirements, eg interface integration, have been tacitly ignored.

Thus the principles set out in part II are a good basis for discussing and comparing IPSEs, even if there are some IPSEs which don't fully espouse the principles. Hopefully this assertion is borne out by the discussion of three current IPSEs below.

III.2   CAPABILITIES OF CURRENT IPSES

Our aim in this section is primarily to illustrate the capabilities of current environments, as far as possible in terms of the concepts we introduced in part II. We discuss three environments which have widely differing characteristics in order to reinforce the range of possibilities encompassed by the term IPSE. The first has been developed as an open environment by an independent software company established expressly for the purpose of marketing IPSEs. The second by a hardware manufacturer as an extension to their standard operating system, both to support "in-house" developments and to increase the sales of the hardware. The third was developed by a system builder, but incorporating commercial products, to satisfy their own development needs. These differences in objectives and commercial perspectives are reflected, to quite a significant extent, in the technical capabilities of the systems.

For readers wishing to find out more about other currently available IPSEs and IPSE research there are a variety of useful publications. There have been several recent IPSE conferences and, in most cases, the conference proceedings are now available, see for example [McDermid1986] and [Sommerville 1986]. Also, in the UK, the DTI has supported a programme known as STARTS which has produced much useful material on software engineering, especially software engineering tools. Their most relevant publication is the STARTS guide [DTI1987] which summarises the capabilities of many IPSEs.

III.2.1   ISTAR

ISTAR [Dowson1987] is an open environment based on UNIX. ISTAR was produced by Imperial Software Technology (IST). IST was set up, with the primary purpose of producing ISTAR, with backing from several large companies including Plessey and British Telecom. ISTAR was thus both aimed at a market and at solving problems as perceived by IST's backers. ISTAR is sold not as a "packaged product" but as a semi-custom product with consultancy and tailoring services to adapt it to the needs of the using organisation. It has achieved some market penetration but it is a high-price, low-volume, product. Philosophically the adoption of a semi-custom approach seems entirely appropriate - the relatively poor commercial performance probably reflects a mixture of technical (eg performance) limitations of the product and a lack of market awareness of the need for the solutions which ISTAR offers.

ISTAR was developed to be consistent with the UNIX philosophy in that it contains a number of workbenches supporting different aspects of the development process. Perhaps its most significant characteristic is that it enforces a particular model of the development process known as the *contractual* model. The contractual model is the crux of ISTAR's organisation and operation. All development work is divided in to contracts with specified inputs and outputs, but within the constraints imposed by these inputs and outputs the developer is free to fulfill his contract in whatever way he pleases. Note however that contracts may specify tools to be used so it is possible to achieve quite tight project control through these contracts.

Fulfilling a contract may involve subcontracting the work to other developers, thus a project will be represented by a hierarchy of contracts. This gives a clear project structure from a managerial point of view, but it also gives a way of partitioning the database to simplify configuration control. In terms of our earlier discussion the contracts provide the domains for team control. Also ISTAR runs on a network and the contract is used as the basis for distribution, one contract being carried out on one workstation.

The ISTAR concept of a workbench is exactly the same as that espoused by UNIX - a group of tightly integrated tools supporting some particular phase of, or activity in, software development. Several workbenches are "imported" directly from UNIX, and some commercial products are directly imported, eg the Alsys Ada compiler and its associated tools. However most of the workbenches were developed specifically for ISTAR.

This is another area where ISTAR is unusual as it makes considerable use of tool-building tools with the aim of being able to customise the environment to the needs of particular organisations. Methods supported through these specially developed workbenches include (a variant of) CORE which is a graphically based requirements analysis method, and a formal method known as Z [Hayes1986]. The Z tools, known as BALZAC, were generated (semi)automatically by supplying the syntax, scope and type rules to a program generator known as GENESIS. Conceptually this tool building approach is very attractive as it not only allows appropriate tools to be produced in the first place, but it also facilitates their adaptation throughout a project. These theoretical attractions appear to be outweighed by the costs (in memory utilisation and performance) of using the tools (judging by the author's experience with BALZAC).

There are also quite extensive project management facilities again related to the contracts. Clearly progress can be represented and monitored by reference to the contracts, and the contracts give the basic mechanism for links between technical and managerial activities needed for management integration. There are also specific project management tools, eg one based on Barry Boehm's COCOMO cost estimating model [Boehm1981]. This is a further area where ISTAR is relatively unusual. As noted above IPSEs give the opportunity to collect project data. However there is a risk of getting biased statistics if the IPSE is not used on a multiplicity of projects.

It is interesting to summarise the capabilities of ISTAR in terms of the five forms of integration identified earlier:

- interaction integration - this seems to have been a relatively low priority although there is some consistency within workbenches; the desire to import workbenches from other suppliers and the operating system make it relatively difficult to achieve this for the IPSE as a whole;
- tool integration - this is achieved by a purpose-built database;
- management integration - this is supported by the contractual approach; arguably this is one of ISTAR's greatest strengths, and it certainly gives more positive assistance in this area of project control than most IPSEs;
- team integration - again this is achieved by means of the contractual approach;
- technical integration - this is achieved for localised activities within the life-cycle by means of the workbenches, but there is relatively little technical integration throughout the whole life-cycle; arguably this is the best that can be done with our current understanding of software development; it is almost certainly the best that can be done with an open IPSE.

Technically ISTAR is probably the most advanced and interesting IPSE available. Commercially it is probably ahead of its time.

III.2.2 DSEE

DSEE [Leblang1984] stands for Domain Software Engineering Environment. DSEE was produced by Apollo Computers to work on their Domain workstations. Since Apollo have recently been bought by Hewlett Packard (HP) work is now being undertaken to make DSEE run on HP equipment and on heterogeneous networks of HP and Apollo machines. DSEE uses a distributed database manager which is implemented at a low level in the system (requiring modifications to the operating system kernel). This is the main reason why the extension to operating with HP machines in non-trivial. DSEE was primarily seen as a way of extending the market penetration of the Apollo computers into the software engineering marketplace, and was also developed to support internal software development projects. It will perhaps only be fair to judge commercial success when DSEE is available on HP machines.

Despite being UNIX based DSEE is quite different from ISTAR, in a number of respects. It is essentially an extension of operating system capabilities to give more direct support to software engineering activities, so it should really be considered as an IPSE infrastructure rather than a "full blown" IPSE. DSEE is intended to support essentially any tool which runs on the Domain or HP workstations. Obviously the available toolsets include compilers, but there are also other software engineering tools such as Cadre's Teamwork which is a set of CASE tools.

A key component of DSEE is a distributed database manager, mentioned above, which is really the true infrastructure. DSEE also incorporates four "managers" which provide tool support for various activities in software development, eg configuration control, however there is no tool installation or customisation service offered with DSEE. In some senses one can simply regard DSEE as a "better operating system".

The History Manager (HM) provides source code control by maintaining histories of source versions, together with changes between versions. Modules and other development items are grouped into libraries and users reserve elements in the library, and have to obtain private copies of the items before they can work on them. Once they have made changes they replace the items and the HM creates a new version from the user's private copy. The HM requires users to identify the changes, and the purpose of the changes, they have made, or intend to make, and at any time users can ascertain which items are reserved, and what is being done to the items. Users can also interrogate the change history. Thus the HM gives basic access control over versions, and allows users to determine the reasons for changes to try to ensure that changes are made consistently and compatibly. The HM also facilitates the production of variants, and merging of variants, although, for the reasons given earlier, there is always a need for checks that the merged changes are compatible.

The Task Manager (TM) provides a way of identifying and tracking low-level changes made as part of some higher-level activity. A task description consists of a title and identified active items, together with a record of completed item changes. Thus a task, at any time, represents work that has been undertaken towards some particular goal (e.g. a bug fix) and the work remaining to be done. DSEE maintains central task lists from which work is allocated. Users work on particular tasks, identified in individual task lists. Thus the TM helps both in planning and scheduling work, and with identifying ramifications if, for example, it is decided to abandon some activity. The TM provides the basic link between technical and managerial actions and plays a similar role to the contract in ISTAR, although the use of the TM is not so strongly formalised.

The Monitor Manager (MM) monitors user-defined dependencies between items (modules etc.) and alerts users in the event of any change to these modules. Thus, for example, it is possible to store dependencies so that when a module is modified the user is notified (reminded) of the need to change the associated documentation. Similarly a user can establish dependencies so that he is notified of any changes in modules on which he depends. The MM uses regular expressions for dependencies so it is relatively easy to specify dependencies on changing items, eg by giving a regular expression over the history of an item. The MM can also be used to notify oneself - thus, for example, a software engineer can arrange to be notified that he should change the associated documentation if he changes a source code module.

The Configuration Manager (CM) may be thought of as an extension to programs such as Make and Build described in part II. However the extensions are quite significant, and it is worth outlining them here. One of the problems with Make is that the language used for describing building operations is quite crude. The CM supports a more sophisticated, block structured, language. This enables the user to indicate much more clearly the structure of the system being built, and the dependencies between the different components. It also makes it relatively easy to specify variants of products, eg to run on different machines, and to have the variants built accordingly, eg by invoking the compiler for the appropriate machine. The descriptions used by the CM are still usually produced manually, although there are some tools for generating CM scripts, eg from Teamwork designs. In general, however, there is not enough information in the purely structural dependencies that can be ascertained simply by analysing a design or a program, and the automatically generated scripts have to be tailored by hand. The CM in conjunction with the HM also provides some facilities for managing team developments.

We mentioned earlier that emerging windowing and interface standards such as X-windows and the Motif "look and feel" were influencing IPSE design. DSEE works on top of X-windows, and can be accessed via Motif, which has a number of advantages. For example, in heterogeneous development systems, it is possible to maintain sources of a program intended to run on one class of computer on the filestore of another computer of another class (instruction set). If there is no cross-compiler from the development system to the execution system then DSEE will transmit the sources to their eventual execution environment for compilation (using CM scripts and X-windows) and can receive the results of compilation for storage on the original (development) machine. This can all be done through the one interface, without leaving the "host" machine. Thus DSEE (and presumably other IPSEs exploiting this technology) can operate effectively even in heterogeneous development environments.

As with ISTAR we can summarise the capabilities of DSEE in terms of the five forms of integration identified earlier:

- interaction integration - this was initiallya relatively low priority due to the desire to import tools from other suppliers and the operating system; X-windows and Motif give some opportunities for interface integration but what is achieved will still be heavily dependent on the individual tool developers;
- tool integration - this is achieved by a purpose-built distributed database;
- management integration - this is supported by the Task Manager;

- team integration - this is achieved by a mixture of the Task Manager, the History Manager with its ability to manage variants, and the Configuration Manager;
- technical integration - this was not an objective for DSEE.

Technically DSEE is less ambitious than ISTAR, but judging from demonstrations and user reports it caries out its more limited role very effectively. DSEE is probably a very effective environment for a medium sized project seeking to use relatively standard software development practices, eg good high level languages and structured methods.

III.2.3 Safra

Unlike DSEE and ISTAR, Safra was concerned with the production of a support environment for a particular project. Safra was developed by British Aerospace (BAe) for the Experimental Aircraft Programme (EAP). The EAP is a prototype advanced fighter aircraft. It is aerodynamically unstable and uses active computer control over the main control surfaces. A flyable aircraft was produced in extremely tight timescales, with software development compressed to about one third of the time that might normally have been available for such a project. Safra was essentially a "one-off" IPSE development. It proved highly successful for its purpose, although it probably wouldn't be very widely useful outside the avionics application domain. BAe are now working on the next generation of support environment (see part V).

The Safra project was quite different from DSEE and ISTAR in that it was more concerned with producing a single coherent method set and supporting that set with tools, than with providing general purpose IPSE mechanisms. Thus Safra represents pragmatic integration of existing capabilities, not an attempt to provide a general open framework.

Safra employs CORE, MASCOT and a detailed software design method based on MASCOT supported by a commercial IPSE product known as Perspective. Perspective was developed by Systems Designers, now SD-Scicon, and supports a variant of Pascal extended to incorporate the basic MASCOT concepts. Perspective also provides facilities for configuration management and host-target working, that is developing software on one machine for execution on another.

CORE is used for expression of requirements. It is a structured method with a well-defined procedure (in the BAe version of CORE there are 11 stages) and a set of related diagrammatic notations. CORE identifies the main independent (potentially concurrently executing) activities and the data and control flows between these activities. It also identifies and defines the structure of the data which flows in the system (as a regular expression). The functionality of the activities is described by means of text. CORE was supported by a graphics tools developed by BAe, which represents the resulting requirements in a proprietary design database known as PSL/PSA.

MASCOT represents systems as sets of processes communicating either in a tightly coupled fashion via "channels" or in a loosely coupled manner via "pools". MASCOT is normally thought of as an independent design description, but in Safra it is strongly integrated with CORE. There is a natural flow from the activities (and data) identified in CORE to MASCOT activities (and to the two types of data flow). Thus the PSL/PSA database also holds MASCOT designs derived from the requirements. This design is taken down to the level where it is straightforward to design the process (or sub-process), because the unit corresponds to a simple algorithm or decision table.

Perspective holds the source programs for the EAP software, and the derived object code. The code is modularised (structured) according to the MASCOT design and the code is kept under configuration control by Perspective. Perspective supports the notion of individual domains, as described in part II and a form of handshake protocol for entering items into, and removing them from, shared domains.

Perspective provides extensive source code debugging facilities both for the host and target. Complete software (sub)systems can be exercised on the host, then transferred to the target, and their execution still monitored in the target. For EAP the software was all developed using Perspective and it's host-target capabilities. Also extensive software testing was carried out on a rig before the software was installed in the aircraft. A number of tests were carried out on the ground, eg high speed taxi trials, before the aircraft was flown. Safra was used for essentially all the activities from requirements, upto the use of the test rig.

The complete software system developed for EAP was 225k words of code running on a distributed embedded multi-processor system. The software included some critical components, e.g. active management of control surfaces, and was mainly "real-time". The evidence from the project was that Safra was very successful, for its specific purpose. On previous aircraft, eg the Tornado, code had been developed at about 250 lines per man year (this is probably typical for such high integrity software). For EAP productivity of 1700 lines per man year was achieved. The investment per software engineer was about £30,000, but BAe estimated that the increase in productivity repaid the investment six times over. The above should not be taken to indicate that there were no problems with the approach adopted - however it should be clear that the approach was effective by comparison with the company's (and the industry's) standard approaches.

We can also discuss the capabilities of Safra in terms of the five forms of integration identified earlier:

- interaction integration - this was not feasible; Perspective and the CORE tool used different, and incompatible (character and raster graphics) terminals so it was not possible to integrate the interfaces;

- tool integration - this was by special purpose code to provide "shells" round the tools and to convert between the existing proprietary databases used;

- management integration - this was not addressed within Safra; management was carried out external to the IPSE;

- team integration - this was achieved by means of domains supported by Perspective;

- technical integration - this was probably the greatest strength of Safra, and the primary reason for its success; there is a strong flow from CORE, through MASCOT to Perspective Pascal, giving a clear technical structure to the project.

Safra is clearly limited in its application domain and, so far as the author is aware, it will not be used again even on future avionics projects. However it serves to demonstrate that a relatively pragmatic IPSE development can prove highly effective.

III.2.4   General Observations

It is interesting to consider the reasons for the differences between the three IPSEs described above. As indicated earlier most of them stem from the different commercial positions of the companies involved.

ISTAR is basically an infrastructure plus a set of tools (and tool-building tools) sold with a set of services. The design of ISTAR is based on the premise that IPSEs are a "semi-custom business" and that it is necessary to be able to tailor an IPSE and its tool set to the needs of a particular customer, or project. Thus ISTAR makes relatively few commitments to particular ways of solving software development problems. The main counter-example to this general observation is the use of the contractual approach - here ISTAR has made a commitment to a particular managerial style and a way of linking technical and managerial activities. However it can be argued that this approach is widely applicable and doesn't cut ISTAR off from any classes of application. Thus the most significant characteristic of ISTAR is that it is intended to be a way of generating solutions to particular software development problems, and IST provide consultancy and other services to develop a solution for a client.

DSEE is essentially an extended operating system plus a set of very general purpose tools which can be thought of as additional operating system utilities. Thus DSEE is primarily an infrastructure and there is little emphasis on end-user tools, eg compilers or CASE tools. DSEE is sold simply as a product and there is no associated consultancy or customisation as there is with ISTAR. This reflects the commercial aims of a hardware manufacturer who is seeking to increase the attractiveness of his products. Presumably this was also one of the attractions of Apollo for HP!

BAe is (primarily) in the business of producing aircraft, not software engineering tools. Thus Safra reflects much more directly end user needs, and was geared towards the production of real operational software. Where necessary, generality and flexibility were sacrificed for effectiveness. Here again the commercial needs are reflected - a tool was needed to assist in the development of a working aircraft, and there was no value to be gained in producing a generally marketable product.

The intention of this comparison is not to praise or denigrate one or other of the three environments. Instead the intention is to indicate the complexity of IPSE design and to hint at the subtlety of the decisions and trade-offs to be made in designing IPSEs. These examples, hopefully, make the point quite forcibly as the different commercial issues have resulted in the development of vastly different systems - all of which can still validly be called IPSEs, and which are effective in their own way.

It is perhaps also worthwhile making some observations on pricing and market penetration. CASE tools often run on IBM PCs, or compatibles, and are priced from a few hundred pounds for simple, single user, tools up to, perhaps, several tens of thousands of pounds for the more sophisticated products. Typically these have sold very well, and often companies have furnished whole development projects with a particular CASE tool. Thus market penetration is quite high with product volumes in thousands, or even tens of thousands. IPSEs, on the other hand, tend to be quite expensive, with prices ranging from the tens of thousands up to hundreds of thousands for systems such as ISTAR. Of course it must be remembered that, with ISTAR, one is buying a service as well as a product, and the environment will support many individuals and possibly many projects. Nonetheless the market penetration of "full-blown" IPSEs is disappointing and few, if any products, have reached a total of one hundred sales in their lifetime, and some are still in single figures.

There seem to be several reasons for the disparity between the sales of CASE tools and IPSEs. Obviously there is the issue of price, but there seem to be several other important reasons. It is quite clear to a manager what CASE tools do - IPSEs although much more pervasive don't quite so obviously "do something", indeed part of their job may be stop people doing things, eg deleting files. Thus it is more difficult to explain the value of IPSEs, especially when they carry high price tags. Arguably this problem has been exacerbated by concentration on developing PTIs, rather than on large tool sets. We return to the issue of evolving PTIs in part V.

The use of an IPSE usually implies an organisational and managerial change, whereas the use of a CASE tool does not. Thus the ramifications of procuring an IPSE are much greater. IPSEs typically don't support management activities very effectively - but with the sums of money involved it will certainly be managers who are making the purchasing decisions. Finally there is relatively little evidence that IPSEs are actually cost effective. The experience with Safra is one of the few really successful projects carried out using an IPSE. Thus it is hard to convince managers of the value of making such major investments.

It seems reasonable to believe that IPSEs will become viable technology both in a pragmatic sense, and in a commercial sense. However the evidence to date is that they are not, as yet, a viable business proposition. We will now turn to a more technical assessment of IPSEs which are currently available.

The capabilities of most so-called IPSEs are somewhat limited when compared against the objectives set out in the introduction. There are three primary areas where the objectives are not met: coverage of all technical and managerial activities, integration and scaling.

Few environments have a comprehensive set of tools. ISTAR is perhaps one of the best of the available environments in this respect, but there are many environments which provide little more than programming support. Perhaps classical examples of this are Smalltalk, and Perspective, each of which are very effective in their own way (object-oriented and host-target development) but which extend little beyond program development and testing.

Integration is strongest in the simple environments such as Smalltalk and Perspective, largely because they have been developed as single systems, and because they are relatively limited in scope. With open environments integration, especially from the interaction point of view, is difficult to achieve and most open environments will suffer from non-uniformity between tools.

Scaling is a less obvious problem. The performance of IPSEs is largely constrained by the ability to access the infrastructure database. Most present-day environments are very slow, even with modest sized project teams. These performance problems prevent the IPSE from scaling to dealing with large projects. Unfortunately, as the

the environment becomes more sophisticated, e.g. the objects stored become finer grained and more relations are held between objects, the performance becomes worse. Also performance becomes worse as the demands on the database, eg for the volume of stored data or for the number of transactions, increase. Thus these intrinsic database problems make it difficult to make more sophisticated environments for big projects - and, of course, it is the big projects that require the sophistication.

Thus, at present, there are limitations on the capabilities of IPSEs and it seems that at least some of the limitations are unlikely to be overcome in the near future. This reinforces our view that it will be some time before IPSEs will be a commercially viable technology.

Part IV: High Integrity Systems

IPSEs are intended to be widely applicable so they should be useful for the development of high integrity systems, ie systems whose failure could be catastrophic either for an organisation, individuals or the environment. The avionics programs for the EAP clearly fall into the class of high integrity software so there is evidence that IPSEs can be used for such applications. However the main concern of this part of the paper is not with the use of IPSEs in high integrity applications, but with the additional requirements which have to be placed on IPSEs for use in the development of such applications.

Given the success of the Safra project it may seem that there are no additional requirements. Our aim in section IV.1 is to indicate why there are extra requirements, and to outline their nature. These requirements can best be thought of as an additional set of control rules which the IPSE has to enforce. In order to articulate the requirements we use a model of the development process and the data stored in an IPSE. The model is outlined in section IV.2 and section IV.3 uses the model to present some requirements on IPSEs for the development of high integrity systems. The model also gives an illustration of the type of data structures which must be stored and manipulated by an IPSE.

It must be emphasised that the material presented in this part of the paper is tentative. The ideas expressed here have been developed in conjunction with the evolution of a PTI standard aimed at high integrity systems (PCTE+). Whilst many of the ideas are based on current practices, eg in high security operating systems, they have not been evaluated in use. Nonetheless it is hoped that this brief discussion will serve to point out those issues which an IPSE for high integrity applications must address.

Finally it is worth noting that one of the reasons why the Safra project was successful may have been that it was concerned with a high integrity application. Typically much labour intensive work is carried out in verifying high integrity systems, and much less effort is put into such activities for less critical software. Even though Safra was limited, it removed much of the potential for error in these critical verification activities (because of the strong technical integration) and will have helped reduce the verification effort substantially. Assuming that this hypothesis is valid, such major gains in productivity would not have been noticed in less critical activities due to the relatively low emphasis placed on verification.

IV.1   INTRODUCTION

High Integrity (or dependable) applications may have to satisfy one, or several, objectives. Typically these objectives are not to do with functionality, but with protection of resources. It is helpful to illustrate some of these possible objectives here, before discussing the requirements for IPSEs. High integrity applications developed using an IPSE might be intended to satisfy one (or more) of the following classes of objective:

- military security - preventing unauthorised access to sensitive (classified) data stored by the application;
- privacy - preventing unauthorised access to (sensitive) personal data stored by the application;
- safety - preventing the computerised system, especially its software, contributing to malfunctions in systems which could lead to injury, loss of life or loss of valuable resources;

• integrity - prevention of corruption of data stored by the application.

We make the distinction that security and privacy are concerned with controlling read access, and integrity is concerned with controlling modify access. Unfortunately the term "high integrity" is also used to embrace a number of objectives, including security - we will use the term integrity for the specific objective, and high integrity as the group name.

Where software is used to achieve, at least in part, any of the above objectives then reliance is placed on the software to carry out some particular function, or to display some properties. In some cases the objectives for the software may be functional correctness but in other cases the objectives for the software might be timeliness, integrity, or robustness. Clearly the development environment affects the ability of the software to meet these objectives - for example if the wrong set of modules are integrated then it is unlikely that the system will be functionally correct. Thus, in this context, the question which we have to address is - "if security, privacy, etc. are the objectives for systems developed using an IPSE, what are the corresponding objectives for an IPSE?"

The general answer to this question is that any of the objectives that relate to logical properties of a system, rather than physical properties of the system's environment, might be required for an IPSE. Thus we might require an IPSE to uphold rules about military security, privacy and integrity, however the most important objective is integrity.

IV.1.1   Integrity

It is first necessary to clarify what we mean by integrity. Following dictionary definitions we can say that integrity means "freedom from corruption or impairment". Thus achieving integrity means protecting something from corruption or impairment. The reason, therefore, that integrity is the key issue for an environment for high integrity systems is that corruption of, say, a program source in the IPSE could lead to incorrect code being loaded in the application, and hence erroneous (eg unsafe) behaviour on the part of the application. We can illustrate this further by means of a stylised fault tree:

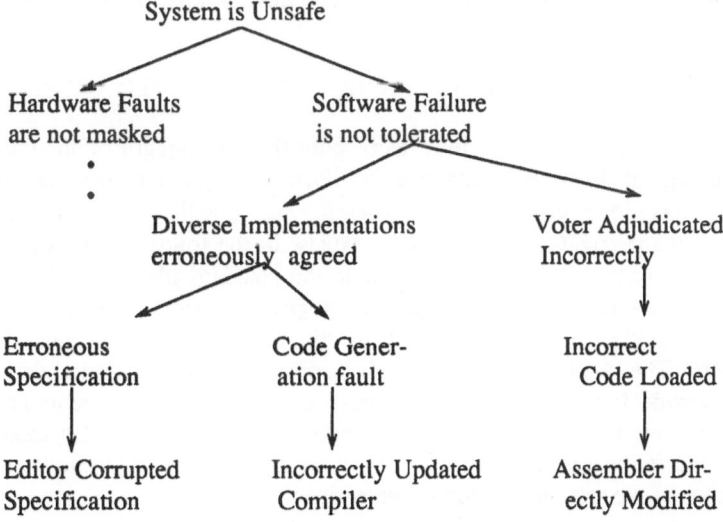

Although clearly oversimplified the tree serves to show the sort of causal relationships that there can be between actions (failures) in the IPSE and in the application. Obviously some of these issues relate directly to the integrity of the tools which is partially outside the scope of the IPSE (even if the tools were developed in the IPSE). However several of the problems can be addressed by control mechanisms in the IPSE. This again can be seen by means of an illustrative, rather than definitive, example:

Fault	Editor Corrupted Specification	Incorrectly Updated Compiler	Assembler Directly Modified
Possible Cause	Programmer Wrote Own Editor	Compiler Used Before all Modules Updated	Programmer Edited Code to Improve Speed
Possible Cure	Control over Tool Introduction	Make Update Atomic (Indivisible)	Deny Direct Access to Assembler
High Level Control Objective	Ensure Integrity of Toolset by making Tool Introduction a Privileged Operation	Ensure Integrity of Composite Operations	Prevent Modification of Derived Items

The high level objectives set out in the bottom row of the above table are clearly control mechanisms which the IPSE infrastructure could enforce and, as such, they are integrity objectives for the infrastructure. In the following we will refer to the notion of "control objectives" meaning the integrity objectives which the infrastructure must seek to enforce.

The notion of integrity in an IPSE is rather more subtle than the above discussion implies. However we first amplify the integrity control objectives, before delving into these additional issues.

IV.1.2 Integrity Control Objectives

There is relatively little work published on integrity although some operating systems, eg the VME HSO referred to above, do support object integrity labels and control over operations based on these integrity labels with the intention that higher integrity (data) items receive higher integrity labels. In the following we will draw on a number of previous areas of work. These include the standard ideas of military security, the notion of integrity labels, and concepts of integrity control as identified by Clark and Wilson [Clark 1987] and Chris Sennett in his work on development environments [Sennett 1987]. The work also makes some use of enterprise model defined by Dobson and McDermid [Dobson 1988]. Although we draw on a considerable amount of earlier work we will try to make the discussion self-contained so the reader should only need to consult the references for amplification on the points made, or to understand the wider ramifications of the selection of control objectives.

We also note that integrity must relate to individuals, as well as programs and data, because many of our controls will relate to what individuals are allowed to do. In this context integrity really means "trustworthiness" and we will think of an IPSE user as having an "integrity clearance" by analogy with a security clearance.

There seem to be three primary aspects of integrity which any set of control objectives should address. These aspects are:

- rights of a user to modify data: these will be based on the user's integrity clearance and the integrity of the data;
- capabilites of a tool to modify data: these will be based both on data integrity and the tool integrity "clearance";
- control over user invocation of programs/tools: this is straightforward access control which might mean, for example, that a user couldn't install a new program - only the IPSE administrator could.

Briefly the reasons for being concerned with these issues are as follows. Control over modification of sources is important as it can impair the integrity of the system being developed in the environment. The rights are contingent on the user (or the role in which he is working), because we would trust the application system architect to modify the system architecture, but we would not trust a junior programmer (or the project manager) to do so. Less obviously we may have varying degrees of trust in tools. For example we may be willing to use an optimising compiler for initial development work, but not to produce the code for system to be tested and installed, because of concerns over the correctness of the optimisations. Finally control over program/tool invocation is necessary as only certain users (roles) should be able to modify certain information, eg user integrity clearances or the set of installed tools.

It may not be entirely clear that there is a distinction between integrity and type (where we could think of the users as having types too). There certainly is a distinction, however, as the example of compiler optimisation should show. Both the unoptimising and optimising compilers would be of type, say, Ada Source -> Assembler, but each would have different access rights because of their (assumed) integrity. Specifically the unoptimising compiler would be able to write object files with an integrity level indicating their suitability for release (or final test) and the optimising compiler would not. Having control over tool invocation based on types is important - but it is not a substitute for integrity controls. We have just hinted at the subtlety regarding the interpretation of integrity by referring to "assumed" integrity. It is therefore appropriate now to consider these subtleties.

IV.1.3   Belief in Integrity

Operations in an IPSE can genuinely change the integrity of an item, eg a compiler fault can corrupt an assembler or binary file. However operations in the IPSE can also affect our belief in the integrity of some item. This can best be illustrated by means of a number of small examples.

Consider a program source entered through a text editor. Initially little is known about it (except who produced it) and it is a reasonable expectation that it is not even a syntactically correct program, ie that it would have impairments that stopped it being a legal progam. However if the program were subsequently compiled then our belief in its integrity (freedom from impairment) would rise. If, later, the program were verified (using a theorem prover of known integrity!) against its specification, then our belief in its integrity would rise still further: the program source is now known (or believed as there may be faults in the proof system) to have no impairments with respect to its specification, as well as with respect to the rules of the programming language. Thus, although the program source hasn't changed (and neither has its real integrity) our belief in (knowledge of) its integrity has, and we might want to change its integrity label accordingly.

Imagine now a less formal program development where a specification is presented for review. The specification developer might "walk through" the specification and get agreement from the others present that the specification is as intended. This again raises confidence and the reviewers might wish to raise the integrity label of the specification. In fact it is possible to use integrity labels as a way of controlling progress through development phases with reviews authorising the step from one phase to the next.

It can be seen that integrity labels are perhaps best thought of as indicative of our believe in something, rather than a true reflection of integrity. Seen in this guise they can be thought of as a useful control mechanism - and perhaps the best guide we have to true integrity. However the discussion also indicates that we need further set of issues to be addressed by the control objectives:

- rights of a user to modify integrity labels: this might include an "n-man" rule which would allow the attendees at a review jointly to uplift integrity labels, but not allow a single individual to do so;
- rights of a tool to modify integrity labels.

It may also be apparent from the above that we need some notion of "integrity flow" where the integrity of some newly created or modified item reflects the integrity of the items and tools used to produce it. Thus an item made with five high integrity items, and one low integrity one, would have a low integrity (because the IPSE users would believe it to be impaired in the absence of any other information).

IV.1.4   Relevant Control Objectives

As indicated earlier there are a number of concerns facing the designer of an IPSE for the development of high integrity applications. We have briefly indicated some of the objectives related to integrity, and we will amplify on these points below. However it is worth pointing out that there will be other objectives to satisfy.

For example if military software is being developed then specifications and program sources may be classified. Thus the IPSE may have to support a conventional military security policy. Worse, the program sources and the application may be constrained by **different** policies, and thus the IPSE may have to support multiple policies simultaneously, eg when debugging the programs. In general the range of policy objectives which have to be supported by an IPSE may be very large and complex, see for example McDermid and Hocking [McDermid 1989b] for a discussion of one possible set of policies.

Integrity related objectives are the most important for an IPSE as integrity must be handled, no matter what the application domain of the system under development in the IPSE. Consequently we will focus on integrity for the rest of this part of the chapter.

However it is important to note that additional objectives may be relevant for an IPSE, and that the objectives may be in conflict with one another, necessitating compromises in designing an IPSE for high integrity developments.

IV.2 ELEMENTS OF THE MODEL

In order to articulate the control objectives for an IPSE more clearly it is necessary to have a fairly precise model of the entities that comprise and interact with the IPSE. The following descriptive model outlines the elements which the author believes are needed in such a model. Space does not permit full discussion of the reasons for choosing this model, but hopefully most of the concepts are clear from consideration of the activities undertaken in software development.

IV.2.1 Overview of the Model

There are five main elements, or entities, in the model, two of which relate to the IPSE users:

- Individuals - the set of people authorised to use the computer system and the IPSE;
- Roles - aspects of organisational structure representing different responsibilities associated with the IPSE or system under development;
- Data - passive "objects" in the IPSE which may be manipulated by the programs (active objects) in the environment;
- Programs - active "objects" which may be tools in the IPSE, or (parts of) the system under development;
- Activities - units of work which individuals undertake in fulfilling a role, eg design review is an activity which might be undertaken in a QA role. Activities can be undertaken "manually", eg by direct user input, or by using tools and data in an IPSE.

These elements appear to be fundamental to a model of software development, and hence an integrity model. To produce a fully detailed model of control objectives would require a specification of the permissible members of each entity "set". For the present purpose no further detail is required but we note that it would be possible to produce a categorisation of the above entities which would be representative of real developments. All the entities are disjoint, including programs and data - because we can regard programs as data before they are loaded and executed. This gives rise to systematic relationships between programs and data which enable us to deal with the "subject-object duality" which arises in program development, see below.

There are attributes associated with the entities in the model which are needed to enable us to articulate the constraints on execution of programs which will form the heart of the model. These attributes are set out below.

There are also a set of relations between the entities in the model. In general these would have to be stored and maintained by the IPSE in order that it could enforce the control objectives. The relations cannot readily be classified in any helpful way. We present a few examples of these relations below.

IV.2.2   The Entities of the Model

Here we briefly discuss the model entities introduced above. We focus on those entities which are most important for the articulation of the control objectives, and aim to give some background information to underpin the selection of control objectives. In some cases we give categorisations to describe the entities because we would expect the control rules to depend on the particular category in question.

IV.2.2.1   Individuals

The individuals are the set of people authorised to use the computer system including the IPSE. There is no useful way of categorising the users of the IPSE except via their roles.

IV.2.2.2   Roles

The roles represent the different responsibilities associated with the IPSE or system under development. An individual may be associated with more than one role, and vice versa. Here the categorisation is more important as access to functions (tools) and to data is determined, to some extent, by the role. The following categorisation is intended primarily to indicate the most salient "integrity related" roles, however project management is included as it is important in software development in terms of allocation of responsibility. The roles chosen by way of illustration are:
- Developer;
- Design Authority;
- Project Manager;
- Evaluator;
- Integrity Officer/System Administrator.

These roles hopefully have a fairly intuitive meaning, but, in practice, roles will be very important in achieving integrity, so it is helpful to expand on each role here.

A developer is responsible for some aspect of program (software system) design and development. This may involve both implementation and testing, or it may simply be a design activity resulting in some specification. There are three significant factors constraining the role. First, the developer may produce something according to a specification he is given, but may not change that specification. Second, the developer may not by himself "sign off" his own work to say that his product satisfies the specification. Third, the developer will be accountable for, but not responsible for, his work. Responsibility will lie with the design authority.

A design authority is responsible for the design of some part of a system. In general, it is the design authority who is responsible for producing the specification to which the developer works. The design authority can delegate authority for some activity, and hence accountability, but not responsibility. Thus the distinction between design authority and developer is a classic case of "separation of role" for achieving data integrity. Typically a design authority will develop a design for some part of a system, this will be implemented by a developer, and the implementation will be signed off by both the developer and the design authority.

In developing a low level specification from a high level one, a design authority will typically also be acting as developer (albeit of specifications not of code). The role of design authority is assigned by the project manager and may not be delegated. Thus in practice, the system design authority will define the system architecture, this will be broken down in to subsystems and design authority for particular subsystems will be allocated to particular individuals by the project manager. These individuals may "subcontract" developers without delegation of responsibility. They can also "subcontract" authority but not responsibility for a design review to the evaluation role.

Both design authority and developer have the ability to create (and modify) technical descriptions of systems - specifications, programs, etc. They can also carry out other activities, eg testing.

The project manager role has the usual responsibilities for ensuring project progress, etc. In the security/integrity context the role has responsibility for defining the design authority for the system as a whole, and for subsystems. This responsibility may not be delegated. Again this is an issue of separation of role. The design authority for the system cannot design the system with potential flaws, then assign himself to design and implement the critical parts of the system. This is perhaps only germane when one is considering deliberately introduced flaws in secure applications.

The evaluators are responsible for independent assessment of the products of development. They have responsibility for assessing the complete system in conjunction with the overall system design authority. In practice this means that the design authority will submit the system to evaluation when he thinks it is satisfactory. Evaluation may also be accountable but not responsible for lower level design reviews if delegated by the design authority. The evaluators are allowed to access, but not modify, all the development data but they may have data of their own which is not visible to design authorities or developers.

The integrity officer or system administrator is responsible for ensuring that the IPSE operates with adequate integrity, and for certain "housekeeping" activities. In general this involves establishing users, projects and project managers, together with assessing the audit trail for potential security/integrity violations. It is desirable to separate administration and integrity roles, but there are difficult issues, eg patching audit files in the event of disc corruption may violate the integrity rules which would apply to a normal user, which suggest that it is not practical so to do. A "two man" rule for certain operations may be appropriate.

IV.2.2.3 Data

The data are the passive "objects" in the IPSE which may be manipulated by the programs (active objects) in the IPSE. In general we have to allow for duality in the sense that objects stored in the IPSE can be loaded and executed as programs. This can be treated by means of suitable relations between programs and data. The categories of data needed are:

- descriptions - specifications, programs, documentation, etc.;
- evidence - test results, proofs, logs of reviews, etc.;
- test data;
- system data - including passwords, access control lists, etc.

The descriptions represent all the results of the constructive aspects of software development, and documentation is intended to include prosaic items such as user manuals, which may have integrity constraints (for example because errors therein may lead to security breaches in the operational system).

Evidence is the information provided as part of the development process, and by evaluators, that the descriptions bear the proper relationships to one another and thus that the system being developed meets its integrity and security objectives. Test data represents the information with which the (partially) developed system is exercised.

The system data represents the data structures necessary to maintain security and integrity of operation. It may appear odd that they are present in a description which is mainly concerned with an IPSE interface, however it is necessary to identify this category in order to articulate certain security and integrity requirements.

In practice a further category may be needed in order to deal with new inputs to the system whose integrity status (category) is not yet known.

There are also attributes associated with the entities in the model. These include:
- Owner - applying to programs and data;
- Integrity Levels - applying to individuals, roles, and data;
- Type - applying to data and programs.

These attributes will be used in enforcing the control objectives.

The categorisation is almost (but not completely) orthogonal to the integrity classifications presented below. It is possible, for example, to have low integrity executable which represents a part of the operational system which is untrusted, and high integrity executable.

IV.2.2.4 Programs

Programs are active "objects" which may be tools in the environment, or (parts of) the system under development. There is a straightforward categorisation of programs:
- tools;
- system (components).

This categorisation is essential as there will be different access rights associated with each category. In practice, a much finer categorisation might be expected, eg related to the number of integrity levels available for the data and tools. Alternatively we may need to draw distinctions between transformational tools, eg compilers, and verification tools, eg test suites, as they can affect (belief in) integrity in different ways.

IV.2.2.5 Activities

Activities fall into three basic classes:
- create/modify;
- transform;
- analyse/evaluate.

This simple categorisation is motivated by the need to represent the extent to which different classes of activity can affect integrity, or are responsible for integrity.

Most creation or modification activities will be untrusted, and their output will later be checked to ensure that it is suitable for "elevation" to a higher integrity class by some transformation activity, or by some manual or automatic assessment activity.

There may seem to be some redundancy between the idea of a role, a tool (as a subcategory of program) and an activity. However these three concepts are related, but disjoint. A role may involve creation and assessment of a number of data items, and thus embody several activities. The activities and role categories do not always bear the same relationship to one another - eg there will be a difference in activities when some transformation is carried out by a trusted tool as opposed to an untrusted tool as, in the latter case, additional assessment will be required. Similarly the activities do not correspond simply to tools. Some activities may be carried out automatically, but some may be manual, eg assessment via a design review. Further, more than one tool may be capable of supporting a particular activity. One example of this is the multiplicity of editors available on most computer systems. Thus there is not a unique association between any of these three entities.

IV.2.3   Attributes

As indicated earlier there are attributes associated with the entities in the model. These are:
- Integrity Levels - applying to individuals, roles, and data;
- Type - applying to data and programs.

We discuss these attributes in the above order, again seeking to give a simple description, rather than a full definition as might be appropriate for a policy model.

IV.2.3.1   Integrity Levels

There is not such a well-accepted view of integrity markings as there is with security markings. Some of the earliest work on integrity was that due to Biba [Biba 1977]. More recently Sennett [Sennett 1987] has addressed the issue of integrity markings in an IPSE. We follow his scheme:
- Classification - a hierarchical marking. For expository purposes we will take only two markings - high and low;
- Categories - a project related "need to modify" marking. Elements of this marking set might be projects.

The reader is referred to Sennett [Sennett 1987] for a detailed explanation of the reasons for adopting these markings. In essence the reason is as follows. If we assume that an IPSE supports multiple projects (simultaneously or perhaps through libraries passed from one project to another) then the ability to change data shared between projects should imply the right to modify information in respect of all projects which use the data.

As we pointed out earlier the idea of integrity levels needs careful interpretation. In practice, the integrity labels really represent belief in integrity.

IV.2.3.2   Types

In general an IPSE will support a type system identifying the classes of data stored in the IPSE database, and possibly the tools which operate upon these data. For a high integrity IPSE the type system takes on greater significance. Some tools will be trusted to change the integrity levels of particular data items, or to generate new data items of given integrity level. However a trusted Ada compiler should not be trusted to generate high integrity object code (binary load images) from project plans. It is arguable that trusted tools should be relied on to "vet" their own input for type correctness, however the use of additional type information to constrain the execution of tools reduces the tool's scope for malfeasance and thus simplifies certification of the tool, increases confidence in the overall IPSE, etc.

Type systems are a complex subject in their own right, and it is not appropriate to discuss them in detail here. However it is clear that, at minimum, a type model is required that supports some form of data categorisation. Ideally a much more sophisticated type model should be used. One possible candidate is the model supported by Ten15 [Foster 1989]. Particular attractions of this type system include the ability to represent the type changes which occur when loading a program for execution. This would enable us to articulate, for example, integrity and security constraints on accessing a program as a passive object in the IPSE database and to state separately the rules that apply to it as an active entity whilst executing. This separation of concerns simplifies the specification of IPSE properties.

IV.2.4   Relations

The set of relations needed to describe the complete model implicit in the set of entities presented above is very large. We simply present here a small but, hopefully, representative sample of relations to illustrate the nature of the proposed model. The relations are presented without constraints. The relevant consistency constraints are illustrated below, and the integrity control objectives are also sketched in terms of these relations. The notation used is that the name of the property or relation is given, followed by the operand names in chevron brackets, ie property/relation<operands>.

IV.2.4.1   Properties

The properties of entities have been indicated above, and include:
- integrity<program> - the maximum integrity level to which a program can write data, ie its integrity "clearance";
- integrity<role> - the maximum integrity level to which a role can write data;
- integrity<individual> - the maximum integrity level to which an individual can write data;
- type<datum> - the type of the data item;
- type<program> - the type of the program.

These properties are those outlined informally in the preceding sections. In practice the detailed control objectives would be expressed as predicates over these properties and the relations described in the subsequent sections. This can be thought of as forming part of the schema for the IPSE database.

IV.2.4.2   Binary Relations

The binary relationships represent some of the basic properties needed to articulate the integrity objectives set out in section IV.3. Again we simply present an illustration - the complete set would be quite large and complex:

- needs<role, data> - data which a role can access - this may be directly an integrity issue or it may reflect access as laid down by a contract (as with ISTAR);
- assigned<role, individual> - simple binding of user and role to which they are allocated;
- accountable<role, data> - data which role is accountable for producing;
- responsible<role, data> - data which role is responsible for producing;
- authority<role, data> - identification of design authority for data;
- evaluator<role, data> - identification of evaluator for data;
- readable<data, program> - data for which program has read permission;
- writable<data, program> - data for which program has write permission.

These relations show the main properties associated with the model as it relates to the "static" picture, that is the assignment of roles, the visibility of data, and so on.

IV.3   Control Objectives

There are many possible values for the relations defined above which would not correspond to a "meaningful" state of an IPSE. The control objectives are intended to ensure that the values are meaningful. We indicate first some basic consistency objectives, then set out some objectives which would constrain operations in an IPSE.

IV.3.1   Consistency Objectives

The objectives are presented informally using the relational notation introduced above. We use the asterisk (*) to represent that an element might be repeated in the relation. Thus "role*" below represents multiple roles in the "valid_assignments" relation.

- valid_delegation<role1, role2, data> - role1 is design authority for data and role2 is of type evaluation or design authority or development;
- valid_authority<role, data> - role is design authority and no other role is design authority for that data;
- valid_assignments<individual, role*> - individual does not have evaluation and design/development/management responsibility for the same data;   integrity level of role is less than the integrity level of the individual.

These are the constraints which derive from the informal descriptions of the entities given in section IV.2 and we would expect them to be upheld by the IPSE. Thus these control objectives are more of the form of data invariants, than control mechanisms. However we would, *inter alia*, require these rules to be upheld on modifying the IPSE state. This is the realm of the transition objectives.

IV.3.2   Transition Objectives

These control objectives are constraints on operations which can be carried out in the IPSE, consequently they govern the state transitions made by the IPSE. The first of the following objectives following represents the direct integrity flow constraint. They are again expressed in a simple relational form - they may be viewed as being stylised post-conditions reflecting the allowable state after the transition (contingent on the state before the transition). The objectives of section IV.3.1 still apply.

- allowable_update<role, program, data*> - the integrity of the data exceeds that of the program and the role;
- validl_tool_installation<program, role*, type, integrity> - tool can be installed if the types of data are visible, and the integrity level of the tool is appropriate, given the roles in which the tool is intended to be available;
- valid_sign_off<individual, role, program, data> - role is design authority for data; individual integrity exceeds that of the data; individual is assigned to the role; program integrity exceeds that of the data and other program constraints satisfied - this represents the constraint to allow the individual to "sign off" an item and so raise the integrity level; multi-role "sign-off" could also be represented easily;
- valid_tool_execution<role, individual, program, data*> - program is a tool; execution is type valid; explicitly referenced data is accessible to user in role on access control grounds; integrity of data written is exceeded by that of integrity of role and tool.

There are clearly other direct controls, but these are some of the most crucial ones.

IV.3.3   Elaborating Control Objectives

We have illustrated the nature of some possible control objectives. If developing an IPSE for high integrity systems, then a complete set of control objectives would need to be elaborated. So far as the author is aware most work on this front has been done in the context of PCTE+ which is an extension of the PCTE PTI intended for use in high integrity, particularly military security, development projects. PCTE+ supports integrity labels, security labels and types (albeit rather crudely). However there does not yet seem to be agreement on a sensible set of control objectives for PCTE+.

IV.4   COMMENTARY

Even the brief illustration of control objectives given above serves to illustrate the complexity of the necessary rules. This complexity is very worrying, because there are already difficulties in producing effective IPSEs even without considering these control objectives. It seems worthwhile amplifying on the issues of producing high integrity IPSEs, before drawing more general conclusions.

There are a number of aspects of the development of a high integrity IPSE which we need to consider. Four important questions are:
- usability - is the user interface intelligible?
- assurance - how confident can we be in the integrity of the IPSE implementation?
- effectiveness - is the IPSE effective for software development?
- cost-effectiveness - does the IPSE give "value for money"?

In many sense the last question incorporates, or sums up, the first three. We treat the points in turn.

If the set of possible rules for integrity (and perhaps privacy or military security) are all directly and independently manifest to the IPSE users then it is likely that the IPSE will prove bewildering to use. However suitable IPSE organisation should make it possible to remove many of the possible sources of confusion, eg by making all the controls implicitly defined by the domain in which someone is working, or the activity on which they are working. Thus it should be possible to reduce, if not eliminate, the complexity of the interface, as seen by the typical software engineer, caused by the integrity controls. However the system management/integrity policy management interface will be very complex, and this may mean that, in practice, it is necessary to live with a rather simpler set of rules.

The implementation of the IPSE infrastructure clearly has an effect on integrity of the software developed using it. Specifically it needs to be of high integrity - with respect to corrupting the programs, specifications etc. - if we are to trust it to develop high integrity software. (Clearly there is a recursion here but we only consider the IPSE itself.) Thus we need to have confidence, or assurance, in the integrity of the IPSE implementation. Estimates for the size of an implementation of PCTE+ (the only PTI to address the integrity issue) vary, but figures of upto a million lines of code have been quoted. There are major technical problems in gaining assurance in systems of such size; it is also likely to be very expensive, even if the "trusted" parts of the system can be minimised.

With effectiveness we are most concerned about the performance of the IPSE, especially where it is layered on top of an operating system and an alternative development environment would simply be that operating system. If tools run much slower in the IPSE then there will be a cost penalty in using it - and also problems of morale among the staff using the IPSE, affecting quality, and other facets of the software. Again taking PCTE+ as a guideline, given the volume of code, it seems far from clear that adequate performance can be achieved. However it is possible to implement integrity controls fairly cheaply as has been demonstrated, for example, with VME HSO. This might mean that it is only viable to implement a high integrity IPSE on top of a high integrity operating system from the point of view of effectiveness. This point will really only be answered by trial implementations and use.

Cost-effectiveness really relates to whether or not there is a cheaper way of achieving the same end result, ie high integrity applications. This is still an open question, but the above observations on effectiveness, assurance, etc. tend to indicate that there would be problems in supporting a sophisticated set of control policies with the currently available IPSE technology, in a cost-effective manner. Perhaps the fact that Safra was used to great effect without any of the controls illustrated above indicates that the presence of any sort of IPSE is a great help, and that "specmanship" in trying to improve integrity controls will at best be neutral or may actually hinder high integrity developments, not help them. We return to PCTE+ and the issues of high integrity developments in section V.1.

Part V: Conclusions

Here we briefly consider the trends in IPSE design and implementation before drawing some conclusions on the "state of the art" in IPSE design and the future evolution of IPSEs. The conclusions are drawn, to some extent, from the "evidence" presented above and, to some extent, are subjective views based on observation of a number of IPSE projects.

Some technical comments are made in this concluding part of the chapter, but our aim has been to focus more on commercial and political issues. Thus, for example, much of the discussion on IPSE trends discusses what is likely to be available in the marketplace in the near future.

V.1   IPSE TRENDS

There are many interesting trends in IPSE design and implementation. Probably public tools interfaces, infrastructure implementation technology (primarily databases), the convergence of CASE tools and IPSEs, and process modelling are the most relevant. In the conclusions we consider the trends in the use of IPSEs.

V.1.1   PTI Developments

It is clear that IPSE developments are expensive. For this and other reasons, eg portability of tools and "portability" of software engineers, it seems desirable to try to develop standard PTIs. We briefly consider the main developments, then make some observations on the viability of the approach.

There is considerable interest in developing and standardising PTIs. The European Commission has supported the development of the Portable Common Tools Environment (PCTE) which is a fairly elementary PTI strongly influenced by UNIX. The infrastructure only supports files, not a true database. Several IPSE infrastructures have been developed to support the PCTE interfaces and there are many projects developing tools to the PCTE interface. Some of these are commercially available. Nonetheless it is generally accepted that PCTE is rather weak, and as a consequence there is a development, known as PCTE+, which addresses such issues as security, integrity and databases. It is worthwhile discussing the international dimension in IPSE interfaces, before returning to PCTE+.

In the USA the Common APSE interface Set (CAIS), and its revision, CAIS-A, have developed in a similar manner to PCTE and PCTE+, but with DoD support. The PCTE+ and CAIS-A interfaces are conceptually similar and there are now proposals to unify the two definitions. Also, in the commercial arena, Atherton Technologies are developing a "standard" known as ATIS based on an existing product, the Software Backplane [Paseman1988] aimed at the same problem as PCTE+ and CAIS-A but which is rather more technically advanced, being based on object-oriented technology (see the next section).

There are massive documents describing PCTE and CAIS. The functions visible at the interfaces are defined in terms of procedures in various programming languages, and these definitions are typically referred to as language bindings. For example, there are definitions of the Ada and C programming language bindings for PCTE+ running to about

500 pages per language. Worse, the CAIS-A definition runs to 1100 pages. However there are few, if any, good overview documents and it is hard to understand these interfaces at a conceptual level from the available specifications. The interested, and persistent, reader can get further information on PCTE+ from Yard Limited in Glasgow and information on CAIS-A is available via the DoD.

One interesting question is - will IPSEs developed using these emerging standard interfaces be cost-effective? Again we are in the realm of speculation because there is no practical experience of the use of the interfaces, but we can draw some observations. An IPSE infrastructure can provide team integration, but only facilitate (although possibly to a large degree) the other aspects of integration, viz: interface, management, technical and tool. The facilities for team integration can be provided on top of operating system facilities, so good operating systems and commercial products such as ATIS, form the "competition" for PTIs, at least at the technical level. We discussed effectiveness and cost-effectiveness of PTIs in section IV.4 above and our views are somewhat pessimistic - bluntly the current PTIs seem to be very complex and costly for the benefit to be gained from using them. However it may not be necessary to rely on speculation for much longer. There are now two competitive design studies for PCTE+ being undertaken in the UK, and an implementation is underway in France. The UK studies also involve evaluation exercises for PCTE+, so some (relatively) firm data should be available soon on the cost-effectiveness of PCTE+.

Another interesting question is - will IPSEs based on these PTIs succeed, and be widely used? This is harder to answer than it might seem. Even if PCTE+ is found technically wanting there is considerable political pressure behind the development and adoption of PCTE+. Further, some companies have expressed their commitment to "make PCTE+ work" so there will be considerable commercial force behind the standard. The history of computing is full of examples of systems (eg languages and operating systems) which are not very satisfactory technically, but which are nonetheless commercially successful. It is possible that PTIs such as PCTE+ will fall into this class.

Thus it seems likely that a major trend in PTIs will be the consolidation of the position of the current publicly sponsored definitions, and a slow evolution towards commercial viability. It is unclear whether or not other approaches, such as ATIS, or improved operating system definitions, such as POSIX, will represent a real commercial challenge to the PCTE "family" of PTI definitions.

V.1.2   IPSE Implementation Technology

One of the most important technical keys to making an IPSE infrastructure work effectively is the database. Early IPSEs used files, but in order to get fine grained control over software development it is necessary to be able to store smaller objects, eg procedures or assertions, and to represent relationships between them. Consequently later IPSEs use some form of database and most are, at least superficially, relational.

Development of IPSE databases has, however, proved problematic. There are strong technico-economic constraints to use existing database technology as many man-decades of work has gone into making the databases fast, efficient, reliable, robust etc. Unfortunatley IPSE databases need to contain large unstructured objects, eg text and object files, and the objects stored are very complex and hierarchical, eg one might wish to inspect a program module as both its source text, its symbol table and its load image. Further it is often necessary to "navigate" about the database much as one would in a hierarchical filestore. Thus, although relational databases are used, they often have to be supplemented or extended in order to give them additional capabilities. It is probably fair to say that the relational basis is not entirely satisfactory for an IPSE infrastructure but the attraction of the mature database technology has often overridden such concerns. A current trend is towards the investigation of object oriented database techniques which it is believed might overcome the technical problems of relational approaches, and which might, in time, become mature technology.

As indicated earlier, object orientation essentially means that programs do not directly access data structures, instead they access data via procedures associated with each data item. These procedures can preserve certain properties of the data. For example if a bank account balance is represented as a real number in conventional programming then it would be quite possible - although quite meaningless - to take the square root of a bank balance. In the object oriented approach such misuse of data would not be feasible as the object representing bank accounts would not allow direct access to the real number representation of the balance and would not implement a square root operation. Thus the object oriented approach supports, *inter alia*, the notion of data integrity. As should by now be clear integrity is very important for IPSE databases and it is relatively easy to achieve data integrity in an object oriented style.

This is a very rapidly evolving area of research and space does not permit a full survey of projects. One project applying OODB technology to the development of support environments is DAMOKLES [Dittrich1987]. However, as with much of IPSE technology, the potential is not yet realised and there are essentially no IPSEs available which are firmly based on the object-oriented approach. The "most object oriented" IPSE is probably that produced as part of the Alvey ASPECT project [Hitchcock1990] and this is very much a research vehicle, not a robust implementation.

There are other trends in IPSE infrastructure and databases. Problems being addressed include the issue of providing effective access to the large volumes of data present in an environment. This is leading to the development of "active databases" which volunteer information to their users at appropriate points. This is essentially a generalisation of the DSEE idea of a monitor manager, and is typically achieved by implanting rules, e.g. in Prolog, in the database (for this reason the term intelligent databases is sometimes used). These rules are "triggered" when certain data values are present in the database and cause further data to be generated, or actions to be taken. One use of such techniques might be to inform a project manager when the end of a task is reached, and the required deliverables have not been registered in the project database. Object orientation and active databases seem highly compatible - one simply requires that one of the method objects is triggered when a specific condition obtains.

In research IPSEs the trend seems to be very firmly towards object orientation and active databases. There is a lot of activity in developing commercial object oriented databases, *per se*, but little on commercial object oriented IPSEs. There are still considerable technical problems to be overcome before object oriented IPSEs can be produced, but the evolution of suitable database products suggests that such IPSEs may become viable commercial technology in due course, bearing in mind the comments above about the need for mature database products to support IPSEs.

V.1.3   CASE and IPSE convergence

We have previously drawn out the distinctions between CASE products and IPSEs. It seems unquestionable that the trend will be for these two classes of product to "move towards one another" in terms of the functionality offered. In the long run we may not draw any distinction between the two classes of product. Arguably those CASE vendors who are also database vendors should have the competitive edge. They already have products which offer good "end user functionality" and the database technology necessary for mature products. Arguably the database vendors are tied by their relational technology, but there is already some evidence that they are developing object oriented databases. Further some CASE/database vendors are working on computer supported cooperative working - and this will probably be a key to the future utility of IPSEs/CASE tools. The trend towards CASE/IPSE convergence is already apparent and seems certain; there may also be a trend for the database and CASE suppliers to dominate the market.

V.1.4   Process Modelling

If environments are to be flexible then they must be adaptable to different development processes, e.g. incremental or contractual, as well as different methods. In order to customise environments it is therefore necessary to be able to describe, or model, the software development process including the set of stages to be gone through, the relationships between the stages, etc.. This has led to the notion of process modelling. Process models are much more detailed than life cycle models - the aim is to be able to produce models down to the level of individual tool invocations, for example in compiling a part of a software system. If these models can be stored in an IPSE then they can, in principle, be used in order to control the development process both constructively, eg to make new facilities available, and in a more formal control sense, eg to enforce certain QA actions before software is released. Of course process models have to include "invokation of the user"so that the creative aspects of software development can be encompassed.

It can be argued that the process model is just a "fancy database schema", or a "fancy makefile" but it is much more extensive than either. It covers issues such as tool invocation, which the schema does not, and it also, in principle, covers the complete development process, whereas a makefile deals only with a fragment of the development process. In practice software process models are not yet at the state where they can be used for complete projects, and clearly there are potential pitfalls implicit in this approach which might result in unnecessarily constraining productivity and creativity. Process modelling is a very interesting topic, but clearly it is still very much a research issue. Some of the most interesting work in this area is discussed in a series of software process workshops [Dowson1988]. From the point of view of trends it is still rather premature to say whether or not process modelling will make its way into commercial IPSE products.

V.2   CONCLUSIONS

IPSEs are conceptually, and in practice, complex artefacts. It is relatively easy to see a set of high level objectives for IPSEs, and much less easy to achieve those objectives in practice. As we have indicated above most of the presently available IPSEs fall far short of the overall objectives that we have identified. Further it is unlikely that the currently available IPSEs will scale up to deal with very large projects although systems such as DSEE have been used on quite large projects. This, of course, is not to say that the currently available IPSEs are without value.

As the experience with Safra shows there are benefits of using IPSEs and they can be applied to the development of high integrity software. At least with the simpler systems, ie those that take a conservative approach of simply extending an operating system, the benefits outweigh the drawbacks for many classes of project. As the technology improves the range of projects which can be handled will be extended, hence IPSEs can still be seen as having potential and there is hope for their future. However there are technical problems which must be overcome before the use of IPSEs can become widespread. We have identified some of these issues and tried to illustrate both the commercial and research trends.

Thus we can conclude that environments are already useful, albeit in limited ways, and that there are research projects which may overcome some of the limitations. As a final point, it is worthwhile considering the role of IPSEs in a wider context. Architects (tempered by company management) are responsible for designing the physical working environment for software development (and other) staff. An IPSE is essentially the *intellectual* working environment for software development staff. In other words, an IPSE (or at least a complete one as outlined in part II) would provide the environment in which a systems analyst or programmer would work for much, if not all, of the day. Thus there is a considerable responsibility on the part of IPSE designers to provide a stimulating and rewarding environment for its users, and to enable them to feel satisfied with the way they are working - not frustrated at fighting the machine. Perhaps, therefore, the ultimate design objective for an environment is to provide facilities to enable software designers and programmers to work effectively, and pleasurably. This is both a major challenge, and a major responsibility, for IPSE designers.

V.3   ACKNOWLEDGEMENTS

The view of IPSEs, and in particular the view of integration, outlined in this chapter has evolved over a number of years and many of my colleagues have provided useful comments and criticism which have helped me to formulate my ideas. Alan Brown and Itana Gimenes have been particularly helpful in providing detailed criticism on this particular presentation of the ideas.

The paper also draws, to some extent, on a number of earlier works on IPSEs. In particular some diagrams and text have been extracted from lecture notes on IPSEs which were presented at an IEE Summer School on Software Engineering for Electronic System Designers held in 1989. This material is used with the permission of the IEE.

V.4   REFERENCES

Biba 1977. J K Biba, "Integrity considerations for secure computer systems", ESD-TR-76-372, ESD/AFSC Hanscom AFB, Bedford, Mass (1977). (MITRE MTR 3153 NTIS AD A039324 (1977)).

Black 1987. W J Black, A G Sutcliffe, P Loucopoulos, P J Layzell, "Translation between Pragmatic Software Development Methods", in Proceedings of ESEC87, eds. H Nichols and D Simpson, LNCS, Springer Verlag (1987).

Boehm1981. B W Boehm, "Software Engineering Economics", Prentice Hall (1981).

Brooks1987. F P Brooks, "No Silver Bullet: Essence and Accidents of Software Engineering", IEEE Computer, Vol. 20 (4) pp 10-20 (1987).

Clark 1987. A Comparison of Commercial and Military Computer Security Policies, D D Clark, D R Wilson, Proceedings of IEEE Symposium on Security and Privacy, IEEE Press (1987).

Cronshaw1986. P Cronshaw, "The Experimental Aircraft Programme Software Toolset", Software Engineering Journal, Vol. 1 (6) (1986).

DeMarco1978. T DeMarco, Structured Analysis and System Specification, Yourdon Press (1978).

Dittrich1987. K.R. Dittrich, W. Gotthard and P.C. Lockemann, "DAMOKLES - A Database System for Software Engineering Environments", in "Proc. of IFIP Workshop on Advanced Programming Environments", Springer Verlag (1987).

Dobson 1988. Security Models and Enterprise Models, J E Dobson, J A McDermid, Proceedings of IFIP Workshop on Database Security, ed. C Landwehr, IFIP Press (1988).

DoD1980. DoD, "Requirements for Ada Programming Support Environments: Stoneman", (1980).

Dowson1987. M. Dowson, "Integrated Project Support with ISTAR", Software pp., IEEE, (1987).

Dowson1988. M. Dowson, (ed.), "Software Process Workshop", ACM (1988).

DTI1987. DTI, "The STARTS Guide, Second Edition", Department of Trade and Industry (1987) Available from the National Computing Centre.

England1987. D M England, "A User Interface Design Tool", in "Proceedings of ESEC87, Lecture Notes in Computer Science", Springer Verlag (1987).

Erickson1984. V B Erickson and J F Pellegrin, "Build - A Software Construction Tool", Bell Lab.s Technical Journal, Vol. 63 (6) pp., (1984).

EURAC 1987. Requirements and Design Criteria for Tool Support Interfaces, GIE Emeraude, Selenia, Software Sciences (1987).

Feldman1979. S I Feldman, "Make - A Program for Maintaining Computer Programs", Software Practice and Experience, Vol. 9 pp., (1979).

Foster 1989. The Algebraic Specification of a Target Machine: Ten15, J M Foster, in High Integrity Software, ed. C T Sennett , Pitman (1989).

Goldberg1983. A Goldberg and D Robson, "Smalltalk-80: The Language and its Impelemntation", Addison-Wesley, (1983).

Hayes1986. I. Hayes, (ed.), "Specification Case Studies", Prentice Hall International (1986).

Hitchcock1990 P. Hitchcock and R. P. Whittington (eds.), "The ASPECT Project", (to appear, (1990).

Hoare1985. C A R Hoare, "Communicating Sequential Processes", Prentice Hall 1985.

Jackson1986. K Jackson, "MASCOT3 and Ada", Software Engineering Journal, Vol. 1 (3) (1986).

Kitchenham1986. B A Kitchenham and J A McDermid, "Software Metrics and Integrated Project Support Environments", Software Engineering Journal pp., (1986).

Leblang1984. D B Leblang and R Chase, "Computer Aided Software Engineering in a Distributed Workstation Context", in "ACM Conference on Practical Software Development Environments" (1984).

McDermid1984. J A McDermid and K Ripken, "Life Cycle Support in the Ada Environment", Cambridge University Press 1984.

McDermid1986. J A McDermid (Ed), "Integrated Project Support Environments", Peter Peregrinus Limited 1986.

McDermid1989a. J A McDermid, "Software Design Methods: Characteristics and Choice", in "Software Engineering for Electronic Systems", ed. A C Davies, Butterworth Scientific (1989).

McDermid1989b. J A McDermid, E S Hocking, "Security Policies for Integrated Project Support Environments", Proceedings of IFIP Workshop on Database Security (1989) (to appear in the IFIP Press, ed. C Landwehr, 1990).

McDermid1990. J A McDermid and P Rook, "Software Development Process Models", in Software Engineer's Reference Book, ed. J A McDermid, Butterworth Scientific (1990).

McGuffin1979. R W McGuffin, A E Elliston, B R Tranter and P N Westmacott, "CADES - Software Engineering in Practice", in "Proc. of 4th International Conference on Software Engineering", IEEE (1979).

Milner1980. A J R G Milner, "Calculus of Communicating Systems", in "Lecture Notes in Computer Science No. 92", ed. G Goos and J Hartmanis, Springer Verlag (1980).

Mullery1979. G P Mullery, "CORE - a Method for Controlled Requirements Specification", in "Proceedings of 4th International Conference on Software Engineering", IEEE Computer Society Press (1979).

Paseman1988. W G Paseman, "Architecture of a Tool Integration and Portability Platform", in "Proceedings of COMPCON" (1988).

Ritchie 1978. D M Ritchie and K Thompson, "The UNIX Time-Sharing System", Bell Sys. Tech. J., Vol 57 (6) pp.1905-1929, (1978).

Rochkind1975. M J Rochkind, "The Source Code Control System", Transactions on Software Engineering pp., IEEE, (1975).

Sennett 1987. The Development Environment for Secure Software, C T Sennett, RSRE Report 87015 (1987).

Sloman1983. A Sloman, S Hardy and J Gibson, "POPLOG: A Multilanguage Program Development Environment", in "Information Technology: Research and Development" (1983).

Sommervilee 1986. I Sommerville (ed), "Software Engineering Environments", .Peter Peregrinus Limited (1986).

Sutcliffe1988. A G Sutcliffe, "Jackson Structured Design", Prentice Hall, (1988).

Thimbleby1986. H W Thimbleby, "Experiences of "Literate Programming" using cweb (a variant of Knuths WEB)", The Computer Journal (3) pp., (1986).'

Took1986. R K Took, "The Presenter - a formal design for an autonomous display manager for an IPSE", in "Software Engineering Environments", ed. I Sommerville, Peter Peregrinus Limited (1986).

3

Reflections on a large software development project

Brian Warboys
Department of Computer Science
University of Manchester
Oxford Road Manchester M13 9PL

Abstract

This paper is an attempt to extract some lessons,with some subsequent and very personal reflections, from my involvement with the development of the ICL VME Operating System. They represent personal views and personal reflections and in no way necessarily reflect those of the company. I present them in the hope that they are useful inputs to the current plethora of noise surrounding software engineering and its application. In particular I am concerned that the experiences gained from the lengthy usage of an early support environment should yield some input to the present round of investments in Integrated Support Environments. The paper attempts to justify the notion that a framework fashioned for Process and Architectural support should be the starting point for the development of the core of such an Environment.
"It takes longer than you expect, even when you take into account Hofstadter's Law" [hof].

Keywords:*Software Development,Operating Systems*

1   Introduction

"The writers against religion, whilst they oppose every system, are wisely careful never to set up any of their own " (Edmund Burke).

It is now some 10 years since I ended my direct line-management involvement with ICL's VME Operating System [bcw80]. This seems to be about the time it takes to be able to look back at those years with an appropriate sense of detachment. However the danger in leaving it this long is that any lessons to be drawn from such a period in our modern fast-moving technological context have, long since, been rendered irrelevant. The production of this paper has unfortunately demonstrated, to myself at least, that this is not the case. It serves to illustrate what has been learnt, a great deal, what is yet to be learnt, and perhaps, most importantly, what has been learnt but has yet to be properly exploited.

1.1 On Soft-ness

The problems, in the main stem from the very term *Soft*-ware. Most seem to originate whenever strenuous efforts are made to deny the very nature of the technology. That is the fact that, by definition, it is meant to be *Soft*. Soft implies malleable and hence in one dimension is associated with a *perceived* low cost of change. Somehow we seem unable to reconcile the confict between malleable and manageable. Thus the term *Software Factory* is much in vogue carrying the implication that if we can *harden* the technology sufficiently then somehow it becomes manageable.

My own opinion is that come the moment when we are, at last, happy that it has become *hard* enough we shall then invent the notion of something *softer* with once again the properties of a low perceived cost of change, albeit in the new factory context.

In my experience the major conceptual difficulties derive from the strange notion that since the technology is soft the definition of its required behavior can be specified in very imprecise terms. The softness of the technology allowing rapid redevelopment of the product to match the prospective customer's needs. This trend is further exaggerated by the fact that most software is used to support management activity of one form or another and hence the requirement itself is also extremely *soft*.

Such a reasoning process has been raised to an art-form by many advocating the exclusive use of Expert System technology in business applications to allow the development of systems by successive refinement of operational prototypes "in front of the vendor's eyes". This process continuing until the customer exclaims that he is happy! I recall hearing about a similar reasoning process during a discussion with a town planner, long ago, when he was explaining to me the design process that led to the development of tower-block housing.

There are two separate activities which are intertwined in all this preamble. One concerned with *process* and one with *technology*. They are often confused. This small case study will, I hope, shed some light on that confusion. It is my contention that we (the software community) have never adequately separated these concerns and that this is at the root of many of our present difficulties.

In particular there exists considerable confusion about the term *integrated* . It is used very loosely to both describe the integration of a set of tools to provide a coherent *product* and the notion of support for an integrated development process which includes supporting tools. The former emphasis on tools integration and the unfortunate separation of the concerns of the tools from the products produced using the tools tends to de-emphasise the paramount importance of the *methods* which the tools support in favour of the tools themselves. It is an unfortunate attribute, possibly of our current market economy, that there is a tendency to market tools as discrete entities rather than as contributors to a continuous development process. The paper attempts to justify the need for a more coherent approach.

2   A review of the historical perspective of the VME project

These reflections, given the current context, are inevitably dominated by observations on the experiences gained by the use of a form of Integrated Support Environment for the development of the system throughout the best part of two decades. The environment in question is known as the CADES [djp, bcw76] system and has been used since 1972 for the support of the development of the ICL Operating System VME [bcw80]. Not surprisingly, given its age, this system accurately reflects the industrial concerns prevalent in the late 1960's. The focus on these concerns was due in no small measure to the two successful (well they were perceived as such at the time) NATO Software Engineering conferences of 1968/69 [jnb, pn] which are arguably responsible for the very term Software Engineering.

Examination of our experiences with this system over the last 16 years lead to some interesting observations on both what has changed and unfortunately what has not during this period. The observations fall into two categories :
- The Industrial Scenario and development concerns of that era.
- The Technology developed to address those concerns.

Perhaps more than anything they are timely reminders at this time, when there is an unseemly rush to standardise Support Environments, that our engineering expertise is still far from being mature. They show us how much has changed (and has still to change) in even our understanding of the Software Development Process. This must lead to concern that in the realisation of the need for an "OPEN" standard we should not hastily define a very closed system.

2.1 Our Industrial Scenario in the early '70's.

Prior to the early 70's ICL (in its various early forms, English Electric,ICT etc.) had produced a number of comparatively small operating systems and associated compilers for the relatively small mainframe machines which existed at the time.

These systems were produced as discrete components and as they gradually grew larger the approach was essentially to treat the enlarged components as collections of programs and to contract out the development of the programs to separate groups of programmers. It was found that this approach was inadequate. Indeed that the cost of the systems compared to earlier systems increased exponentially rather than linearly with their increase in size.

Thus in 1971 when ICL set out to produce a major operating system, VME, for its new range of Mainframes (what became the 2900 and the Series 39 ranges) it recognised that it had a major task on its hands since all the indicators were that the development would never finish. In a sense this has proven to be the case since some 200 development staff have been continually developing the system since that time. The result was to establish a development support project to develop a rigorous system development methodology, Structural Modelling, and a Computer Aided Development and Evaluation System, CADES, to support the methodology.

2.2 The perceived problem circa 1970

At that time the problem was perceived as being dominated by product structure concerns. Early documents [bcw76] state :

> "The large development team would need to be able to identify and preserve the overall structure of the operating system. Experience on earlier systems had shown how difficult it was to protect a large system from structural decay. The team would need to be able to distinguish between features which affected the overall structure of the system and those which were merely cosmetic.

The methodology and computer aided system would have to facilitate all stages of the operating system development process, i.e. high level design, low level design of implementation, construction, system generator and maintenance. They would have to encourage the codes of good practice which prevailed within the computer industry, i.e. structured programming, data/entity driven design, delayed fixing and binding, design for resilence etc."

Two years later, in a much earlier reflections paper [bcw78] on the problems of developing large software systems, I was to draw the following observations/conclusions on our approach.

"There are a number of points that experience in the development of large and complex software systems highlights :

- The importance of determining a good structure for the system and recording this structure and its history.

- An ability to be able to invert the product structure to provide the diverse views required by external requirements.

- Allow the product structure to determine organisation structures.

- A need for strict control over system versions.

- Interfaces which are flexible but can be tuned allowing scope in development for effective customisation.

- A continuous design/ implementation/ integration process because of diverse organisations.

- A central definition of the system and its variants to provide control."

2.3 Observations on this view of the Perceived Problem

Reflecting on these perceptions which were produced "in the heat of battle" - not an unrealistic analogy given the intensity of management and technical interactions which result from the undertaking of such a venture - it seems that there are four separate strands which emerge :

- Architecture and Product Structure

- System Representation

- The Development Process

- Implementability/Testability of Product

2.3.1 On Architecture and Product Structure

To a large extent our emphasis on the avoidance of "structural decay" has paid handsome dividends. This is due in no small measure to the early work done in the then ICL New Range Planning Organisation [jkb] in creating an Architectural Framework for what was to become the 2900 (and then Series 39) systems. This was in place before our Operating

System design began and we merely needed to decide on our complementing Architecture. From the beginning I recall that design discussions were soon punctuated with protestations of "That's not architectural" and the design group soon developed an intuitive and shared understanding of the required architectural constraints. This has lasted throughout the two decades of development and one cannot overstate the importance of such an understanding.

It is my experience that the *primary* cause of failure in developing large systems is the absence of such a strong sense of an architectural framework. In this sense I am using the notion of Architecture as being :

- the *constraints* which must be obeyed by a component to ensure that it is integrable

- the *rules of composition* which ensure that when components are taken together they also form an integrable component.

This view of Architecture, as an *active* framework for design is an important topic, not yet adequately addressed even in the research domain. We have been developing some thoughts on this topic and it is explored in a little more detail in a recent paper, [ph], on the subject.

However the existence of a strong architectural model did not enable the effective re-use of components, be they designs or implementations. This problem is wider than architecture and I shall return to it later in the paper.

2.3.2 On System Representation

The naive development route hinted at in the quotations in 2.2 above contained no mention of the process of Specification. This is perhaps the most significant change in our understanding of the means of Software Engineering which has emerged over the last decade. Our "top-level" activity was termed *Design*. Specification was an informal process, although not in the sense of being unstructured. In fact the process was extremely well structured in terms of Requirements definition, Facility Design, Module development implications etc. It was informal in the sense that its outputs were English narratives.

The process was useful but suffered from a "Write many-read once" property. That is great insight was generated as a result of narrative production and, I believe we were in the vanguard of those introducing formal inspection techniques, but it was virtually impossible to use the results as a systematic means of control for the refinement of such specifications into implementations. To achieve this important property in ensuring the means of a "continuous development process" we would have needed to adopt a more formal mathematical approach (e.g. [cbj86]). Unfortunately the important tools and expert support were not available to us and to a large extent are still not. Until such support appears (hopefully during the next 5 years) widespread use of such techniques will not become the norm and we shall continue to suffer the consequences of inadequate specification processes.

2.3.3 On the Development Process

The emphasis on "a continuous ... process" was, and is, of paramount importance. Much of this was achieved by the development and use of the CADES system. The inadequacies, such as they were, were in my view due to the emphasis (admittedly my own) on product structure as the prime determinant of all control. This emphasis ("allow the product structure to determine organisational structures") in both process and product was I now believe too gross an over-simplification. Although it does have the merit of being a good simple management message. On reflection I would now argue that we must recognise that the development process for systems of this complexity is going to be a heterogeneous assemblage of differing process fragments. That the regularity required for consistency should come from the twin frameworks of some form of support for active Architectural Constraints and a Development Process Harness which together allow for the embedding of differing sub-components be they product structures, language representations or management processes. We are currently experimenting with such notions within the Alvey IPSE 2.5 Project [ras1], [bcw89]. The impact of such a Support Environment is discussed later in this paper.

A significant aspect of "a continuous ... process" was the mid-life introduction of the constraint of *incremental development*. The key feature was the vision of developers, at individual module levels, being able to release product increments, after significant regression testing, directly into operational systems. Although the vision was never fully implemented, and possibly should never be, it acted as a simple management device for focussing attention on the means of moving away from large development increments with all the attendant problems that such batching implies. The effects were all-embracing and had a good influence on all stages of the development process. The emphasis, from requirements through design to implementation being on the need to preserve system integrity in a very direct way. In this sense it was the management analogue of architectural constraints. It is a classic example of the need to construct frameworks for development consisting of simple messages at both architectural and process levels.

2.3.4 On Implementability/Testability of Product

"We may have invented immortality but it will take forever to test it!" or again as Djikstra remarked at the 1969 NATO Conference [ewd] "Testing shows the presence, not the absence of bugs". The previous remarks on representation are relevant. The absence of systematic refinement of specifications leads in the end to the problem of testing. The well known (for some 20 years) relationship between cost of error correction and the development phase of discovery (that the later it is found the more it costs to correct) serves to underline this link. There is no doubt that the single largest cost to ICL and the VME customers was the revalidation of releases and the cost of non-conformance caused by the non-confirmation of the "absence of bugs".

I can only re-iterate the links between the front and back-end phases of the life-cycle. The role of language (and representation) in all of this is very clear. The bold, for that time, decision to write VME in a *real* high level language (see below) and provide extensive module-interface support with CADES led to the formal "absence" of whole classes of errors. This is a clear pointer to the solution to the problems in specification and its refinement. For the last decade we have been experimenting with more formal approaches and we are certainly nearer to acceptable solutions than we were!

3 Structural Modelling and the CADES Approach

Structural modelling was first described in detail in [djp] in 1973. It followed the philosophy that system development should be primarily a data-driven top-down process. We had digested the lessons from the NATO conferences!

The emphasis was on the modular structure of the system being designed to manipulate defined data items, rather than data items being invented to support the encoding of abstract functional requirements. Each code entity was termed a holon, a term borrowed from Koestler [ak] to describe utilities in an hierarchic system.

A language called SDL (System Development Language) was devised to allow the expressions of holon-holon and holon-data relationships. It should not be confused with the SDL of the CCITT recommendation SDL-88; they are unrelated. SDL is also used to describe how each holon uses its relationship with other holons and with data items in order to carry out its particular functions. The hierarchy of SDL Holons represents a gradual refinement of the total description of the system, each level being a complete description of the system at that level of design, the level being fixed by the accompanying data tree decomposition. At the lowest levels this use of SDL merges completely into the implementation programming language, S3 (a close relative of the expression oriented language Algol68).

The CADES database was set up to record information about the various holon-holon, holon-data relationships and this was then used as the basis for version control and other management support purposes. It had become, of course, a Support Environment.

By far the most important development was that the database was established from the very beginning of the project as the *only* source of all product components. Source code could only be produced by the execution of an Environment Processor (the EP) which processed design information from the database to produce S3 source code. An early example of process enforcement through the use of tools.

3.1   Observations on the CADES Approach

Within the size and scale of this paper it is only feasible to attempt a very superficial analysis of the approach but the more significant highlights are :

- The approach is based on the notion of constructing a multi-level model of the product to be developed and then using this hierarchy as the means of development management. This, of course, reflects the aforementioned strategy of emphasis on product structure as the means of control. This leads to some good and bad attributes. The best is perhaps that the architecture of the system plays at least some active role in the subsequent design decomposition. The theology of the product approach is reflected directly in the tools used for development. Thus both the architecture and the tools system have survived the test of time. Essentially the same system is still used 16 years and some 3000 man years later. It has demonstrated that Support Environments can have longevity!

  The worst attribute is that the process of development is necessarily made subservient and thus although the product has not suffered structural decay the process of development has not been able to adapt properly to more modern influences at both language and technique levels. As was mentioned before it is particularly noticeable that the "total life cycle" outlined above made no mention of specification. Further the granularity of the database is product oriented and thus the granularity of the supported process is of necessity constrained to the level of the product modularity. Management of the process is therefore conducted at the holon level. Re-use, optimisation, version management and all the other Engineering concerns are thus also constrained to operate at this level.

- The approach is essentially one of "Structure design followed by structure evaluation". Support for iteration is provided but essentially the system is oriented towards design capture of new and modified functions followed by the use of conventional (Codasyl based) database technology to invert and evaluate that design. The notion of prototyping is missing and the ability to reason about the design is essentially restricted to structural analysis.

  Again the primary goal of managing the avoidance of product structural decay was realised but the granularity of design entities essentially restricted the ability to reason except at holon-holon level. In practice abstraction was limited to essentially establishing a functional scope for subsequent holon decomposition.

- The system is a closed one. Not really in the sense of current Open Systems concerns since one could easily define a "Public Tools Interface" to the system but in the sense that any tool added to the system is constrained by the core style of schema representation. New tools have to be totally integrated and the resultant costs severely restricted the ability to experiment with new toolsets, to rapidly discard and acquire new tools and generally to adopt a flexible tools strategy.

- Many mundane issues are of fundamental importance. In the end most development effort on the CADES system was expended on Version Control and it is clear that it is of paramount importance that such issues are addressed in such a way that they are all embracing and transparent to tools providers.

3.2 Subsequent conclusions for the future

- It is clear from the above that the principal constraint to a flexible support environment is, not surprisingly, the basic architecture of that environment. The environment is after all, itself, a product and hence the previous remarks concerning the role of architecture are clearly appropriate. Clearly, given that the ultimate goal in the building of *conformant* systems is that there is a seamlessness between the architectural constraints actively applied throughout development and those applied to the run-time system, there is an important relationship between the architecture of the development environment and that of the developed system.

  Such a link has much to do with the language used to express designs but clearly the architecture of the development environment needs to be based on some alternative to a *product-structure base* since there is little commonality in the range of products we would wish to develop at this level.

  In our case the decision to base the granularity of the database at a predominantly holon level had an all-embracing impact on both the approach to an open tools policy and to the type of development process which the tools enabled (and/or supported). In fact the decision to base the environment core on the granularity of the entities to be developed was the key factor. Our experience is that any attempt to base the Support

Environment on the entities to be developed rather than the process to be used for the development is doomed to the same constraints as the CADES system imposed.

In particular we should now take the view that it is axiomatic both that software development is an iterative process and that this process should be managed and changed actively rather than as a transparent side-effect of the product or organisational structure. This implies the need to support considerable process change as development proceeds. Moreover it is now clear that this process is, in practice, a collection of separate process fragments rather than being a simple coherent development cycle. The attempts over the last 20 years to produce a single simplistic representation of the software development cycle have not served us well. They have merely resulted in an over-simplification. The approach has had the effect of actually increasing the separation of the real process from that perceived by the management system.

The result, in many cases, has therefore been to establish a more impractical process than previously existed. Further the dynamic and heterogeneous nature of the process has not been recognised and this has had a negative effect on many well-intentioned engineering improvements. The provision of an attractive workstation interface to such simplistic process models will, I am afraid, only delay not cure the sense of disillusionment with such systems.

- The "Structure design then structure evaluation" strategy of CADES had highlighted the constraints on better approaches to development. In particular the need to reason about our specifications, designs, implementations is fundamental to good software development. This ability to reason implies a level of integration of process and tools which needs to be determined by the nature of the interaction between the reasoner and the tools and not by the product modularity constraints. As workstations increase in power with improved screen and "tactile" support so the notion of a reasoning assistant will become increasingly tractable [cbj1]. However it is also clear that the Environment is still required to support the conventional level of granularity as represented in the CADES system.

A major influence on software support systems should therefore be the desire to achieve the integration of these coarse and fine grain support systems. There are also implications on the user interface in terms of the management of vast quantities of fine-grain entities and their subsequent projection via coarser-grain entities, for example to allow the browsing of entities of management interest such as plan impacts.

- The closed nature of CADES had highlighted the constraints which such an architecture placed on flexible tool acquisition and disposition. Increasingly there is a need for greater flexibility in creating hybrid design processes and this implies flexibility in levels of tool integration. A simplistic "Operating System" style CASE will not, in itself, by concentrating on the store-plus-tools level of integration enable the rapid construction of Integrated Support Systems as distinct from the support for heterogenous tools systems. OPEN systems imply a speed of change as well as community-wide ownership. It is important to ensure that the community wide ownership desire does not inflict upon us a closed system in terms of development paradigms.

Thus another major influence ought to be the desire for the process based core to be the *means* of flexible and very cheap alien tool interworking, essentially a generic "meta"

Public Tools Interface. Hence it is considered of vital importance to an Open CASE system that it provides a standard means of construction of Public Tools Interfaces rather than any one Interface per se.

- The notion of Component Re-use had been an early motivator in the CADES system. The hope was that by the use of Database support a generic approach to "Libraries" could be developed, indeed that such commonality would be established at many levels. In practice this did not happen. The means of Specification and then subsequent browsing were not available, but again, even if they had been, the fine-grain integration which such "pattern-matching" implies would not have been realised by a totally "entity"-based core. Again some support for the recognition of the development process in order to enable re-use was required. It was also clear that the development process was such that the re-use of process fragments was as great a contributor to productivity as any design component re-use. CADES did not aid the long period of gestation concerned with the construction of a process,in many cases a heterogeneous assemblage of sub-processes, to solve large scale problems. This need to employ a variety of solution strategies in any given system development is, I believe, of great and growing importance.

4 On future Support Environments

The purpose of these kinds of Support Environments is to provide the means by which the process of developing, maintaining, supporting and enhancing information systems is made more efficient, in both quality and productivity terms. Traditionally such Environments, be they for the support of programmers or the support of projects, have been considered as tools to support people who have tasks to carry out.The view we should take is to stand back from this position of "users and tools" and consider the problem as a whole.

The process of developing, installing and changing information systems is one which involves the co-operative efforts of many people. People are involved in this process because of the intellectual nature of the various tasks. We should not forget that no tool, as yet, can remove the essential involvement of the human being. As Dijkstra [ewd] said in 1972,

> "We shall do a much better programming job ..... provided we respect the intrinsic limitations of the human mind."

The next generation of Integrated Product Support Environments (IPSE - a term coined by the Alvey programme [alv]) should be the means of supporting the whole process rather than just being a collection of tools which assist particular activities or classes of activities within that process.

The essence of the integration component of an IPSE should be based on this notion that an IPSE is about supporting the process of systems development, a process in which people (the "users" of the IPSE) play a very significant part. In many ways this is the logical successor to systems such as CADES where the environment is seen as providing the components out of which the process is formed, but in a completely general way which is ignorant of process.

5 Conclusions

To understand the relevance of such a generic approach based on the notion of a core system providing support for a process framework rather than the stylised "operating system" core, beloved of many CASE offerings, there is a need to examine the current context within which we need to engineer software.

Major changes have taken place in the industry structure, the technology and the market since we developed the CADES system. Most of these emphasise the need for an Open system, in a Process sense, and in terms of flexibility of Tool interworking.

The Industry is, in general, no longer concerned with the development of discrete software components. Instead the major concern is with the "glueing" together of components to provide the IT component of some larger ecosystem. There is a need to recognise the endemic nature of IT, to recognise that our traditional software component is but one component of a much broader control system.

Further there must be a recognition of the need for the support of mixed componentry, much of it never to be specified in terms to which our software development methods can sensibly relate. There is a need to recognise the ever increasing variety of methods, languages and toolsets, to recognise the need for support for system development "in the large" and for component re-use of a wide variety of component types.

In particular this paper has attempted to highlight the need for a support framework containing support for the embedding of some representation of architectural constraints together with a form of process model harness as being of paramount importance. It has attempted to justify the need for such support in order to enable an approach to system development based on the recognition that the development processes dealing with a heterogeneous assemblage of process and components are rapidly becoming the norm.

6 Acknowledgements

I am indebted to all the people involved in the VME development who provided me with such splendid support during my time with the project. I am further indebted to both ICL and the University of Manchester for allowing me to pursue the recent stages of my career with ,as it were, the very best of two worlds, those of Industry and Academia. The mix of the two has had a substantial effect on my reflections in this paper.

References

[ak] A.Koestler "The Act of Creation" Macmillan 1964

[alv] Alvey Programme Software Engineering Strategy, November 1983

[bcw76] B.C.Warboys and G.D.Pratten "CADES - Principles" Seminar Oxford University February 4th 1976

[bcw78] B.C.Warboys "The Manufacturers Problem in producing large Operating Systems" Paper presented at IEE meeting on The Design and Performance of Operating Systems London 9th Feb 1978

[bcw80] B.C.Warboys "VME/B a model for the realisation of a total system concept" ICL Technical Journal November 1980

[bcw89] B.C.Warboys "The IPSE 2.5 Project : Process Modelling as the basis for a Support Environment" Procs Software Development Environments and Factories Conference Berlin May 1989

[cbj86] C.B.Jones "Systematic Software Development Using VDM" Prentice-Hall 1986

[cbj1] C.B.Jones and R.Moore "An experimental user interface for a Theorem Proving Assistant" IPSE 2.5 document SE13/29/234

[djp] D.Pearson "CADES" Computer Weekly,July 26th,August 2nd,August 9th 1973

[ewd] E.W.Dijkstra "The Humble Programmer" CACM No 10,Vol 15 1972

[hof] D.Hofstadter "Godel,Escher,Bach : an eternal braid" Penguin Books

[jkb] J.K.Buckle "The origins of the 2900 Series" ICL Technical Journal May 1978

[jnb] J.N.Buxton and B.Randell "Software Engineering Techniques" Report on NATO Science Conference October 1969

[ph] P.Henderson and B.C. Warboys "An architectural framework for systems" ICL Technical Journal May 1989

[pn] P.Naur and B.Randell "Software Engineering" Report on NATO Science Conference 1968

[ras1] R.A.Snowdon "IPSE 2.5 Technical Strategy" IPSE 2.5 project document 060-00131-2.2

4

A LARGE EMBEDDED SYSTEM PROJECT CASE STUDY

Bob Malcolm
Malcolm Associates Ltd
Savoy Hill House, Savoy Hill, London WC2

ABSTRACT

This paper presents a discussion of why large software projects go wrong. It attempts to cut through the swathes of myth and misrepresentation, and to dig deeper than the press and other superficial pundits. The various commonly quoted sources of disaster, and especially 'the software', are analysed in the context of a case study which is representative of the typical 'project disaster'. It is shown how bad design decisions are made not because people are stupid, technically incompetent, using the wrong technique, or badly managed, but because they are people - operating in an environment which encourages parochialism and petty politicking, and afflicted by perversity.

INTRODUCTION

Embedded real-time systems typically comprise chains of different types of information processing in and out of a central computer-based information presentation and decision support system. The input chains start with analogue signal processing of the raw data from 'front-end' sensors, followed by digital signal processing, and then the digital data processing of a computer-based system, which may have associated digital electronics, such as operator work-stations, often purpose-built. The output side is much the same in reverse, starting with the computer-based system controlling digital, possibly microprocessor-based, sub-systems which in turn control analogue actuators and transmitters. This is a greatly simplified picture of just the primary information channels of a system. In addition there will be many subsidiary control loops comprising special-purpose digital circuitry and perhaps several microprocessors within each box.

The case study project was for the bespoke development of just such a system.

96

Apparent and real causes of problems

After the disaster come the recriminations - attempts to apportion blame to the design, the design method, the designers, or the management of the project:

"Whose fault was it? It *must* have been a bad design. They must have used poor (ie Not Invented By The Critic) design techniques. They should have had a quality management system. The whole thing was mismanaged wasn't it? It *must* have been the software, mustn't it?"

And, of course, there is much argument over the requirements. "Did they or did they not keep growing?; did they or did they not keep changing? Was it really the customer's fault?"

"How *could* they do it?"

But there isn't a 'they'. *They* are individuals, usually well-qualified, well-intentioned, well-motivated - at least as competent as their critics.

The body of this paper examines the requirements, the design, the quality assurance, and the management of the project, looking at both the commonly blamed problems and the real problems. This is followed by an analysis of the underlying factors which created the environment in which the technical difficulties arose, and an attempt to draw some still-tentative conclusions.

REQUIREMENTS

Well, did the specification grow like Topsy? Yes . . . . and No. Towards the end there was a fairly typically bitter contractual battle which led as usual to all parties leaning on the written word, whatever had been the spirit and intent of the contract. The customer went back to the original few pages of outline requirement, which was the basis for the proposal and thence the contract, and say that it had not changed. Indeed it had not: but the requirements had moved on somewhat. *Apart from* official contractual changes, the actuality of the requirements - the fleshing-out and interpretation - was embodied in a myriad documents, designs, undocumented decisions, and assumptions. Nevertheless, and perhaps as was only to be expected in such a difficult situation, the customer, publicly at least, flatly denied the relevance of anything outside the original flimsy statement.

In fact, very early in the project it was recognised by both customer and supplier that there were likely to be problems with the requirements. They decided to establish a group to resolve uncertainties. It was to be small, so that it could make decisions *very quickly*, with only three parties represented - end-user, supplier, and customer's technical advisers.

The road to a project disaster is also paved with good intentions. Ten years later this small, fleet, group had become a *committee* with over a score of customer representatives from various departments. It met every six months. So the multi-humped camel was born, though really it never got beyond gestation since, by this time, what was actually happening on the project bore little relationship to the formal committee statement of the long-term requirements.

What about the software requirement specification?

During tests and trials with the real hardware in a real environment, there were reports back from both the customer and the trials team that the software was not coping well with the demand. The software team tried to ameliorate the problem with a series of changes, but this 'software problem' did persist. Only when one of the managers who had been involved in the early design work became involved did reality reveal itself. The demand with which the software was having difficulty was *more than two orders of magnitude greater than the design target*. A software problem indeed!

But the supplier should not be complacent in a situation like this. The software might well satisfy the software requirement specification, and in the case study dramatically beat it. The hardware might even have met its specification, though it did not in this case. But if the real world load is greater than expected, then the customer will not be happy if the supplier tries to hide behind the specification. In the case-study project, the whole system would have been quite useless if the software had simply met its specification. The supplier might have a legal case, but if it comes to an argument, then the battle is already half lost and a disaster imminent.

This is yet another case of the distinction between meeting the specification and *real* quality - providing customer satisfaction.

DESIGN

Design philosophy

We must take care to distinguish between the design philosophy and the actual design. The software philosophy was simplistically expressed at the beginning as "1. Don't rush (ie don't introduce into the design unnecessary real-time constraints); 2. Do only one thing at a time". In essence this meant message-passing, interrupt-free, design - some years ahead of its time.

The philosophy worked well. The first build of the system integrated successfully in *one week*, rather than the expected three months, much to the surprise of the software manager who had not been in favour of this newfangled philosophy.

But the ultimate vindication must surely be that although it was creaking badly, the system did actually cope with more than one hundred times the original expected data rate, with a consequent combinatorial explosion in some aspects of the data-handling.

However, there were indeed some horrors in the actual design of the "How *could* they?" sort. And there were some design decisions which have since been criticised but which were well-founded at the time. Which is which is usually clear: but not always. Some of each type will be recounted in this section.

Hardware-software interface

One of the ways to 'avoid rushing' was to buffer data. There were therefore large 'software' buffers in the main computer, to temporarily accommodate input data which did not need an instant response. In addition there were buffers in the hardware lines, prior to transferring data into the main computer. But the function of these hardware buffers was slightly different. When they were not full, they acted simply as buffers. But, unusually, they were kept as small as possible, consistent with not losing data under normal circumstances. This provided a simple and cost-effective counter-measure to spurious unmanageable surges of noise. The idea was that the little hardware buffers would be deliberately overwritten in the event of such surges - and there a lot of these in reality. In this way most of the noise would be lost, and the main computer would not be overloaded. (Some real data would be lost as well but not, relative to the noise, a significant amount, and it was better to let the computer spend its time processing clean data from less noisy areas than clog it up trying to sort wheat from chaff with a low probability of success.)

Years later there were some problems with the main computer servicing of its buffers. It transpired that, somewhere along the line, the software manager, finding that he was running out of store, had persuaded the hardware team that the hardware buffers should be expanded, so that the software buffers could be shrunk. Now, not only was the hardware not limiting noisy input data, but the main computer had less capacity to absorb the load. Is it any wonder there were problems?

A box too few

Fairly early in the project it came to light that a major function had been completely left out of the initial design. Its natural place lay between the digital signal processing and the digital data processing. Between is right: it transpired that both the design managers responsible either side had assumed that the other had dealt with it. They sat in adjacent offices, could not stand each other, did not talk, and certainly failed to communicate.

Despite recognition of this oversight, the effect persisted. Years later, in trying to sort out some interfacing problems, it became clear that the missing functionality had been 'bolted on', along with some other forgotten bits and pieces.

It had, for instance, been a stated starting assumption of the software team that there would not be spurious multiple copies of the same input data, and also that the data would already be sorted on arrival. Both of these assumptions were 'remembered' - ie rediscovered - when the serious effect of them not being satisfied became evident. Again, these functions had been belatedly 'bolted on' in another peripheral processing unit.

But by this time such inelegances were everywhere as people and teams optimised their own sub-system at the expense of others and the whole. Sometimes they were grabbing responsibility for functions from others - either to build empires or because the new bit was technical fun. Sometimes they were dropping responsibility for functions to reduce the load on themselves and on the processing capability in their bit.

A box too many

And sometimes these things happened for no obvious reason at all: thus it was with the interfacing unit. This box was originally devised as a solution to the interface limitations of the first main computer. Again, quite late in the project there were some technical difficulties. The design team eventually called in help so as to better understand the function of the unit. Again, only when one of the old hands became involved did he realise that this box was still in the system. The original computer had been replaced some years previously by one with far superior interfacing capability, completely obviating the need for the interface unit.

"We'll just do it in the software"

There were a lot of other interface problems, with both the main computer and with the subsidiary microprocessors which had sprung up throughout the system. Often the hardware engineers relied on 'doing in the software' jobs which would be simple in hardware but horrendously difficult and expensive in software.

There were wires soldered the wrong way round, so that the least significant bit was where the most significant should have been and vice versa. ("Is bit 1 or bit 16 the most significant bit? - or should that be 0 or 15?") The software was expected to turn every data word coming across that interface back to front, bit by bit.

Elsewhere some microprocessor software received data from a specially built keyboard. Now, electromechanical keys have a tendency to 'bounce' for several tens of milliseconds after being pressed. The effect, if not handled properly is to generate a stream of spurious data. It had been common practice for years to build in simple 'contact debounce' circuitry at the interface. Later this became encapsulated in standard chips. But in this case the hardware engineer did not know about them, or forgot, or couldn't be bothered to use them. So the software was expected to do 'contact debounce'. It is *possible* in software, but it is very painful.

Elsewhere again, in another microprocessor, the software was 'thrashing'. It was having to inspect an input channel so frequently that it had no time to do any actual processing of the data. The software team were struggling, being criticised by the hardware team for poor performance, until the fight got so bad that yet another old hand was brought in to referee. It turned out that the hardware team had failed to put in a one word register as a buffer which would have latched the data - stored it temporarily until the processor was ready.

But one of the biggest interface boobs of all concerned the distribution of peripheral functions from the main computer to local subsidiary processors. Even before the availability of microprocessors such distribution had been part of the design philosophy. The approach was then novel and well-publicised, being presented at international conferences.

The original, and well documented, design concept, was that each packet of data should have an identity related to its source. This identity would be passed to the subsidiary system. When the subsidiary system required more information from a particular source, it would request it from the main computer, referencing this identity, making it a fairly simple matter for the main computer to find it. Nowadays we would talk of 'object oriented design', but again this project was ahead of its time.

Unfortunately, as the project progressed and personnel changed, a hardware engineer, in order to save a small amount of store, decided not to bother to save this identity. So the only information passed back to the main computer was the value of some of the data already sent. The main computer then had to work out from which of several hundred possible sources of data this packet had come.

The original concept was intended to simplify the interface, and reduce the associated processing so that it was virtually negligible. The consequence of the actual design was to bring the main computer to a near standstill. (Later this was rectified, to some extent.)

Yet another example of corporate forgetfulness, despite clear documentation, concerned the Built-In Test Equipment (BITE). Simplifying, this takes two forms. Static BITE is a facility to monitor such things as voltages in analogue circuitry, to ensure that components are operating properly. Dynamic BITE often requires some input-to-output test to check that the functional operation delivers expected results. The need for both was recognised and an outline approach documented. It was pointed out that the dynamic BITE needed further consideration. It got it - but years later, after the kit had been built without it.

Good programming practice
Moving onto the software design *per se*, the problems were different, but just as perverse.

Only when a new programmer had to amend an old module of someone else's code did its rather curious structure come to light. The input to the module was a single piece of data, together with a number. The data was to be placed into a table of data. The number was a pointer to the right place in the table.

This job *could* have been done simply with just a single program statement (an array assignment). Instead of which it went on impenetrably with a long chain of if's and then's: "If the pointer value is one then put the data into the first place in the table else if it is two then put it into the second place else if ..." and so on for half a page. (Luckily the table did not have a million entries!)

Of course, the programmer of the original had thought that he was simply following the company's very thorough and copiously documented structured programming rules. It is rather like someone, having been told that the shortest distance between two points on the globe is a great circle, sets off from London to Brighton - heading north. It *is* a great circle, but...

More seriously in effect, it was realised quite late on that at least ten per cent of machine time was spent shuffling unused - that is not worked on - data about the main store, ending up unchanged exactly where it started. This was discovered only when a performance analysis was done to see where processing time might be saved. But it had not been done unknowingly. The particular designers thought that it was 'good' programming practice to make local copies of data which might be needed, before execution of a subprogram. Indeed that is what some of the text-books taught. But nobody at the time saw, directly, the effects of this 'good' design. And who would have thought that they would go one stage further and copy it all back again after it had been 'used' (ie, usually, *not* used).

Estimates and resources

On the general subject of estimation and performance, this project was much like any other. The estimates for the requirements which had been the centre of attention during feasibility studies were not *too* bad. But lurking beneath the waterline were the other nine-tenths of boring, forgotten, and late-coming bits. For instance, the estimate for one suite of 'subsidiary' software facilities was sub-contracted out to a firm of software specialists. The store estimate was 200 words. Ten years on it was 600K and rising daily - now two-thirds of the total main computer store requirement.

Partly because of the performance problems, the choices of computer and programming language both came in for criticism. Apart from upgrades, there was one mid-development change of main computer type. At that time there had been some support in the supplier organisation for shopping abroad. But there was then a clear and well-documented instruction from the customer to "Buy British". Interestingly, this seemed to get forgotten during the later recriminations.

By the end of the project the programming language chosen was considered by many to be passé. But at the beginning it was the only available high level language for this type of application. It was also the customer's standard. It was ahead of its time - so far ahead that an appropriate compiler did not exist at the beginning. And throughout the project there was a running battle with the compiler suppliers to support it adequately. (A familiar story?)

The possibilities of changing horses in midstream - whether of language or the main computer again - were frequently explored, with thorough studies of the options available. Each time it was felt that the technical advantages would be outweighed by the management disadvantages in simply being able to handle such a massive change. So the less than perfect choices were made not by default, but consciously, carefully looking at the tradeoffs.

QUALITY ASSURANCE

Quality Management System

At about the same time as the project was getting under way, the company was one of the first anywhere to introduce an explicit software quality management system with a dedicated software quality department.

At least ten per cent of software costs were allocated to the quality management function. Its operation was regularly vetted by the customer, and in general got a clean bill of health.

Closely associated with the quality system was the training department which, in essence, taught the technical and procedural standards for the project. All new staff, however highly educated, went through an intensive four-week course in these.

Some features of the quality management system might now be considered old-fashioned but, essentially, at first at least, it worked. But the reason that it worked, and the extent to which it worked, and the way that it worked were due much less to *what* was done than to *why* it was done.

The benefits were to a great extent in *communication* - giving a large and changing team a common way of doing things, of pulling teams together in some direction.

It also gave everyone a good feeling to know that they were trail-blazing these new techniques - that they were held up as a shining example to others of the bright and better way to do things. So what, if anything, went wrong?

Structure and style: procedures and paper

First and foremost the creation of a large and separate quality department, certainly *in the form which it took here,* caused some of the problems. The approach is quite common in the industry and it is taken for good reasons. Even if given explicit responsibility for performing quality-related functions, development staff notoriously treat them with lower priority than their current technical or managerial challenge. Furthermore, it is often felt that the independence of a separate department enables it to act as a kind of corporate conscience.

But that separation led to different goals, different styles of operation, and a different type of staff. Unable to see into the technical content of the project to directly assess its actual quality, they concentrated on execution of the procedures, and on providing documented evidence of the execution of the procedures. Paper, paper, and more paper. Rows and rows of filing cabinets full of forms. After all, this was what was needed to have the quality management system 'registered'.

So programmers came to look on 'quality' as something to do with form-filling - nothing more than a boring clerical task.

They willingly relinquished control, chairmanship, and conduct of their design reviews to the willing expansionist quality department. How else, on such a project, could "Not Applicable" have been accepted as the answer to a standard checklist question of "Have the real-time constraints been satisfied?"

Elsewhere, they encouraged the configuration control clerk to fill in the configuration control forms for them. Of course the consequence was that the forms might have had all the right numbers in all the right boxes, but absolutely **no** content. This was fine for registration, but clearly, without real content, the forms could never have been the basis of *control.* And indeed they were not, since most of them were completed as a matter of form (!) some time after changes had been made.

Configuration management: pretence or reality

Behind this superficial problem lies a much bigger problem associated with software configuration management generally. Part of the problem lay in the fact that the way it was done (and in many places, still is) was based on received wisdom. And because the development team had abdicated responsibility for these issues, no-one there looked closely enough to analyse the problem and see, and be brave enough to say, that received wisdom was wrong.

Software configuration management procedures were based on those for hardware. But few software quality managers realise that the hardware procedures are generally concerned with change *embodiment*. That is, they are concerned with the control of changes to production, *after a design change has been decided.* The control of consideration of *design* changes is something else entirely. So software designers were being asked to give details of their proposed change which they could not possibly do until they had actually designed it and convinced themselves that it was satisfactory. In software, though, that means 'until they had actually implemented the change and tested it'.

The forms could be completed *only* retrospectively, and therefore perfunctorily - which means probably badly and, often, plain wrong.

Some might say that even if the quality system did not properly *control* what was done, at least it would provide the information to know *what* was done. Oh yes? It only took *three months* to find the right sources so that the accepted system could be rebuilt from registered library components.

And hereby hangs another tale... To some extent the difficulties experienced in rebuilding the system from library components was because the procedures, such as they were, had anyway been ignored in the heat of last minute panic before customer tests.

In recognition of this the quality department had accepted a streamlined procedural system for use during tests and trials, but this was also being ignored. This time it was because of the cavalier attitude of the front-line test-support team who felt themselves to be above such things. After all, they knew what they were doing, and what they had done: nobody should interfere with *them*.

Meanwhile, just before each test, the software project manager was faced with both the customer and his own management asking for eleventh hour changes, while his own team were unearthing bugs and proposing fixes. *And* he was supposed to know what was going on.

Procedures with purpose

And that was the starting point for the solution - to recognise that the project manager had *really* to be in control. Faced with all the demands, he needed to have at his fingertips knowledge of what options were available - what he could and could not do, both technically with respect to the software design, and in terms of deploying effort to different tasks.

New procedures were devised. They were simple but effective. They were based entirely on the needs of the project manager to be able to answer questions about possible rescheduling of changes. Some paper was involved, but not a lot. The emphasis was now on real *information*, not on *documentation*. And the information demanded from the team was now driven by genuine need from the top, rather than by some abstract idea of what documentation 'should' be provided. So those who had to provide it were brutally made aware of that need. They soon learned to cooperate.

The quality manager took some convincing - or telling. Reluctantly he accepted that photocopies of the project manager's information - basically three sheets of paper, with many annotations, were all he was going to get. He did not readily accept that these were the best records he could possibly have, and that they were worth far more than all the filing cabinets full of (literally) meaningless forms.

From the need for information, there were also implications for the information flow. These led to other major changes to the structure of the project team, which are described further later under the topic of project management.

MANAGEMENT

Running on from the organisational issues associated with quality management, we will first investigate some general aspects of organisational structure and management, before returning to the specific question of project management.

Organisational structure

One of the criticisms levelled at the project in an external audit during its last few years was that the software team was separate from the rest of the project. It was, in effect, acting as a subcontractor. In consequence there had developed an 'us and them' attitude between the software division and the division holding the main contract.

This was to some extent true. Right from its initial establishment it had been a bone of contention within the company. However, after an acrimonious paper war just as the project was beginning, 'The Programming Group' was born.

In the later criticism of the separation, the benefits were forgotten. By having a single group responsible for all the software in the company's different projects, this 'programming group' was able to develop a critical mass which could sustain a proper infrastructure of a development bureau, a software support group, the quality department, the training school, and a research and development team.

It enabled a career structure for software staff, who would otherwise be a difficult fit in a company dominated by electronic engineers. A corollary was that it had, to some extent, pay scales of its own, in recognition of the general shortage in supply of suitable software staff. This did cause some problems of resentment elsewhere, but it was felt to be better to have staff and put up with the resentment than not to have staff.

And if all these failed to satisfy an individual software engineer, the organisation was resilient to staff changes.

Project management

Turning now to project management specifically, there were, in addition to the handling, avoidance, or otherwise of the problems described earlier, other difficulties. These were primarily to do with project scheduling.

Early in the project there arose what seemed like the sensible idea of software prototyping. Even today there is discussion and argument about the appropriateness of different approaches to prototyping. Then it was thought that there should be just a few, discrete rather than evolutionary, prototypes. Each new prototype would learn from the previous, in a process of refinement. The first would be simply to evaluate functionality. The second would accept changes arising from the first and test them with realistic-seeming hardware, but not the actual kit. Finally there would be a 'final draft' for use with near-production hardware, as the basis for the deliverable system.

This all sounded fine - until the project schedules were collapsed. So the second prototype development began long before the first was finished - even had it not been over-running. There was then no chance to use lessons learned from the first in the second. The two developments continued in parallel, with the first becoming more and more of an academic exercise, necessary for the supplier to meet its contractual obligations and to get payment; hated by everybody for consuming resources (ie people) and diverting attention from the main goal.

But even *that* lesson was not learned later on. Some years later, the same thing happened again, with knobs on. The next prototype was, of course, late: and the overall schedule was foreshortened because a trials version was required early. So the concept of a prototype was abandoned, and the prototype already on the stocks transmogrified into the first of a string of deliverable versions, now relabelled phase 1, phase 2, etc.

This all sounded highly plausible while work proceeded on the first phase, and indeed even during the early days of the second phase. It was only during the middle of the second phase that it was realised that the software delivered from the first phase, and now looked after by a separate team, had evolved considerably in response to feedback from trials.

Of course, the first phase team were supposed to keep the others informed of all the changes. But we have already heard how successful the procedures had been. Perhaps they would have got round to filling in the paperwork some time. But you know how it is under trials conditions...

However, there was now no way that the customer would accept a second phase deliverable which did not incorporate the changes incorporated into the much evolved first phase. Of course, to change the second phase to incorporate the first phase changes would have been a mammoth task, even if the trials version were not changing daily.

And after the second phase, waiting in the wings, were the third, fourth, fifth, ...

Eventually the management team bit the bullet. The second phase was, as a separate and parallel development, abandoned. The first phase was taken in hand and controlled properly. The second phase functions were designed as add-ons to be gradually incorporated along with changes arising from trials and with other changes in the customer requirements arising from the changing world of the customer.

There was now just a single stream of development - incremental, evolutionary, development.

At about the same time, major structural changes were made to the project team. The impetus for the changes came from the new software project manager who had inherited a deep, compartmentalised, hierarchy and who wanted much better visibility and understanding of what was actually happening on the project, and of what relationship it bore to the present requirements. This was connected with the new approach to configuration management, which demanded real information, rather than mere documentation (discussed above under 'quality assurance').

The new structure was very 'flat', with a loose collection of 'task force teams' grouped by the different functional areas of the system. Senior subordinate managers who would usually be assigned sub-projects within a hierarchy were instead given functional rôles - responsible for knowing precisely, at any moment, the status of the present work packages, the availability and suitability of staff for new work packages, the available flexibility for rescheduling, the financial position, and the technical position - in depth, not just that it was said to be alright, or that there were problems, but the precise nature of any technical problems.

The senior technical staff responsible for knowing this last set of information would, on many other projects, have been promoted into administrative positions in the hierarchy. Now they were placed in the various functional areas as team leaders. (Though these were relatively low-level in hierarchical terms, it was clear to all that they were by no means junior.)

The project manager could now know the precise *actual* position at a moment's notice; was able to discuss new and changed requirements with his own management or with the customer on the basis of good information; and knew and was able to discuss technical problems as they arose, with the support of top-flight technical advisers who had equally good information.

This approach is not recommended as a recipe for all projects and all project managers. It was just one way of achieving *real* control, rather than a paper pretence, and one way of achieving proper project communication (see later section on "what might be done").

In addition, the structural changes included a clear separation between the development 'task force teams' and the integration team. This removed the bottleneck which conventional integration techniques had imposed. This in turn enabled a dramatic increase in the effort which could be applied to the development - by an order of magnitude.

In parallel, and in addition to the major changes to configuration management procedures discussed earlier, there were detailed alterations to working practices - like removing all private temporary storage so that all work went through the project library.

Within six months of these changes the next software delivery took place on schedule - the first time this had happened since the minutes-before-the-deadline delivery of the proposal, ten years previously.

From then on there would still be problems. The incremental development was not always as flexible as was hoped, since the sequencing of the incorporation of some features was sometimes quite critical. Some things could not be done a bit at a time. Some were just hard. But there was no longer the threat of tens or hundreds of man-years of work simply being shelved.

Except, of course, that that is precisely what happened to the project as a whole.

ANALYSIS AND DISCUSSION

Did it go wrong?

Was it a disaster? If a disaster is something which adversely affects human beings then yes. Maybe the politicians, empire builders, and plain dimwits simply got their due comeuppance. But the majority who suffered sweeping redundancies, or other more subtle damage to their psyches and careers, were honest hardworking engineers who had achieved great things. Perhaps, though, we should reclassify it as a natural disaster, given the combination of perversity and inevitability.

Why did it go wrong?

Why was it a disaster? Well, it was not at source the software, nor any of the other commonly quoted culprits. Certainly there were things wrong with all of them, but that is to ignore the many things which were right. Now getting some things right - even, with cooler retrospection, a lot of things right - can hardly be an excuse for getting others wrong. But it does indicate that the problem lies deeper than a simple change of management team. After all, these were mostly well-qualified, well-intentioned, well-motivated people, intrinsically capable of making decisions at least as sensibly as their critics.

To simply say that if this had been done or that had not been done then the project would have been a success is flawed in two respects. Firstly, it is to ignore the beneficial aspects of many of the decisions, without suggesting how those benefits might otherwise be obtained (the grass is greener effect). Secondly, to say that decisions could have been better is to beg the question of *how* they might have been made better.

It is difficult to see what might be done better to foresee the undesirable side-effects of otherwise well-considered and sensible decisions. It is facile, though perhaps true, to talk of learning from experience and consulting widely in order to tap into the experiences of others.

Parochialism and politics

So what of bad decisions? The case study illustrates that, in general, on a large project the problem is not *directly* that people make the wrong decisions. They do this as a *consequence* of approaching the decision from the wrong direction. They look after their local interests, acting parochially. Sometimes this is *because* they forget or are never aware of important considerations outside their own area; sometimes it is perhaps *why*.

'Parochialism' may, though, sound more pejorative than intended. It has overtones of deliberate ill-will to others, but that is rarely the case - at least in the beginning.

There are *some* bad guys, who start out by seeing a project as one round in their fight to develop a career *rather than* a system. It is not that they want to do a disservice to the customer, just that doing a good job is not their number one priority. So why not build a career by building a good system? Well, on projects which last more than ten years, in an industry in which career steps - and even salary assessments - may be no more than six months apart, being seen to perform in the short term can easily be more important than the real thing in the long run. 'Performance' is the right word - as in *acting*: they are the corporate politicians.

But the majority at least start out with goodwill to all men.

For an analogy, look at life on the farm - a coherent food-production organisation, when viewed abstractly and from a distance. Now step inside. The pigs see other pigs and a sea of mud. They may through cracks in the pig-sty door see a glimpse of the world beyond - perhaps the side of the sheepshed - and wonder what sort of pigs there are on the other side. The sheep see other sheep, some straw, and, at lambing-time when they most want to be alone, a lot of human heads. The farmyard geese see quite a lot as they strut up and down. Sometimes they see the horse's head sticking out of the stable door. Given its size, they muse on the strength of its two webbed feet. The battery hens don't see a lot. And we have all heard the one about being a mushroom.

So it is on a project. For all the best reasons we encourage small teams to have a strong sense of identity; we minimise the number of people reporting to each line manager; to avoid confusion we insist on formal communication channels - the pig-sty doors. So we create deep management hierarchies and the mushroom syndrome. How many times have senior managers been appalled that their junior team members did not even know who the project manager was when he visited (let alone the customer).

So both managers and members of teams within a large project end up pursuing local goals. What is this but modularity, and separation of concerns, after all? - a good thing, surely? It is not (at least not always - see later) that they would not *like* to identify with the overall project goals. Indeed they perhaps think that they do, but as in the farmyard, who knows? In its mild form the symptoms are no more severe than parochial decision-making, though as discussed above the technical consequences can be very damaging. But there is only a thin line between parochialism and politics. It takes only a little resentment between individuals or teams for the one to degenerate into the other, and for long-running feuds to form and fester.

And then, to compound the difficulties, things go wrong. Even if each manager had not been set an impossible task, delivering to time and budget is rarely easy and there is rarely any contingency for any difficulties which might arise. Once the budget is blown, careful, steady, conscientious management is not easy. Getting away with the bare minimum and justifying it becomes more important than the customer's needs or even the boss's.

So even the good guys can, under pressure, be more concerned with self-preservation than cool, honest, appraisal of the situation. Who can blame them? Only those who have never been there. And can anyone tell which are the bad guys and which the good guys in a bad mess?

And these last two problems - of both bad guys and good guys under pressure - are not restricted to teams within large projects, but to the senior project managers and company managers as well.

Politics and parochialism affect not just suppliers, either: customer organisations can be equally afflicted. We talk simplistically of 'the customer', but in large organisations there may be several departments responsible for different facets of the acquisition of new systems. (Think of the twenty-odd on the case-study requirements committee.) There can, for instance, be a continual tug-of-war between end-users and their centralised 'buying department'. On one project, worse even than the case study, these customer departments could not even agree on which one of them was legally responsible for the contract. The supplier could not find out who to sue for non-payment, after difficulties with delays and disagreements on the specification.

In these situations a project can be just a pawn in the political manoeuvring of different customer departments. Even if it does not start out like that, when things begin to go wrong the same forces as in the supply side will start to surface. There will be those trying to save face with their superiors and colleagues (ie competitors in their own rat-race), and those trying to make capital out of the problems. Those faces which were so friendly during all the fun of feasibility studies can turn very sour when their owners are in big internal trouble.

Perversity

After parochialism, whether of the benign farmyard variety, or of the malignant political kind, comes perversity. This is not, in this context, deliberate wilful waywardness of individuals. Rather, it is the failure of 'the system' - the people system: failure to communicate, despite every effort; corporate forgetfulness. "People squared equals perversity".

Such perversity characterises those examples given earlier in the paper where, with *apparently* good communication between teams working together, and nobody acting parochially, still things went wrong.

In some cases the requirements evolved, invalidating the original design assumptions. Hence the basic form of the design was no longer appropriate. Then that form of design became a shackle, constraining both performance and the further enhancement of the design.

In others, where the design assumptions were still valid, the design evolved for other reasons. In doing so it diverged from the original design concepts. No-one remembered them or recognised what was happening. So the bastardised remnants of the original design actually degraded performance, and hindered further design enhancement.

Some of the unexpected side-effects of otherwise good ideas seemed quite perverse, too.

It seemed like a good idea to base the software design on an assumption that modern signal processing hardware would produce clean data; like a good idea to use advanced techniques like message-passing software design; like a good idea to reuse existing hardware change control standards.

Indeed it sometimes seems that any attempt to improve things is to tempt fate of the perverse kind. We know and try to anticipate the obvious opposition from reactionaries and entrenched NIH. But there is also a basic problem with novelty itself. New approaches are simply not understood. In a way they are not even understandable if they are not part of the 'culture' of an organisation or the discipline. The new ways are not easy to adopt. Applying them can seem contrived. It may be easier to choose a 'worse' solution which is 'understandable' (ie personally familiar) and which conforms with the existing culture (ie corporately familiar).

But these are not the *really* perverse problems of novelty. *They* arise when the new techniques *are* applied, but without understanding. Thus the strange, but perfectly well-structured, program module.

SO, WHAT MIGHT BE DONE?

A problem in perpetuity?
The historical pattern is that we begin with an individual. This individual designs or in other ways works with a set of mental building bricks - concepts, or even physical components.

To do more than can be achieved by one individual, we form teams, and teams of teams - big projects.

From asking a single monkey to write "Hamlet", we now expect co-operating teams of monkeys to deliver the Complete Works of Russell.

We can improve the process in a variety of ways to enable an individual or a team to do more, or the same but better. We can give the individual 'bigger' concepts or components. We can develop design techniques which enable the individual to make better use of existing concepts (such as structured programming). And we can try to better order the organisation - in the most general sense, including the project organisational structure, the development schedule, the procedures.

The biggest advances, since they allow equivalent sized and organised teams to do better, come from 'bigger concepts'. But, in general, individual team members, project managers, and even companies have little control over these. They evolve from the industry at large. Individual organisations may have their in-house design techniques, and usually have their own approaches to company and project organisation. But, as we have seen, conventional procedures, however carefully conceived, are not necessarily enough for large projects.

So it *is* worth looking for generically applicable ideas, not encapsulated in standard management techniques, about how to do things better.

It might be argued that the problems will go away as we give designers bigger and better concepts and components, since they make projects smaller and simpler. But that would require that we exhaust the capacity of application domains to find new and ever more complex requirements. Yet there is little evidence that we will cease to stretch our capabilities, and sometimes to over-reach them - to bite off more than we can chew.

There is even an argument that it is good and stimulating for society to take on at least some high-risk projects. But high-risk of some means almost certain failure of at least a few. Which customers will volunteer for disaster projects in the interests of cultural enhancement?

So what does make big projects go right?

Looking at *good* decisions and well-managed projects and working out who were the people behind them, the important factors seem to be luck, together with parochialism, power, personalities, and so on - all the same factors - which by, happenchance, happen to lead to success rather than failure. In other words - people, again.

But there do seem to be some common success factors. Not counting luck, two stand out. The first is a good project manager; the second that the team have done it - or something like it - before. These tend to be discounted by technologists, perhaps because they have so little control over them - like the adage about choosing one's parents more carefully.

At first sight there are no obvious connections between these factors and those which led to the mixed bag of successes and failures of the case study. But what is it that the 'good project manager' *does*? We talk of 'a strong sense of purpose', 'commitment', 'knowing what he wants' coupled with an ability to communicate those things and to motivate everyone else.

Moreover, this is a two-way process. The 'good manager' will also be a listener - able to pick up the 'vibes' from the project team; able to sort out the wheat from the chaff of project reports and meetings; able to appreciate what he is hearing so that his actions are based on understanding rather than rote and rule-books.

Is this not just one approach to overcoming the problems of parochialism and lack of understanding of, and identification with, the real customer requirements and with the design concepts? In other words, a 'good manager' may be able to achieve the effects which we seek. We must try to achieve the same effects without necessarily having any choice over the project manager.

Out of a project employing several thousand people, perhaps only a handful *really* appreciate the customer's requirements; only a handful really understand the design concepts; and if we are lucky these handfuls may overlap. Many of the problems of the case study were a consequence of a breakdown in (effective) communication of this appreciation and understanding. A 'good manager' is one way, and we may always be better with a good manager than the alternative. But if we recognise what it is that he does, then we may be better able to facilitate the achievement of the same effects in other ways.

In a way, that is one of the purposes of design reviews and requirements reviews - to ensure that proper communication has been achieved. When viewed in this light it becomes clear why it is so important to have customer participation at such reviews (at the appropriate level). It also becomes clear why they should not be treated as an administrative formality.

But there are more fundamental things we can do which can have a bigger effect. Thus the 'flat structure' described above for the software team, towards the end of the case study.

The purpose of that structure was originally to give the software project manager hands-on control - counter to received wisdom on management style. Not only was that achieved, the benefits were much more. The 'trusties' embedded into the development teams were placed there to give the project manager good information. But clearly this worked both ways. All members of the development teams were much more aware of the customer's needs, of the design strategy, and of how their own work contributed and fitted with the overall design and the work of other teams. Moreover, morale was thereby improved.

There may be other ways of achieving the same effect: one alternative is to have a 'flying squad' of technicians who are made guardians of the design, its integrity, and its coherence with the (perhaps evolving) design concepts. This has the additional advantage of separating the rôles of technicians - perhaps not the best managers - from management. It may have the disadvantage of separation and isolation from the line management - it will need a determined project manager to make it work. In a way, the 'trusties' of the case study fulfilled this rôle, but without becoming remote from the line.

Turning now to the second oft-quoted success factor, should only those organisations familiar with the type of work undertake new projects?

Let us set aside political considerations such as the drive to open markets up to new suppliers, to provide opportunities for small and medium-sized enterprises, and generally to encourage competition. Let us further set aside concerns that innovation would be inhibited. Let us instead ask what is meant by 'corporate familiarity'.

Even if a supplier has done a similar large project before, it would probably also have been a lengthy project. And an organisation is a collection of people who, in this fast-moving industry, will mostly have moved on - as will the technology which they used, and indeed the operational requirements. So we are unlikely ever to find the *same* project team which has even done the same *sort of* thing before.

What we have instead is a collection of people who might know something about some aspects of this sort of job. The message is the same - we must organise to communicate this knowledge, rather than leave it locked up in a few isolated heads. (Though care must be exercised so that over-conservative individuals do not stifle innovation.)

But: as the case study demonstrated, *documentation* - however thorough, and however carefully design decisions and the reasoning behind them are documented as well as the design itself, and even if there are no hidden assumptions - is not enough if no-one will read it. The organisational structure must be such that those who have the knowledge, or who know it exists, are able to make sure that it is applied effectively.

So far we have talked of ways in which we might get the best out of people, their knowledge, and the technology they use.

An alternative approach is to attempt to build into the management and technical organisation mechanisms for monitoring and feedback. So we would have a 'closed-loop' development system, rather than rely on the 'open-loop behaviour' of the project team. But this is what quality control is supposed to do and, as with quality control, it might sound fine on paper; it *might* even work in 'peacetime'; but it will probably break down in the heat of action, when the urgent takes priority over the important.

We should not expect procedures based upon some ideal, but unrealistic, model of development to turn untidy reality into the tidy ideal. And it is often at the very time that control is most needed, that the control mechanisms break down. We should avoid *reliance* on monitoring mechanisms. As in so many control systems, the greater the dependence on feedback, the greater the risk of instability.

We have heard how the case study was awash with procedures and forms, driven by the needs of certification. But the forms did not say anything useful, and the procedures did not help anyone actually *control* anything. The institutionalisation of the procedures - leading to abrogation of responsibility to a separate quality department - diminished their value still further. Finally, they were ignored anyway in the heat of last minute panics. But this last should not really be seen as an additional problem: it was more a *consequence* of the contempt felt for the official system.

It was only when the project manager took full responsibility for both his own needs for control *and* the needs for quality assurance that the procedures and paperwork were redesigned to provide, use, and record the real information required for the real decision-making. *Then* there was real motivation to make the procedures work.

So there is a positive conclusion here. Procedures should *primarily* be designed not to check that the right things are done, but to facilitate the doing of the right things.

SUMMARY

We spend a lot of time agonising about which techniques and tools to use in future - and even whether to suffer the trauma of a mid-term change to solve today's project problems. But who cares what colour we paint the hangar when we should have been building a ship?

Most designers can do a good job with the techniques and tools they have to hand, as long as they understand their capabilities and limitations, and as long as they understand what they should really be doing. But there are no technical fixes for problems of understanding, nor for fundamental organisation and management problems which inhibit that understanding.

It is sometimes said that all we have to do with a large project is make it a collection of small projects. The argument in this paper is that that is not enough. It is not even enough to make it a collection of the *right* small projects. It must be more than the sum of its parts, and that added value has to come from communication and cooperation, and from structuring the project, the project team, and the procedures to achieve effective communication. Else the sub-projects will, first through parochialism, and then politics, and peppered with perversity, fragment and fail.

Final footnote on the 'software problem'
The first instance of a 'software problem' given in this paper was the difficulty that the software had in coping with more than two orders of magnitude more data than the design target. To conclude, here is another 'software problem'.

One day a serious software fault was reported. Apparently, the screens had simply gone blank during tests. From the subsequent 'fault investigation' the following story emerged.

During previous tests the customer had complained of an annoying rattle in the metalwork of the system. The mechanical engineers had cured the rattle by adding a metal brace to the offending panel. Unfortunately this brace passed across the duct for a cooling fan. The fan was that for the main computer which, some time during the later tests, overheated and quite properly tripped out, switching off automatically to avoid damage. The screens went blank and in the history books - in this case the system fault log - was entered another statistic - yet another 'software problem'.

--ooOoo--

5

DESIGN OF A FLIGHT AND RADAR DATA PROCESSING SYSTEM FOR THE SUPPORT OF AIR TRAFFIC CONTROL

S C WILLMOTT
UK Civil Aviation Authority

ABSTRACT

An Air Traffic Control Centre is presented as an example of a Large Software System thereby enabling characteristic concerns to be illustrated. The Air Traffic Control problem domain is explained in terms of airspace structure and the roles of the people involved. The processing chain of flight and radar data from source to destination is described, together with their interaction. A generic system architecture is discussed. A subsystem life cycle covering planning, procurement and operation is outlined. Finally concerns characteristic of Large Software Systems in general are discussed with reference to the above framework.

1.   INTRODUCTION

1.1   This paper is based upon a presentation for the Centre for Software Reliability Sixth Annual Conference in September 1989. The conference's emphasis was on the real problems of software engineering for Large Software Systems. All figures referenced appear at the end of the paper.

1.2   The paper endeavours to provide insight into the various software systems which are linked together to support Air Traffic Control (ATC). The intention is to allow an appreciation of the size and complexity of such systems. Examples are loosely derived from Flight Data Processing (FDP) and Radar Data Processing (RDP) at the London Air Traffic Control Centre (ATCC). Airports are the other major component of a national Air Traffic System (ATS). In order to generalise they are considered to be analogous in this paper's terms to a scaled down ATCC. The vital areas of voice communications and navigational aids are not considered. Neither is the dissemination of relatively static information, such as airport status or air space maps, considered.

1.3   Firstly a simplified view (figure 1) of how airspace is structured is presented in order to provide some oversight of ATC. This is enhanced by illustrating the various roles of personnel at an ATCC. The overall complexity of a national centre is then indicated by a structured viewpoint breakdown (figure 2) which places the FDP and RDP subsystems in context.

1.4   Flight and radar data are considered to be different representations of the same entity. The former relates to the intentions of the aircraft's pilot while the latter corresponds to the actual position of the aircraft in the air. Both aid the dialogue between the ground based controller and the airborne pilot, the purpose of which is the safe, orderly and expeditious flow of air traffic. Consequently the relationship between FDP and RDP is overviewed (figure 3) before considering each in more detail. The chain of processing from remote source, through processing at the centre and to display on an ATC suite is outlined for FDP (figure 4) and RDP (figure 5). A view is presented of how these two chains of processing could be more closely integrated in the future (figure 6).

1.5   Systems such as these require significant engineering investment in terms of planning, procurement and operation. This is illustrated by a simplified subsystem life cycle (figure 7).

1.6   The paper concludes with a discussion of concerns characteristic of Large Software Systems in general and in particular with reference to the framework established.

2.   SIMPLIFIED AIRSPACE STRUCTURE

2.1   Figure 1 illustrates plan and elevation views of the air space controlled by an ATCC. The International Civil Aviation Organisation (ICAO) defines airspace in terms of national and international Flight Information Regions (FIRs). This airspace is generally stratified into Lower, Middle and Upper Air Space. The major components in Middle Air Space are Airways which have volume and are known collectively as Controlled Air Space. Aircraft flying within Airways must satisfy certain mandatory requirements (eg. must file a prior Flight Plan and carry a Secondary Surveillance Radar transponder). ATC here is active in so far that the pilot, who carries the ultimate responsibility for his aircraft, must obey ATC instruction unless he has good reason to do otherwise. In this event an incident would be declared and investigated. The bulk of civil commercial aircraft fly in Airways and are deemed to be en-route from departure to destination airports within the FIR. Point to point routes are also designated for en-route aircraft in the Upper Air and which are over-flying all or part of the FIR. Upper Air flights are also under active ATC. Aircraft flying outside Airways are known as off-route traffic and the ATC service is passive or advisory. In general all traffic in an FIR is controlled from one ATCC, en-route from one Operations Room and off-route from another. In the UK the former is manned by civilian Air Traffic Controllers and the latter by military.

2.2   When en-route aircraft enter the environs of a major airport complex they enter special airspace known as a Terminal Maneouvering Area (TMA). Final approach and departure occur within a Control Zone which surrounds the immediate airport vicinity and the ATC service is provided by the Airport. Aircraft in the Upper Air and in Airways fly in generally uniform level flight, whereas aircraft in the Middle Air tend to be military and fly in a more unpredictable fashion. Aircraft in the TMA also require more effort to control as they are descending into or climbing out of an airport or being held in stacks when busy. In order to organise ATC the FIR airspace is sectorised so that only one Air Traffic Controller is responsible for the aircraft in a designated volume of airspace. Hence the controller's task is divided between directing the pilot and coordinating with other controllers.

3.   AIR TRAFFIC CONTROL ROLES

3.1   Civil ATC is manned in watches which provide a 24 hour service. Each watch is managed by a Supervisor who keeps the ATC workload under constant review. It is the Supervisor's decision when to impose or lift restrictions on the number of aircraft being controlled in the en-route FIR. Each civil sector is controlled by a civil suite, which is often separated for example into east bound and west bound. The sector/suite team is managed by a Sector Chief Controller, who will look for impending problems. Active ATC is provided by a Radar Controller, who concentrates on the Radar Data Display and talks on a designated radio frequency to all aircraft under his control. The Radar Controller is assisted by a Support Controller who handles all inter-sector coordination. This ATC team is complemented by ATC Assistants who prepare and present flight data as appropriate.

3.2   In addition to the ATC sector teams there are a number of more general ATC tasks. These include Flow Regulator Controllers who are active when the airspace flight capacity has been restricted. Their prime function is to allocate departure slots for scheduled and unscheduled flights from airports. A Low Flying Advisor will provide details of traffic in the Lower Air such as crop sprayers. Any pilot in the open FIR who is not receiving any ATC service can radio in for advice from a Flight Information Service.

3.3   Military ATC is also provided in 24 hour watches. Each watch has a Supervisor who oversees the Operations Room. New ATC tasks are assigned by an Allocator Controller to sectors in his geographic area according to available workload at these suites. Each suite is manned by a Radar Controller as for civil and he is supported by an Assistant who undertakes coordination functions. A significant number of off-route flights fly through Airways and as such present coordination problems which are resolved by Civil/Military Joint Area Controllers who form another component of civil sector teams. All emergencies, ranging from hi-jacks to pilots who are lost, in the FIR are handled by a military Distress and Diversion ATC team. Special flights, such as Royal Flights, are handled by a Special Tasks ATC team.

3.4   In addition to the ATC watches there are 24 hour Systems technical watches. These are managed by a System Controller who is responsible for the performance of all the technical systems supporting the operational ATC watches. Each system has a designated System Engineer who is backed by a Support team. The prime purpose of the Systems watches is to maintain the necessary level of operational support using individual system online redundancy and major component replacement. Repair of offline system components is performed by day specialist staff. Development of systems is also undertaken by specialist day engineering staff, however, final testing of changes has to be scheduled into the 24 hour operational service - generally at night and during the relatively quieter winter period.

4.   VIEWPOINT STRUCTURE FOR AN ATCC

4.1   The viewpoint structure shown in figure 2 is derived from a study done by the Royal Military College of Science. Only solid nodes are expanded and the diagram is not considered complete. The root of the hierarchy is to be interpreted as the ATCC itself in the Air Traffic System environment. The Air Traffic Services provided by the ATCC are factored out from a context of interaction with other ATCCs, users such as airlines and pilots and airports. The above Systems Control and Support Services viewpoints are also recognised. Remote radar stations are considered below.

4.2   In the next two levels in the hierarchy the different ATC functions alluded to above are identified, but only civil ATC is expanded in any detail. Flight plans are received by the ATCC and stored. Flight details are presented at the relevant sector just before the planned airport departure or arrival at the FIR boundary time. When the flight is confirmed as active more details are displayed at all relevant sectors in the ATCC. Furthermore as the flight progresses these details are updated.

4.3   Radar Data Processing (RDP) is broken down into previous RDP and display systems, which are being superseded by the mainstream RDP and its backup bypass system. The functional aspects of full RDP are described below.

5.   OVERVIEW OF FLIGHT AND RADAR DATA PROCESSING

5.1   Figure 3 presents an overview of the interaction between Flight and Radar Data Processing. In general the Flight Data Processing (FDP) of data associated with a flight is concerned with the intentions of the flight. In theory before a pilot departs he files his intentions in an ICAO standard format which is propagated over a worldwide flight data network to those ATCCs from which he will require an ATC service. In practice each airline files its scheduled flights in a batch of repetitive flight plans. Only one-off flights are filed by individual pilots. However, there are ICAO standard message formats for amending these filed plans. These plans and their amendments are stored at each ATCC and presented to and amended by operational controllers as described below. Relevant changes, such as boundary time estimates, are sent automatically to ATCCs in adjacent FIRs.

5.2   The actual position of an aircraft in the air is detected by radar stations remote from the ATCC. For an aircraft entering the FIR this detection is generally the first positive indication that the flight is airborne, whereas flights departing from major airports in the FIR are notified directly to the ATCC. This interaction between Flight and Radar Data is captured in a common Flight/Radar Database which forms the heart of the overall FDP/RDP system. The display of radar data to the ATC Radar Controller is tailored interactively by the controller. Furthermore with full RDP he is able to interact with flight data via his radar display interface. Knowledge of the flight's intentions is also valuable in resolving some of the radar processing problems identified below.

6.   FLIGHT DATA PROCESSING CHAIN

6.1   Figure 4 shows the Flight Data Processing chain in more detail. Flight plans and their amendments are received over telegraph networks, via telephone and on magnetic tape. They are processed initially to check them and enable their manual repair before storing them. The most complex part of a flight plan is its route field. This together with the filed departure point is processed in order to determine the initial departure path from the airport in the FIR. The estimated time of departure and the initial sector are derived so that proposed or warning flight information can be displayed at appropriate sectors at the appropriate time.

6.2   When the flight becomes airborne or is handed over from an adjacent FIR the flight plan is activated. This is done manually or triggered automatically by RDP. The route field is processed again in full in order to estimate arrival times at established reporting points. This processing depends heavily on the FIR airspace route structure. Wind information is also used to compute ground speeds. Active flight data is output to all sectors in the ATCC along the flight's route. In principle the same processing is done for en-route and off-route, but different display media are used. FIR boundary estimates are sent to and received from some neighbouring FIRs automatically.

6.3 Only one controller at a time is responsible for the flight and only he can update its flight data. However, all updates must be distributed to all interested sectors. Handing over this responsibility to the next sector controller is defined formally in the Manual of Air Traffic Service procedures and supported by interactive processing. En-route traffic tends to flow uniformly and these procedures are streamlined. Off-route traffic is more unpredictable and handover procedures are more flexible.

6.4 When an adjacent FIR places restrictions on the rate at which it will accept traffic Departure Flow Regulation comes into force. Up to two hours before the filed departure time an airline can request a departure slot. These requests are displayed at the flow regulation suite together with the known planned departures and flow restrictions. The Flow Regulator then allocates a slot and advises the airline. The aircraft must depart within the 20 minute slot or another slot must be requested.

7. RADAR DATA PROCESSING CHAIN

7.1 The various radar data flows from the radar head through to the radar display are shown in more detail in figure 5. Primary radar is a passive surveillance system. A pulse of microwave energy is reflected by the aircraft back to the rotating radar antenna thereby enabling the range and azimuth relative to the radar head to be determined. The aircraft can be struck by about ten separate pulses as the antenna turns. The analogue signals are digitised and processed. The central aircraft return is determined. Fourier techniques enable stationary objects or slow flying flocks of birds to be filtered out leaving discrete radar returns known as plots. Plots are tracked and correlated over successive rotations of the radar antenna so that spurious single returns can be discarded.

7.2 Secondary Surveillance Radar (SSR) is an active system. The SSR radar emits groups of microwave pulses which are decoded by an SSR transponder on the aircraft which returns a train of pulses encoding an aircraft identity or a readout from the aircraft altimeter. Again these signals are digitised for processing. Aircraft range and azimuth are determined as for primary radar, but use of monopulse techniques enables increased accuracy. Transponder replies have to be correlated with interrogations by the SSR concerned. Replies triggered by other SSRs are ignored. Furthermore as the SSR replies are stronger there is a greater probability of misleading reflected returns. Plots are correlated over successive scans as for primary.

7.3 En-route radar sites have both primary and SSR with either synchronised or co-mounted antennae. An aircraft should be detected by both systems and the two processed plots are combined into one plot message. Otherwise returns are composed into their own discrete messages as they would be from a single radar site. All these messages are transmitted over landlines or microwave links to the ATCC.

7.4 Radar data received by the ATCC is routed to different systems. Furthermore Airways and the TMA are covered by two or three overlapping radars. Mainstream RDP fuses this radar data into an integrated picture. Radar input processing time-stamps and converts all radar plots into system cartesian coordinates based upon an Earth model. Each radar head is registered as a fixed point and different radar heads at the same site are collimated from a single reference point at the site. This processing enables continuous monitoring of radar quality. Overall SSR is preferred as it is very much cheaper for long range cover. It carries more data in terms of aircraft identity and altitude. The latter enables accurate slant range correction. In the absence of a radar derived height the flight plan is used instead.

7.5 Correlation of radar plots from different radars and over their consecutive scans prepares radar data for tracking. Tracks are initiated when uncorrelated plots from previous scans are recognised as a credible track. Flight data assists in this recognition. Conversely track initiation can automatically activate a flight plan. New plots are associated with existing tracks. Where there is more than one track in the association volume this correlation process can become complex. Plots which do not become identified with a track are passed on directly to radar picture composition.

7.6 The tracking process naturally includes updating the track data with the new plot. This enables more accurate prediction of where the next plot is expected, thereby reducing the association search volume. Optimal tracking is recursive. If an expected plot is not received the track is able to coast until a plot appears within an ever increasing search volume. Finally if no plot is received after a certain time the track is dropped. Ordinarily this occurs in response to a flight data update canceling the plan when the flight lands or passes out of the FIR.

7.7 Radar returns are prone to random and systematic errors. These can lead to erratic display of an aircraft in uniform flight. Tracking is used to smooth out these errors. However, this smoothing also tends to disguise the display of an aircraft turning. The adverse consequences can be reduced if the track is matched with a flight plan and the plan indicates a manoeuvre.

7.8 Full tracking also enables longer term prediction of flights - thereby enabling conflict alerting to warn a controller of an impending incident and giving him time to redirect aircraft.

7.9 The integrated radar picture is composed of tracks, plots and map data. It is broadcast to all radar displays. Display of uncorrelated plots covers problems in track correlation. However, generally there is too much information for an individual controller and he selects that information which is relevant eg. he limits the range of airspace displayed.

7.10 Owing to the complexity of the above mainstream RDP an ATCC will have a backup RDP path. This generally processes individual radars through to display. In this scheme it becomes important to be able to convert the SSR aircraft identity code into its callsign. This conversion is derived from FDP. A simple route designator is also supplied for display against the radar symbol.

7.11 The Systems Controller is able to remotely monitor and control which radar head and supporting electronics is in operation.

7.12 Finally radar data is recorded so that it can be replayed to enable investigation of any ATC incidents. For example in a real incident a radar replay was able to pinpoint quickly the area where an aircraft crashed into the sea.

8. INTEGRATED FLIGHT AND RADAR DATA PROCESSING

8.1 With modern computer technology there is greater opportunity to integrate and consolidate much of the above processing. One possible architecture is illustrated in figure 6. Use of Wide Area Networks would enable the FIR ATC function to be distributed between several smaller ATCCs and Airports. These would provide contingency cover.

8.2 It would still be necessary to have a central computing complex for the global processing needed to support conflict alert, sector load prediction etc. This would probably be a complex of coupled fault tolerant mainframes.

8.3 Within an ATCC, Local Area Network (LAN) technology would greatly simplify the distribution of processed flight and radar data. Multiple redundant networks would improve the overall system resilience.

8.4 ATC suites would be based on high powered workstations in groupings of one, two or three. The display of flight and radar data would be integrated. Reconfiguration of the Operations Room would be handled consistently. It would be sensible to integrate voice communication channel selections so that it would be straightforward to set up a particular suite for a particular airspace sector.

8.5   This type of architecture would support a progressive failure strategy. Failure of central processing would not prevent suites from communicating over the LAN. Failure of the LAN would not prevent local workstation support. These failure modes would allow existing airborne aircraft to be handled safely until they landed or left the FIR. When traffic has decayed to an acceptable level the ATCC could be recovered.

9.   SIMPLIFIED SUBSYSTEM LIFE CYCLE

9.1   Large Software Systems such as described for an ATCC require significant investment. This must be planned and controlled by reference to an overall life cycle. Figure 7 shows how various life cycle activities interact. In order to meet corporate objectives it is necessary to develop strategic plans which capture the evolution of the system and its component subsystems. Programmes of one or more projects are established to create or change systems. Completion of a project results in operation of a new function, which improves the ATC service.

9.2   Each subsystem develops over a life cycle. Most subsystems are embedded and it is important to explore the requirement and perhaps architectural design during the conception phase. This culminates in a specification which enables competitive procurement. Production is done under contract and results in a delivered subsystem which has to be integrated into the operational environment. During its operation, the performance of the subsystem is monitored so that a timely decision can be made with regard to planning its replacement. Conventional project management covers the activity from specification to introduction into operational service.

9.3   ATC is a regulated service and as greater demands are made of the supporting systems it is becoming more important for the above development to take place under approved quality management procedures - both on individual systems and across the organisation.

9.4   Configuration management is also a major issue. It is paramount that changes to connected subsystems are coordinated when proposed and when implemented. A hierarchy of Configuration Control Boards can be defined which in turn relates to an overall system/subsystem decomposition.

10. CHARACTERISTIC CONCERNS

This section raises a number of issues arising from the above. These serve to illustrate the types of problems that can arise in the development of Large Software Systems.

10.1 <u>External Constraints</u>: The laws of physics are fixed. There is a finite amount of airspace in the FIR and airports are sited according to sociological and political demands. Although there is scope for increasing air space utilisation this requires changes in ATC procedures and system support. New ATC procedures have to be modeled carefully to establish the benefits. Sometimes extensive live simulations are used which also assist in the specification of the system changes. Furthermore changes in airspace structure and ATC procedure are constrained by international agreement. This illustrates international constraints.

10.2 <u>Intuitive Skill Problem Domain</u>: The overall integrity of the current system depends heavily upon the skill and motivation of the Air Traffic Controllers. The former is established by extensive training and validation on a particular sector before a controller is permitted to undertake radar control at that sector. This indicates that it is difficult to define the ATC role in formal terms.

10.3 <u>Complex Human Computer Interface</u>: ATC is done by closely knit teams. The efficiency of the team is greatly affected by the system Human Computer Interface. Motivation could be undermined by injudicious use of computer support. Computers are good at routine monitoring tasks whereas humans cope well with exceptions. Over-dependence on the computer may lead a controller into not fully assimilating the air space picture which in turn may result in a dangerous situation when the computer fails. Generation of false alerts can be very disruptive. It is also important that unsolicited changes to flight data are effectively notified to the controller.

10.4 <u>Historical Functional Decomposition</u>: The role of an established ATCC in the FIR will have evolved over decades. En-route and off-route traffic have different characteristics. Civil and military controllers have different organisational ethos. These factors lead to different functional emphases which in turn may lead historically to suboptimal functional structures.

10.5 <u>Historical Design Architecture</u>: The diverse technical requirements at an established ATCC will have been satisfied by different engineering groups over the decades. This as above may lead to a suboptimal ATCC architecture which reflects the engineering and procurement organisational structure.

10.6 <u>Lack of Control Over Data Capture</u>: There are a number of problems associated with the capture of flight plans as they arrive from sources on worldwide networks. Although they are based on the ICAO international format their quality varies considerably eg. route fields are inadequate to derive FIR and sector involvement. Flight plan amendments arise from similar sources and these can lead to duplicate plans which are similar but not identical.

10.7 <u>Flexible Data Display</u>: Display of flight data is not standardised. Predominantly civil ATC use printed flight progress strips. These are resilient to power failure and are easily amended with coloured pens. The strip is slotted into a strip holder which forms a very effective physical token which is moved manually around a flight strip progress board in relation to the aircraft's general position in the air space. Military ATC has much experience with the electronic display of flight information. These displays are smaller and can even be integrated with the radar display. They are updated interactively with the computer which enables an up to date flight database to be maintained. This in turn is interrogated by other controllers who need to know the intentions of aircraft not under their control.

10.8 <u>Integrated Remote and Central Processing</u>: Local tracking is performed at the radar head in order to correlate plots over successive scans. Local track numbers would assist in resolving ambiguity in plot to track association in central RDP. They would also enable quicker track initiation. Mode S is a new SSR interrogation technology which greatly reduces SSR radio space pollution. It interrogates individual aircraft. However, it must emit an all-call interrogation to capture new aircraft and individual Mode S ground stations must pass these identities on to other stations. This represents wide area distributed RDP processing which overlaps central multiple RDP.

10.9 <u>Long Processing Chains</u>: The physical radar return undergoes many transformations before it is displayed to the Radar Controller as representing the actual aircraft position. More rigorous specification techniques could be used to minimise the risk of error at each step.

10.10 <u>Complex Data Fusion</u>: In central RDP there are a variety of techniques in fusing radar data from several radar sites. These range in computational effort. The simplest is to allocate preferred radar coverage to discrete volumes of airspace and pass only those plots on to the tracking process. Full multi-radar tracking is optimal, but computationally expensive. A complex smoothing filter is needed to handle different error variances at irregular time intervals. For each aircraft a system track is updated by all correlating plots.

10.11 <u>High Integration Architecture</u>: Full integration of functions leads to greater impact on the ATCC when a subsystem fails. Transition management of system changes is more difficult. The management of redundant intra-centre networks is complex - particularly when the impact on operations is to be minimised.

10.12 <u>Systems Planning</u>: The strategic planning of the development of systems in an ATCC requires the capture of a functional and architectural design in a structured fashion that aids visibility of design change proposals. As there will be several development programmes in place, each at different stages in a timescale of several years, these planned designs need to be correlated. Owing to the size and complexity of such programmes modern computer aid is necessary to make this process effective.

10.13 <u>Software Engineering Standard</u>: Subsystems at an ATCC will have been built over the decades with a variety of Software Engineering methods. The advantages of standardisation are recognised, but it currently unclear upon which particular approach it would be reasonable to standardise, bearing in mind the scale of the above applications.

11.   CONCLUSION

11.1 A contemporary ATCC has been illustrated as a Large Software System. A number of issues relating to its development have also been discussed. These concerns take on greater significance when it is appreciated that ever more performance is being demanded without jeopardising the integrity of the ATC service provided. Furthermore these issues are of general public concern.

Fig 1. SIMPLIFIED AIR SPACE STRUCTURE

FLIGHT INFORMATION REGION

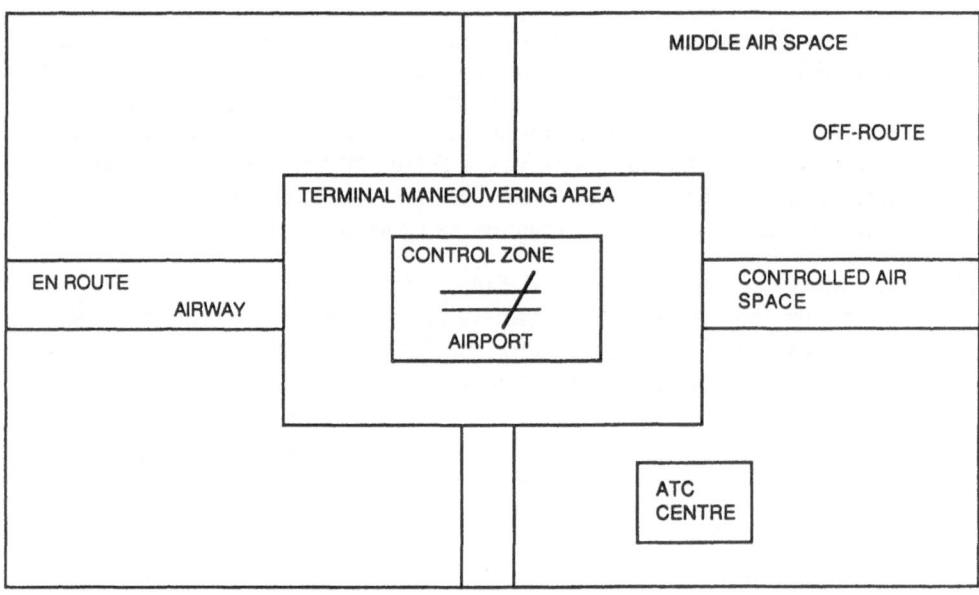

PLAN VIEW

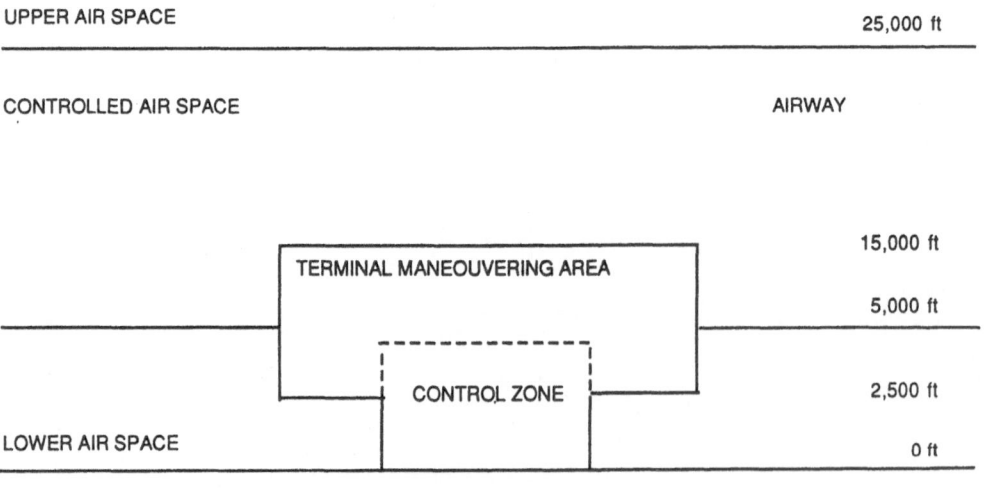

ELEVATION VIEW

Fig 2. VIEWPOINT STRUCTURE FOR AN ATCC

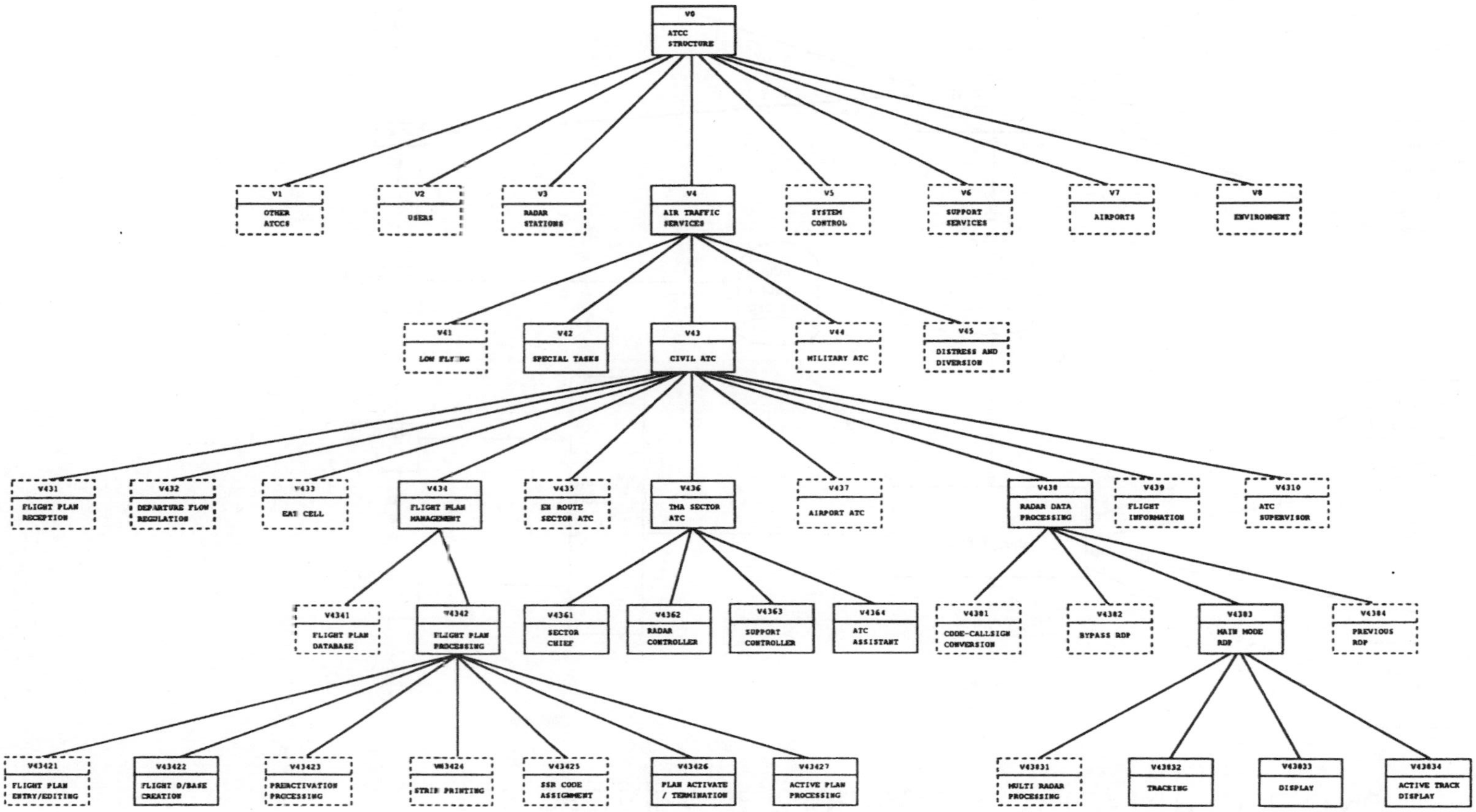

Fig 3. OVERVIEW OF FLIGHT AND RADAR DATA PROCESSING

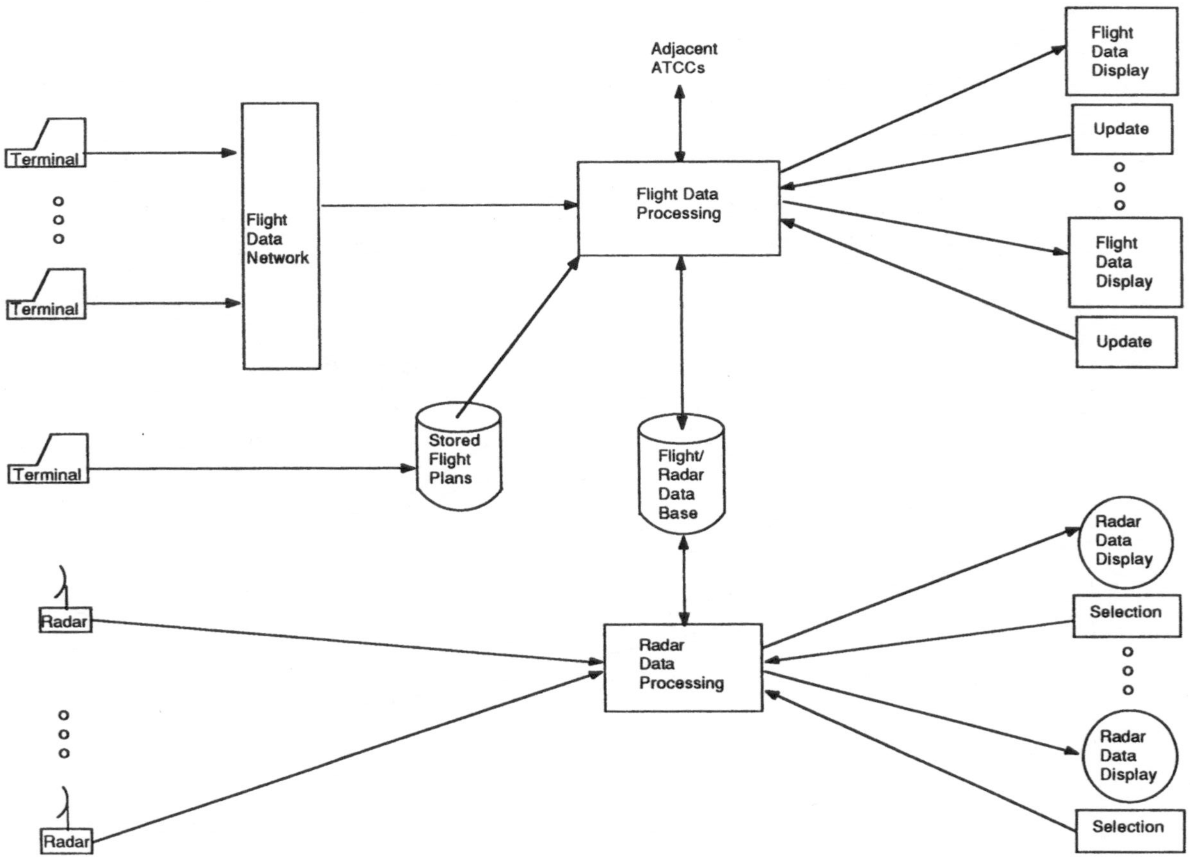

137

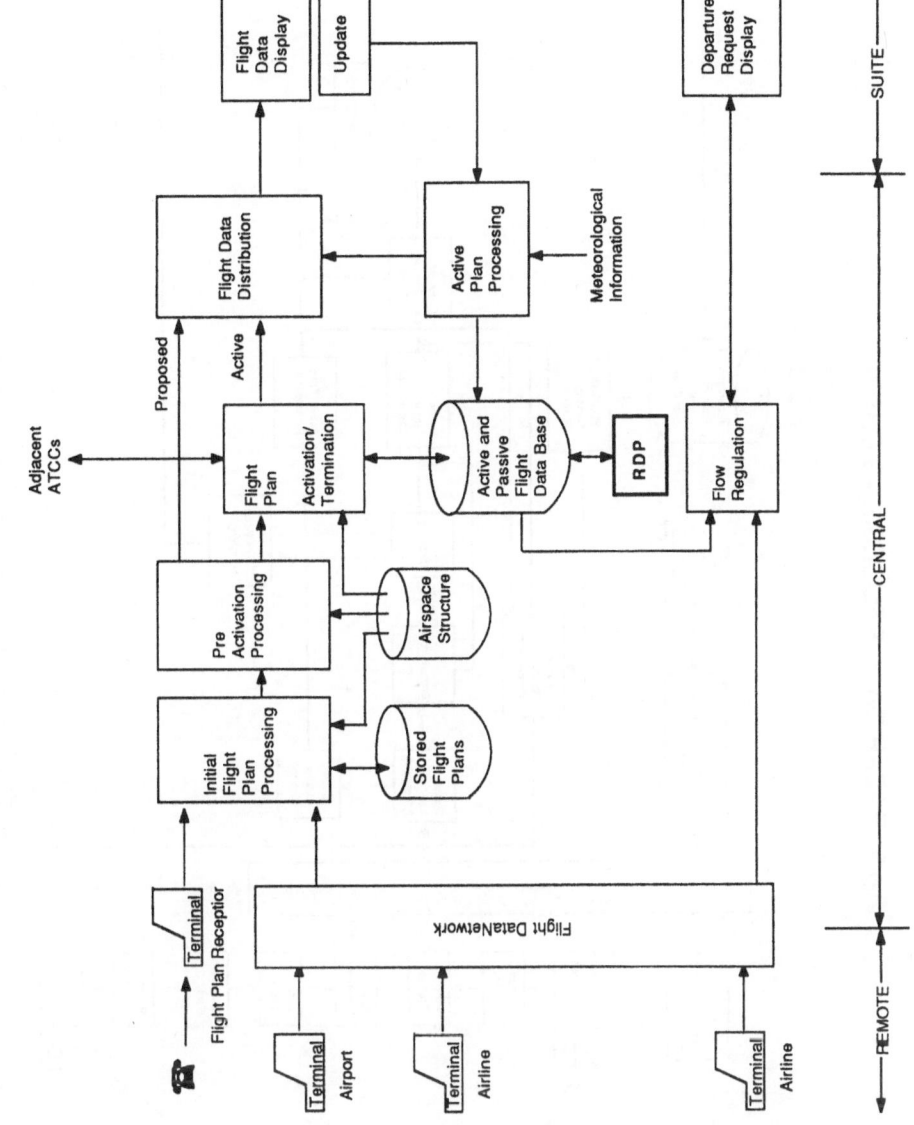

Fig 4. FLIGHT DATA PROCESSING CHAIN

Fig 5. RADAR DATA PROCESSING CHAIN

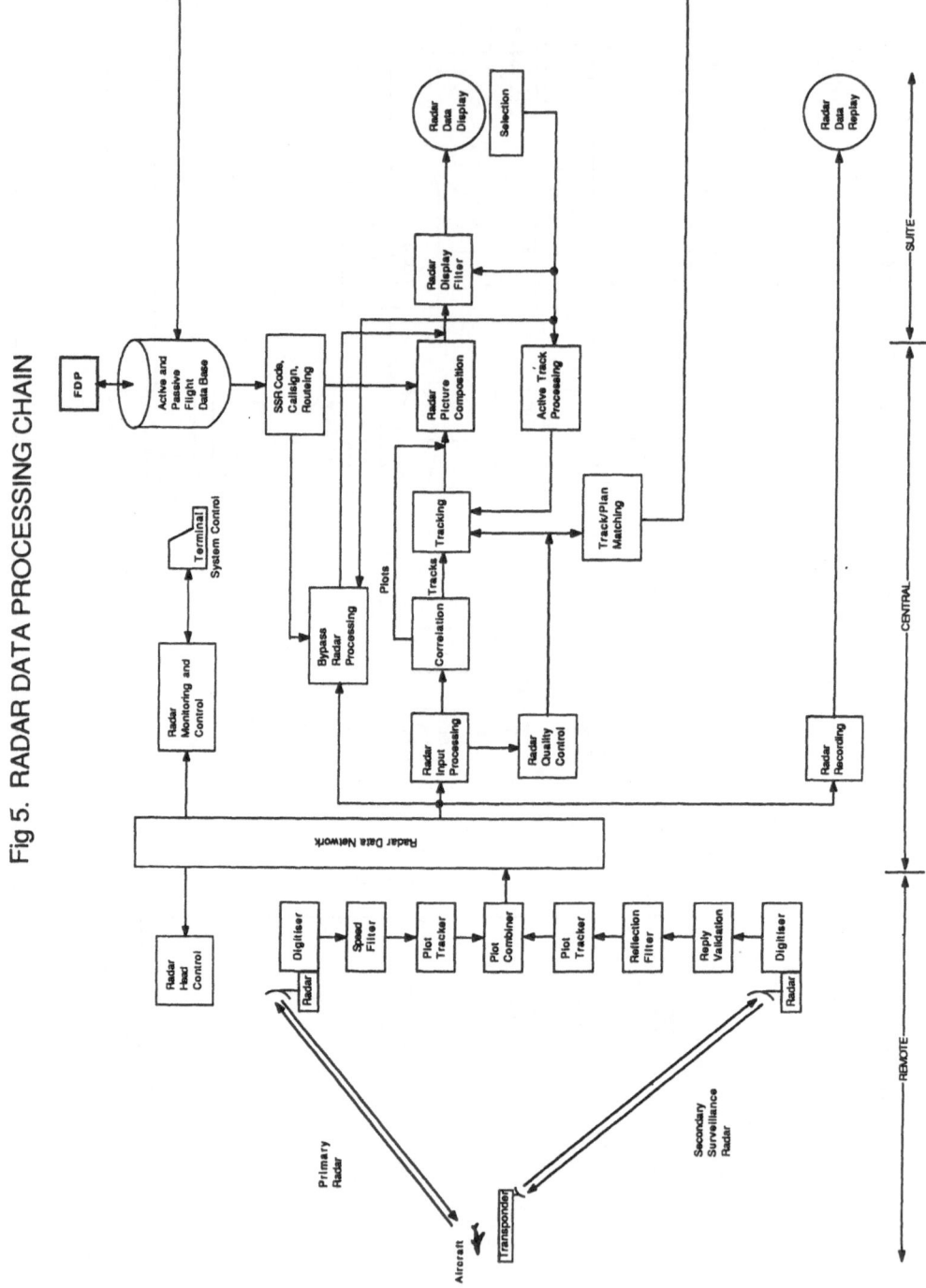

Fig 6. INTEGRATED FLIGHT AND RADAR DATA PROCESSING

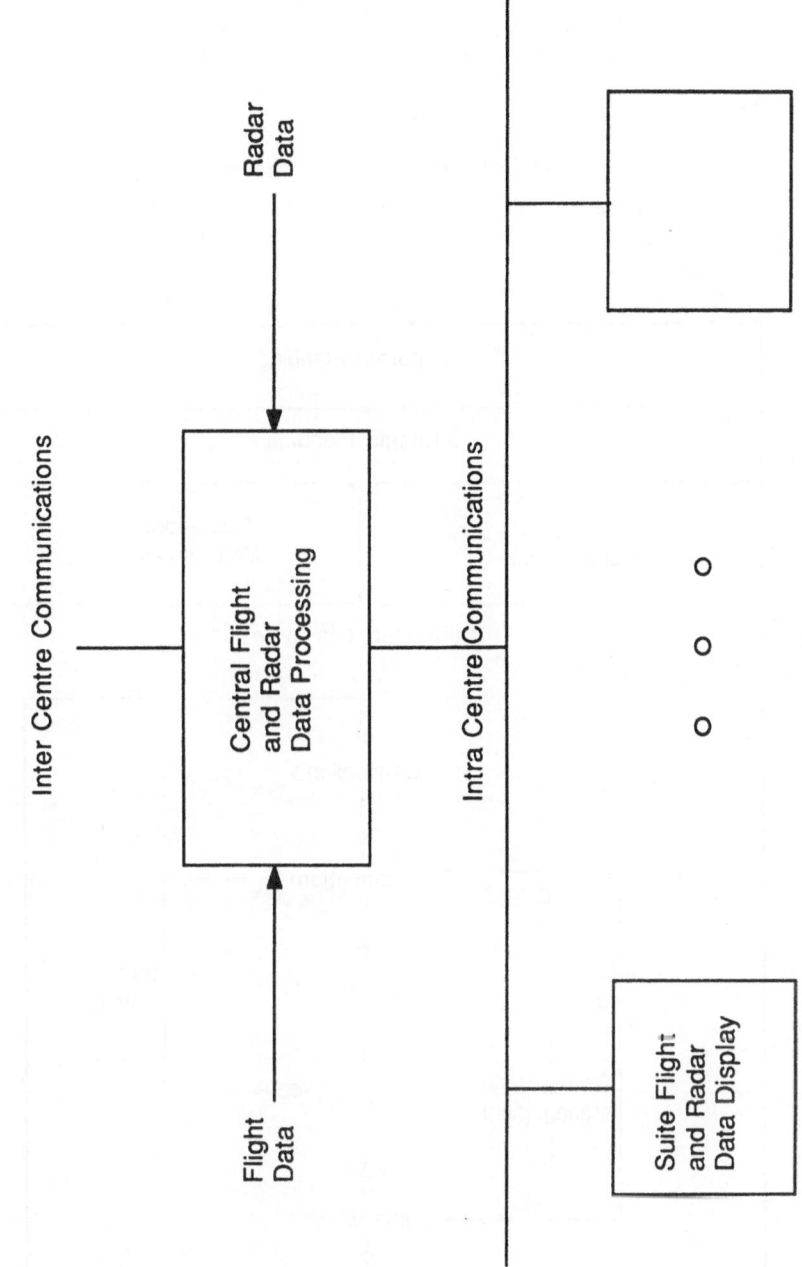

Fig 7. SIMPLIFIED SUBSYSTEM LIFE CYCLE

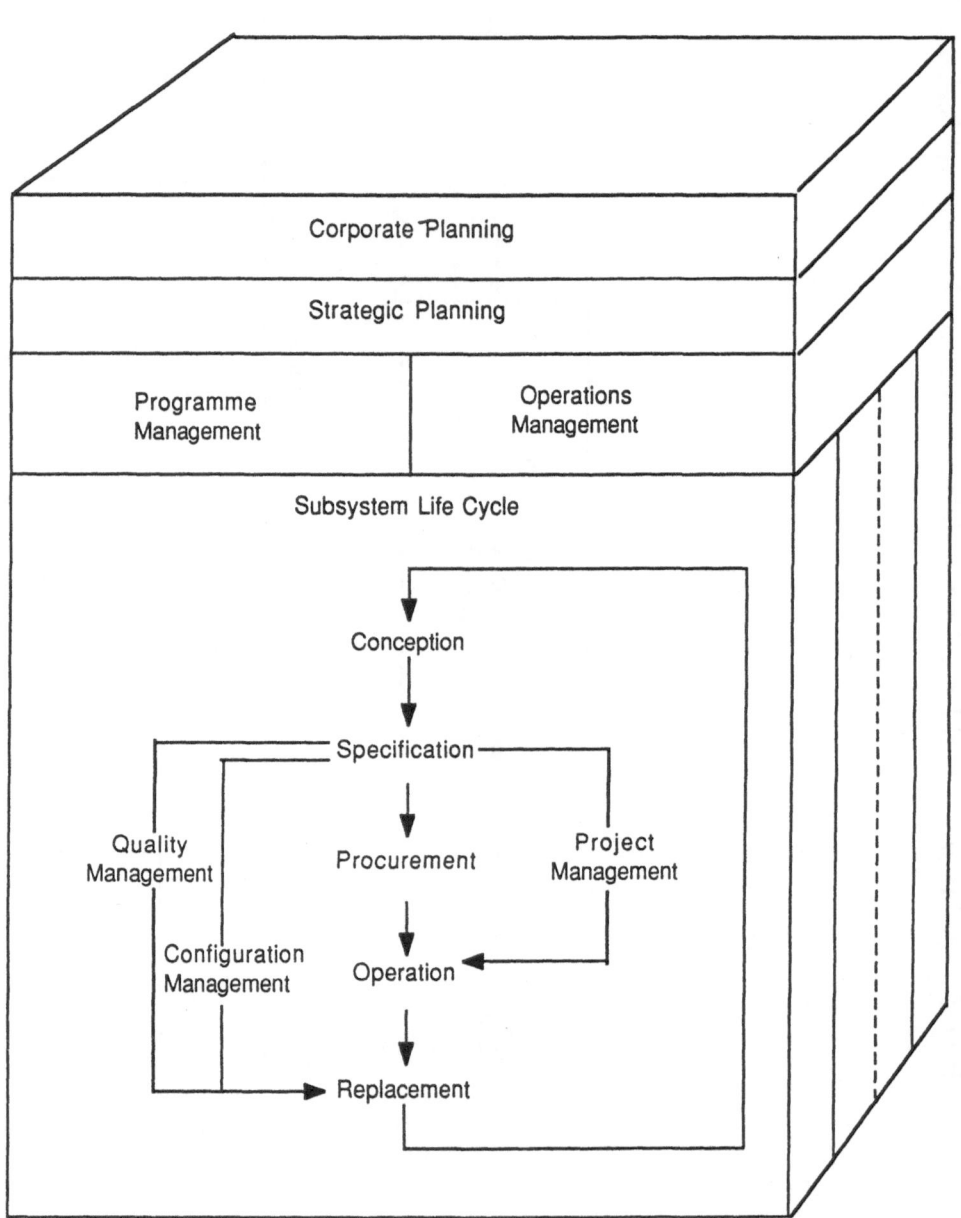

6

AN ARCHITECTURE FOR MULTI-VENDOR SYSTEMS

JOHN DOBSON

Computing Laboratory
University of Newcastle upon Tyne
NEWCASTLE NE1 7RU

ABSTRACT

The Integrated Systems Architecture (ISA) project is a major ESPRIT project which is intended to provide an architecture for interworking computer systems that embodies and exploits the best distributed computing system concepts, and that plans to provide a basis of future international standards in the area of open distributed processing.

1.   OVERVIEW OF THE ISA PROJECT

The ISA project has the prime objective of the establishment of open international standards for interfacing applications operating with distributed resources that come from more than one supplier.

Specification of standards without feedback from practical implementations can lead to flawed and impractical standards. It is necessary to ensure the widest possible validation of the concepts and specifics of standards before they emerge from the necessarily protracted standardisation process.

As the enabling electronics technology (semiconductors, fibre optics, etc.) continues to press ahead remorselessly, and the availability of this technology is continually expressed in new products and services (e.g. multi-media communications carrying data, sound and vision), standards must be produced that apply to these new technologies. This requires that the framework of the ISA project has to take into consideration today's futures which will be tomorrow's actuality.

The work done in the Alvey and the (first phase of the) ESPRIT research programmes showed that it is possible to produce a reference model for distributed processing systems that is comprehensive. That model must be produced and agreed by all the projects and manufacturers working in the various different domains of distribution, since it is the framework in which both current and future work must reside. The ISA project has undertaken to produce this framework and agree it with the other projects working in the field.

Once produced and agreed, the model will then be freely available to all active workers, be they academic, industrial collaborative research, industrial collaborative technology implementations, or purely commercial implementations. The early transfer from research and advanced development projects to actual implementations provides much of the feedback necessary to invest the standards process with practical demonstrations of applicability that are needed to underwrite the quality and validity of the standards.

The ISA project will undertake some practical work of its own both to investigate difficult concepts before they are promulgated and to assist other workers to more readily take up and pursue those concepts in their own implementations. The ISA project will make the results of this work available both in a written form (i.e. a manual), and in the availability of source code. The objective for this activity is to assist European industry to move rapidly, and with an informed understanding, to the provision of products and services for open distributed applications executing on multi-vendor systems. In order to facilitate both this objective and the generation of open standards openly arrived at, the ISA project will impose no constraints whatever of the kind associated with intellectual property rights.

2.   INTEGRATION and STANDARDS

The ISA project has two themes: *integration* and *standards* . It will enable the integration of application systems from multiple vendors both by creating a set of common architectural constructs for distributed computing systems and by utilising these constructs in the development of standards. The evidence for the achievement of integration will be the development of practical demonstrations of application interworking, based on standards derived from the project.

The project will concentrate on *enabling* rather than *providing* integration; that is, it will concentrate its efforts on defining models, interfaces and standards based on work already done by other distributed system projects so as to create a common infrastructure or platform through which separate applications can achieve true interworking. The ISA project will seek acceptance of its results by other projects in the distributed systems arena (in all application domains). It will encourage those projects to implement the functional interfaces defined by ISA which will be needed to generate practical application products.

The many applications that form an integrated system will not only require different functionality from the supporting infrastructure, but will also place differing emphases on quality attributes such as response time, throughput, security, and reliability. This in turn demands a unified approach which pays careful attention to many technical, human and managerial issues, and treats them all as facets of a single architecture. The ISA project will use such an approach to define an organised selection of solutions to a wide range of common integrated processing problems.

3.   DIVERSITY and FRAGMENTATION

3.1   Diversity

Human organisations are distributed in nature: people work in different places and information is acquired and stored at different locations. People increasingly rely on computers in their work, and efficient user support, providing fast response to user actions, can be provided by a distributed computer system which reflects the distribution of the human organisation it serves.

But human organisations are subject to changes and these too must be accommodated by the computer systems supporting those organisations. Also, technology will provide opportunities to develop computers with new functions and improved performance. Whilst enterprises may wish in time to replace old equipment with new, the related costs and effort involved are likely to become prohibitive since technology is changing so rapidly. Instead, owners will call for gradual and continual evolution of their systems, and consequently systems will be thought of as collections of distributed components rather than as a single resource.

Integrating multiple computers of the same type is relatively easy. Such computers can be combined so that to the application designer they appear to be one very large computer. Application designers can then exploit existing application design processes for non-distributed applications.

But this approach does not always lead to satisfactory solutions, because different applications lead to different operational requirements. For example, factory automation applications require real time response and a high degree of reliability; applications in the design department may require high security but place fewer constraints on timeliness. This diversity of application requirements demands a diversity of hardware and software support; and this heterogeneity in turn complicates the design of a distributed system and the integration of its parts.

3.2   Fragmentation

At the moment there is no public architecture for building distributed systems on a multi-vendor basis which can span multiple application domains. It is just about possible to install a multi-vendor system in a single application domain where standards are relatively mature (e.g. office applications, CIM) and where the manufacturers have a common forum for determining agreement (e.g. ECMA). However, the increasing importance of value-added network services and the extension of the computing arena from offices and factories into homes and schools means that there is a real need for a common architectural approach which incorporates the very significant differences in policies and patterns of communication arising from these extensions. There has not yet been much opportunity to integrate the technology used in the domains of computing, telecommunications, and value-added networks.

Another aspect of the problem of fragmentation is that European IT companies are at a disadvantage in the breadth of products they can supply to meet the new demands in the expanding areas, by virtue of their smaller size compared with the market leaders in Japan and the USA. Since European companies are not able to compete in breadth, they concentrate on their undoubted capacity for specialisation in depth. In many cases, however, this specialisation has been done in isolation. There is now a need to provide some common architectural framework that will enable system integrators to focus on a particular market area. The European IT industry therefore needs an enabling mechanism to provide scope for market-specific suppliers to survive by selling to a wide range of industries and system integrators, and a structure to aid integration of market-specific components from different suppliers in different countries servicing different application domains.

It is important to recognise that the scope of this problem is wider than that of mere communications interconnection, a sub-problem which can be solved (at least at the lower levels of the OSI Reference Model) by building subsystems conformant to the standard protocol definitions. Integration at the system level requires careful attention to issues such as information, processing, communications, distribution, management and administration, specification, human factors, and the application environment. Currently these are treated piecemeal whereas what is required is an architectural approach which treats them all as facets of a single problem.

4.   STANDARDS and INTEGRATION

4.1   Standards

Standards first emerged in the field of engineering. Bodies were formed to agree such things as dimensions for mechanical parts and engineering practices. In this form of standardisation, the issues are well-understood and the task is one of choosing between alternatives.

The IT industry in Open Systems Interconnection (OSI) standardisation started in a similar way. The OSI Reference Model was developed by analysis of extant proprietary and CCITT communications protocols, and many of the OSI layer standards were achieved by selecting from protocols that existed at the time with only minor modification. The OSI standards, including the Reference Model, are currently under the control of the ISO/IEC subcommittee JTC1/SC21.

OSI has assumed importance in the IT industry since it opens up an alternative communications platform to proprietary standards. Before OSI, vendors of communications-related applications typically announced them for specific proprietary standards. This had the effect of benefitting the providers of those standards to the detriment of other suppliers. With OSI. vendors have joined together to achieve an OSI platform at least as important to application providers as any proprietary standard.

There has been a consequent effort to extend OSI standards to achieve extended communications functions, such as transaction processing, electronic mail, office document transfer, and so forth. Many of these are relatively new areas with which there has been but little practical experience. Consequently ISO committees often find themselves inventing standards rather than choosing them. This is a dangerous strategy, since the vendors who align themselves with OSI now depend upon the technical expertise of committees with changing memberships that meet barely four times a year and are distracted from their technical goals by the intense politics of international standards making.

Within Europe a new approach to standards making has begun, illustrated by the X/Open consortium. Here the industry has come together and funded a technical group to develop and extend Unix within the forum of X/Open members. In this way momentum and excellence is maintained since there is a permanent group devoted to technical progress.

X/Open is developing an applications platform based on Unix. Unix is a mature system and its origin is as an operating system for a standalone machine. However, a new generation of operating systems has emerged which is oriented towards distributed processing (MACH, CHORUS, AMOEBA, V etc.). These operating systems are qualitatively different from UNIX and place greater emphasis on performance and distribution. It is these sorts of operating system that will be the foundation of future high performance distributed processing. It is imperative that work be done in a similar fashion to X/Open for this next generation of systems so that they can be developed into products with guaranteed interworking sooner rather than later. Fortunately for product evolution, most of these systems are able to emulate UNIX with no loss of function (and sometimes increased performance).

4.2   Integration

This section highlights some of the techniques available for integration that are considered important by the ISA project.

4.2.1 Programming languages

Distributed processing can be made more accessible to the programmer by adding distributed processing features to language libraries and compilation systems. This is possible if distributed processing functions are presented as extensions to, or refinements of, the data and control structures found in conventional programming languages. At the leading edge of this approach are the various object-oriented programming languages, several of which both support distributed processing and embody the benefits of a rich type structure.

4.2.2 Remote procedure call

Remote procedure call (RPC) has become dominant as a way of providing communications from local to remote processes. RPC enables a client program running on one computer to invoke server processes on another, potentially remote, computer in a way that conceals whether or not the client and server processes are co-located.

4.2.3 Parallelism

RPC and similar techniques have made possible the design of distributed programs. In distributed programs there is potential for parallelism and this has led to much research into the problems of consistency: the private data associated with each process must be protected from interference by other processes; access to shared resources must be carefully controlled if chaos is not to result. Much work has been done on advanced transaction-based systems drawing on record-locking techniques. Another approach, having the same goal of ensuring atomicity, is that of optimistic concurrency.

Distributed programs also provide the opportunity for replicating a program in different locations in order to improve dependability and performance, and have also been employed in fault-tolerant systems. Bulletin boards extend the concept of a replicated object and lead to a decentralised approach to programming where several computers co-operate to achieve a common goal.

4.2.4 Operating systems

Distributed processing requires the coupling together of the local operating systems in the networked information system so as to provide a global network level operating system. This is facilitated by the techniques mentioned above and also by a number of trends in the design of operating system resources: large virtual memories, lightweight processes, and fast interprocess communications.

Two styles of extending operating systems of networked computers into an integrated distributed environment have emerged: networked operating systems (e.g. ACCENT, AMOEBA, CHORUS, MACH and V) and distributed operating systems (e.g. EDEN and EMERALD). In networked operating systems the linked computers preserve much of their autonomy and are managed by interaction with their local operating system; however, all resources are uniformly accessible on whichever system they are located. In distributed operating systems, system management is global, and individual computers have little autonomy. This is possible only where there is tight coupling between the operating system kernels of the systems involved.

A number of experiments have been made to explore how UNIX could be extended to provide a distributed operating system (e.g. LOCUS, UNIX UNITED). Such systems offer greater performance and dependability than a single node UNIX system since several computers are used to support it. They provide mechanisms within the kernels of the interconnected UNIX systems which give the user the illusion of a single large UNIX system, insulating the applications programmer from any of the effects of distribution. This has the great merit that applications written for ordinary UNIX can run unchanged in the distributed UNIX environment.

4.2.5 Protocols

Many aspects of protocol design have been revisited using systems engineering techniques rather than traditional communications engineering. The application of end-to-end principles has led to a focus on reducing buffer management and processing overheads at network nodes. Consequent review of the layering of protocol implementations together with simplification of the protocols has allowed the implementation to be moved out of processors into microprocessor-based network interface units.

4.2.6 Multi-media integration

Most kinds of information-related activity involve mixtures of data, text, pictures, graphs, charts, the spoken word, and synchronised sound and vision. People work naturally with multiple media, and have always been able to do so until the limitations of information technology raised an artificial barrier.

Many networking technologies can now transport both isochronous forms of information (voice, video) and anisochronous information (image, graphics, text, data). Several systems have been built to support interactions involving all these forms of information in an integrated fashion (for example within a conferencing application).

5.   SYSTEM ARCHITECTURE

As indicated in the previous section, the subject of integrated system architecture is beginning to receive considerable attention. The increased scope of design and levels of complexity of integrated systems implementations are forcing the use of some set of logical constructs for defining and controlling the interfaces and integration of all the components of a computing system. Since our current technology permits the distribution of large amounts of computing resource in small packages to remote locations, some kind of architectural structure is imperative, because decentralisation without structure is **dis**-integration. In this and the following sections the ISA framework for rationalising the various architectural concepts and specifications is explained. This framework is seen as being necessary to enable clarity of professional communication, to enable improvement and integration of distributed development methodologies and applications, and to enable agreement on a set of standards which reflects the common culture of the European approach to integrated systems architecture.

5.1   The Role of an Architecture

The role of a systems architecture is to systematise practical experience into an engineering design discipline. A systems architecture is not simply a descriptive tool: it creates a style and an essential logic of design which allows common use of both components and design methods.

The creators of an architecture must analyse possible, proposed, and existing solutions to design problems. The analysis must identify both the common functions found in different solutions and any common configurations of function. Once found and described, the functions and configurations can be named and this can clarify the dialogues between designers and system owners and hence reduce the burden of design work. The architect's job is then to summarise, analyse and systematise knowledge and experience about the functions of the systems and their components.

5.2   The Contents of an Architecture

An architecture contains both a set of concepts and a method for modelling a system in terms of those concepts. These are required to support a description of the constraints that the architecture places upon a designer when decomposing design problems and composing systems from subsystems and components. The constraints are expressed as a set of components, rules, recipes and guidelines, together with a set of formal notations which are used to express or represent the design.

The *components* are "standard" system building blocks. A set of relationships may exist between these components, and a set of rules constrains how the components may be related and hence the design choices open to the designer. These *rules* form the conformance criteria: any model satisfying all the rules conforms to the architecture; and a system conforms to the architecture if it is a correct implementation of a conformant model. Non-conformance is more likely to lead to failure when the system is in service.

The *recipes* describe useful structures of components to meet particular needs. They represent particular ways to satisfy design requirements effectively. The use of recipes should reduce design effort and provide extensions to the architectural style, but is not mandatory. It is likely that components used in recipes will become the most widely available ones, since following the recipes will be a quick way to design a system.

The *guidelines* explain how components and recipes can be applied to tackle problems of design, and why the rules are reasonable constraints on designs. They explain the problems that can be encountered and how they can be avoided; and they give general techniques for constructing models of systems rather than the more explicit instructions that are contained in the recipes.

An architecture, then, is *not an abstract design for some universal distributed system* but rather a designer's toolbox of useful components and standard constructions. A single system design could not scale to span all possible distributed processing requirements; instead, the ISA project will provide the designer with an organised selection of solutions to a wide range of distributed processsing problems. The designer must make an appropriate selection and estimate the necessary trade-offs between interworking capability (by restricting the choices available) and optimisation of quality attributes (which requires flexibility of choice).

5.3   The Process of Architecture

As mentioned in the previous subsection, the results of an architecture can be expressed in the form of components, rules, recipes, guidelines and constraints. These results have to be developed as the outcome of some architectural process. Some existing architectural projects have analysed the evolution of their work, and have arrived at a view of the architectural design process as consisting of five distinct phases. These phases do not always follow in strict sequence, and thought often goes back and forth between the phases. Nevertheless, it is usually found possible to ascribe any instant in an individual's activity or thought to one or other of these phases; and in general they do follow each other roughly in the sequence outlined.

The first phase consists of development of concepts and theories. During this phase, ideas are examined, refined and rejected; key ideas emerge and are seen in relation to each other; a vocabulary is defined, using natural language or some (semi-formal) restricted variant. The purpose of this stage is mainly to define what the architecture is *for* ; that is, its relation to human intentions and concerns as reflected in the basic concepts that are expressed by the vocabulary.

During the second phase, the concepts and their relations are cast into a more formal language, possibly with some simplifying abstractions and assumptions. In some projects, the expression of this stage takes the form of a 'reference manual' or 'reference model'. The purpose of the manual or model is to define what the architecture is *about* ; that is, what can be said in the language of the architecture.

During the third phase of the architectural process, the formal expression defined during the previous phase is used to generate the specifications of the basic architectural components and the rules which explain and constrain how they are to be constructed and combined.

During the fourth phase, a prototype or demonstrator is designed together with the essential instrumentation which will allow the architect to measure performance, determine the site of problems or inefficiencies, and quantify its dependability. This is a phase in which tools are of prime importance: tools to build, to measure and to analyse.

During the fifth phase of an architectural project, the prototype is built, exercised, measured and demonstrated. The purpose of this phase is validation of the adequacy and suitability of the architectural concepts for their intended purpose, rather than the demonstration of a marketable product.

6.   PROJECTIONS FOR SYSTEM MODELLING

As mentioned previously, existing architecture projects have begun to co-operate and to analyse their results. This analysis has also revealed five styles, or *projections*, for describing systems. These are called the enterprise, information, computational, engineering, and material projections. Each projection has its own viewpoint on the nature of distributed processing, its own set of concepts and language, and its own set of decisions to be made during system design. Every computer system can be described in each of these projections, each description having a different purpose.

6.1   Enterprise Projection

A model in the enterprise projection explains and justifies the role of the computer system within the whole organisation. Enterprise models describe people's and systems' actions, goals and policies, and embody a set of statements about the organisation's missions and values. Design decisions made in the enterprise projection address *what* the system is to do rather than *how* it is to do it, and requirements are expressed purely in functional terms.

6.2   Information Projection

A model in the information projection identifies and locates information and describes information processing activities. The value of information to modern business makes this model useful to managers as well as designers. Information models enable analysts to describe enterprises, including any distributed systems operating within them, in terms of information resources and information processors. Such models describe the structure, interpretation, value, timeliness, and consistency of the information (possibly from multiple sources) that can be collected, processed, and presented in different places at different times. Design in the information projection concerns the nature and role of information in the system, and the design decisions are epistemological in nature: who knows what, and where can information flow?

6.3   Computational Projection

Computational models help programmers by structuring programs for modularity and parallelism, for integrating separate applications into packages, and for making programs independent of the computers and networks on which they run. These models provide a description of the system which explains how integrated application programs may be written for it. The description is in terms of information representations, programming languages, system services, and program specifications.

6.4   Engineering Projection

An engineering model describes distributed systems in such a way that designers can reason about the performance of the systems built to their designs: e.g. whether efficient use of system resources is achieved. Engineering models define families of system building blocks and explain how to interconnect and organise them. Engineering level decisions concern trade-offs between quality attributes such as performance, dependability, and scaling.

6.5   Material Projection

Models in the material projection act as blueprints of systems during their construction and maintenance. They are intended for the use of system builders, and are expressed in terms of physically realisable components and standard interfaces.

6.6   Common Foundations

Each projection represents a particular viewpoint of distributed processing and each has difficulty addressing the concepts used by the others. Historically, each viewpoint has been developed separately from the others with little interaction between them. It is important to realise that a system must ultimately be modelled from all viewpoints simultaneously; each viewpoint is equally valid and it is meaningless to argue which is the most fundamental. However, the projections will not be of equal significance in any specific context.

The main reason for the historical separation in that there is no common foundation for expressing the interactions and relationships between the projections. This lack of a common foundation is an architectural issue that is being taken very seriously in the ISA project. The models resulting from the five projections contain similar logical constructs. These have been explored and a common logic developed, capable of describing all of them. Although the five projections are related in complex ways, by developing this common foundational logic, the task of managing the projections becomes tractable.

7.   TECHNICAL ASSUMPTIONS FOR ISA

Although the ISA project is most definitely not a project to build a distributed operating system for its own sake, the architectural approach to the design of an integrated system clearly requires a distributed operating system as a prerequisite. Common to nearly all recent distributed operating systems are two assumptions that will be adopted for the design of ISA. The first assumption is that communications bandwidth is increasing and that network throughput is becoming less of an important constraint than network latency. The second assumption is that processes can be inexpensive. This requires operating system support for lightweight processes and requires that each such process be able to communicate with remote processes easily and efficiently. However, both of these assumptions lead to problems of scaling in large distributed systems. This tradeoff is also being investigated by the project, since it is intended that the ISA architecture be equally applicable to very large networks.

Several engineering principles are common to the technical developments reviewed earlier, and these will be adopted for ISA: encapsulation, indirect binding, strong typing, distribution transparency, dependability, performance optimisation, and language integration.

Encapsulation requires that program module boundaries should be enforced by 'firewalls', either through hardware protection domains, through strict compile time checking, or through some combination of both.

Indirect binding is the provision of communications via intermediate objects. Indirect binding permits further objects to be transparently inserted into the binding to cope with remoteness and heterogeneity.

Strong typing insists that access to objects should be via interfaces which are specified independently of the implementation of the objects and that a binding between a set of objects is possible only if they have consistent interfaces.

Distribution transparency is the provision of mechanisms that cope with the complexities of distributed processing and that provide the programmer with a high-level set of application-oriented primitives so as to enable the programmer to exploit distribution to good effect.

Dependability is that property of systems that justifies users in placing reliance on the services they deliver. Dependability includes reliability, availability, security and safety. Reliability can be achieved by the use of design diversity and various other mechanisms; availability by the use of replication techniques, and security by the use of encapsulation and encryption techniques. Safety can be enhanced by these measures, but is ultimately a system design and specification problem.

Performance optimisation is achieved by using parallelism, the deployment of caches, process switching, end-to-end handshakes and the avoidance of data copying, so as to overcome network and operating system delays to remote operations.

Scaling is the art of designing systems which neither occur high overheads nor break down as the number of computers involved increases or as their interconnectivity changes (for example because of increased physical separation).

Language integration requires that distributed processing be accessible to programmers in terms of the control and data structures of ordinary programming languages. A distributed system should be an extension of the programming language development and run-time environments.

To provide a standard applications interface and yet allow for a variety of requirements, ISA will define a set of architectural building blocks which may be used to build interfaces between application programs and other parts of the distributed system in order to provide the basic infrastructure functions. These components will hide the complexity of aspects of the distributed nature of the system.

The figure below provides a simplified illustration of the relationship between the components in a typical ISA system. The *base and operating systems* represent the computers and networks used to provide the processing, memory and communications capability. The *ISA nucleus* components provide the minimal level of support to applications. The services in each nucleus co-operate to provide an *applications platform* spanning the base systems. The ISA components that provide *transparency* make use of the support for distributed processing provided through the platform and provide a transparent interface to the applications. Together, the ISA components help support *applications* on geographically dispersed, heterogeneous computing components and allow for *interworking* between applications.

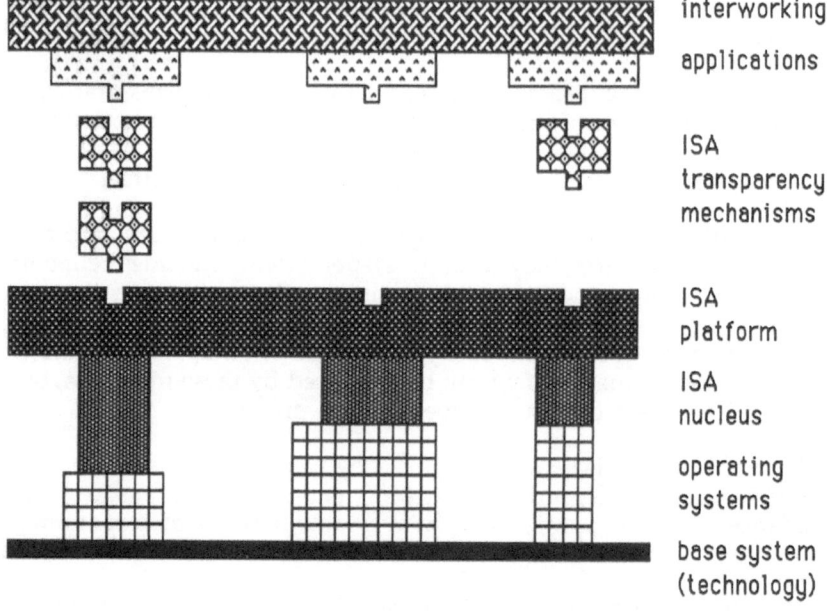

interworking

applications

ISA
transparency
mechanisms

ISA
platform

ISA
nucleus

operating
systems

base system
(technology)

Provision of a common architectural framework, though necessary for communication between design teams, is not sufficient to enable communication between applications. It is a starting point of the ISA project that although an architecture should provide a reference model, it is more than a set of architectural statements about the reference model; it must also show the reference model in application and use. The ISA project will therefore make public and explicit all aspects of its architecture, including in particular the application platform interface, so as to encourage the common culture of practical applications integration.

8.   SUMMARY OF THE ISA PROJECT

In summary, therefore, the architectural goals of the ISA project are threefold:

1) A *standardisation goal* is to achieve international standardisation of the application interface (i.e. the upper level of the ISA platform and transparency mechanisms).

2) A *collaboration goal* is to work jointly with application oriented projects to ensure that the architecture adequately provides the platform they assume and to assist them in the design and construction of their own platforms.

3) A *development goal* is to demonstrate implementations of the ISA platform within the context of a set of applications capable of being turned into products at an early date.

ACKNOWLEDGEMENTS

The ISA project is closely knit and collaborative. The words used in this paper are the several and joint efforts of the whole project team rather than those of the nominal author. Nevertheless, although he cannot claim any credit in reusing the words of others, the author as spokesman must take the blame for their deficiencies.

7

INCREMENTAL DEVELOPMENT AND DELIVERY FOR LARGE SOFTWARE SYSTEMS

DOROTHY R. GRAHAM
Software Engineering Consultant
Grove Consultants,
Grove House, 40 Ryles Park Road,
Macclesfield, England SK11 8AH, UK

ABSTRACT

Life cycle models have arisen in order to bring control to the process of software development. Two aspects of life cycles have provided benefits: the ordering of development phases, and the modularisation of the development process to give discipline and control. The third aspect, production of systems monolithically, is not beneficial for large systems.

Incremental development is the development of a system in a series of partial products, generally with increasing functionality, throughout the project timescale; incremental delivery gives those increments to the users when they are completed. An increment is complete when all the associated life cycle products are finished, including testing, training, and documentation. There are significant benefits both for developers and users, but there are also significant problems. In particular, more discipline is needed to manage incrementally, particularly good configuration management.

An earlier paper [1] gave an extensive bibliography of incremental development and delivery. This paper summarises the types of incremental development with particular reference to large system development, and gives additional recent references.

INTRODUCTION

Life Cycle models such as the Waterfall or V-models have been developed in order to bring control to the process of software production. There are three key aspects embodied in such models:

- do things in a certain order (design before code, requirements before design, etc.)

- modularise the process, so that "chunks" of work can be reviewed at checkpoints, i.e. increase discipline, apply standards, ensure documentation is done

- deliver the entire system as the single end product of the entire development process

It is my contention in this paper that the first two aspects of monolithic life cycle models have provided the benefits which have been achieved, but the third aspect does not scale up for large system development and may actually be detrimental.

SOFTWARE DEVELOPMENT PROBLEMS

Although significant improvements in the development of software systems have been achieved in recent years, there are still significant problems remaining. Monolithic software development is generally fixed at the earliest possible time, both in terms of cost and schedule. In order to meet tight contractual restrictions, the Requirements Specification is produced either before or soon after the start of development, and is then "frozen"; i.e. changes to the requirements are strongly discouraged.

Estimation

It is difficult to estimate the cost, effort, time or size of large systems with a high degree of accuracy. This is not unique to software development projects, it also affects other engineering disciplines. Being able to foresee the future with unerring accuracy is not a task which is easily done, by people or by machines. The real world does not stand still while large systems are developed; new products and processes are discovered, underlying assumptions are invalidated, new laws are passed, and developers learn new things, which would have enabled them to build a better system, if only they had known those things at the beginning. It is a common experience at the end of development to know how it should have been done.

Changing Requirements

Knowing how it should have been done is also a common reaction of users when they first see the new system they have asked for. A widespread response when using the new system for the first time is: "That is not what I want". It is much easier to "know it when you see it" than to say what it is that you want before you see it.

This effect occurs even when users have been extensively involved in specifying the system (but then they should add, "even though it is what I asked for"). User knowledge also grows throughout system development; the users cannot ask for what they will really need because they cannot see into the future with unerring accuracy either.

The point is made by Floyd, Reisen and Schmidt that "requirements are not 'given' and therefore cannot, strictly speaking, be analyzed." Rather, they are gradually established through interaction between users and developers. [2]

These two aspects of developing knowledge are illustrated in Figure 1 below. Both user knowledge and developer knowledge increase with time. System A, which is specified at the beginning of development reflects the minimum of that growing body of knowledge for both parties. System B is the system which the developer would have built with hindsight, and System C is the system which the customer would have asked for with hindsight. System D is the system which is actually required at the end of development.

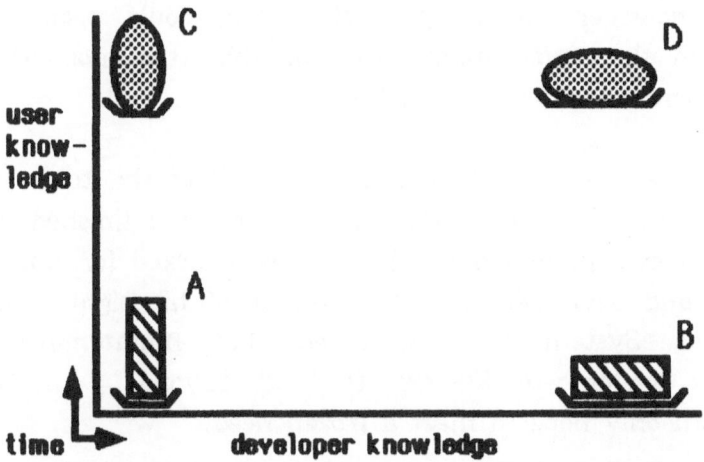

Figure 1. Increasing knowledge throughout development.

Testing and Maintenance

Significant problems are experienced in the testing and maintenance of large systems. Testing typically takes 40% of the software development effort for any sized system, with testing of real-time systems often taking up to 80% of the development time. Testing of large software systems is difficult, but with the monolithic life cycle, the major dynamic execution testing of the software is done at the end of development. Verification and validation procedures help to produce better quality intermediate life cycle products, but they are no substitute for testing the real end product.

If development takes longer than expected and schedules slip, then it is likely that testing will also take longer than expected. However, the end date has a tendency to remain fixed in time, so the testing schedule is compressed rather than extended. Problems which are built into the software are only discovered late in development, when there is no time to put them right. If testing is difficult, why do we leave it till last?

With some types of development, testing is constrained by the development of hardware, for example, so that testing cannot be done early. However, other types of system could begin testing much earlier in the development timescale than the monolithic life cycle implies, with considerable benefits.

Maintenance can typically account for 80% of the total system costs. A major aspect of the early maintenance of a finished system is to create the system which should have been asked for and built, if only users and developers had the benefit of hindsight. In the diagram above, System A is delivered, but maintenance then progresses the system to System D (and beyond). A frozen specification can only hope to meet a frozen need.

Customer Confidence (lack of)

Figure 2 below illustrates the confidence levels which occur with both monolithic and incremental development models.

Confidence is initially high with both approaches, probably higher for the monolithic approach at the start because it is the accepted way to do things.

During lengthy development, however, customer confidence drops off, as no working product is yet visible, developers talk in techno-speak, and delays are announced. If delivery of the system comes before all confidence is lost, there is hope of recovery, but if confidence goes below a certain point, then no matter how good the system is technically, it will not be accepted by users.

This user resistance may be dormant during monolithic analysis and implementation, emerging when the system becomes operational, and taking the form of sabotage, scapegoating, or incorrect use of the system. [3]

An incremental approach produces a working product much earlier than a monolithic approach. The initial reaction to seeing this is usually "This is not what I want", leading to an initial loss of confidence, although the delivery of an increment on time is generally a refreshing change for customers.

By developing incrementally towards the needed system (rather than the specified system), confidence is restored to a high level which is then maintained and increased.

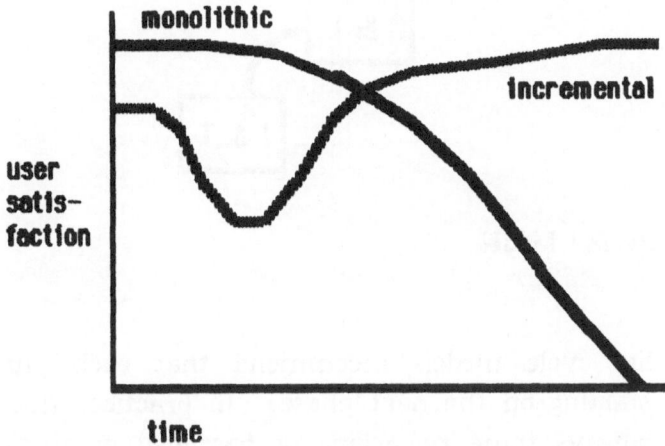

Figure 2. Customer Confidence throughout development.

THE THREE-DIMENSIONAL WATERFALL MODEL

The Waterfall model is taken as illustrative and representative of monolithic life cycle models. It is usually shown in a form similar to Figure 3 below. The Requirements Specification (RS) should be done first, followed by System Design (SD), Detailed Design (DD), Code and Test (C&T), and Integration and Test (I&T).

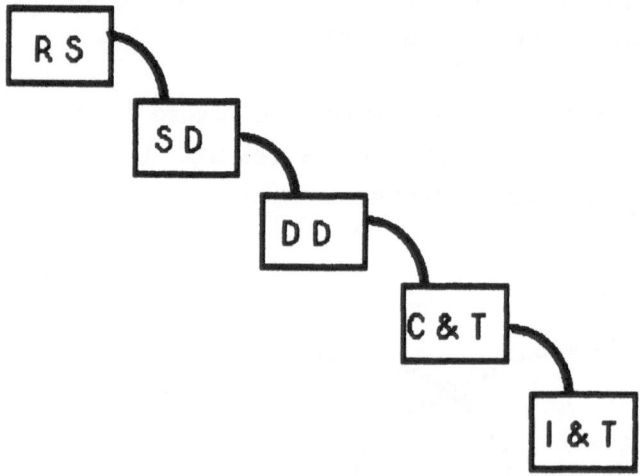

Figure 3. The Waterfall Model

Monolithic life cycle models recommend that each phase be completed before starting on the next phase. In practice, this never occurs; there is always some reworking of baselined products from previous phases.

In monolithic development, the working system in its entirety is delivered at the end of the whole development process.

The waterfall model does not show what is actually being recommended, however. It is really a two-dimensional representation of a three-dimensional object. A three-dimensional model, Figure 4, shows more accurately the time sequence of development. Each horizontal "slab" should be completed before starting on the next one.

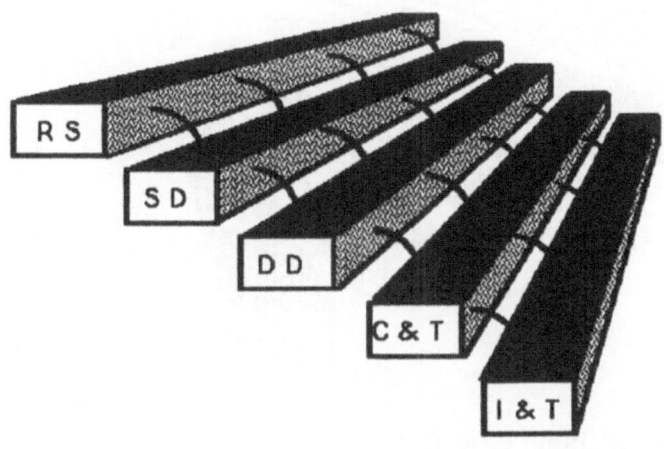

Figure 4. The Three-dimensional Waterfall Model.

INCREMENTAL DEFINITIONS

An incremental approach postpones detail in some or all phases to produce working software earlier in the project development timescale. The basic idea is to develop the system in a vertical **slice** rather than a horizontal **slab**.

Incremental Development

Incremental Development is the development of a system in a series of partial products (increments) throughout the project timescale.

INCREMENTAL LIFE CYCLE MODELS

Incremental Build and Test

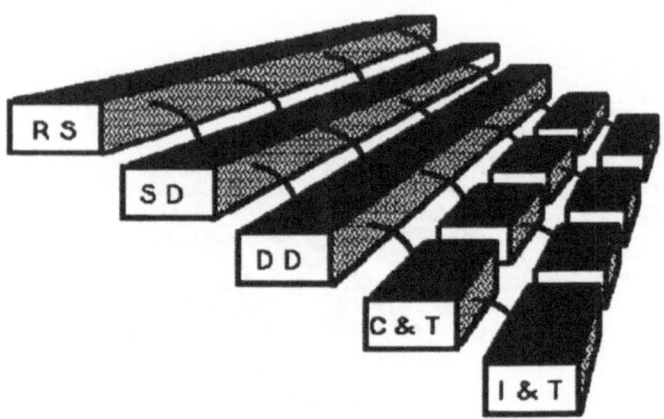

Figure 5. Incremental Build and Test.

The incremental build and test approach begins the incremental development in the coding phase, with the previous phases being monolithic. Examples are given in Deutsch [4] and Wong [5] among others.

Many developers go some way toward this approach informally, although often without the complete set of life cycle documentation. Since this is not what is recommended by the monolithic waterfall model, the developers may feel guilty that they are not following the model correctly; better results will be obtained from following the incremental build and test approach intentionally rather than accidentally.

Incremental Delivery

Incremental Delivery is the delivery of increments to the customer/users at intervals throughout the project timescale.

Note: A system can be developed incrementally without being delivered incrementally to users, but not vice versa.

Increment

An Increment is a self-contained functional unit of software, together with all supporting material, including:

- requirements specification,
- design documentation,
- test plans, cases and results,
- user manuals and training,
- estimates, plans, schedules, resourcing,
- quality assurance information (e.g. review reports)
- configuration management information.

An increment produces (or alters) a cross-section of the final system deliverables, related to a functional portion of the final system.

Incremental development is the construction of a software system in a series of small mini-life-cycles, rather than construction in one large monolithic life cycle.

In the following sections, a number of incremental life cycle models are shown.

Evolutionary Delivery

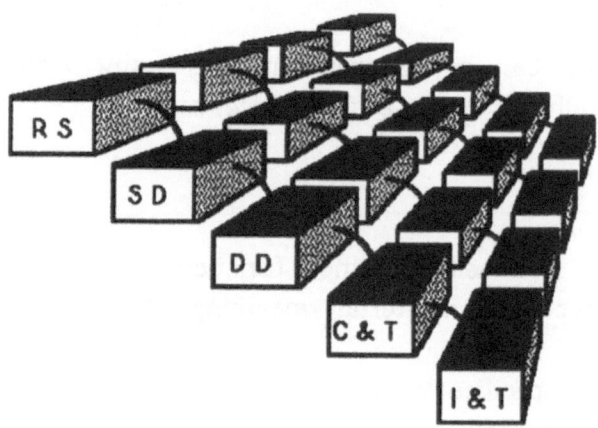

Figure 6. Evolutionary Delivery

Evolutionary delivery as described by Gilb [6] is shown in Figure 6, and is the most extreme incremental approach, defining the increments from the top of the life cycle. Gilb's method includes incremental delivery as well as incremental development, and therefore has useful working facilities available to the customers much earlier than other life cycle models.

The diagram shown actually does not do justice to the evolutionary delivery method, however, since there is a higher level process which precedes the incremental steps, consisting of setting system and business objectives, open architecture design, planning and quality assurance.

The evolutionary deliveries are made at frequent intervals (possibly as small as a week), and consist of some function, facility, or organisational change which is useful to the customer and relatively easy to produce. In fact that ratio is used to determine the order of the increments.

A major effect of evolutionary delivery is to elicit requests for change, mainly from users ("that isn't what we want"). However, these change requests may be "folded back" into the development process at significantly less cost than for monolithic models, for two reasons. First, change is expected and planned for, so it does not come as an unwelcome surprise. Secondly, when requirements have been completely detailed and designed (in the monolithic approach), changes which are requested will affect the work already invested in the frozen specification. With incremental development, requested changes which affect those areas which have not yet been completely detailed, do not result in discarding work already done. Change can be turned to advantage, provided it is controlled.

Framework Incremental Life Cycle

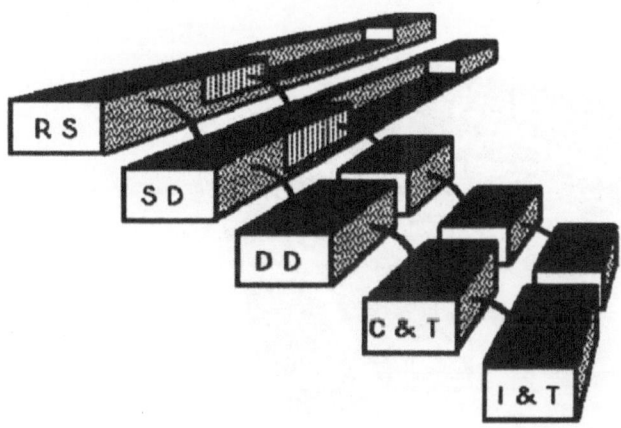

Figure 7. Framework Incremental Life Cycle

Just as one extreme being wrong does not imply that the other extreme is right, a framework incremental approach may be the "best of both worlds", by providing a compromise between the monolithic waterfall and Gilb's evolutionary delivery. Enough of the initial requirements specification and architectural design is done so that the direction and structure of the system produced is clear enough to direct the software development process. This approach can still give useful products very early in the development timescale. An example of this type of approach is the specification of the structure and interfaces for a database, with detailed facilities to be specified later.

A similar method recently described by Hill [7] as a hybrid between "conservative" and "radical" top-down approaches has been found to work successfully. See also Redmill [8] and Krzanik [9].

Phased Development

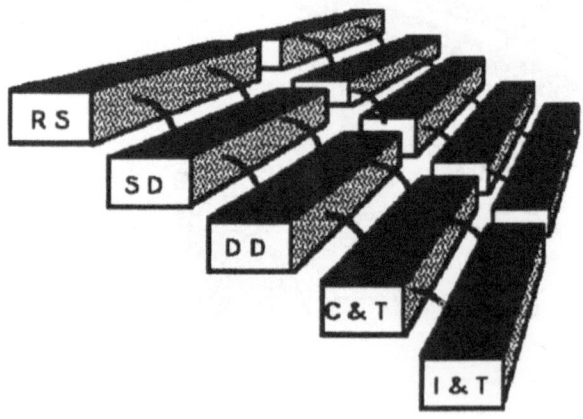

Figure 8. Phased Development

Phased development has frequently been used in the development of large systems, and is a step in the right direction. The difference between a very small phase and a large increment is not distinct. However, phases tend to be large and growing; there is a tendency to put as much as possible into the current phase. There is also a temptation to compensate for timescale slippage by bringing forward the later phases to overlap the earlier ones. This approach can result in severe incompatibility between successive phase products. The emphasis with incremental development is to include as little as possible, i.e. as little as would be useful into each increment.

Prototyping

Prototyping is usually regarded as the building of a small system (or two) before building the big one. The knowledge gained in either building or using the prototype is then used in building the "real" system. A good description of the prototyping approach, combined with risk analysis, is given by Boehm [10].

"Rapid prototyping" is used to describe the building of systems using software tools such as code generators, report generators, or Fourth Generation Languages (4GL's). A recent book called "Structured Rapid Prototyping" by Connell and Shafer [11] gives guidance in the development of systems incrementally.

Prototypes are used to reduce risk in the applications area (a novel design, function or performance), or to reduce risk in the user interface area. (The users should then recognise the final system as what they had approved as a prototype.)

However, in a long development timescale, with several years between deliveries of prototypes, the requirements may change extensively, so that it is difficult to relate new requirements to the old prototypes. New hardware capacity, newer user interface styles and graphical capabilities seen on personal computers can make a prototyped user interface seem very old-fashioned.

It is not always possible to predict in advance of development whether a prototype will be thrown away, incorporated or built upon. Prototypes are classified in terms of their use into experimental, exploratory, or evolutionary prototypes. (Floyd [12]) Prototypes can also be classified in terms of their relationship to the life cycle as Throw–Away, Incorporated, or Incremental,. (Ince and Hekmatpour [13]).

Throw–Away Prototype

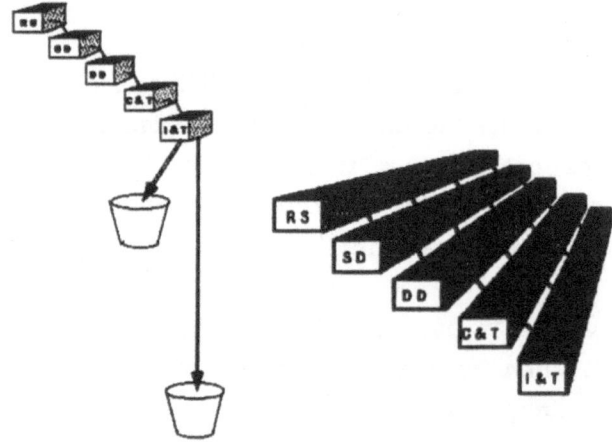

Figure 9. Throw–Away Prototype

If the prototype is written with the intention of throwing it away, then it is unlikely (and unnecessary) for it to be developed to the same standards as a "real" development. This type of prototyping is sometimes called "quick and dirty". The prototype can be discarded as soon as development of the large system begins (the first bin in the diagram), or it can be kept and possibly used by the customer until the large system is actually delivered and finished (the second bin). There is a tendency for users to become fond of a well-used prototype and be reluctant to throw it away.

A throw-away prototype can be used as an animated requirements specification; if the prototype looks and interacts in a way which is liked and approved by the customer, then the final system can be tested to ensure that it looks and behaves in the same way.

Incorporated Prototype

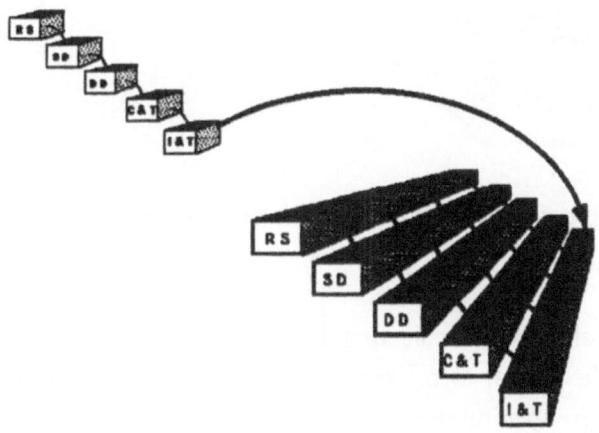

Figure 10. Incorporated Prototype

Part or all of the prototype can be incorporated into the final system software product, either code, design, or requirements. If a prototype has any possibility of becoming incorporated, the software engineering discipline and standards applied to its development should be consistent with the desired quality of the final product.

Incremental Prototype

An incremental prototype is the development of the system in a series of prototypes which are integrated together to become the final system. This therefore looks the same as the Evolutionary approach shown in Figure 6, but possibly without incremental delivery or the higher level of overall objectives, open architecture and planning of Gilb's approach.

Tool-intensive Incremental Development

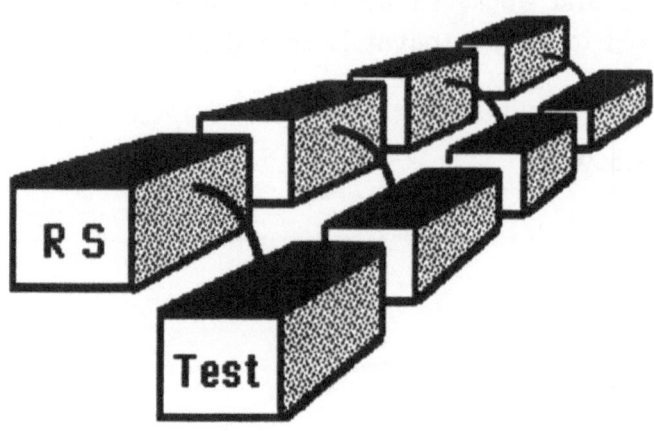

Figure 11. Tool-Intensive Incremental Development

Software development tools are becoming capable of automating "higher up" the life cycle, i.e. code can now be generated directly from detailed design specifications. At the same time, requirements are being specified in increasingly more formal notations.

These two trends give the possibility of eventually automating the entire life cycle. Semi-formal specification methods such as SSADM, Jackson, Yourdon and others may eventually be automated. Mathematically based formal methods such as VDM, Z, and OBJ are rigourous enough to automate now. There is already a commercial tool (ObjEx) [14] which automates specifications written in OBJ.

Although current approaches suffer from severe performance limitations, future hardware and software development will continue to ameliorate performance problems. Ultimately we are left with only two phases: specifying requirements and testing. If this happens, it would not be sensible to specify all requirements before getting something working, and software development will naturally follow an incremental cycle.

INCREMENTAL DEVELOPMENT RESEARCH

There is a large body of research in the area of incremental development as described in Graham [1] for a comprehensive overview, Gilb [6] for historical development and general inspiration, Ince and Hekmatpour [13] on prototyping, Agresti [15] for discussion of new paradigms, and Law and Longworth [16] for strategic considerations.

Guidance for implementing incremental development and delivery can be found in Deutsch [4] for incremental build and test, Gilb [6] for evolutionary delivery, Connell & Shafer [11] for tool-intensive (4GL) development. An interactive incremental development methodology called "STEPS" (Software Technology for Evolutionary Participative System Development) is given in Floyd, Reisen and Schmidt [2]. Michael Jackson has recently launched an incremental development methodology called "ISE" (Incremental Software Engineering) [17].

Reported experience in the use of incremental development is scarce. The design of a prototype for a large system is described in Harker [18]. Other references have been given in Graham [1].

It is interesting to note three instances of successful use in other papers included in this publication: Warboys [19] on the success of CADES, Chatters [20] on the fault-free factory approach, and Malcolm [21] on the first on-time delivery in ten years, albeit in a project which was probably already doomed (due to the loss of user confidence). Willmott [22] also felt that incremental re-development of an air traffic control system would be safer than one-time replacement.

The successful IBM "Cleanroom" approach [23], described at an earlier CSR conference, is also an incremental approach.

INCREMENTAL STRATEGY

Suitability

Large systems are particularly suitable for incremental development. Monolithic development is suitable only for small systems of short duration, where the requirements are well known at the beginning of development and unlikely to change, according to Krzanik [9], and for commercial packages such as a database package, operating system, or word processor, according to Connell and Shafer [11]. Gilb maintains that any system can be developed using evolutionary delivery. [6]

Deciding which form of incremental development to use should be based on the risk factors for the particular system to be developed. If the system requirements are very uncertain and highly likely to change, then prototyping may be suitable. If the system architecture is critical, e.g. a database, then the framework model may be suitable. If development funding is uncertain, then evolutionary delivery may be most suitable. Incremental development is quite feasible for fixed-price contracts, but may well be easier without incremental delivery.

Partitioning the System into Increments

Deciding how the system can be divided up into self-contained functional increments, particularly for incremental delivery to users, can be difficult when incremental techniques are initially tried. (Deciding how best to partition a system for development is never easy anyway.) There are a number of good design methodologies for producing a loosely coupled architecture of non-overlapping functions (which is good design practice in any case); incremental development does not require any particular or specific design technique. The involvement of outside consultants with knowledge and experience of incremental development can be very helpful in the initial stages.

The initial difficulties experienced in designing increments are often due to thinking about the system in ways which are quite different to the monolithic approach. Monolithic thinking is directed toward completing all requirements first, but incremental thinking takes a small requirement subset toward implementation first.

The objectives which drive the partitioning process are to keep the increments as small as possible, provided they will provide a useful function to the users. The temptation to continually increase the functionality within each increment should be resisted. It is also essential to retain control over the content of each increment, and prevent developers from incorporating other "good changes at the same time", which then becomes undisciplined and uncontrolled.

Prioritising and Scheduling

The scheduling and sequencing of development is based on three aspects: first, any parts of the system which must be in place before functional increments can be implemented should be completed first, but only the minimum needed.

Second, the broad strategy for the next series of increments should be defined. Alternatives include the development of the most critical increments first to minimise risk, the development of interface increments first to test control, or the development of functional threads first to achieve a working partial product. The latter is needed as early as possible in order to use incremental delivery effectively.

Within the broad strategy, there will be a choice of increments among equal priority. The third scheduling aspect is based on a ratio of two things: the user benefits and the development cost. The user benefits for the selection of proposed increments should be analysed and prioritised by the user organisation, if that is feasible. The development costings should be estimated by the developer organisation.

This ratio of benefit over cost determines the scheduling priority. This is technically called "the juiciest bit" (Gilb, [6]) Thus an increment with a high perceived benefit with high cost may be developed before one for a low cost and low perceived benefit, but those with both high benefit and low cost will be earliest.

The increments to be prioritised will not stay fixed for long, but need to be re-analysed in the context of recently delivered increments; error correction increments may take precedence over other planned increments, for example.

PROBLEMS OF INCREMENTAL DEVELOPMENT AND DELIVERY

In this section, various problems related to incremental development and delivery are outlined. Possible solutions are suggested where appropriate. Further discussion, particularly of management problems, can be found in Redmill [8].

There are many aspects of software development which are not affected by incremental development or delivery, such as the need for good management, quality assurance, configuration management, and the training of staff in software engineering principles. Additional training is needed, however, when departing from development techniques which are widely accepted, even when extensive benefits can be gained.

Hardware Related Problems

Risk of inadequate choice: The choice of hardware for a system to be developed incrementally will be based on intentionally incomplete specifications, with the risk that an inadequate choice will be made. In fact monolithically developed systems often make the wrong choice of hardware as well, but the risk is increased in incremental development. A hardware upgrade may be a possible solution.

Response times: If a small number of increments have been delivered on the target hardware, response times should be extremely good at first, but will gradually deteriorate with increasing functionality, to the disappointment and frustration of users. To overcome this, it is possible to "simulate the final user environment", i.e. put in slowing-down code to be removed during system tuning. If response times are severely affected by a single increment, this can be an aid to identifying system bottlenecks, which can be difficult to localise with a slow system which has been developed monolithically.

Development hardware: If the target hardware is delivered with the early increments, additional hardware may be needed to continue the development of the system. This problem is normally postponed until the maintenance phase of monolithic development, but needs to be faced earlier in incremental delivery.

Embedded systems hardware: The parallel development of hardware for embedded systems may constrain the definition of the increments.

Life Cycle Problems

Incremental development is not an alternative to applying life cycle discipline; the phases of the life cycle still need to be followed in the right order and with all of the associated controls. Each increment is a small life cycle in its own right.

Requirements specification: Requirements still need to be specified for the limited area which comprises an increment, and need to be frozen while the increment is developed (icecubes instead of icebergs). This enables planning, estimation and scheduling to be done in the small. The Requirements Specification is needed to define the boundaries of the system and of the increment.

Design: Design is needed in order to preserve a coherent structure to the software system throughout the changes which will occur during incremental development. The overall design should be defined in the first increment, but each increment should also be designed, and the design must work towards preserving the integrity of the overall architecture. This requires effort, as Lehman and Belady point out in their second law of program evolution [24]. The difficulty of providing a good overall design without a full definition of requirements should not be underestimated.

Testing: Testing is needed to ensure that each increment fulfils its requirement, and has not adversely affected the rest of the system. With incremental delivery, more extensive regression testing will probably be needed, since any change to the system results in a changed system. All tests should be run again to ensure that there are no adverse side-effects of the change.

There are additional considerations for a system which is tested extensively using a purpose-built simulator or test harness. If the production software is developed incrementally, the test software needs to be ready for use early in the development timescale, and so may also need to be developed incrementally. This will have an effect on the scheduling of effort between the software product and the test software. Note that the test software needs to be tested as well, before it can be relied upon to test the production software.

Redmill has found that there is a tendency for users to perform thorough acceptance testing only for the first increment with the testing of subsequent increments being skimped. [8]

Other life cycle products: Documentation, user manuals, training, and quality control procedures should not be skimped in the excitement of having something working. They are still needed in order to retain control over the development process. A good configuration management system is essential for keeping track of increments in various stages of completion. Although working code may be produced quickly, the extra documentation required for additional releases may be seen as a greater overhead than with monolithic development.

Management Problems

Living with uncertainty: It is unsettling to live with uncertainty; this is one reason why developers prefer to specify complete requirements before beginning to design a system. However, incremental development requires a certain level of uncertainty to be tolerated within the context of controlled development. There are levels of uncertainty with monolithic development as well, but we tend to hide them from ourselves by attempting to resolve specification uncertainties on paper.

Team coordination: The coordination of teams of people working on different parts of the system, and being in different life cycle phases at once, presents a challenge to management. Corrections found in the use of a delivered increment have to be incorporated into the system as part of an increment further "down-stream". Configuration management is essential.

System releases: Releasing a system to a large user base incrementally is even more of a challenge, and may prove very difficult even with a good configuration management system.

Scheduling and prioritising: The scheduling and prioritising of increments is a process which is constantly being altered by the results of earlier incremental deliveries; management must be prepared to spend effort in supporting this continuing process.

Balance between original specification and desired changes:
Development may tend to proceed in two directions at once; pulled
toward the original specification by the developers (who can easily
become "locked in" to local goals), and pushed toward new changes by
the users.   Management needs to keep the balance between these
two.   The requests for change should not be allowed to "hijack" the
original system objectives, but some change must be allowed or the
benefit of incremental delivery will be lost.   Changes need to be
controlled at a strategic level, in order to take the widest view of the
system objectives into account.

Organisational cultural change: Changing the way a large
organisation develops software is not easy and cannot be done
overnight.   Effort is needed in introducing incremental development
ideas, to assess and then convince of the benefits.   Effort is also
needed to ensure that the concepts are being implemented correctly;
for example, the temptation to merge increments together in order to
meet a timescale should be resisted.   Without continuing pressure,
attitudes and habits will revert to the earlier ideas, even if the new
words are used.

The development organisation may find strong resistance even
from those departments which stand to gain from incremental
development or delivery, for example contracts,   quality assurance,
and higher management.

Financial/Contractual Problems

Contracts: Contracts for the development of software systems
are generally based on a statement of requirements, under the
assumption that development will proceed monolithically.   There is no
reason why incremental development or even delivery cannot proceed
from a "completed", i.e. frozen, Requirements Specification.
However, many of the benefits of the incremental approach will be
lost if user and developer knowledge were prohibited from being
incorporated into the development process.

To allow the format of the contract to determine the development strategy appears to be putting the cart before the horse; surely the contract should be the servant of development, not its master. However, a new contractual approach may also involve significant organisational culture changes.

Competitive tendering: Competitive tenders using an incremental approach as opposed to a fully specified requirement may not enable the purchaser to evaluate like with like. The unspoken basis for pre-specifying the full requirement is the assumption that the requirements can be fully known in advance, which is rarely completely true.

A working prototype may be more convincing to a potential customer than a 250-page document, however.

Estimation: Estimation of system development effort is even more difficult when you don't know what you are going to build. Estimation methods and tools are the wrong way around for incremental development; they tell how long for a known (guessed) size, whereas an incremental estimate wants to know what functionality (size) can be achieved with known effort.

Management accountability: Accountability to higher management may be distorted by incremental development. Effort will be spent on the original specification, corrections and change requests. If management are tracking only effort on the original specifications, they may not have a true picture of the system being produced. On the other hand, incremental development may be the means of forcing out into the open what is really happening, which can be hidden in monolithic development.

De-stabilised development environment: If a developer is funded for only a small number of increments rather than for a full development, this may lead to a de-stabilised development environment, i.e. insufficient commitment to the project from the developer because of the uncertain future of the project. This may produce an inadequate product, a new search for a more suitable developer, with delays and additional expense. However, it is preferable for the purchaser to discover the limitations of the supplier after only a few increments than after a lengthy monolithic development.

If a contract is awarded before a full specification is produced, the buyer may become "locked in" to an unsuitable supplier. It may well be cost-effective to fund more than one developer to produce an early increment, particularly for a large system.

User-Developer Relationship Problems

User expectations: Users need to be involved in the process of setting goals and requirements for each increment, and need a thorough understanding of what is to be achieved by each one; their expectations can become somewhat inflated if they are not kept in touch with realistic proposals. User perceptions of what is easy and difficult to achieve are notoriously inaccurate.

ADVANTAGES OF INCREMENTAL DEVELOPMENT

The advantages of incremental development are given separately to those of incremental delivery. Incremental development without delivery gives advantages to the developers, and incremental delivery gives advantages to the users.

Improved Team Morale

Success breeds success; if the team can see the end product actually working, it is a great boost to morale and can lead to greater productivity.

Early Solution of Implementation Problems

Problems which are discovered during implementation can be put right before the rest of the system is built according to the same (faulty) assumptions. Testing the software early in development leads to improved quality of the finished product.

Reduced Risk of Disaster

If you are going to have a disaster, it is much cheaper to have an incremental one; you will have lost only thousands or tens of thousands rather than millions.

Improved Maintenance

The maintenance of incrementally developed systems is easier than monolithically developed systems because a maintenance environment is started early on in development. Good maintenance is continuous controlled change, and so is incremental development. Increments which are not designed to be easy to change will not survive the incremental development process.

Control of Over–engineering or Gold–plating

If best–value increments are developed first, that leaves the worst–value increments until last, where their true cost can be seen. Additions to specifications are often agreed for political reasons at the beginning of a project; if the benefits to end users drive the production schedule, the political enhancements may well be quietly forgotten.

Measurement of Productivity

In monolithic development, productivity is measured in terms of lines of code produced per day, or pages of documentation. If parts of the system are working, "product"–ivity can be measured in terms of the actual product.

Estimation Feedback

Estimates are produced in the large, for the whole system, but also in the small for the increments. If the first increment's actual effort is out by a factor of two, for example, it is possible that the global estimates are also out by the same factor. In monolithic development for a project taking say 6 years, you may not find out how inaccurate your estimates are until 4 years have elapsed; with incremental development you will find out much earlier, say after 2 months.

The feedback from incremental estimation can either modify or confirm both the global estimates and the estimates for subsequent increments. Either way management has better information sooner than with monolithic development.

Smoother Staffing Requirements

With monolithic development, the project will need teams of analysts, followed by teams of designers, coders, and testers in sequence. With incremental development the need for specialised teams is distributed throughout the development process.

ADVANTAGES OF INCREMENTAL DELIVERY

The benefits of incremental development for developers are significant, but the greatest benefits come from both incremental development and delivery to users.

Useful Product Early

Seeing something working which will actually benefit their needs is the greatest reward for users. Users may well be worried about their decision to invest in a software system and may remember hearing tales of disaster in related areas. Having something which can bring business or operational benefits early in the development process gives them the beginning of a return on their investment without having to wait years for anything tangible.

Increased Confidence in Developer

The users' confidence in their developer is greatly enhanced by having something working early; actually this applies whether the increment is delivered or not. An improved working relationship results from better morale.

Better Quality Software

The software which is produced benefits from the developers' increasing knowledge being "folded" back into the developing product.

Longer Useful Life

The system will have a longer useful life, because it will be easy to maintain, having been subject to a great deal of controlled change throughout development. Products which can evolve easily to satisfy changing business needs last longer and are more cost–effective than those which are so difficult to change that they are abandoned and replaced.

More Flexible Options

If a project does suffer from cost or time overruns, some later increments can be eliminated, and the most useful parts of the system will still be produced within the original financial constraints.

Something Useful if Cancelled

If a monolithic project is cancelled, the only things produced are piles of paper (requirements, design documents, etc.). If an incremental project is cancelled, the increments already produced form a working product of some sort.

Increased User Acceptance

If users actually have some say in the way the system is developed, their sense of "ownership" is improved, which leads to better acceptance of the system by the user organisation.

Increased System Assimilation

The assimilation of a major new system into working practices can be traumatic for the user organisation. People are resistant to change, but they resist large changes more than small ones. Most problems of system use stem from people problems rather than technical ones. Incremental delivery allows small areas of the organisational procedures to be altered at any one time; when the problems are overcome, those areas are then established, so the system has a foothold in the organisation. This also increases the sense of system "ownership".

Increased Understanding of Requirements

Incremental delivery gives the users something real. Their first reaction is "this is not what I want", but now they have a much better idea of what they do want, and can progress toward their true requirements.

System can Meet Real Need, not Frozen Need

The increasing user knowledge gained during development can be "folded" back into the development process, so that the eventual system is much closer to what is really needed at the end, rather than what was thought to be wanted at the beginning.

SUMMARY OF EFFECTS

A summary of the effects of incremental development and delivery is shown in Figure 12 below.

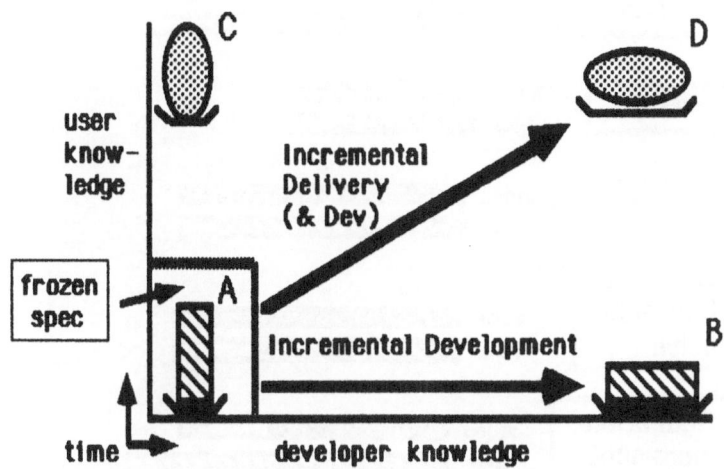

Figure 12. Effect of incremental development and delivery.

Incremental development moves the final product from the initial specification, System A, towards System B, what the developer would have produced with hindsight.

Incremental delivery cannot occur without incremental development, so it is not possible to move from System A to C.

Incremental development and delivery moves the final product from System A towards System D, the system which is wanted at the end of development.

Monolithic development confines the system to System A, the frozen specification. Neither user nor developer knowledge can be incorporated into the software system product.

COMPARATIVE COSTS

The comparative costs of monolithic and incremental development for a hypothetical project are shown in Figure 13 below.

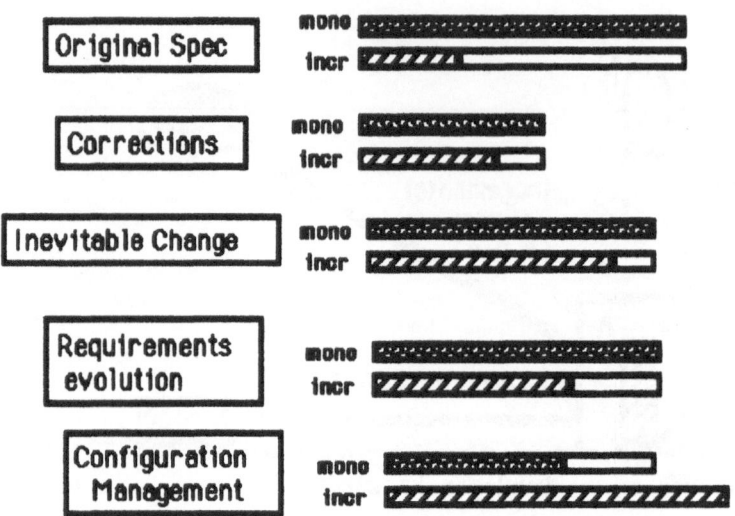

Figure 13. Comparative Costs of Monolithic and Incremental Development

Original Specification

With monolithic development, the cost of developing the original specification must be met in full in order for the project to produce anything useful. With incremental development, it is possible that the original specification would still be produced, but is more likely that only part of the original specification will be produced.

Corrections

The cost of corrections is no more, and should be less, for incremental development than for monolithic, since errors of analysis, design or implementation will be discovered earlier in development and will not have propagated through the rest of the system requirements, designs and code.

Inevitable Change

It will not be any more costly to respond to inevitable change, such as a changed hardware environment or new work practices. It should in fact be less costly for incremental development, since a system which has been developed incrementally is accustomed to frequent change.

Requirements Evolution

It will not be any more costly to implement evolving requirements, and in fact should be less in incremental development, since many changed requirements can be incorporated into the final system without having to discard work already done on superseded requirements.

Configuration Management

Configuration management costs are likely to be higher with incremental development than with monolithic development, particularly if the existing configuration mangement method and/or tools are fairly primitive. Configuration management is more essential for incremental development and delivery, although it is a good idea for any software development.

COMPARATIVE SCHEDULING

The comparison of scheduling differences between monolithic and incremental development is shown in Figure 14 below.

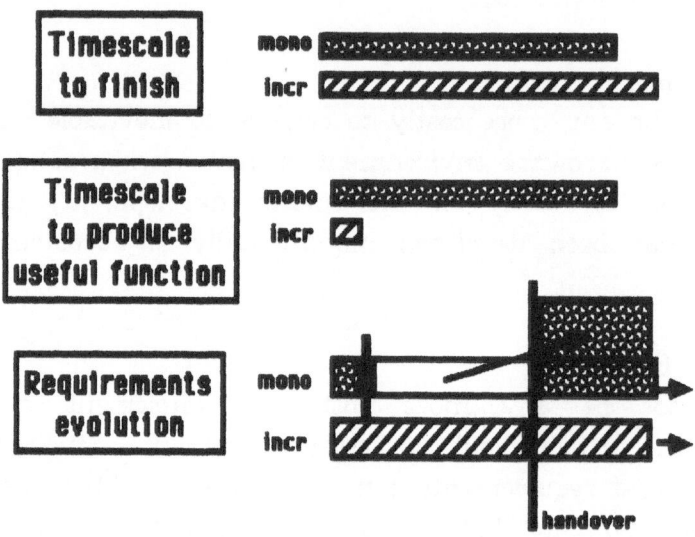

Figure 14. Comparative Scheduling for Monolithic and Incremental Development

Timescale to Finish

The elapsed time to finish the total development may be longer for incremental development than for monolithic development, but it is not as critical.

Timescale to Produce Useful Function

The timescale until something useful is produced is much shorter with incremental development and delivery; this is the main reason for using incremental models. This is also why it is not as critical if the elapsed time to finish the total system is greater than with monolithic development.

Requirements Evolution

Real requirements do evolve, whether the developers take note of the changes or not. In monolithic development, only a limited number of requirement changes are permitted; the remaining changes are therefore stacked up waiting until after handover to be implemented. In incremental development, the evolving requirements can be incorporated into the evolving product.

After handover, the incrementally developed system merely continues to adjust to changing requirements in much the same way as it did during development, but probably at a reduced rate (fewer new facilities being included).

The monolithic system has two problems after handover. First, it must become a maintenance-type environment capable of handling changes in a controlled way, which may involve some "teething" troubles. Second, it must deal with the backlog of changed requirements which have been stacked up and prohibited during development, in addition to coping with the on-going requests for changes.

SUMMARY AND CONCLUSIONS

This paper has given definitions of incremental development and delivery, and emphasized that an increment should be a complete self-contained functional unit of software, including all life cycle documentation, test documentation, and other support such as user manuals and training.

Essentially the incremental idea for large system development is to develop a series of small systems, which will eventually become the large system. The main strategy is to postpone some detail in order to get something working as soon as possible. A vertical "slice" of the life cycle model is taken, rather than a horizontal "slab" at once.

Incremental development can reduce many of the risks of large system development, but it is not without problems. The problems of incremental development centre around the management and control of software and associated products in a different time ordering to monolithic development.

In order to "think incremental", there are three guidelines:
- Think Small (ask not how much can be done, but how little can be done to provide a working partial product)

- Think Useful (the benefit to the end users is the primary driving force behind incremental development and delivery)

- Think Complete (an increment is a mini–life–cycle in its own right).

As software developers begin "taking their own medicine" by adopting software tools, I have predicted [1] that incrementally developed tools will be more successful than monolithically developed tools; this is already supported in the experiences of implementing IPSE's as reported by LeQuesne [25].

Barry Boehm once said that developing software from requirements is like walking on water; it's easier if it's frozen. However, it is easier to freeze a pond than an ocean.

Software is the most flexible, malleable and adaptible medium ever known; isn't it strange that the first thing we do with a software requirement is to freeze it? Incremental development and delivery can help to put the "soft" back into software.

REFERENCES

1.   Graham, D. R., "Incremental development: review of nonmonolithic life-cycle development models", Information and Software Technology, 1989, **31**(1), 7-20.

2.   Floyd, C., Reisen, F.-M., and Schmidt, G., STEPS to Software Development with Users. In Lecture Notes in Computer Science, Vol 387: ESEC '89, ed. C. Ghezzi and J. A. McDermid, Springer-Verlag, 1989, pp. 48-64.

3.   Hirschheim, R. & Newman, M., Information Systems and User Resistance: Theory and Practice, The Computer Journal, 1988, **31**(5), 398-408.

4.   Deutsch, M. S., Software Verification and Validation: Realistic Project Approaches, Prentice-Hall, Hemel Hempstead, 1982.

5.   Wong, C., A Successful Software Development, IEEE Transactions in Software Engineering, 1984, **SE-10**(6),714-727.

6.   Gilb, T., Principles of Software Engineering Management, Addison-Wesley, Wokingham, 1988.

7.   Hill, G., Radical and Conservative Top-down Development, Software Engineering Notes, 1989, **14**(2), 32-38.

8.   Redmill, F., Computer System Development: Problems Experienced in the Use of Incremental Delivery, to be presented at SAFECOMP '89, 5-7 Dec, 1989, Vienna, Austria.

9.   Krzanik, L., Anomalies with evolutionary innovation project control strategies. In The art and Science of Innovation Management, ed. H. Hubner, Elsevier Science Publishers, Amsterdam, 1986.

10. Boehm, B. W., A Spiral Model of Software Development and Enhancement, ACM SigSoft Software Engineering Notes, 1986, **11**(4), 14–24.

11. Connell, J. L., and Shafer, L. B., Structured Rapid Prototyping. An Evolutionary Approach to Software Development, Yourdon Press Computing Series, Prentice–Hall, Englewood Cliffs, 1989.

12. Floyd, C., A Systematic Look at Prototyping. In Approaches to Prototyping, ed. R. Budde, K. Kuhlenkamp, L. Mathiassen, H. Zullighoven, Springer–Verlag, 1984, pp. 1–17.

13. Ince, D., and Hekmatpour, S., Rapid Software Prototyping, Technical Report 86/4, Open University, 1986.

14. Gerrard, C., ObjEx, Gerrard Software, Macclesfield, 1988.

15. Agresti, W. W., New Paradigms for Software Development, IEEE Computer Society Press, 1986.

16. Law, D., and Longworth, G., Systems Development: Strategies and Techniques, The National Computing Centre, Manchester, 1987.

17. Jackson, M., Jackson Information Update: Conference 1989, 30–31 October, Eastbourne, Computing, 19 Oct 1989, p. 52.

18. Harker, S., The Use of Prototyping and Simulation in the Development of Large–Scale Applications, The Computer Journal, 1988, **31**(5), 420–425.

19. Warboys, B., Reflections on a Large Software Development Project. In CSR: Sixth Annual Conference on Large Software Systems, ed. B. Kitchenham, 1989.

20. Chatters, B., Software Reliability Improvement – The Fault Free Factory (A Case Study). In CSR: Sixth Annual Conference on Large Software Systems, ed. B. Kitchenham, 1989.

21. Malcolm, B., A Large Embedded System Project Case Study. In CSR: Sixth Annual Conference on Large Software Systems, ed. B. Kitchenham, 1989.

22. Willmott, S., Design of a Flight and Radar Data Processing System for the Support of Air Traffic Control. In CSR: Sixth Annual Conference on Large Software Systems, ed. B. Kitchenham, 1989.

23. Dyer, M., A Formal Approach to Software Error Removal, The Journal of Systems and Software, 1987, 7, pp. 109–114.

24. Lehman, M. M. and Belady, L. A., Program Evolution: Processes of Software Change, Academic Press Inc. (London) Ltd., 1985.

25. LeQuesne, Individual and Organisational Factors and the Design of IPSE's, The Computer Journal, 1988, 31(5), 391–397.

8

Independence in Verification and Validation

RICHARD N HALL
Software Project Manager
GEC Avionics Ltd
Airport Works, Rochester, Kent ME1 2XX, UK

Abstract

Large software systems are very complex and their development may involve hundreds of man years of skilled effort with correspondingly large budgets. Add to this the rigorous constraints applied by a real time and safety critical applications and this makes for an extremely challenging verification and validation task throughout the software lifecycle. The software proportion of system costs has increased dramatically over the last decade. Good verification and validation has a crucial part to play in ensuring software project success.

This paper discusses the concept of independence in the software verification and validation task and in more detail presents experiences in setting up an independent software verification group covering several large projects within GEC Avionics. As discussed below the inclusion of independent V & V methods can provide increased productivity and reliability during software development.

Software will always contain errors. V & V must be about how efficient we can be in pulling out the errors. The right attitude to V & V is important. Case tools and formal methods will not solve all of the problems of developing software for large systems. V & V is here to stay and independence can help!

Introduction

In order to place my experience in the area of software verification, validation and testing in context, an overview of the systems development environment in which I have worked follows:

GEC Avionics

GEC Avionics is one of the GEC-Marconi group of companies. Head office for GEC Avionics is in Rochester, Kent. Other sites are at Nailsea, Welwyn Garden City, and offices world wide.

Products

Our product area which mainly consists of civil and military aviation systems, also includes systems for land vehicles, ships, submarines and subsea energy production.

Achievements

World wide sales are made to over 70 countries and GEC Avionics has won 14 Queen's Awards to Industry for export and technology produced. For example, we have provided systems for;

- Automatic Flight Control and Blind Landing System for Concorde,

- Head Up Displays (HUDs) for all General Dynamics F-16 aircraft,

- Flight Control System for Tornado and UK Experimental Aircraft Programme (EAP),

- Slats and Flaps Control System for Airbus.

- Standard Central Air Data Computers for 37 types of USN/USAF aircraft, and

- ASW systems in fixed and rotary wing aircraft - for RAF/RN and export.

Experience

There is a capability in the company covering all facets of research, design, development, production management and support for electronic systems.

Systems frequently include multiple processors and large amounts of software.

For example, one recent Tactical and Acoustic system had 19 processors, and approximately 1.3 Mwords of flight software in ROM.

ASET

Advanced Software Engineering Taskforce

Due to the increased importance of software activities as a proportion of projects' activity the Advanced Software Engineering Taskforce (ASET) was set up to encourage internal company dialogue on software engineering with the aim of identifying and promoting good software engineering practice, methods and tools.

ASET funds evaluations of new tools and methods. Reports and seminars spread this information throughout GEC Avionics and other GEC Marconi Companies. It is against this back drop that my experience of software V & V was gained.

Verification and Validation

What is V&V?

In order to clarify any discussion about V & V it is necessary to define the terms verification, validation and testing. Almost everyone has their own ideas about this but throughout this paper I shall assume the following definitions, which I believe are most useful:

Verification is about checking that all intentions of the previous phase are embodied in the next phase; e.g. Intentions of a detailed design are completely covered in the code. Another way of looking at this is that we have a blue print and we are concerned with accurately reflecting its content in each phase of development. Verification may be static or dynamic.

Testing is dynamic verification. Testing is searching for errors by multiple execution of code with results compared against some previously determined expected results. For an example of other definitions see MYERS (2).

Validation

Validation is about checking that software is fit for purpose. This is more narrowly defined as checking a lifecycle phase output against the customer requirements (usually a specification). Using the blueprint analogy with validation we are asking the question "Does the blueprint show what the customer wants?"

The Software Lifecycle

LIFECYCLE

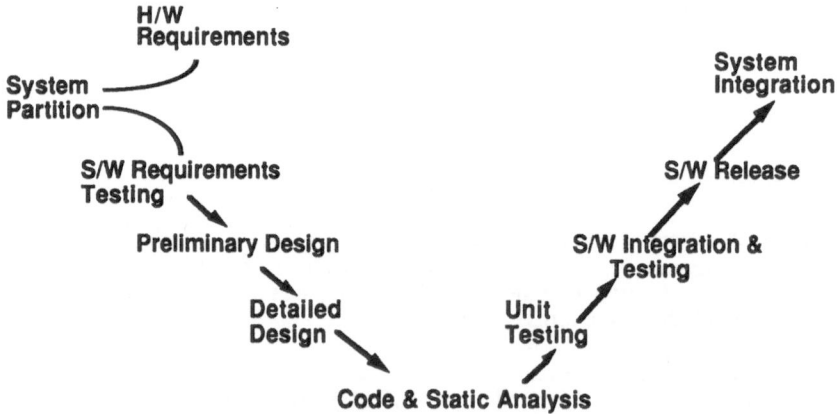

Figure 1. Typical Software Lifecycle

V & V activities must span the entire software engineering lifecycle. A typical example of the 'V' (shaped) lifecycle is shown in Figure 1 above. The 'V' lifecycle is a great improvement on the old waterfall model of software development as far as V & V is concerned. This is because it shows with great clarity that when code is available, the job is only half done and much hard work remains in the various testing and debugging phases to push the software project up the right hand side of the 'V'. The 'V' lifecycle also forces the recognition of levels of testing e.g. unit, unit integration and software subsystem testing. These levels are closely related to the levels of requirement and design decomposition.

Finding errors

The value of finding the inevitable errors in software is clear if one considers the cost benefit of increasing the quality of (or confidence in) of a piece of software. So finding errors gets us nearer towards our goal of delivering software or systems containing software to a required standard.

Having defined testing as multiple execution of code with the aim of finding errors, let us look at why we should also aim to catch them as early as possible in the lifecycle.

Finding errors early

The pay off for finding errors early (e.g. in the design rather than the testing phase) is a reduction in cost to develop a system to a particular quality standard. See Figure 2 .

FINDING ERRORS

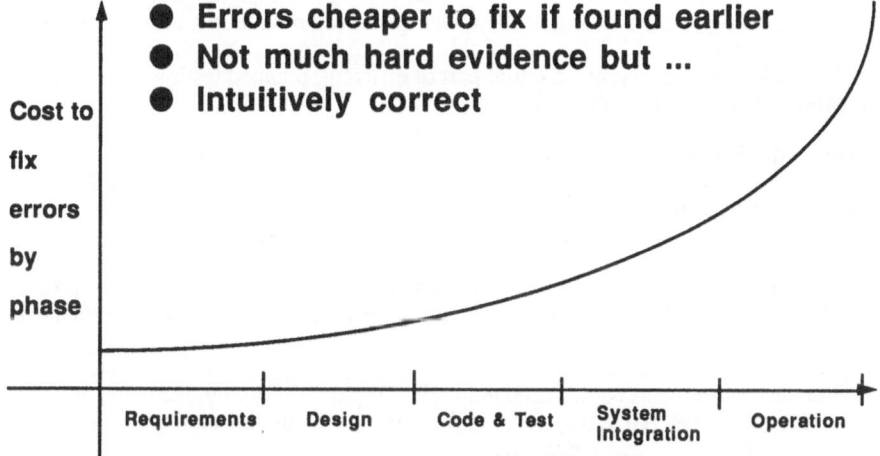

Figure 2. Finding Errors - Relative Cost versus Lifecycle Phase

This belief, which I also hold, is difficult to prove but must intuitively be true. Consider the case of an error discovered at a preliminary design phase which needs around a man day to correct all the relevant document sections. The same error if overlooked until the system reached service would have rippled through preliminary and detailed designs, code, and passed various testing phases, which unfortunately missed it, to reach a customer.

The cost here must be considered as the effort required to correct the design and code and to add appropriate tests to test documents and then to re-run old regression tests plus new tests , to check the correction before re- releasing the system, and retrofit new software in EPROMs to systems in customer use. Clearly more than half a man day cost! Belief comes in to the argument when we are asked to interpolate between these two extremes and accept that the sooner an error is trapped, the less will be the knock on effects, thus the cheaper it will be to fix. For further comment on this topic see HENNELL (7).

Techniques for Verification

Static verification may be done with or without the use of software tools. Any document may benefit from a review e.g. requirements, design or code reviews. Often the terms review, walk-through or inspection are used as interchangeable. However, I prefer to use "review" as a generic term covering any meeting with the purpose of checking the output of a software lifecycle phase. Walk-throughs are effectively the human execution of test cases with a peer group present to spot errors. An inspection aims to collect errors from a review team in the most efficient way without necessarily walking through test cases, MYERS (3).

Static code analysis by tools such as SPADE, MALPAS and LDRA Testbed allows the automation of checking for inconsistencies and the use of programming standards. This usually would not replace the other review techniques but would be in addition to them where deemed necessary.

Dynamic verification (testing) must be accomplished with the help of tools to enable test stimuli to be applied to the software under test and to monitor the results. The environment used may be either simulated on a host computer (e.g. VAX) or on target (e.g. M68020) in a system context with test harnesses built around the software under test.

Regression testing is the running of tests to verify that software changes have not adversely effected the original software. Software changes carry more risk than the production of original code. However, the regression testing of these changes is often done in a hurry. Everyone gets bored with repetition so the only way around this problem is to automate testing wherever possible. This aids repeatability, an essential part of efficient, planned testing. Automation also helps to maintain investment in planned testing.

Techniques for Validation

If we take the earlier definition of validation as checking any lifecycle phase output against customer requirements, there are a number of ways of achieving this.

By far the most efficient way is to do as much validation during the early part of the project as possible. This is to ensure that the software requirements accurately embody what the customer wants.

Methods include requirements capture and animation, rapid prototyping, formal expression of specifications and reviews. All aim to assist in flushing out misunderstanding and ambiguities early in the software (and system) lifecycle.

In an ideal world this would be enough, and we would then only need to verify that we were building the specified software accurately. In practice the successive refinement and decomposition of designs can cause divergence from the original customer requirement. The skill and experience of the staff producing systems and software is crucial in trapping this divergence and correcting it. This may be done either formally, in reviews, or informally through the curiosity of staff. In both cases, validation is taking place. Formal reviews are essential but won't find all the problems!

ASET has created a Formal Methods panel and currently 8 studies in the following areas are being progressed including:

- Requirement Animation Study

- VDM v Yourdon comparison

- Z study

- The integration of formal and structured methods

Independence

Throughout this paper we have concentrated upon what is to be done and when it should occur in the lifecycle, without considering who should be performing V & V activities, BEIZER (6). This is where the idea of independence in V & V must be considered. This concept in its must basic form simply says that V & V activities are performed more effectively when someone other than the software designer or programmer is involved. The degree to which that involvement happens is debatable but the concept is clearly considered useful by the MOD since the draft DEFSTAN 00-55 (9) mandates the use of independent V & V teams when developing safety critical software. This is still under discussion but it shows that "independence" in V & V is gaining favour.

First let us consider the entrenched attitudes to V & V and the benefits to be gained from independence.

Attitudes to testing

"Testing is boring"

'Testing is boring!' is one of the attitudes I have heard expressed. Traditionally programmers have disliked documentation most. Their second worst dislike must then have been testing, for it had (has?) a reputation for being repetitious, undemanding work. The grudgingly done unit testing simply seemed to delay the process of design, code and "getting the system working" by large amounts of intuition, head scratching and overtime. One difficulty with this attitude is that if it is hard to get a programmer to do testing thoroughly, it is almost impossible to encourage him to take the "King's shilling" in order to "press gang" him into being a full time tester!

Though these attitudes may be difficult to remove, it is well worth the effort to do so. If left in place the risk is that any testing will be performed in an inefficient way with much of the testing unplanned and each test being created off the top of the programmers head. This allows no use of identical regression tests as each test run has to be re-invented. The investment in testing is not maintained for re-use later on. Clearly a full time dedicated test engineer could bring an improvement by creating and performing planned tests.

Testing - an afterthought

Testing becomes an afterthought when it is overlooked due to early project pressures or when an unenlightened attitude is taken.This is generally a management problem.

The thinking goes like this : "I'm short of staff, have tight timescales so let's get on with design and coding and leave testing until later. After all, if there's no code, there's nothing to test!"What makes this attitude so insidious is that there are grains of truth about it. However, "testing" is often used as a general word encompassing all V&V activities, but V&V cannot be bolted on at the end of the coding stage of a software project. Considering the software lifecycle makes it clear that V&V needs to happen from start to finish. While the designers are designing, the V&V plans, and tests should be in preparation. This is ideally done in parallel by an independent V&V team who may also be reviewing the designer's output. This team, given their role, will be keen to speak up for V&V from requirements analysis onwards, so the project is not allowed to forget V&V until it is too late to be effective. In fact without well documented, testable requirements the V & V team cannot begin their preparations, so they have to apply pressure to clarify requirements at the earliest possible time. This can only benefit the quality of requirement specifications which in turn serves to benefit the whole project lifecycle, IT STARTS DEVELOPERS' GUIDE (8).

To "prove" the software works...

The wrong definition of testing may explain problems with inefficient testing. How often have you heard someone say that testing is done to "prove" that the software "works"! This is so imprecise as to be useless and even damaging to efficient testing if allowed to go unchallenged. This must be changed.

A test case is like a scientific experiment. An hypothesis must be held about the behaviour expected to be exhibited.

This is expressed in terms of inputs or stimuli, and associated expected results, based on an hypothesis. A test, or experiment, is now performed with the aim of disproving the hypothesis, or in other words, finding an error in the software. With a successful test or experiment we learn something new. If the test or experiment exhibits the expected behaviour we have only confirmed expected behaviour in one specific set of test or experimental conditions. This does not constitute proof of behaviour in any other conditions but does increase confidence. However, when the test or experiment does not result in the expected behaviour we have proved that an error exists either in the hypothesis or in the behaviour of software or experiment, and have added to our knowledge.

Added value

Armed with the knowledge of a software error we may then search for its cause and correct the error. This adds value to the software by increasing its quality.

Good tests find errors

The result of this change in the definition of testing leads to the conclusions that a "good" test finds an error or errors and that one must never plan testing with the assumption that no errors will be found, MYERS (3).

The benefits of independence

What then are the benefits of having independence in V & V activities? Some have already been mentioned:

The encouragement towards planned testing which is more efficient and maintains the investment in testing through the use of test planning documentation.

The consideration of testability throughout requirements analysis and design is encouraged. When there is always someone purely responsible for testing it is less likely to be overlooked.

Better management visibility of testing progress by measuring the success of testing as proportional to the number of errors found.

Objectivity in testing leads to more efficient error detection, BEIZER (5).

Objectivity

One of the most important benefits of independence is objectivity.

Most of us, if we have written software, have had the experience of looking for an error and being unable to spot anything wrong at all, only to have the first person who glances over your shoulder point it out immediately! This success can often be put down to objectivity. We all find it difficult to find mistakes in our own work. Thus someone independent to carry out testing, who is not limited by the possibly subconscious belief that all is well, is more likely to cast an objective eye over software and will be more efficient at tracking down errors.

How to achieve independence in V & V

If you are now convinced that some measure of independence is required in V & V activities we must now ask how to achieve it and consider the various ways.

Peer reviews

A peer review is the process by which individuals in the same software development team reviewing each others work with the aim of discovering errors. It relies on a co-operative atmosphere in which constructive criticism is directed against the software not at individuals, WEINBERG (1). This works best in small, friendly projects and when timescale pressure is not too high. Organisation problems increase with multiple teams and when timescale pressure is exerted it is generally the reviewing task, rather than the programmer's own design and code work, which is hurriedly done. Some of these problems may be overcome by formalising the process. Methods of review include the walkthrough and inspection as mentioned earlier.

Code swap testing

Code swap testing is rather like peer review, except that individuals produce their own design and code.Another programmer writes unit tests from the top level design and detailed design and then runs these tests to find errors in code produced by the original programmer, who fixes any errors found. As with peer reviewing this technique adds some independence where the overhead of a specific independent V&V team is not warranted due to small project size but the same problems apply and close monitoring by managers to ensure equal attention is paid to these activities is essential by planning both implementation and testing activities explicitly for each resource and carefully monitoring progress. An active software QA department can often assist the manager with close monitoring of the lifecycle activities, provided sensible control gates are defined between phases.

Audits

A tester or other programmer may be called upon to check the procedures used, documentation generated and technical content of a programmer's work for errors. The software QA department could well be involved in this activity but would not usually be expected to comment on technical content.

Independent Verification team

Full time V&V staff

The independent V&V team, consisting of software engineers engaged in full time testing, is the best method for achieving objectivity and effective V&V. The degree of independence depends to some extent on to whom the team report but the essential benefits accrue from someone other than the designer/programmer performing the V & V activities.

Who should make up the team?

Experience helps in any task and IV&V is no different.

Arguably, some of your best staff should be tasked with setting up the IV&V team before the development teams begin work. This will pay dividends in flagging early the misconceptions, omissions and mistakes which are rife at the start of any project, allowing them to be put right before too much damage is done. It requires good experienced staff in the IV&V team to criticise tactfully some of your equally experienced designers when they occasionally get it wrong. We all make mistakes!

It also requires time to develop an IV&V team. They do not grow overnight and much training and development is required to encourage the right methods and attitudes.

What does an IV&V team do?

An IV&V team is involved throughout the software lifecycle from requirements through to software acceptance always with the aim of finding errors. This involves attending a multitude of reviews and in parallel developing planned testing. When code is available the team's role concentrates on software integration, although this can be assisted by the designers, and software testing. It is important that the IV&V team run a well kept problem record system that allows them to track errors until they are seen to be fixed by the development team. In my view the IV&V team should never fix the code otherwise the designers would miss out on feedback as to where errors were found in their code and the independence of the V&V team would be compromised.

How to measure the success of an V&V team

The ultimate measure of success for an IV&V team must be the errors raised set against the cost of finding those errors.

As exhaustive testing is considered impossible for anything but a trivial piece of software, testing must therefore be an economic process. So, contrary to the feelings of many managers, the IV&V team are more successful, the more errors they find. One word of warning, however; the IV&V team are also finding errors prior to testing, so one must take account of all the review errors identified by the IV&V team in order to obtain a fair indication of their success. A good review record system helps with this task.

Problems

Although the concept of independence in testing has been around for some time, MYERS (3), and much lip service has been paid to the benefits of having an "independent" person, usually taken as simply a "different" person, to review and/or test a piece of software, relatively few independent test teams exist, to my knowledge. Possibly because initially a management belief in the benefits has to be held in the face of the unavoidable initial increase in cost of allocating a fair proportion of project effort to work solely on the V&V side of the lifecycle.

It must be admitted that over the past decade managers with a predominantly software background have not been common, although numbers are growing, and with little knowledge of software and scant evidence to back productivity claims it is little wonder that individuals with a belief in IV&V have been thin on the ground. For developers of large software systems this is exacerbated because large software systems have more problems both managerial and technical. Thus they have more to gain, but the very size of the problem does not lend itself to taking risks with a new method on the basis of belief. Who can afford to run experiments alongside that crucial large software development in order to gain the appropriate proof?

Independent Organisation

Here the independence in V&V activities is achieved by engaging a company separate from the prime software or system developer to perform V&V on the end products. As the most extreme form of IV&V one might think it gained the maximum advantage and this is probably so if limited to final acceptance testing of an entirely functional nature. However, it falls down on a number of points which may result in problems for both customer and supplier. These are :

Testing, especially acceptance testing, can never create high quality software it may only serve to catch a selection of the errors which may remain in a piece of software at the end of the lifecycle.

Quality is built into software throughout the lifecycle and an IV&V team can assist in reviews from requirement to implementation to improve the final product. This role, in my view, is unlikely to be offered lightly to an external and possibly competitor company. The success of this area of activity improves with better co-operation between design and test teams

The in-house IV&V team would take on board much testing of a structural nature, e.g. integration of software units and again good working relationships between design and test teams are essential to find problems and fix them in a timely fashion. This degree of involvement is unlikely to be achieved by an external agency.

The MASD Experience with IV&V

Background

Maritime Aircraft Systems Division produce aircraft mounted submarine detection systems which process and display data from submarines via a variety of sonobuoys. These systems have been fitted to both fixed wing and rotary wing aircraft for use by the RAF and Royal Navy and have significant export sales to their credit.

The division has the capability to perform all aspects of design, development, production and support for these systems and this includes a large software development facility.

Task Explosion

Since the late 1970's, the capability of microprocessors and associated memory components has exploded. With this vast increase in capability of the devices came an expectation of dramatic improvements in system capability. This in turn expanded the tasks and the problems involved with developing reliable software for large, multiprocessor, real-time systems.

Increased Problems

These were problems of scale. In a division where in the mid 1970's around 3 staff were dedicated to only software work, by the mid 1980's one particular project alone had approximately 250 software engineers engaged in development work. Clearly methods and organisation would have to progress in order to cope. Of course, it was a gradual process, but one of the ideas tried was first to allocate specific staff to system integration and testing (including software testing) and then to extend the idea and attempt to find errors as early as possible in the lifecycle by creating an I V & V team on a single project as a trial exercise. This proved successful enough to be extended into an IV&V group involved in all software projects within MASD.

How the IV&V Group was developed

<u>Initial experiences</u>

On the first project which had the benefits of an IV&V team, the emphasis was very much on developing the concepts about how the philosophy which instigated this team was to be useful in practice. It took time to work out the ground rules for supplier-customer and customer-supplier relationships between the design and IV&V team and the IV&V team and system integration team respectively. The ideas were quickly taken up but in practice each software handover necessitated negotiation regarding specifics. No matter how good the codes of practice are in the area of software testing and responsibilities, the first time your fledgeling IV&V team reject a piece of software due to lack of some piece of documentation, or insufficient module testing, you will have a lot of feathers to smooth down if the relationship is to remain co-operative and the criticism is to remain constructive. See BEIZER (6). The concern felt at this stage will be at least equal to the elation felt when the IV&V team complete a successful software handover having raised armfuls of problem records and meticulously checked all of the fixes from the designers.

<u>Creating an IV & V Group</u>

To create an IV & V group to cover eventually all software projects, more staff were clearly required. Also, as these projects already had software teams of some experience, there was a need to assure them of the good intentions behind the new organisation. Convincing presentations from myself and the IV&V team leader were instigated to sell the idea of IV&V as a useful contribution to the software development activity and that to be a part of that team was intellectually challenging. In recruitment the stress was placed on recruiting "test case designers" rather than the more general term "tester" , to emphasise their rightful equal status with implementation designers, BEIZER (6). The job title "software engineer" was kept for the "test case designers" to stress their involvement with the whole software lifecycle.

The aims were to automate testing wherever possible and otherwise to engage technical assistants to run repetitive tests thus freeing the test case designers to spend more time reviewing, producing planned tests and evaluating results.

Clearly we had to dispel the fear of week after week of repetitive test running as being all V&V was about. The idea that testing was boring was largely overcome and a number of recruits joined the group.

<u>Training - a mechanism for change</u>

Initially, training was essential to encourage the right approach, and a suitable course, designed by the NCC, was identified which was eventually brought onto the GEC Avionics site for software V&V training.

I believe that, although software tools may facilitate V&V, as with all parts of software development, it is attitude which distinguishes a good IV&V team. The psychology of V&V or even the methods are rarely given emphasis in software engineering degree courses, but V&V can account for around 50% of project costs. See IT STARTS DEVELOPERS' GUIDE (8). Until this mismatch is addressed in higher education, companies must look to provide suitable ab-initio training to allow designers to begin to think like true testers.

In order to practice what we preach, our own trainee software engineers (TSE) do a "tour of duty" with the IV&V group, as they do with other groups in the division during on-the-job-training and often wish to return when their training is complete.

The college which provides our TSE's with general training has been encouraged to include more time on V&V in the custom designed HND Software Engineering course taught to our TSE's.

These initiatives have become on going processes by which enlightened attitudes to testing are encouraged across all software engineers and new blood is found for the IV&V group to enable it to become self perpetuating.

Team Identity

As with all teams or groups, the encouragement of group identity by clearly defined roles and responsibilities, and by opportunities for social gatherings assists the group to stay coherent and share aims for future progress. Organising a V&V group Christmas meal or a celebration for the 1000th problem record raised help with building a group. This is especially necessary when that group are involved in an activity which is considered new within an organisation as this tends to create insecurity. The insecurity is probably well founded because it it unlikely that the first use of IV&V teams will meet with unanimous approval and an early success is always helpful in consolidating a new position.

The disadvantage may, however, be turned to an advantage in team building. The psychology of groups is such that an external threat, whether real or perceived, tends to enhance group (team) identity. Given a great deal of hard work, early successes will come and if acknowledged, as above, serve to create team pride which enhances team identity and should finally put to rest any doubt that staff had about belonging to a test group.

Important lessons

The most important lessons to come out of this experience with V&V are:

- it improves planned testing markedly

- it does find errors earlier but don't expect software to be completely error free as system integration often identifies software to software subsystem interfacing problems and the errors missed by the prior testing.

- it improves management visibility of real and measurable progress in software development.

- it is crucial that the IV &V team are run by managers and team leaders who understand the concept and believe in it. A V&V team will wither if run by a manager intent on getting the code finished, and leaving V&V until later, and who is then disappointed when errors are found. The IV&V team must be independent enough to be allowed to go for errors in a determined way, and to be supported by their team leaders and managers when they find problems. To be fair, it is extremely difficult to give the judgement of Solomon between generating software within timescales and finding the maximum amount of errors. Better to have two managers argue it out; it's easier than arguing with yourself!

Summary

Not only is V & V currently important, but it will remain so despite new methods and CASE tools. The effectiveness of V & V activities can be greatly improved by the use of staff separate from the design and implementation activities. The degree of this independence appropriate depends upon the circumstances. However, any independence is better than none.

Why should you use I V & V teams? Given that the CSR conference theme is "Large Software Systems" the delegates are certain to have an interest in finding ways to improve the outcome when producing large amounts of software. In this area IV&V is most pertinent.

Give it a try. Don't expect miracles over night, but when in place, I believe you should see improved management visibility of the software development process, more effective planned testing and an improvement in the quality of software being released to customers or to the next phase of system testing, depending on your circumstances.

References

1.   G.M. Weinberg, The Psychology of Computer Programming, Van Nostrand, New York, 1971, pp 52 - 64.

2.   G.J. Myers, Software Reliability, John Wiley & Sons, New York, 1976, pp 169 - 195.

3.   G.J. Myers, The Art of Software Testing, John Wiley & Sons, New York, 1979, pp 4 - 16, pp17 - 35.

4.   B.W. Boehm, Software Engineering Economics, Prentice-Hall, New Jersey, 1981, pg 37.

5.   B. Beizer , Software Testing Techniques, Van Nostrand, New York, 1983, pp 5 - 7.

6.   B. Beizer, Software System Testing and QA, Van Nostrand, New York, 1984, pp 179 - 182, pp 315 - 317, pg 317.

7.   Hennell, M., Testing Throughout the Lifecycle. In Software Engineering - The Decade of Change",Ed. D. Ince, Peter Peregrinus/IEE, Stevenage, 1986.

8.   IT STARTS Developers' Guide (Version 1), NCC, Manchester, 1989, pp 2.25 - 2.30, pp 8.12 - 8.35.

9.   00-55, Interim Defence Standard - Draft Issue, MOD, 1989.

9

THE RECOVERY OF SOFTWARE PROJECTS

DR SINCLAIR G STOCKMAN, AFIMA
Systems and Software Engineering
Research Division
British Telecom Research Laboratories
Martlesham Heath
Suffolk
UK

KEYWORDS

Management, Software Management, Project Control, Process Improvement

ABSTRACT

The past 5 years have seen significant improvements in the management of software projects. This is evidenced by the introduction of quality management systems into software development organisations and the progress made in the certification of such systems (Ref[1,2,3]).

A situation which has faced many project managers during this period has been how to introduce improved management and technical methods and tools into a project which has already started, but is suffering from many of the symptoms of a project which is out of control, and which would benefit from these new methods and tools.

In this paper we will present practical guidance on how to bring 'problem' projects under control, so that the advances of software engineering can be made use of, if appropriate, by the project manager. This process is referred to as project recovery.

The paper will start by discussing some of the common symptoms of a 'sick' project. Knowledge of what to look for can enable project managers to identify problems at an earlier stage and thereby take more effective corrective action.

We then move on to setting out the steps which can be taken to achieve project recovery, and how these steps should be implemented. There are many important issues which have to be addressed here. The introduction of new techniques into an existing project is fraught with difficulties. If the process is mismanaged, the project can end up in an even worse state.

Following on from this, the paper will identify how the use of software tools can help in the above recovery process. Several tools, ranging from documentation aids to management and technical tools will be discussed. Again the dangers, as well as the benefits, of the introduction of new tools will be presented.

In addition to the 'technical' problems inherent in the implementation of a recovery program, the paper will address the issue of staff antagonism towards recovery programs. It is essential that managers address this issue actively, otherwise their efforts can be frustrated by staff who misinterpret changes in management practices as a threat to their status.

2   WHY RECOVERY?

Despite claims that the software crisis is over, all is not well. Often the project manager is faced with the task of recovering a project which, for various reasons, is not performing adequately. It is this problem which this paper aims to address - the recovery of software projects - for it is only by the proper management of this recovery process that the project manager can hope to bring to bear the promised advantages of the new generation of software engineering methods and tools.

There are many causes for a project slipping into a state where it is in need of recovery. One, which is likely to become more prevalent in future years, is the increasing volume of 'old' software systems which will be in use and which will require further enhancement. We are becoming more successful at delivering systems to the marketplace. These systems often have a lifetime of greater than 10 years. During this time the software will probably have to go through several phases of enhancement and be transferred between several support and development teams. In these circumstances, the likelihood of a project being in need of recovery, is high. It is therefore vital to understand how to realise the recovery of a software project, in order to be able to make use of the advances likely to occur in software enabling technology.

Projects which are still in the initial development phase can also be in need of recovery. Problems may have arisen due to slack management or the project suffering from a series of false starts due to changing requirements.

Whatever the reason, if some form of recovery process is not applied to these types of project, they are likely to slip further into chaos, and, after a period of being a heavy drain on scarce resources, ultimately collapse.

3   THE SICK PROJECT

A sick project is one which is in need of recovery. Two issues are addressed in this section.

1.   Firstly, what are the symptoms of a sick project.

2.   Secondly, what are the causes of sickness.

Sickness takes many forms, from transitory to severe. In this paper I will focus on the symptoms of severe sickness, that is those symptoms, which if they are not addressed, will result in the project eventually collapsing.

3.1 Symptoms Of A Sick Project

Things to look for include:

1.   The busy team - lots of panic - firefighting -

Many projects are populated by staff, both managerial and technical, who thrive on chaos. It is important to recognise this element of enjoyment because often, in the initial and intermediate stages of sickness, staff on the project may appear to be happy with their lot. In evaluating whether a project is in trouble, one must be able to differentiate between a project where the resources are being effectively utilised to meet tight deadlines, and those where staff are busy running around in circles, achieving little. The latter is often characterised by a large number of 'key' staff e.g. 'Only Fred can do this" - or - 'The project manager has it all in his head'. This type of chaotic situation can only continue for a limited period of time, after which the project team will start to breakdown and ultimately the project will grind to a halt.

2.   Everyone is busy, yet few statistics on what is being done -

Closely related to this theme of the busy team is the situation where everyone is busy, but there is no information on what is being done.

Consequently it is impossible to manage the project out of any crisis because the manager has no feel for how any change in strategy or procedure will affect progress.

Useful statistics to look for are:

1. What time is being spent on problem evaluation and fixing?

2. How many problems are being cleared per month?

3. How much time is being spent on development, management, testing?

3.   No future release plans are in place -

The absence of release plans is a clear indication that a project is in trouble. Effectively the project team is being focused on sorting out today's problems to the exclusion of any development effort for the future. The team are working in a strategic vacuum and ultimately the project will be suffocated and die.

4.   No effective configuration management -

This ranges from uncertainty on how to build the system to no knowledge of the parts which comprise the system.

Inevitably software systems consist of a number of parts, which when combined function in a particular way. Yet a large number of software projects have given little if any thought to how they are going to control these parts. It is frightening that in many cases not only is there ambiguity about how the parts are put together, but the release team do not know which parts are supposed to go into the release.

A consequence of this type of scenario is that valuable effort is being wasted rewriting build files, making a set of releases in quick succession as errors in the previous builds are discovered, and expending significant effort on all of the activities associated with the release process.

5.   On-site bug fixing -

Having released a system with a large number of problems, the software flying squad is sent in. This team dive straight into the code on the customer's site and attempt to effect immediate solutions. No time is spent addressing the design or trying to analyse the problem. This team are effectively hacking the system, sniping at problems and probably aggravating problems.

This is one of the classic features of a sick project.

6.   Ineffective plans -

Sometimes no plans, sometimes out of date plans, sometimes plans which can't be used for control either because they contain too little information, or because they are too complex.

Plans act as a framework within which to exercise control. They are a model of the project. Where there are no plans, there can be no control.

Where the plans are out of date, the control will probably be misdirected.

Where the plans are not being read, efforts at control will be misinterpreted and often ignored.

Where a plan does not contain provision for control, for example by not giving any visibility of potential problems until the end of a project, then it cannot be used as a basis of control early in the project.

7.   Unclear product strategy -

A major cause of wasted effort and consequently project sickness, is that staff on a project do not understand what the objectives of the projects are.

In this environment, staff can often take what they think is appropriate action only to find that they are causing further problems.

Where there is not a common vision within the project team, then it is not surprising to find the members of the team all working towards different goals. Large numbers of staff simply do not understand what they are trying to achieve.

8.   Growing problem lists -

Sick projects often have the major proportion of their resource being expended on fixing problems. Yet often, the number of problems continue to rise.

In addition, often their is no process of prioritorisation in fixing problems. So effort is expended on fixing problems which are not perceived as a major problem, while major problems remain unfixed for months.

9.   Cost and schedule overruns.

Cost and schedule overruns are in themselves not indicative of a sick project. They become problems when no action is being taken to bring these overruns under control.

A point worth emphasising is that the staff working on a sick project are often highly competent, dedicated and hardworking. They may even have to hand the correct tools. But a project is not simply comprised of individual parts - it is in itself a system and it is this system which is sick and needs to be subjected to recovery.

What, therefore are the causes of this sickness. A general cause, often given, is lack of a managerial and strategic framework within which the project can progress. This is part of the story - certainly if such a framework does not exist, then a project will run into problems. But the existence of a managerial framework is in itself far from sufficient. A much more common cause of sickness is failure to actively manage a project at various levels.

4   KEY ISSUES IN RECOVERY

Given that you are faced with a sick project, how do you set about recovery?

1.   Recognition

If you don't know you have a sick project, you are unlikely to plan any recovery treatment. Yet this is where most problems arise. If identified early the treatment can effect complete recovery, if left undetected, the illness becomes so severe, the project is beyond recovery. The symptoms discussed previously are indicators. Project managers and quality auditors should always remain on the lookout for these symptoms.

2.   Staff

The staff are the most valuable and important asset in any project. In many ways, the management of the recovery process hinges on the effective management of the project staff.

3.   Planning

Recovery will not happen by itself. The process needs to be planned and resources made available.

4.   Tools

As with any process, any aids to automate the process will make it more effective.

5.   Finally control.

As stated above, it is not enough to plan for the recovery. The process must be managed, and by its very nature, an intensive level of management is required for the recovery process to be successful.

There are several issues which must be stressed.

Firstly, recovery is not easy. It must be planned strategically and often calls for management of the highest calibre. If the recovery process fails, it is likely that the project will collapse. When a multi-million pound project is involved, this is obviously a major economic failure. If the project is a strategic component of a set of developments, then the ripple effects of this failure will spread outwards into these related projects.

Secondly, recovery is long-term. It cannot be effected within a few weeks and requires continuous effort, often over a number of years to sustain recovery.

Lastly, the project may 'reject' recovery. It is important for managers responsible for effecting project recovery not to assume that all those involved with the project will welcome their efforts enthusiastically.

These points combine to make project recovery a difficult task, requiring skilled management, hard work and a clear vision, not to say a steady nerve.

5   A TALE OF RECOVERY

I will now try to illustrate what is involved in project recovery with an example scenario.

Firstly, what were the symptoms. The project was a critical project, involving the use of state of the art system architecture. The target market was volatile. The original plans were optimistic. Software was being developed in advance of the hardware being available, and the specification for the hardware was not fixed. There was a firm release date for the first system, which could not be slipped, but no defined release plan. The project team was highly skilled. The team was, however, involved almost exclusively in fire-fighting, trying to cope with a combination of changing requirements, changing hardware and a growing list of problems with the software. Consistent configuration management procedures were not in place and the project was not going to meet the required deadlines.

Against this background, what was to be done. The first crucial step was the realisation that there was a problem. The next was admitting to the existence of the problem and planning recovery action. This was not easy. For management to admit to serious problems requires them to accept that they have not been successful in performing their primary task. It requires a constructive culture to ensure that management teams feel able to admit to problems.

The course of treatment was carefully planned. Firstly the interfaces between the team responsible for technical development, the team responsible for product release and installation and the sales team were clearly defined. This was crucial in allowing priorities to be identified and individual managers to be identified with clear responsibility for certain areas.

Next, the project priorities were identified and agreed. This process involved accepting that everything couldn't be defined as a high priority. A picture was created of the strategic requirements for the project, initially over a six month period and ultimately extending to several years. This has to be set against the pre-recovery situation, where the picture rarely extended beyond a few weeks.

The current role of the staff involved on the project was then established. This is essential for several reasons. Firstly, the staff need to be convinced that they are an integral part of the recovery process. Secondly, it is necessary to obtain a clear picture of what the staff perceive as their priorities and roles - often this differs from that of their management, or between different teams in the project, notably the development team and the product release team. Thirdly, it is important to identify early on where the weaknesses in the current organisation lie. These often result from overall development being impeded by a bottleneck in the development team, because one staff member has too much responsibility.

The third step in the recovery process was to get on top of what existed. Understanding what the system does can come later - for the time being accept that it does what it does. If you are to gain control of a project and start to plan strategically, then it is essential to establish definitively what the component parts of the system are and how they are combined to produce the product in its current form. This provides a firm foundation for any future system changes.

Following on logically from this, well defined configuration management and change control procedures were introduced into the project. Failure to do this has been the death knell of a large number of projects.

Having completed the above, it was possible to begin to manage the actual recovery.

The first step was to determine how much effort was being expended on strategic development and how much was being expended on firefighting. A plan was created to decrease the % of firefighting activity over a time period of 12 to 18 months.

All known problems were identified and prioritorised. Then timescales were agreed on when these problems would be fixed and they were built into future release plans.

Release plans for the project with well defined contents for each release were created and agreed.

It goes without saying the creation of acceptable release plans is not an easy task, nor is there any set formula to follow. It is a skilled management task, requiring vision, determination and realism.

The next step, having put in place a work program to achieve the above priorities, was to establish an up to date specification. This acted as an essential reference point for future work on the project. In parallel with this, the project documentation was updated in line with development work being undertaken on the project.

The tactic here is to update documentation as and when it is needed, rather than expend a large amount of scarce resource updating documentation on parts of the system which may remain untouched for a considerable time period. A normal first step is to establish the structural design of the system. Next put in place test programs for the project. This will have to be effected in stages, with the most critical and troublesome components of the system receiving priority attention. Given the structural design of the system, it is possible to identify the key components and ensure that there is more than one staff member who understands that component.

6   THE WEDGE

A key objective of this type of recovery process is to establish a well defined plan for the upgrade of the system and a clear timetable for increasing the % of effort being expended on strategic development to a level which allows the project to progress relatively normally.

Having achieved the above, you now have a framework into which you can introduce new technology to assist with increasing the overall productivity of the project.

Whilst the above list of actions may seem somewhat obvious, it is surprising that this type of approach is not more commonly used. A more normal approach has been to try to throw more technology and more staff at the problem, all of which is more likely to compound the problem than solve it.

For example, tools are bought in the absence of defined methods or procedures for their use. Valuable time is wasted trying to learn how to use them and then, when they finally come on line in the project, they do not fit in with the other methods already in use. Often different tools are bought by different parts of the team to solve the same problem. This tends to reduce the level of communication across the team.

7   WHAT CAN GO WRONG DURING RECOVERY

The previous set of actions seems relatively straightforward, but needless to say there are many pitfalls. A few of these are addressed below.

Firstly configuration management. During a recovery process, or indeed during any software development process, management must give a high priority to establishing clear procedures for configuration management and change and build control. A common problem which arises during recovery, if these procedures are not established, is that either no one knows how to build the system, which normally results in numerous erroneous releases which further compound the chaos the project is in, or worse still, no one knows what parts actually comprise the system, again resulting in much the same effect.

Configuration management tools are brought in, but no procedures are established for their use and code modules can 'disappear' into the bowels of the system, never to reappear.

Secondly, a common pitfall is in the area of project management. Recovery is a management rather than a technical exercise. Management is a decision intensive activity. During recovery many management decisions will have to be taken, and these will have to be taken in such a manner to ensure that the project does not reel from left to right getting nowhere. The worst that can happen to a sick project is to have either a manager who is over cautious, or a manager who reacts instantaneously to problems.

An inappropriate level of quality control is a third prime cause of failure in recovery. It is essential to effect quality control during recovery, introducing change control, reviewing and testing. It is equally essential, however, to ensure that the quality control being exercised does not grind the project to a halt. When undertaking recovery, one is already in a risk situation; that is the risk that the project may fail completely. To come out of this situation, one cannot expect to remove all risk, rather one must aim to minimise risk. So the management must exercise active control over their quality control program and have a clear understanding of the risks they are taking.

8   TOOLS FOR RECOVERY

The philosophy of the recovery process outlined above is to establish a relatively stable framework within which software enabling technology can be introduced to assist with the progression of the project.

A maxim which should be followed is that 'simple is best'. There is much which can be achieved with simple tools and these should be exploited. Taking a few examples.

Configuration management tools. These are essential. Having established well defined procedures, tools such as CMS, SCCS (Ref [4]) etc are invaluable in providing a vehicle for effective, efficient change control. They allow management and the development team to have an accurate picture of the composition and change history of the product.

Documentation tools allow for the development of consistent documents and greatly ease the interchange of information between project team members (Ref [4])/

Planning aids, for example pert and gnatt planning tools allow management to create and communicate plans in a clear, unambiguous formats. In addition, the automation of the planning information, allows the plans to be kept up to date.

Testing tools provide information on the test coverage, and allow managers to identify gaps in the current quality control procedures which will require strategic planning to clear in future releases (Ref [4,5]). Even simple testing tools which provide an online facility for recording test results and provide an automated summary list of test which have been run and those which have not been run can be invaluable for improving the level of visibility of testing to management.

Each of these tools in themselves is of assistance. But they are made all the more effective when available through an IPSE type framework, which provides for interworking of the tools and communication of information between project team members (Ref [4.6]).

It is the contention of this paper that the recovery steps outlined earlier provide a framework within which this type of IPSE technology can become available to the project manager faced with the task of bringing a sick project under control. Further in the absence of such a recovery framework, even IPSE technology will be of no use in bringing this type of project under control.

Assuming that the tools are being introduced within the recovery framework outlined above, there is still much which can go wrong. Tools are automatic aids. They run on computers, and usually they are very expensive on machine resources. If one does not plan for their introduction, then configuration management and testing tools can bring the development to a standstill by overloading the development environment computing facilities. This further highlights the need for careful planning during recovery.

Another point to note is the need for the tools to be appropriate. While there are many attractive design tools currently on the market, they are unlikely to make a major impact on a project which is in the throes of recovery, unless they automate an already existing method. To introduce a new design method without allowing a substantial lead time, will probably result in the development team falling even further behind in schedules because of long learning curves and unnecessary duplication of development activity.

If planned, tools are key in ensuring the success of a recovery program. A good example is a configuration management tool set which, when introduced in conjunction with a well defined set of procedures, can result in control and stability returning to the release phase, a significant reduction in avoidable system construction errors and a substantial reduction in the amount of effort being expended on post release problems.

9   STAFF

Turning now to one of the most important aspects of any recovery program, the project staff. It is unlikely that a complete change of staff when you start a recovery program is either feasible or desirable.

The project manager responsible for the recovery process must remember that project staff are likely to feel vulnerable. Many of the technical decisions and managerial decisions they have taken in the past are likely to be brought into question. Often these decisions, when considered in the light of the information which was available at the time they were taken, may be found to be reasonable, but with the benefit of hindsight and a clear strategic understanding of what the project is trying to achieve, they are obviously incorrect. In this situation, management must ensure that the staff do not mistakenly suspect that a witchhunt is in progress.

Project staff must be involved in the review of the project and the process of establishing clear procedural frameworks. They must also be involved in identifying which tools should be introduced into the project. This does not mean that the project is run by a committee, for in a recovery situation strong management is called for; but time must be taken to ensure that the project staff are given the opportunity to place their ideas on the table - and the project manager must ensure that he gives these ideas due consideration.

Staff are likely to feel very possessive about the code they have written. When trying to introduce a recovery process, it is essential to 'depersonalise' the code, by dismantling the expert cartels within the project. This process can be perceived as a threat by staff who may feel that being an expert gives them extra status. This perception must be countered by the project manager. The advantages of depersonalising the software, for example less weekend working, greater flexibility in leave entitlement, improved career flexibility, must be stressed.

There are occasions when even after these advantages have been pointed out, some staff members will try to resist the efforts being made to effect recovery - that is, they are rejecting the treatment. In these circumstances, the manager must take strong action to replace such staff members as soon as possible. If possible, they must be taken off the critical paths and ultimately off the project. Hopefully this will be the exception rather than the rule, but the manager must not sidestep this problem when it arises.

Another point to note is that managers must not underestimate the advantages the introduction of some new blood can have on a project. Often new staff can quickly clear problems which have baffled the 'expert' staff for several months.

During recovery, the project manager must establish a working team hierarchy. While retaining overall control, significant responsibility for the recovery program must be devolved to the team leaders. This guards against a team of indispensable technical experts being replaced by a single managerial expert, a situation which would represent a clear backward step.

10   CONCLUSIONS

Project recovery is not an exact science, rather it is a process built up from experience. The objective of the process is to establish, or re-establish a project framework within which it is possible to exercise state of the art project management techniques and make use of software technology approporiate to the needs of the project i.e. to minimise the amount of firefighting and maximise the amount of strategic development work.

The process discussed in this paper has been and continues to be successful.

The main messages of this paper are:

1.   The need to plan recovery, in terms of technical activities, quality procedures, staff utilisation, computer resource utilisation and release planning.

2.   Commitment - Recovery is not an easy process. It requires a high level of commitment on the part of the management team and the staff involved. It also requires commitment from the funding management and an understanding of the timescales involved. Recovery must not be viewed as a short term process when making the decision on whether to proceed with it or stop the project.

3.   Vision - The process requires vision, particularly on the part of the key management.

4.   The process requires a high degree of level headedness. There are many things which can and probably will go wrong along the way and the management will be required to make many difficult decisions. It will only be possible to make these within the framework of a recovery program spanning a timeframe of 6 to 24 months, otherwise the project will veer from side to side before finally foundering.

Acknowledgement

Acknowledgement is made to the Research and Technology Board of British Telecom for permission to publish this paper.

11 REFERENCES

1. International Standard on Quality Systems, ISO9000, 1987.

2. AT&T Technical Journal, Vol 65, Issue 2, 1986.

3. Proceedings of First European Seminar of Software Quality, April 1988, EOQC, Brussels.

4. Department of Trade and Industry STARTS Guide, 2nd Edition, 1987, National Computing Centre Publications, UK.

5. On Software Testing for Multi-microprocessor Systems, 10th EUROMICRO Symposium on Microprocessing and Microprogramming, North-Holland Publications, 1984.

6. Project Support Environments, Computer Systems (GB), Vol.5, No.3, March 1985.

10

SOFTWARE RELIABILITY IMPROVEMENT - THE FAULT FREE FACTORY (A CASE STUDY)

BRIAN CHATTERS
ICL Mainframe Systems,
Wenlock Way, West Gorton, Manchester M12 5DR

ABSTRACT

Effective quality management is fundamental to achieving high reliability in complex software developments. This paper discusses the role of quality management in the development and maintenance of a mainframe operating system with particular emphasis on Quality Specification and Measurement. The importance of the relationships between software engineers and quality professionals is explored.

Through a case study, the paper describes the tools and techniques adopted, how they have evolved over time together with their relative benefits and the overall quality improvements that have been achieved.

The tools and techniques form part of a long-term strategy to establish a fully-integrated software factory producing error free products.

INTRODUCTION

ICL, part of the STC group, is an international company applying the latest generation of information technology techniques in order to provide high value customer solutions to today's and tomorrow's business problems.

The operating system for the medium to large range of processors is called VME. It is used worldwide and in the UK is the most popular of all available major systems, being installed on more mainframes than the operating systems of any other supplier.

VME is a very large development. It is a general purpose operating system which includes basic facilities for running user programs in a multi-user, shared environment and addresses such aspects as job scheduling, resource management, file handling, cataloguing, security, data management and transaction processing. It is an evolutionary system which is delivered to its customer base at regular intervals to provide enhanced capability as the user requirements evolve with time.

The major challenge of the tools and techniques used to develop the software is to enable new facilities to be integrated into the existing software system and continually to seek quality improvement with each subsequent release. Each incremental release represents a maintenance version of earlier releases and captures error clearances of previously detected problems. It is a fundamental requirement for VME to cause no disturbance of the customer systems as a result of the installation of each subsequent release. This is defined as "non-regression".

However, having the right tools and techniques to perform the tasks is only half the answer. It is equally important (maybe more so) to ensure that there is effective management of the development route and that the workforce is trained in the use of the tools and techniques.

This paper discusses the role of quality management in the development of VME and describes how the emphasis on quality management has brought about significant improvements in the reliability levels of the systems.

QUALITY MANAGEMENT

Quality Management is an essential part of the software system development process. It serves two major purposes:

*   To ensure that quality issues are specifically addressed during the planning and implementation phases of software development. It is now well established that product quality is not an "add-on" feature that can be included after the product has been built. Consequently, a clear statement of requirements is required prior to implementation and "quality plans" are needed to ensure that these requirements will be satisfied.

*   To give assurance that the development process is being adhered to and to give assurance that the product will perform as required against the quality attributes in its target environments.

Requirements for a product come from three sources.

*   Market requirements: state such things as user-oriented functionality, price, performance, markets, etc.
*   Company strategies: determine the types of products that will be produced.
*   Quality processes: state how the product is to be produced and how the development activities will demonstrate that all requirements are satisfied.

No development route can be effective in delivering quality products unless it is supported by a suitable quality management system with adequate quality control. Specifically for VME, this means:

*   An on-going Quality Improvement Process: fundamental elements of the process are management commitment, communication and awareness, education, measurement and corrective action.
*   Conformance to acceptable Quality Control System standards. Mainframe Systems is approved against ISO9001 (BS5750).
*   Formal quality checkpoints throughout the development route with objective criteria which must be satisfied before further progress can be made.
*   A documented set of procedures and processes for education and reference.

Quality Attributes

Many have argued that quality is subjective and that it cannot be
quantified. Fortunately, these views are now very much in the minority.
Before quality can be planned and implemented effectively, the activities
need to be defined in objective terms. One way in which this can be
achieved is to categorise the quality requirements into standards areas
known as "quality attributes". Checklists can be generated providing
standard attributes which are then used at the requirements setting and
planning stages. Because of the different characteristics of software
systems, there is no universally accepted set of quality attributes which
apply to them all. Even when there are common attributes, their
significance to the overall quality may be radically different.

In addition to providing a more objective definition of quality
requirements, attribute checklists also ensure that non-functional aspects
of software systems are considered and planned at the initial stages of
their development (eg installation and maintenance considerations).

Attributes used in the planning of the VME Operating System software
are known as "abilities". Significant ones used are:

* issueability,
* functionality,
* compatibility,
* availability,
* reliability,
* maintainability,
* performance,
* usability.

Responsibilities

A major factor in achieving quality is to have an effective organisation
with complementary functions and shared responsibility between teams. The
biggest dilemma that a project manager faces is when he is up against
timescale pressures and he needs to make trades. Traditionally, because of
a lack of understanding of quality, this is the area that is traded first.
This lack of understanding is also a major reason why unrealistic schedules
are established in the first place.

The role of the Quality Assurance Manager is to establish quality
requirements with the project manager which translate the market
requirements into quantifiable quality attributes and then to ensure that
these requirements are met before product delivery. The Quality Assurance
Manager has a peer relationship with the project manager and has the
authority to veto the release of a product if the requirements are not
satisfied. However, the role is seen as supportive, helping the project
manager to meet his requirements rather than a policeman enforcing rules.

Management Checkpoints

A key technique for the management of a project is to use a defined
development route which identifies phases. Each phase is terminated by a
checkpoint where an assessment is made of

* the achievement against the plan for the phase
* revised predictions of the quality attributes based on the
  measurements taken during the phase.

Such assessment is formalised and controlled by someone who is
independent from the development team (eg the Quality Assurance Manager
performs this function in VME).

MEASUREMENT

The purpose of measurement is to provide feedback to the development projects to ensure that requirements continue to be met and to allow objective corrective action to be taken when problems are identified.

Measurement is seen as a fundamental tool for the achievement of delivered quality. A key element of establishing a quality plan is to determine the measures and the targets that will be used to demonstrate achievement of the quality attributes. The activity of determining the measures is probably the most difficult one with respect to planning. Success or otherwise of a project is critically dependent upon establishing the right measures which will give assurance that the delivered quality will be met. The challenge is to establish measures throughout the development process which will give assurance that targets are met without recourse to actually measuring the market requirement. For example, a reliability trial for systems with a high meantime between failures may be impossible to stage.

The key to success on measurement is to ensure that the measures are established and owned by the team which is responsible for the implementation of the phase of the development route in which the measures are to be taken. It is a recipe for disaster to impose measures which are not understood by the development teams and which do not enable ownership of problems to be identified. The role of the Quality Assurance Manager is to help in the establishment of the measures and to ensure that they are agreed and documented in the quality plan prior to implementation.

A number of techniques can be used to establish measurement (eg T. Gilb [1], Dr V. Basili [2], etc). Whichever techniques are chosen, the experience of VME has identified a number of basic rules with respect to the selection of measurement techniques. These are:

* Keep the measures simple. The fundamental use of measurement is as a tool to manage development (either from an engineer's or from a manager's perspective); thus, simple and well-understood is far better than precise and complicated.
* Do not over-metricate. A few effective measures are normally sufficient.
* Ensure that the measures are owned by the development projects (ie the problem owners). This re-emphasises the prime purpose of measurement being to manage corrective action when problems are identified.
* Establish the measurements and targets before implementation. Never compromise on their achievement.
* Carry out regular reviews of the effectiveness of a measurement with respect to demonstrating delivered quality.
* Almost any (intelligent) measure is better than no measure.
* All measurements are relative. Keep consistency in measures between versions of the software.
* Avoid comparison with different types of measurements in order to determine quality. A mistake often made is to attempt to measure against "industry norms". In most cases, there are no such things!
* Different measurements will be required at different phases of the development process to determine the quality of the different quality attributes.

Measures that are most effective in the VME development environment are:

* Software error detection rates per development phase (eg design, code,

test,etc). If the development phase covers a long period, the rates should be measured at regular intervals throughout the process (eg weekly or monthly measures).

* Software system break rates. The long-term establishment of this measure means that it is well understood and long term comparisons can be made between different versions of the product.

Data Collection
Where possible, data collection should be integrated into the development process and tools should be provided for their collection and analysis. However, significant quality improvement can be achieved using simple manual methods of data collection. The key to successful data collection is to establish a clear objective for the measurement and to seek commitment from the development teams to gather the information. Unless there are clear benefits to the development process, any data collected will be of poor quality and the collection process will deteriorate. Periodic review of the data and feedback to the "collectors" is essential.

If an automatic data collection process can be established, additional benefits arise. The development of analysis tools allows projects to use the information in costs models and for verifying prediction models.

TOOLS AND TECHNIQUES

When considering any tool kit, the tools in it must complement each other and the selection of any tool or method will depend upon a number of factors. All tools and methods should be integrated into a coherent development route; often, it is not possible to attribute the success of a project to one particular technique.

VME has traditionally used a number of proprietary automated tools in the development process; particularly in the areas of configuration management and the control of customer queries, product modification and system construction.

Other key tools and methods used in the VME development route are described below:

Basic Software Architecture and Design Features
Structured design techniques and basic architectural features need to be established at an early stage to ensure that problems can be easily identified and that the faulty component can be isolated and the underlying faults detected and, hence, corrected.

The VME system is divided into functional subsystems which comprise a set of code and data modules. The subsystems take advantage of basic hardware features which provide facilities for having separate code and data modules and for the protection and security of data by preventing illegal access [4]. The system knowledge required by a subsystem is restricted to a formally controlled set of interfaces to other subsystems.

Fault tolerance is integrated into the design of the system by the establishment of specific error management subsystems which are protected from corruption by the modules which they manage.

Development Techniques
Significant quality improvements will be achieved by the careful selection of techniques used during software development which will help to prevent errors or to remove them effectively. For VME, the most significant techniques are:

* Use of a high-level language (known as S3) which incorporates basic validation facilities which will prevent certain classes of errors occurring in the source code.

* Use of a low-level design language (known as SDL) which is an algorithmic language providing for the localisation of data structures and managing the control of the links and consistency checks between modules.

* The establishment of an automatic set of tools to support development. For VME, a system has been established known as CADES (Computer Aided Design and Evaluation System) which supports SDL and provides rigorous configuration management of the software modules.

* The use of tracing and journalising techniques to provide an audit trail to assist the diagnosis of problems.

Standards
The use of acceptable standards allows for a common understanding of design, code and processes and has dual benefit to software development. Firstly, they prevent the introduction of a lot of errors and secondly, if errors do occur, they allow the faults to be detected more readily. For example, if a peer group all use a common standard, it may be more effective for the group to investigate and resolve a problem rather than leaving it to the original coder.

Formal languages are not used for high-level design but a well-structured set of design documents which conform to a set of standards and provide a clear mapping between the control documents can be very effective. Control documents managed in this way by VME are:-

- Market requirements
- Specification
- High-level design
- Low-level design
- Code narrative

Indeed, one of the arguments against introducing formal design languages is that the state of the art at present only provides for improving a few of the control documents whereas it is the integrity of the design throughout the whole of the development route that is important.

Considerable effort has been put into the establishment of external standards. For VME, the policy is to converge to the IEEE standards which allows the development route to benefit from external research and allows new recruits to relate their experiences more readily to VME.

Organisation
Management of processes is more effective if the organisation is made to fit the chosen development route and that clear responsibilities are established within the projects. One should not be afraid to experiment with organisational changes as a means of improving quality but this is one area where "what is good for the goose is good for the gander" may prove to be disastrously wrong. It is important that one recognises the psychology and culture of the teams before experimenting with organisational changes but the results can be very rewarding if an organisation is structured sensibly. The experiences of specific organisations within VME are as follows:

* Design authority - the design integrity within VME has been maintained by having an effective designer career structure which allows individuals to progress through the ranks to senior design positions. A design authority outside of the jurisdiction of the development projects has been established for VME since its inception. This authority is responsible for the VME architecture and for ensuring that design meets market requirements. Most of the individuals within the design authority have progressed from being low-level designers and implementors of the VME subsystems.

* Test authority - this is one area where there has been a lot of experiments on finding the best organisation for testing with varied degrees of success and failure. (see section on "unit test" later).

Testing Tools and Techniques

If an error is detected in a released version of the software, it may be fixed by the delivery of a code patch to the site which has encountered the problem. At the same time, the source of the code is amended with an architecturally acceptable solution for inclusion in the next release of the software.

For each incremental release of VME, specific emphasis is placed on non-regression testing to ensure that

* facilities released in earlier versions continue to work in each new version of the software
* problems fixed in the maintenance process by emergency patches are cleared permanently in the source code

The list of techniques described below apply both to new code testing and to non-regression testing. Because of the long life of VME development, not all code will have been subjected to all the techniques. It should be recognised that only a small percentage of code is changed with each incremental release and so each release has a legacy of extant undetected errors in the old code. Thus, an effective feedback machanism from the maintenance process is necessary to improve the quality of such code.

Design Reviews: Design reviews allow a peer assessment of whether a design meets a set of requirements. Such requirements are often not explicitly stated and the success of a design review is dependent upon the experience of the staff who take part. There is unlikely to be training in a design review process.

Design reviews have traditionally been an effective way of eliminating problems early in the development route. Acceptable quality control system standards demand a degree of formality in design reviews requiring minuted evidence together with an audit trail of the results of decisions made at such reviews.

Inspections: Formal Inspection is a technique which is aimed at finding errors in a document by comparing it with some higher level document. The technique was pioneered by Michael Fagan of IBM in the 1970s and the process has become known as "Fagan Inspections" [3].

For the technique to be most effective, there are two basic rules which must be satisfied:

* There must be a formal documentation structure which eases the mapping between the control documents for each of the phases of the

development route

* The procedural rules must be rigorously followed. It is very easy for a group of designers of high intellect to stray from the "boring" rules to the more interesting design debates but such indiscipline can ruin an inspection and jeopardise the quality of the product.

The VME experience of inspections began in about 1980 when a pilot study was carried out on a few subsystems to inspect code against the low-level design. This study demonstrated that inspections could eliminate 50% of coding errors before the test phase. However, over time, the effectiveness of code inspections has reduced. There are three reasons for this:

* Programmers get smarter! The inspection process allows programmers to identify classes of errors which can be prevented before code reaches the inspection stage by tightening up on the code standards.

* Rigour in following the processes decays with time. Continuous review of the effectiveness of the process is carried out through measurement and feedback.

* Lack of adequate training. The lack of training is also a reason for a breakdown in following the discipline of the process. All individuals involved in inspections should be <u>formally</u> trained in both theory and practice.

Almost "anything" can be inspected. The VME experience has been to extend inspections to the organisational interfaces where they are considered to be most effective. Specifically, inspecting specifications against market requirements brings about major improvements. Another area where inspections are of major benefit is by checking test cases against the design of the code.

Note that inspections are not a substitute for design reviews. Their purposes are totally different; inspections detect errors between two sets of documents whereas design reviews check out the integrity and validity of a design.

<u>Unit Test</u>: Unit test is defined to be a set of tests designed to find errors in a component (unit) of a system. For VME, the unit is a set of modules which are designed to meet a specific functional requirement. These modules are normally contained within a subsystem. Unit testing is usually a debugging activity.

The most important aspect of unit testing is that it is treated as seriously as software production. Tools and methods used for the design and development of test cases must be of an acceptable standard, equivalent to that of the tools and methods used for software development.

Unit test cases are normally developed from an intimate understanding of the design of the software and they are usually considered as "white box" tests. Some time ago, VME carried out an experiment to have separate organisations responsible for code production and unit test. The objective of the experiment was to ensure that testing was not sacrificed in order to maintain schedules. The results of the experiment were mixed:

* The objective as stated was met and one of the results of the experiment was the introduction of more formal testing techniques.

*   The effectiveness of the unit testing was reduced. This was due in part to the split responsibility which caused a degree of conflict and in part to the need to transfer the design experience to the tester.

The outcome of the experiment was to transfer the unit testing responsibility back to the development projects but to retain the more formal testing techniques which are checked for conformance by the quality assurance processes.

Some consideration has been given to the use of structured testing techniques for defining test cases but these have had limited success in improving the effectiveness of testing. The most important factors which produce effective unit tests are:

*   Acceptable standards for designing and producing test cases. The discipline of documenting test schedules and retaining test results for audit certainly focuses the mind!

*   Intimate knowledge of the design of the subsystem and its interfaces under test (gained by experience)

*   Inspections of test schedules against design.

One technique that is extensively used for unit testing is to provide a test bed on which to run the test cases. A test bed is a tool which simulates the target system environment for the subsystem. The main benefits of a test bed are:

*   The unit tester does not have to be concerned with the way the rest of the system works. The test bed can be set up so that no errors can occur except in the software under test.

*   The tests can be run in a more efficient manner as resources required by other parts of the system are not needed in a simulated environment.

*   Additional diagnostic aids can be built into the test bed.

Within VME, test beds are produced locally within the development projects for particular subsystems. Their most effective use has been with communications software which has benefited enormously from their introduction. It is possible to generate more general test beds for a number of different projects but some of the advantages may be less effective as a result. The cost of producing test beds should not be underestimated; the investment in the design and development of a test bed may be as high as that needed to initially develop the software but the returns on such investment can be very worthwhile for software which is enhanced and issued frequently.

System Test: System testing differs from unit testing in that it uses a "black box" approach by designing test cases from a product specification without the need to have an intimate understanding of the design. For VME, the experience is such that it is best to have a separate system test group from the development projects which takes unit-tested components and integrates them into a target system version.

Some of the techniques for system test are the same as for unit test. viz

*   Acceptable standards for designing and producing test cases
*   Programmer experience
*   Inspection of test cases against specification

The system testing activities carried out by VME serve three distinct purposes:

*   Debugging of new software (unit testing also serves this purpose)
*   Verification that the system is non-regressive against earlier versions
*   Verification that the new functionality works in the target system

Because of the nature of VME incremental releases, great emphasis is placed on ensuring that the versions are non-regressive against earlier versions. Two techniques are employed to improve the effectiveness of non-regression testing:

*   Automation of checking the results of test cases.

    When a test case is generated, its results are saved and subsequent runs will compare their results with those stored. Provided that there is a match of results, a "results file" is updated to indicate that the test has succeeded. If there is no match, diagnostics are generated to allow analysis to take place to determine the cause of the problem. Standard subroutines are called by the test cases to allow this process to be effective. In this way, the output only needs to be examined for failed tests and many hundreds of test cases can be run with minimal effort.

*   Enhancement of the test cases through the use of standards.

    As new test cases are generated (as a result of new facilities being incorporated into the system or as a result of a problem being detected after release and a source clearance being generated), they need to be captured in the "regression test suite". This is achieved by imposing standards on the way that test cases are generated.

Note that system testing is designed to validate all attributes of a system such as product installation, performance, maintainability, etc. Different techniques are used for specific attributes; for example, benchmarking is used extensively to demonstrate system performance.

System Trial: The nature and usage of the VME Operating System software is such that it needs to support a very large number of software and hardware configurations. The parameters that determine these configurations are:

*   the combinations of hardware and software components delivered by ICL
*   additional components supplied by third parties
*   customers own developments and applications
*   user data and filestore
*   time
*   user literacy
*   site procedures (eg housekeeping style)
*   combinations of work profiles

The challenge is to establish techniques which reduce the risks of errors caused by such a multitude of different configurations. The techniques employed by VME are as follows:

* Tight control of interfaces through a well-defined software architecture
* effective training in the use of the system
* System trials on internal systems to provide a degree of "random" system testing.

VME versions are produced by creating a series of internal increments. These increments are installed on a number of internal (non-customer) services to provide random system test. Specific services are:-

1. The VME development service. As a matter of policy, all VME increments are installed on the service which is used for the production of the VME code targetted for inclusion in subsequent increments.

2. Other ICL development services.

3. System Validation Services. Collaboration with major customers allows the generation of services which simulate these customers' anticipated usage. The customers provide workloads and databases which are used by ICL to destructively test the system by running it at its limits. Secondment of customer staff provides a degree of independence in designing suitable tests.

Concluding Remarks: The following points summarise the experiences of using problem identification and correction techniques for testing very large incrementally developed software systems:

* Select the right tools for the job and ensure that the tools in the set are complementary to each other.

* Invest in the development of testing techniques. Effective testing cannot be done on the cheap.

* Programmer experience and standards are the most effective means of improving the effectiveness of testing.

THE CASE STUDY

In the early 1980's, VME was a stable product, performing in line with the original design standards set for it and it had been available since the mid 1970's. A new series of processors, known as Series 39, was being developed to exploit the latest chip and fibre optic technologies and the corporate strategy was to port VME to the new range.

At the same time market requirements for operating systems were changing. Customers were demanding:

* increased reliability as businesses became more and more dependent upon computers
* more rapid resolution of problems to eliminate or minimise the impact of computer defects upon business performance
* improved facilities as the demands upon computer systems and the range of applications software in use became more sophisticated

The task facing ICL's software development engineers was therefore twofold:

* firstly, to modify VME to run on Series 39 so that existing users could purchase the new processor without having to change any of the existing applications programs;
* secondly, to build improvements into the modifications that would meet the more stringent requirements being demanded by customers and eliminate or reduce perceived current deficiencies.

During the 1970's, the VME development route had evolved into an effective tool kit for the production of software to meet the requirements of the time. However, the tools alone were no longer capable of meeting the demands of the 1980's and a new look at the processes and the management of them was required.

Initial Planning
Having identified the changes in requirement, the approach was to:

* size the problem
* identify the changes in the management and development processes needed to secure improvements
* establish objective measures to track progress
* identify, define and implement any necessary training requirements
* incorporate the lessons learned into standard working practice

The First Steps
An action plan was formulated to introduce both tactical and strategic changes to the development processes, with increasing emphasis on management control using quality techniques.

Gathering Pace
In parallel with the Action Plan, the investment approval criteria were modified to make quality standards an investment justification in their own right.

Investing in Quality: An explicit Quality Investment Case was formulated. Activities were concentrated in four main areas:

* The existing Software Quality Manual was completely re-worked. A working party was established to undertake this task, with representatives from each of the development teams. In addition to ensuring that proposed practices were workable and acceptable to each team, the composition of the working party ensured that ownership of the processes was held by those accountable for their implementation.

* A programme was put in place to accelerate the rate at which the design changes were made and thus reduce the number of patches awaiting clearance. At the same time, procedures were improved to guarantee that changes in the operating system design were made concurrently with the implementation of the temporary on-site solution.

* A more formal process of defect analysis was introduced to determine the underlying causes of product error detected by the customer. Early analyses identified a number of defects in the processes for

generating and testing on-site solutions (patches) to specific customer problems. A number of improvements to these processes were introduced to eliminate the defects. In the first year, the number of patches that failed to provide a solution first time decreased by a factor of four.

*   A field reliability improvement programme was introduced to: ensure accurate and timely feedback to the development teams on on-site performance; set improvement targets; and to take any action necessary to achieve the performance improvement targets set.

    Quality Training: To reinforce the product improvement programme, a complementary process of quality education was introduced. This was a company wide programme using a training package tailored by ICL for local needs.

    Effectiveness Measures: In parallel with the establishment of these initiatives, a series of new or revised measurements were introduced to track progress. Eight key complementary measures were used, based on customer performance priorities:

*   "Meantime Between Software Breaks (MTBSWB)" (Three measures for different ranges of processors). The elapsed calendar time between one fault occurring and the next

*   "Bug Backlog". The total number of customer-reported faults that remain unanswered

*   "Incident Rate". The total number of customer-reported faults per unit time

*   "Bug Factor". A measure of the responsiveness to customer-reported faults based on the degree of urgency indicated by the customer and the length of time taken to respond

*   "Repair Quality". The percentage of temporary solutions (patches) supplied to customers that work first time.

*   "Repair Count". The number of repairs for new product errors reported since the previous release of the product.

    Where applicable, each key measure was underpinned by a subset of measures appropriate to the responsibilities of individual development teams.

    Progress against the measures can be summarised by the chart below. Each parameter is compared against a datum measure of 100 at the start of 1986 and shows the values at the end of each year (cf FT index).

TABLE 1
Progress against quality measures - 1986 to 1988

Measure	1986 start	1986 end	1987 end	1988 end
MTBSWB 2900 systems	100	225	887	2005
MTBSWB Small series 39	100	203	1230	3530
MTBSWB Large series 39	100	752	4527	13853
Bug Backlog	100	113	553	818
Incident Rate	100	118	184	204
Bug Factor	100	123	296	444
Repair Quality	100	375	375	1000
Repair Count	100	439	659	989

Management Review: The management review processes were revisited and refined to give focus to the quality initiatives.

*   line management were involved at all stages of the process and were held accountable for successful implementation

*   targets were established for each unit

*   progress against both the key measures and unit targets was subject to regular management review at all levels in the company.

Maintaining Momentum
The initial successes were encouraging. Good progress had been made against the objectives set: field reliability had improved significantly; and the demand for on-site support had not increased in spite of a significant growth in the number of VME customers.

Sustaining Performance Improvement: The next challenge was to build on this success. New initiatives were taken to further improve customer support. Under the code-name PENTAGON, the overall objectives were to:

*   reduce the backlog of unanswered customer-reported faults by 60%.
*   reduce the period a fault remained unresolved.

* reduce the average bug factor per customer-reported fault by 60%.

The following results were achieved:

* the number of unanswered customer-reported faults reduced by 80%.
* there were no unresolved faults older than the target period.
* the average bug factor per unanswered customer-reported fault reduced by 65%.

Education and Awareness: The Quality Education System, was further extended to include training for all employees. The course introduced the concepts of the Quality Improvement Process. It was delivered in ten two-hour modules to classes of fifteen students over an elapsed period of ten weeks per class.

In addition, a series of seminars and workshops on measurement techniques were given by a leading expert in the field of software engineering. The content was specifically tailored to the needs of software development and built upon the measurement processes introduced as part of the quality improvement process.

Consolidation

Today, the VME improvement programme has been fully integrated into the Quality Improvement Process. The management of its future development has been built into the standard quality processes that are adopted throughout Mainframe Systems Division and the rest of ICL. All the key measures and targets set are still in place, with progressively more ambitious goals being set to reflect competitive levels of performance.

In addition, the mechanisms for identifying and resolving "roadblocks" to further improvement were progressively being implemented. A formal error identification and correction system was introduced, enabling development teams to initiate "Corrective Action Requests", a means of reporting actions needed that would improve process performance. Examples of the results achieved include:

* the introduction of a computer-based system to hold the quality control procedures. The benefits of the system are:-

- immediate access by all development staff
- latest information available in a more timely manner
- ability to locate procedures easily and effectively

* a revision of the planning procedures and tools. Better procedures have been introduced to improve the quality of plans; standard checklists are included to ensure that quality requirements are met; more accurate cost predictions can be made through the use of standard prediction models; measurements are incorporated to monitor progress; and computer-based tools have been introduced to improve the accuracy and efficiency of plans.

Summary

The improvements as a result of implementing the Quality Improvement Process can be summarised by the following measurements:

* A 40-fold improvement in the reliability as measured by the Meantime Between Software Breaks.

*   A four-fold reduction in customer reported defects against a background of an increasing customer base.

*   A four-fold improvement in the response time to customer reported defects.

CONCLUSIONS

Initially, the need for improving the quality of VME arose from the business requirements to allow ICL to deliver its new range of processors. Whilst the intellectual capability to solve quality problems had always existed, the focus on Quality management at all levels has ensured that quality will forever remain in the forefront of all the development activities. It has allowed the organisation to achieve levels of quality which, hitherto, would have been considered impossible for a project as complex and as large as a general purpose operating system.

Software engineers and managers now believe that they can ultimately produce error-free products which fully conform to customer requirements.

The processes established have provided a platform for continued improvement of the quality and customer satisfaction levels.

A Software Factory Strategy has evolved which will ensure that VME continues to be developed using the most advanced and effective state of the art quality oriented software engineering tools and methods. The objective of the strategy is to continue to improve both productivity and quality levels through a continuous programme of improvement in three key areas:

*   Awareness and Understanding: increased use of measurement and process modelling using the most advanced tools

*   Phase Automation: use of improved tools for all processes

*   Process Integration: computerisation of the process model to guarantee the integrity of the development route and to control its maintenance, evolution and improvement

REFERENCES

1. Basili, V.R. and Selby, R.W., Four Applications of a Software Data Collection and Analysis Methodology., Software System Design Methods., NATO ASI Series Volume F22

2. Gilb, T., Design by Objectives., Gilb-DBO-84

3. Fagan, M.E., Design and Code Inspections to Reduce Errors in Program Development, IBM Systems Journal, Vol. 15, No. 3, 1976

4. Parker, T.A., Trust in a Large General Purpose Operating System., Procedings of CSR Sixth Annual Conference

11

STRUCTURING TRUST IN A LARGE GENERAL PURPOSE OPERATING SYSTEM

T A PARKER
PRINCIPAL SECURITY CONSULTANT
ICL DEFENCE SYSTEMS, ESKDALE ROAD,
WINNERSH, WOKINGHAM, BERKS RG11 5TT

ABSTRACT

This paper describes the approach taken in ICL to
ameliorate the problem of evaluating the security
of a large operating system in which the number
of Trusted Computing Base and Trusted Process
code procedures is large enough to make
exhaustive detailed scrutinisation more than
exhausting. The approach is applicable to any
structured large general purpose system that
enables a convential TCB/ Trusted Process
architecture to be implemented, though it is
described in the paper with particular reference
to ICL's VME operating system.

INTRODUCTION

In a large and flexible general purpose system like ICL's Virtual
Machine Environment Operating System (VME) [1] [2] the size of the
Trusted Computing Base (TCB) and Trusted Processes is also large, and it
is an onerous task to analyse fully all of the security properties of
all of the code that needs some form of trust. This paper describes how
the task of analysing this code is made as easy as possible.

The ideas described here can be applied to any large general purpose
operating system aiming at a security quality equivalent to B1 or B2 on
the DoD scale [3], provided it has a structure that enables the
different responsibilities of the different parts of the system to be
clearly separated. The structure required is the conventional one of
protected TCB policing all accesses to protected objects from multiple
distinguishable processes as illustrated in Figure 1.

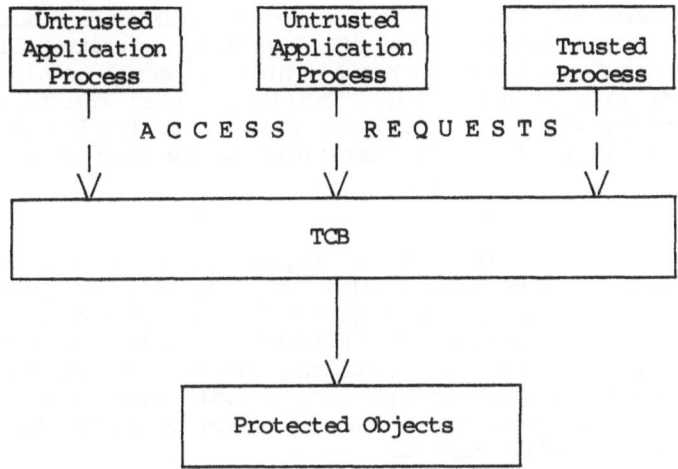

Figure 1. Conventional TCB Architecture - An Illustration

Even in level B3 or higher security systems the Trusted Process problem remains a thorny one, since formal proofs of trusted process security properties are notoriously difficult, and exhaustive scrutinisation is critically important; the fine grain attribution of trust described below would therefore be of value in improving its effectiveness.

The approach used is based on an extension of the simple white/black distinctions of 'trusted' - represented by the TCB and Trusted Processes, and 'untrusted' - represented by all other code. In the VME system a graded series of categories and types of trust are identified; this enables the task of examining the code in each code procedure to be confined to ensuring that the particular trust invested in that procedure is not betrayed. It will be seen later than this can often greatly simplify the examination process.

In the VME system the various trusts allocated to non-TCB code are formalised by markings, and each VME code library is marked with the type of trust that is invested in the modules (collections of procedures) in that library. These marks are used by the TCB code to allow or disallow the use of certain functions, each function representing either the breaking of a mandatory security policy rule, or the execution of some other security related action. Trust can be affected by the current process state; for example a particular trust is lost if any code not having that trust is loaded into the execution environment. Other factors can also affect trust, including the identity of the end user on whose behalf the process is executing; these are described in more detail in the appropriate section.

In VME, both security markings and integrity markings are supported as labels which control the operation of a mandatory security policy, but a sharp distinction must be drawn between high integrity or high security processes and trusted processes. The former obey the rules of the mandatory policy, the latter can make them and/or break them, but are trusted not to do so in a way that violates the true security of the system.

On a certified system, trust is not lightly given to a piece of code since any level of trust demands that the code be scrutinized in some way. If certification is not required (for example in a commercial system) or if further bespoke certification is to be undertaken, trust can be used more freely to extend the capabilities of installation written application code. Indeed, bespoke additional certification is only feasible if a proper trust identification mechanism is in place, supported by run-time TCB controls.

First however we briefly consider the TCB itself, and the next section describes how code within the TCB can be categorised to separate out the parts that are active in and therefore critical to security, from those parts that are passive and therefore less critical. This is conventional design technology required by the B2 criteria, but it is useful to compare and contrast with the trusted process structuring described in the rest of the paper. In these later sections, the different degrees of trust invested in the various trusted processes are described and justified. With one or two notable exceptions (detailed in a later section) these types of trust differ in nature from the distinctions within the TCB, since the trusted processes are policed by the TCB to execute within the confines of their allocated type of trust.

The Trusted Computing Base

The machine architecture within which VME executes has a hierarchic ring protection structure consisting of 16 Rings [4]. The VME TCB is defined to be all of the code running at or below Ring 5. In VME, this code is not one monolithic lump, but is highly structured into subsystems whose interfaces - with each other, and with non-TCB code - are tightly controlled by means of design rules supported by a set of automated development tools known collectively as CADES [5]. These are further supported at run time by hardware protection mechanisms. Each subsystem can be pictured as shown below:

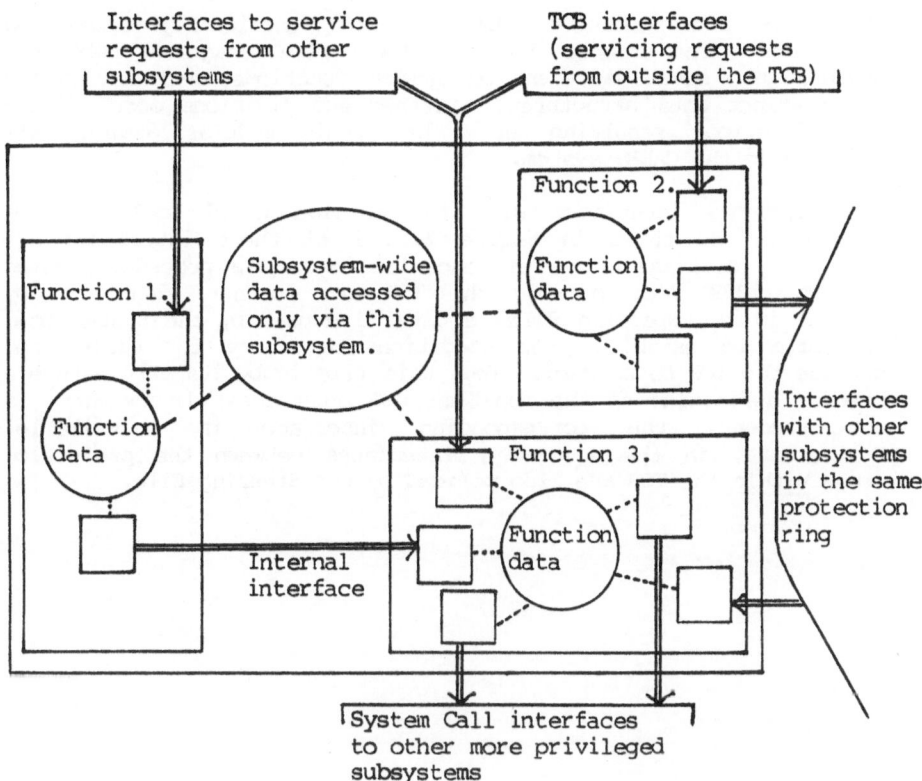

Figure 2. Structure of a VME TCB Subsystem

Figure 2 illustrates the following important points:

* Data is controlled entirely by the subsystem to which it belongs. It is not accessed by other subsystem code except via procedures in the owning subsystem, and then only rarely, since each subsystem is data driven by its own data.

* The internal multi-ring structure of the TCB further reduces the potential for one subsystem to corrupt the data of another. Each of the rings is protected from corruption from code executing in less privileged rings by run-time checks supported by basic hardware mechanisms.

* Subsystems are themselves divided into functionally orientated components. For example the block level file management subsystem divides into seven different management functions, each having its own distinct data structures. Further sub divisions occur within each function, resulting in a hierarchic modular design, all modelled in the CADES system.

* A subsystem's interfaces with the outside world world can be categorised as shown in Figure 2. All of these interfaces are defined by database cross-reference listings. The procedures which support calls from outside the TCB are further identified by entries in the Steering File, a data file used by the System Load subsystem to establish the conditions necessary for calls from outside the TCB to succeed. Thus this file is by its very nature a precise definition of the run-time TCB interfaces; if an entry is not present, the corresponding interface is unavailable. Furthermore, in the same way, interfaces between the protection rings <u>within</u> the TCB are also policed by the Steering File.

Classes of TCB Software

The structured nature of the TCB allows us to define a clear partitioning of the security responsibilities of its code procedures. This partitioning simplifies the scrutinisation process, by enabling it to concentrate only on those security attributes that are required for a procedure to fulfil its specific security responsibilites in the TCB.

The classes are shown below:

1. Procedures that are never executed in the version of the system being offered for certification. Examples of these might be procedures supporting the use of particular peripheral devices, or procedures supporting functions that are not to supporting functions that are not to be present in the evaluated system.

2. Procedures internal to the TCB that have no responsibility for nor influence on the handling of the model objects policed by the Mandatory Policy. Such procedures have a responsibility for not corrupting data which directs other procedures that have greater security responsibility. Denial of service should also be considered. An example of this kind of procedure might be one concerned with low level process scheduling.

3. Procedures internal to the TCB which either support accesses to the objects appearing in the security model or provide the infrastructure by means of which the objects themselves are defined and supported. These procedures must either be functionally correct, or any functional deficiences should not create a security compromise.

4. Procedures responsible for security checks and the implementation of security related functions. These procedures form a TCB subsystem of their own; we shall call it the Security Handler subsystem. The procedures of this subsystem are critical to the security of the system and will be required to pass the most stringent inspection.

5. Audit procedures which, although candidates for the previous section, would not directly cause a first order security violation if they were to fail functionally.

6. Procedures that can be called from outside the TCB. They must be resistant to malicious callers who may pass invalid parameter values or make calls in unusual circumstances with unusual parameter values. These procedures implement the TCB interface, and where appropriate should perform security checks by calling the Security Handler sub-system of the TCB. Four different subtypes can be identified; each requires a different evaluation approach:

* The interface relates to none of the actions defined in the security model (e.g. a procedure which replies to requests for current date and time).

* The interface is to a procedure which does its job within the context of a previously established access capability (e.g. block transfers from an already authorised filestore file.)

* The interface maps on to a subject-access-object action of the model (e.g. a procedure which deletes a file).

* The interface supports a trusted function of some kind, requiring the resultant action to be checked (via Security Handler), and audited.

TRUSTED PROCESSES

Many of the standard functions of VME, required in almost all processes are implemented via system code which runs at a less privileged Ring level than the TCB. Examples of these functions can be found in:

- The System Control Language Subsystem
- The Record Management Subsystem
- Parts of File Controller above Ring 5
- Parts of Name Handler above Ring 5.

In the great majority of processes, this code requires no special trust to operate successfully (ie. it obeys the security policy rules imposed by the TCB) and no evaluation of the code's security properties would on this basis be required. There is however a small number of special kinds of process which engage in system or security related activities; examples are the process which handles user authentication, the process which spools output, and high level scheduler processes. Such processes require the functionality offered by this non-TCB code, but also require to be trustworthy in some respect because of the nature of the job they are doing: they either break the rules in some way or are directly responsible for some security related activity. Such processes are known as "Trusted Processes"

The concept of 'breaking a security rule' needs to be clearly understood in the context of an operating system's mandatory security policy. The need to break such rules can arise from the way in which real world security requirements are imperfectly and over-cautiously reflected in the rules applied by the TCB. The major 'problem' rule is the *-property of Bell and LaPadula [6] which reflects the real world requirement that data from high security sources should not be output to low security sinks. Because the TCB is insufficiently sophisticated to monitor all data flows that might take place within the non-TCB code that it is policing, it imposes the crude but safe rule that no low security sinks (output channels) can be available to a process while high security sources of data are present. This rule is applied because unevaluated code cannot be trusted not to cause actual data flows which would violate the real world requirement. A Trusted Process on the other hand could be permitted to violate the TCB's rule provided that it was scrutinised to ensure that no actual data flow leakages take place.

Some of the code executing in a Trusted Process is clearly special to the kind of process it is and the job it is doing, and will never be executed (nor available) in normal user processes. For example the code directly concerned with the user authentication logic will appear only in the process(es) responsible for user authentication. This is in contrast to the code responsible for breaking down hierarchic object names into their elementary components for example, which is part of a service function used in every process.

Suppose the system were simply to treat all such code as "trusted" in the blanket sense that the TCB will allow it to break any of the rules whenever it wishes, or perform any security related operations it wishes, in the knowledge that the code would not take advantage of this freedom; such an approach would pose a heavy workload on the evaluators of the system since a potentially large amount of code is involved, and it must all be inspected in great detail since it has been granted wide powers.

The VME approach follows the principle of least privilege, in the sense that each individual trusted execution environment is allocated security privileges which are precisely enough for it to do its job and no more. This is done using the VME 'Trusts' system.

CATEGORIES OF TRUSTED PROCESS

The amount and nature of the trust required by the different Trusted Processes varies widely; different categories of trust can be defined and within these categories, types.

The first category of Trusted Process consists of those that are a direct part of the mechanisms supporting or enforcing the security rules of the system. These Trusted Processes could usefully be thought of as agents of or extensions of the TCB and we shall call them TCB-Processes. For example the user authentication process is part of the security enforcement mechanism: it enforces the authentication rules. The trusted functions of such a process cannot by their nature

be policed by the TCB proper, the TCB has not been designed to
understand user authentication. This is not to say that some of the
authentication logic does not run at or below Ring 5 - it does, but
these routines are slaves to the controlling authentication logic
outside the TCB.

The following are examples of TCB-Processes in VME:

> Login   (authenticates end users)
>
> Spooler (labels output)
>
> Security (establishes the security parameters of the system,
>   establishes user clearances and performs downgrade
>   and upgrade operations).
>
> Comms Network Controller (handles network connections)

The second category of trusted process consists of those that have no
direct concern with security but require to break the *-property rule
in some way in order to do their job. Such processes must be trusted
not to leak information through the write-down channels that are now
open to them. An example of such a trusted process is a Scheduler
process, which needs to acknowledge receipt of requests from processes
using its services. In order to be able to receive requests from
untrusted processes it needs to run at a high security level (otherwise
the sender might fail with a *-property violation); this means that
return acknowledgements will usually violate the *-property. No other
trusts are required and the *-property is to be permitted to be broken
in this manner only. In some trusted processes in this category the
risk of accidental leakage is negligibly small but the trusted code
must be evaluated to ensure that it does not maliciously cause
deliberate leakage. The scheduler processes are a good example of
this.

There are other types of second category process in which the risk of
accidental leakage is more significant because of the nature of the job
that the trusted process performs. An example of this is the Filestore
Management System (FMS) process, responsible for taking backup copies
of files, and restoring them. FMS works by merging the files to be
backed up into one large file. During file restoration, this file is
broken down into its component files, which may be of differing
security classifications. The "combine and split" approach of FMS is
possible only if the *-property can be violated. If FMS were to
confuse the component files a security leak might result.

Some TCB-processes may at times require also to break the *-property,
and in this respect belong to both categories. Risk level distinctions
can also be drawn between the different TCB processes.

TRUSTWORTHY ENTITIES

So far trusts have been described only in relation to software, their purpose being to define and control the parts of the system outside the TCB that require inspection by the evaluators. This is the fundamental function of the trusts approach, and controlled evaluation of the system critically depends on it.

There are however three other kinds of entity to which trusts can be applied:

- Human users (represented by VME usernames)

- User terminals

- Software environments

When applied to these entities, each trust can be viewed as a kind of security privilege, similar to a security clearance. Trusts when applied to users, realise in operating system terms the users' real world security rôles, rôles which do not relate to clearances but to security responsibility. One might be the ability to downgrade the security classification of an object. A user's clearance determines the limits of any downgrade capability he may possess but does not determine whether he possesses it or not. This will become clearer in the next section, where some other trusts of this kind are described, but first we shall see how the trusts associated with all of these entities are combined.

Typically a human user will log in at a particular terminal and a process will be made available for his use. This process will have associated with it a certain basic software environment which determines the facilities that can be made available in that process. In due course he may load software of his choosing, or it may be automatically loaded for him to execute in that process.

The number of trusts which is finally associated with the user's process is determined by taking the greatest lower bound of the trusts associated with the four components involved: the user, the terminal, the software environment, and any code subsequently loaded. Untrustworthiness is contagious; it infects everything it touches.

TYPES OF TRUST

Examples of a few of the many different trusts understood by VME's TCB
are given below. They are grouped together under the two categories
defined earlier.

First Category - Security Related Functions

CHANGE-PASSWORD

Allows the process to change personal security data such as the
authenticated user's own password.

CHECK-PASSWORDS

Allows the process to check the password of any user.

CONNECT-TO-DEVICE

Allows the process to connect directly to a device such as a VDU,
card reader or line printer. Having this trust allows direct
output of information to an output device or direct interception
of data from an input device.

DUMP-SUPERVISOR-TABLES

Allows the process to obtain diagnostic dumps of various Operating
System tables.

Second Category - Breaking the * Property

BROADCAST-MESSAGE

Allows the process to broadcast a message to other, possibly lower
security processes. This would normally only be given to a system
process acting for an Operator.

VOLUME-ACCESS-FOR-DISC-WRITE

Allows the process to connect to a whole disc volume for WRITE
access. This is needed for initialising discs or to support their
recovery from tape archives.

WRITE-DOWN

Allows the process to break the general mandatory policy rule that
does not permit high security information to be available while a
process has a low security output channel open to it.

TRUSTED PROCESS EVALUATION

In the preceding sections, using VME as an example we have described the basic principles underlying the ways in which trusts can be implemented in an operating system. This section goes into a little more detail, with the aim of showing how to identify the critical code procedures involved.

In VME a particular code procedure is deemed to possess a particular type of trust if it is loaded from a code library which is labelled with that trust. In this respect the Protection Ring in which the code will run is irrelevant (as long as it is outside the TCB limit of Ring 5). The critical factor is the library from which the code has been loaded.

The trusted libraries in early releases of the product are labelled with all of the trusts that the system supports, though later experience of use of the system will enable a finer grain allocation. A number of other libraries, in some cases very large ones indeed, are present on VME but are not trusted in any way. In practice, the least privileged Protection Ring in which this code would run would be Ring 10, but this is not significant. If it ran in Ring 6 it would gain no advantage from the point of view of the trusts system (or for that matter any mandatory policy controls).

Together, the trusted libraries contain a substantial amount of code, all of which is required in principle to be evaluated at least to a minimal extent. In the VME system there are two main techniques that can be applied to maximise the amount of code that requires minimal scrutinisation and minimise the amount that is required to be analysed in great detail:

Well Defined Execution Threads

Trusted code can only realise its trustworthiness if it excutes in a process which is associated with a VME software environment that also possesses the trust. On the version of the system to be evaluated in the UK, the only environments that possess any trust will be defined by ICL, and will impose strict controls over the level of functionality supported by the processes running in them. This means that the execution paths through the code loaded in such processes can in principle, though not necessarily very easily in practice, be determined by analysis.

Consequently substantial parts of the code in question are never executed in trusted environments, although they might have been loaded. This can exempt much of the code present in the trusted processes from detailed evaluation. Even when code does execute, it will be constrained in the trust that it possesses by the clearances limits imposed by the environment in which it runs.

Neither is the code that is actually executed subject to any stress from end-users. An attacker wishing to break into the system by finding and exploiting functional weaknesses in trusted processes has a very limited range of interfaces at his disposal and can execute no code of his own to help him in his task since this would cause the process to lose its trusted status. Contrast this with the resilience required of the TCB, which must be assumed to be subject to complex code driven attack over a wide variety of the complex interfaces it supports.

Particularly important in this context is the System Control Language (SCL) subsystem which provides a rich and complex language interface used by many processes including trusted ones, but which executes outside the TCB. Because it is used in a number of trusted environments the SCL subsystem must be trusted. The VME design confines trusted processes to the use of only a very few of the possible SCL capabilities. This greatly simplifies the analysis and test requirements since use of other linguistic constructs will always be untrusted, and potentially malicious end-users will be limited in the ways in which SCL in trusted mode can be stressed.

We have already said that it is only the code that is actually executed in the performance of the various functions that needs to be evaluated. However it is unrealistic to have units of trustworthiness smaller than a procedure, and if any code at all is executed within a procedure we should deem that procedure to be required to be evaluated as a whole.

Procedures in the trusted paths will often be quite general purpose, and often used in non-trusted environments with each of these procedures having many external references to other procedures. The procedures which satisfy these externals, and the procedures that in turn satisfy their externals (and so on) form a tree of potentially executable trusted code that at first sight appears to get very bushy, but as the diagram below illustrates, there are two factors which allow us to prune the tree:

- when Ring 5 or below is hit, we have reached the TCB

- we only need to consider external references that are actually followed on the trusted paths.

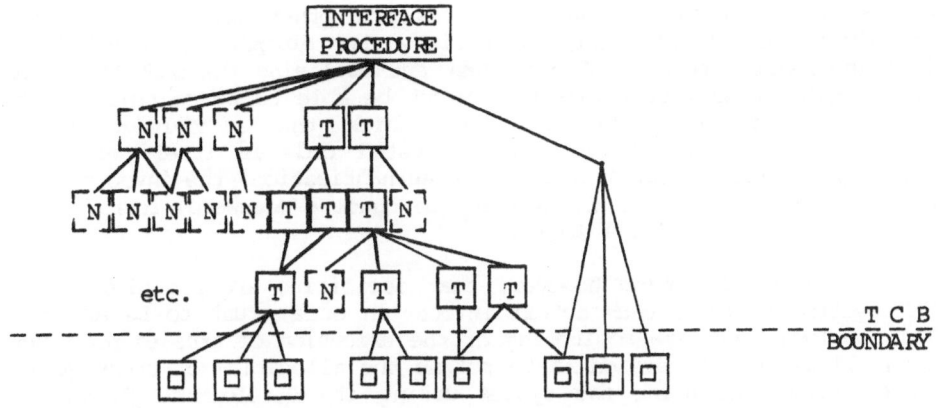

$\begin{bmatrix} N \end{bmatrix}$ = Not called on trusted path

$\boxed{T}$ = Needs to be evaluated

$\boxed{\square}$ = TCB procedure.

Figure 3. A Trusted Execution Tree.

In practice of course, the kind of tracing described here will be difficult to achieve, since actual execution paths can be distinguished from potential paths only by using intimate knowledge of the functional properties of all of the code involved. Construction of the main tree is however greatly aided by tools which are available to trace external references from named procedures.

Clearly Identifiable Trust Invocation Points

When a Trusted Process wishes to invoke a trust, it must do so by making use of one of a number of specific TCB interface procedures. It is this procedure which both makes sure that the process possesses the necessary trust, and if necessary audits the fact of the trust's invocation. The CADES system under which VME is developed has built into it facilities to list all of the procedures which call a nominated procedure. By nominating each of the trust support procedures we can find all the points in the trusted processes from which the actual trust is invoked. By examining the logic related to these invocation points it may often be possible to relegate other executed procedures to only a minor level of scrutinisation. For example when a Scheduler is acknowledging receipt of a request and utilising the SEND LOW CLASS TASK MESSAGE trust, scrutinisation might be able to be confined to the code local to the procedure from which the acknowledgement is triggered. Clearly however, when trusted code is itself executing security related functions (e.g. user authentication) the invocation of any specific trust (e.g. the ability to check a password) forms only a small part of the critical logic.

It is also worth noting however, that facilities are provided in the VME system to cause each actual invocation of a trust to be audited. This optional run-time monitoring of the execution of trusted processes both allows the ICL designers to refine the allocation of trust, based on experience of using the system during its development phase, and helps a live system's security manager to detect on a spot check basis any anomalous use of trust.

CONCLUSIONS

Not only is it possible to structure the TCB into separately identifiable components with different responsibilities, it is also possible to provide a fine grain categorisation of the different degrees of trust vested in the trusted processes. By identifying the points in the processes where trust is invoked, this categorisation can in many cases be used to structure the scrutinisation of the trusted processes themselves. This greatly reduces the size and complexity of the evaluation task.

ACKNOWLEDGEMENTS

The author is indebted to Allen Kitchenham and Dave McVitie of ICL whose original ideas and active involvement in detailed design have made this paper possible.

REFERENCES

1. VME/B. A Model for the Realisation of a Total System Concept, ICL Technical Journal, Vol. 2 Issue 2, 1980, B C Warboys.

2. VME Security Option Product Overview, ICL Internal Document.

3. Trusted Computer System Evalution Criteria, DoD CSC, Fort Meade, Md, August 1983.

4. Security in a Large General Purpose Operating System: ICL's Approach in VME, ICL Technical Journal Vol. 3 Issue 1, 1982.

5. CADES - Software Engineering in Practice, ICL Technical Journal Vol. 2 Issue 1, 1980.

6. Secure Computer System: Unified Exposition and Multics Interpretation, ESD-TR-75-306, Mitre Corporation report MTR-2997, January 1976, D E Bell and L J LaPadula.

12

SOFTWARE RE-ENGINEERING - AN INTERMEDIATE APPROACH

Richard H Warden BSc MIQA
Research Manager
K3 Group Limited
Great Britain

This paper describes an approach to re-engineering software based on the application of modern structured programming techniques. From a case history, the paper describes the steps of the re-engineering methodology, the tools that may be used and the types of problems which have to be solved. This form of re-engineering is considered to be an intermediate step in the goal to develop full reverse engineering methods. The understanding of the issues gained from commercial scale re-engineering can only contribute to the overall body of knowledge needed to solve the reverse engineering problems.

Richard Warden is currently the research manager for the K3 Group in Worcester. He has spent the last three years researching and developing methodologies, tools and techniques to address both the management and technical problems of software support and maintenance. These tools and techniques have been used in a wide range of field assignments.

1.0 INTRODUCTION

1.1 Context

This paper describes some of the practical software re-engineering work performed by the K3 Group. The re-engineering methodology described was designed to offer a practical solution to the needs of commercial software re-engineering projects.

Although the methododology used is based on structured design and programming principles, the paper does not seek to justify the methodology other than by commercial cost/benefit justification.

Therefore it is left to the reader to associate the findings from this work with theoretical descriptions of how re-engineering or reverse engineering may be accomplished.

The term 'methodology' is used as a generic name for all of the principles and methods required for a re-engineering project. It is beyond the scope of this paper to discuss the detailed design of the methodology. However important methods will be discussed.

1.2 Definitions

The terms reverse engineering and re-engineering are used freely today, often without any definition. Other terms such as inverse engineering, recycling and restructuring are also used. In this paper it is necessary to be precise in the use of these terms so that the work described here can be seen in its overall context.

Full reverse engineering is defined as the abstraction of a formal specification from code, from which forward implementation is performed into the required language and operating environment.

Re-engineering is defined as the use of structured design and programming principles to modify significantly existing code and data structures within the current language and operating environment. It, too, requires the generation of a specification, but not for re-implementation in a different environment.

1.3 Motives

The motives for re-engineering need to be considered. The main objective is to improve significantly a system's maintainability and extend software life. Within this objective there is a need to keep/re-use any code or data structures which are sound. This requires an intelligent and selective approach towards the task.

It should be noted that code of any age may be re-engineered.

1.4 Overview

This paper will use case history data to highlight the major _technical_ aspects of the K3 approach. There is a _business_ judgement area outside the scope of this paper covering the initial justification of a re-engineering project. In the case history this process was performed by K3 with the support of an expert system based tool developed for the analysis of software maintenance operations.

Therefore the rest of this paper will describe the K3 re-engineering method under the following headings:

- the case history
- the pilot project
- the main project
- the results
- conclusion

Although the paper focusses on technical aspects, the business justification must not be ignored. If re-engineering and reverse engineering are to become accepted techniques in industrial practice then they must be proven on cost/benefit grounds. Failure to do this will lead to these techniques becoming nothing more than interesting concepts to be pursued in academia.

2.0 THE CASE HISTORY

2.1 The project background

A financial services company had developed core systems in the early 1980s using, largely, non-structured techniques. The systems were implemented in COBOL on an IBM mainframe and had been significantly modified over their five year life. Following a take-over, the company had adopted a more aggressive business plan with high growth targets. This plan would mean significant changes to IT systems.

2.2 The problem

Certain areas of the systems were considered to be very difficult to maintain. It was accepted that in their current state they would not support the new business objectives which required significant changes. The long term aim is to redevelop these systems completely, but in the interim it was decided to re-engineer the the most unmaintainable parts.

About 10% of the code inventory of 400,000 lines was shortlisted initially for re-engineering. This represented about 40,000 lines of non commentary source code. Of this code 24,000 lines were procedural logic. The programs were a mixture of batch and screen based programs. The programs ranged in size between 1000 and 5000 lines of non-commentary procedure source code.

3.0 THE PILOT PROJECT

The first step of the re-engineering was to conduct a pilot project. This took about two months.

3.1 Purpose

The purpose of the pilot project was to:

- calibrate the estimating method

- identify re-engineering criteria

- identify tools requirements

3.2 How it was conducted

The pilot project was conducted in two phases. The first phase consisted of:

- manually re-engineering a program

- examining tools available for the client's environment, which led to the development of a procedure code analyser

The second phase consisted of:

- defining the criteria by which the re-engineering
  would be judged

- using the code analyser to analyse all the
  procedural code

- estimating the project using the above data

3.3 Estimation

In the case history it was estimated that it would take
approximately 65 man weeks to complete the project.   As
the project would re-engineer about 40,000 lines of code
this represents a re-engineering productivity of about
125 lines of code per man day.   It should be remembered
that not every line will be changed; indeed the project
will aim to keep/re-use sound code.

Estimating re-engineering work is difficult. There are
no accepted methods.   K3 used its own method which
looked at a number of key factors about each program.
They included:

- program length

- complexity

- status of specification

- severity of structural problems

- severity of control flow violations

- severity of data structure problems

The pilot program was used to calibrate the method for
this particular environment.   Clearly, the estimation
process requires a lot of judgement to take these
criteria and turn them into work estimates.

3.4 Re-engineering criteria

A key task was to set criteria by which re-engineered programs could be evaluated. From the manual re-engineering the following criteria were set, which included:

- achieve a procedural structure which has good factorisation and depth

- split large procedures to improve functional cohesion

- amalgamate arbritary procedures into in-line code

- remove unnecessary files

- remove data usage violations

- minimise access to file I/O sections

- minimise working storage duplication of data structures

- simplify complex control flows by removing knots and control flow violations

- remove redundant code

- make cosmetic changes, e.g. standardise data names and improve code layout

- maintain original performance

Each of these criteria can be defined in more detail. For example in checking for control flow violations it was necessary to include site programming standards such as, no PERFORMs of paragraphs, and no jumps out of PERFORMed code.

3.5 Tools requirements

The mainframe environment already supported a passive data dictionary which provided static data usage information. To help analyse procedural code, an existing static code analyser was modified for this project.

The analyser was run on a PC. Source files were downloaded to the PC via a terminal emulation program.

The analyser had a number of features not usually found
in commercially available COBOL analysers:

- it used true graphics techniques to produce good
  graphical representation of program structure and
  control flow complexity; these displays could be
  edited interactively and printed

- it could check for possible recursion

- it could analyse programs larger than 10,000
  lines with a 640K RAM PC; PC based analyser are
  often only guaranteed to analyse small programs
  of 1000 lines

- it could handle incomplete procedure code, i.e.
  unexpanded source files, a useful facility if
  copy libraries only contain small, common
  routines

This analyser was developed by K3 specifically for
re-engineering work due to the limitations found with
commercially avalilable tools.

4.0 THE MAIN PROJECT

4.1 The processes

The main project involved performing the same processes on each of the program units selected. These processes were:

- updating the specification

- analysis and production of a re-engineering specification

- cosmetic re-engineering

- structural re-engineering

- testing and acceptance

The following descriptions will concentrate on the re-engineering processes.

4.2 Updating the specifications

The original specifications had been largely paper based, and contained many unincorporated change documents. Therefore revised specifications were written and stored on computer media. These documents provided functional descriptions of programs which were the basis for program validation. The majority of this work had to be performed manually although some data from the code analyser was incorporated. This phase took 22% of the time.

4.3 Analysis and production of re-engineering specifications

Each program was analysed against the re-engineering criteria to produce a list of re-engineering changes. This list was reviewed with the client, and the final re-engineering specification was agreed.

Although many programs required a common set of changes, there was significant individual work required for each one. This indicates that re-engineering cannot easily be automated. This phase took 16% of the total effort.

4.4 Cosmetic re-engineering

Cosmetic re-engineering was performed on the programs. Work included:

- prefixing of data names

- reordering of data names

- addition of section summary descriptions

- insertion of called and calling data

- 'beautification' of code

Cosmetic re-engineering on its own goes some way to improving code understandability. This phase took about 5% of the total effort.

4.5 Structural re-engineering

Structural re-engineering involved the major improvement work done to both data and procedural code. The re-engineering criteria described earlier are put into practice. Clearly this is a skilled task and one which is very difficult to automate in any way. It took some 30% of the total effort.

At any time during the re-engineering the programmer could analyse the current version of a program, check various metrics and look at the current procedural and control flow structures.

The work of this phase is best illustrated by describing some of the problem types found and solved. However one general conclusion was that very often the lowest level of processing code was sound. The actual processing of a transaction was correct. The real problems were more concerned with poor design structure and data usage which made the programs difficult to understand and maintain.

The following are some examples of the problems which had to be addressed.

4.5.1 Excessive fan-out

Some programs displayed high fan-out, with one example expanding from 5 to 46 sections over one logical level of its structure chart. Investigation revealed that there were no transaction centres involved. Instead there were many small, singularly accessed sections which could be incorporated as in-line code.

4.5.2 Recursion

The code analsyer identified recursion between PERFORMs of sections. This is meant to be illegal in COBOL. As the code was written, it was not thought that the right conditions could occur for recursive paths to be executed. However, pity the poor support programmer who may have to understand and modify these structures, and ensure that recursion still cannot happen.

4.5.3 Multiple data structures

Apart from problems with procedural code, it was necessary to deal with a data related problem which had a large, negative impact on program maintainability. Over time, many working storage copies of record structures had been declared for new processing requirements. This appeared to be defensive programming. Rather than use existing working storage records, new copies were created. This saved having to understand how existing record structures were used, but meant that it became increasingly difficult to understand data usage in these programs due to the multiplicity of data.

4.5.4 Unwanted files

Another type of design problem was the use of temporary run-time files to store relatively small amounts of data from intermediate calculations. This required additional I/O and JCL code and gave another source of error for run time failure. These files were replaced by internal tables.

4.5.5 Poor factorisation and cohesion

Poor factorisation and cohesion was found in two forms.

Some sections were found which contained significant control logic mixed with processing code. Often these sections were quite deep in the logical structure of the programs.

Other sections were found to be very large, perhaps 33% of a program, and contain > 50% of all predicates. These were amorphous control sections which had grown over time and did many things.

The solution to these problems was the intelligent
re-design of the program structure so that there are
higher level controlling sections with well defined
functions, and lower level processing sections.

4.5.6 Logic splitting

Logic splitting was found in a number of programs. This
tended to be concerned with error handling. For
example, after I/O a common status routine would be
called, and if an I/O error had ocurred the program
would terminate in this routine. This meant that the
error was not handled in the context of the process
which had requested I/O. Instead, status checks were
made at the process level, so that errors could be
reported in their context. The result of these changes
increased the McCabe complexity.

4.6 Testing and acceptance

This phase took 15% of the total effort. Validation of
the re-engineered code was performed by parallel running
them against the original versions. For batch programs
these runs could take advantage of existing test sets.
However for the screen programs the problem was more
difficult. An automated screen testing product was
evaluated at this phase. However, some of the screen
programs had been changed from field to full screen
validation in the re-engineering. Whilst the underlying
program functions were unchanged, the changes to the
screen response sequences made the use of an automated
tool difficult.

5.0 THE RESULTS

5.1 Introduction

It can now be examined as to whether the initial justification to re-engineer has been supported by the results of the project by looking at costs, benefits and other findings.

5.2 Costs

The cost of re-engineering the code varied from one program to another, but were in the £1.50 to £3.00 per line range. The actual productivity achieved was about 100 lines of data/procedural code per man day, some 20% less than the estimate. Although 20% is not a dramatic difference compared with some software estimating, it is necessary to know where the estimation went wrong. There were two main reasons:

- it took longer to revise the specifications than estimated

- the productivity associated with deep re-structuring was lower than anticipated

An additional cost item was 25 man days spent modifying and running the code analyser for this work. However, to have manually generated the code analyser information would have taken over 100 man days.

An alternative to re-engineering is a complete re-write, or full reverse engineering. However it is difficult to re-write part of a system when it has to fit in with overall system restraints. The major benefits come from an entire system re-write. Clearly this would be a very much more expensive option.

5.3 The benefits in detail

Quantitative benefits were measured. For example:

- individual programs reduced in size by a few percent to up to 30%

- control flow violations were removed

- recursion was removed

- the McCabe measure was reduced by up to 28%, indicating the removal of unnecessary predicates

- structure diagrams showed the simplification of program structures, e.g. reduction in multiple links to I/O sections by up to 40%, or the reduction of excessive fan out

- control flow displays showed the improved flow in controlling routines, e.g. removal of backward jumps in a section so that processing was sequentially down the code

- program performance was improved by up to 15%

Some important qualitative benefits were also recorded:

- few programs had had good specifications; now they all have, with additional data from the code analyser that has not been available before

- the standardisation of data, section and paragraph naming conventions has greatly improved the readability of the code

5.5 The benefits generally

The overall subjective comment is that where these programs were once very difficult and costly to maintain, they are now straightforward to maintain.

This particular case history has been reported a feature article in the computer press (Computer Weekly 29 June 1989). The company concerned has recorded a doubling of maintenance productivity on the re-engineered code.

This is a very important result as it indicates that re-engineering can produce valuable benefits for commercial scale systems. If IT users can be convinced that software re-engineering is worthwile, then this paves the way for the introduction of reverse engineering.

5.5 Some other findings

Here is a summary of other findings:

- the pilot project should include at least two programs to improve the basis for estimation

- the cosmetic re-engineering should be performed before the main analysis which determines the re-engineering specification

- it would be significantly more difficult to perform re-engineering without tool support

- the McCabe measure showed a remarkable correlation with program length, and was not considered very useful; its main help was as a basic measure of testability

K3 had previously had code processed through a leading code re-structuriser to determine how such a tool could help with this project. The code re-structuriser would not have helped for several significant reasons:

- some of the constructs it produced were considered significantly less maintainable than the original code

- the tool only addressed a small subset of re-engineering problems as it had no concept of structured design (as opposed to structured programming)

- the tool caused code expansion of 40% in the trial, whereas a code size reduction was measured in this project

Although these findings relate to a specific tool, they do show that a relatively simple application of restructuring algorithms, based on structured programming (not structured design) principles, ignores significant problem types and are very likely to produce less maintainable code.

Code restructuring tools raise a deeper question. If it has not been possible to automate the software design process in the development phase, is it possible to automate a re-design process in re-engineering? Both tasks appear to be knowledge-based tasks of a complexity level which has not been automated.

6.0 Conclusion

One of the major problems associated with full reverse engineering is that of dealing with arbitrary or problem design structures. Design problems may be either in the procedural code or the data structures.

If the current design of the code and data addressed in this project had simply been reverse engineered into some higher level description, then many of the design shortcomings would be present in a forward implementation into a new environment.

This problem becomes more severe as the scope of reverse engineering is widened. If an objective is to reverse engineer an entire large scale system, then any approach, manual or automatic, must be capable of analysing the architecture of the system as well as sub-system or program design.

There is a limit to the application of manual techniques to very large systems. This dictates a tool supported approach which may have a mechanistic front end, i.e. one based on code and data analysis, but after that there need to be intelligent tools.

To develop such an approach is clearly a very significant task. However, by performing re-engineering projects of the type described here, it may be possible to build a set of knowledge which may be the starting point for an intelligent knowledge-based approach to reverse engineering.

13

THE MAINTENANCE OF LARGE, REAL-TIME EMBEDDED SYSTEMS FROM THE PERSPECTIVE OF KNOWLEDGE ENGINEERING

KEVIN J PULFORD
GEC-Marconi Software Systems
Elstree Way, Borehamwood, Herts, WD6 1RX, UK.

ABSTRACT

Looking at the process of maintenance from the perspective of knowledge engineering can lead to useful insights. A generalisation and extension of work carried out in applying knowledge engineering to maintenance and Software Engineering for real-time embedded systems are discussed. Support for maintenance is discussed including recent research results and areas for further extension are identified.

INTRODUCTION

This paper looks at the maintenance process from the perspective of knowledge engineering. The ideas in this paper are based on work carried out within the ALVEY SOCRATES project to implement a Software Diagnostic Aid for a large real-time embedded system and in the ESPRIT ASPIS project building knowledge based CASE tools. Looking at the maintenance process from the knowledge engineering viewpoint gave us new insights into how it worked and how knowledge based systems could support maintenance. This paper contains an extension and widening of scope of the original ideas to examine the process in general, the sorts of knowledge used and the possibilities of extending tool support.

267

In the next section we give some background to the nature of maintenance of large real-time embedded systems. This is followed by an interpretation of the maintenance process from the perspective of knowledge engineering. We then look at the techniques used at the moment to support maintenance and how these are seen in the context of knowledge engineering, with a look at recent research and how this fits in with the knowledge engineering. Finally some pointers are given where futher developments would be promising.

BACKGROUND TO THE MAINTENANCE OF LARGE REAL-TIME EMBEDDED SYSTEMS

Large real-time embedded systems are characterised by being complex and requiring large teams for their development. An embedded system project often involves the development of new hardware as well as software. This leads to the sorts of problem of ensuring that in building a piece of equipment that the design of the software must match the version of the hardware - this is not always as trivial as it seems and allows great scope for error if not controlled.

The customer for embedded systems demands a quality system. In the sorts of environments that embedded systems are used system failure and the failure to return the system to operation can be acutely embarrassing if not fatal. Also such systems can have a field life of 15 years or more. Part of the quality requirement is to ensure that the system can be maintained if necessary by someone other than the original system builder. A large part of the quality aspects is ensuring proper and adaquate design documentation. In the discussion which follows this is assumed to be available. Because of the complexity of such systems and the need for adaquate documentation the volume of the documentation is vast and can take up many feet of shelf space.

One of the complications of real-time systems is the need to split functions into several ports and execute them separately because of the need to execute several functions at once. The use of a multi-programming executive may be ruled out because of the safety critical nature of the application.

The process of software maintenance consists of three main types of activities:

   i) Fault report clearance

   ii) Upgrades to take into account changes of hardware

   iii) Upgrades to extend system functionality

Fault report clearance involves the diagnosis of faults when the system does not perform to specification and the generation of repairs to correct the behaviour of the system. However, it is often the case that queries relating to bugs are about combinations of circumstances which are not covered in the requirement specification but for which the customer believes the systems response is not appropriate. In this case the appropriate changes to the requirement will need to be decided with the customer and system engineer.

We have identified three main steps in the maintenance cycle. These tend to be similar across the types of activity identified above. The steps are:

   i) Modify requirement; to determine how the requirement needs to be change if at all.

   ii) Develop the modified design; to make the system conform to the revised requirement.

   iii) Test the modified system; to verify the system now runs according to the revised requirement.

In the Modify Requirement step for a fault report clearance it first must be established that the fault report indicates a deviation from the requirements. Sometimes this is obvious but often, and especially on large systems, the bug report may relate to behaviour under a combination of circumstances not covered in the requirement specification. In this case the behaviour that is required in these circumstances must be discussed with the system engineer or the customer. To support this discussion the maintenance engineer may well have to extract details of the behaviour of the system relevant to the fault to supplement that given in the specification and which gives a wider and more general view of the behaviour. The engineer may well go down to the code to ensure that the behaviour is implemented exactly as in the design document. During this process the engineer must be able to relate the design and code to the behaviour of the system. Once a modification has been agreed the engineer needs to ensure that the modified behaviour of the system does not have any adverse consequences when it is placed in its operating environment. This means a much more extensive search of behaviour of interacting facilities than in the fault report and also needs experience of the way facilities can and will interact.

In the design modification step the engineer will need to identify the mechanisms within the system which are associated with the changes in the modified requirement and then develop a modification of them. During this process the engineer will need to understand the relationship between the requirement and the design. In the fault report case the engineer seeks to isolate the mechanisms which have deviated from the original specification. Part of this process in the case of embedded systems is to decide whether the hardware or software is at fault. The next stage is to understand the mechanism that needs to be modified. This will involve extracting the relevant pieces of information from the documentation. A mechanism is an abstraction from the design representing the sequence of operations to implement the behaviour of a facility. Mechanisms are simple enough for the engineer to reason about and develop modifications of the mechansim to adjust the behaviour to match the modified specification. In level of abstraction they are mid-way between code and system level and so that once the modification has been developed in terms of the mechanism it can easily be translated to a code design change.

Following this he will check for interactions with other parts of the system to ensure that the modification does not cause any adverse affects.

Often there is a pause in the middle of this activity while it is decided when to implement the modification and if there are any go-arounds that can be issued. If the software is part of an embedded system which is being produced in any quantity then a decision has to be made on which production batch to start including the modified system and whether to issue upgrade kits for systems already delivered into the field.

The final step is to test the system and check the results against the expected results. Usually there are sets of tests used during the development phase and it is merely necessary to extend these to cover the modified system. If the modification is small the engineer may elect to run only a sub-set of the tests. This will be determined by the criticality of the system and the ease with which it is possible to isolate the required tests.

Part of the nature of the maintenance process is that it is needed only occasionally. Only sporadically do bugs need fixing or new features need to be added to the system for example during mid-life updates or to respond to new military threats. This means that the staff used to maintain the system are sporadically required to work on the system. Over a period of time the details of how and why a system was implemented tends to fade from the mind or an engineer may leave or be transfered thus necessitating using different engineers. An important element of the maintenance process is the need for engineers to learn or refresh their memories of the design of the system. One of the problems associated with large systems that makes this very difficult is the size and complexity of the documentation.

KNOWLEDGE USED IN MAINTENANCE

In general the sorts of knowledge required for software maintenance are similar to that required for the development process. The maintenance engineer will need background knowledge in software techniques such as coding strategies, computer languages, design methods, testing strategies, software aspects of driving hardware, operating systems and many others. In addition it is helpful if the engineer has some broad understanding of the sorts of system he is working on and its intended to uses. For example, if he is to work on Radar Software then he needs to know in outline how radars work and what they are used for. However, he need not know the details of radar and microwave engineering nor have any deep understanding of the Radar Equation.

Within the system specific knowledge used by the engineer two broad categories of knowledge which the engineer seems to use independently. These are

a) Application knowledge which is abstract knowledge about the application which the engineer uses to develop and modify system designs and diagnose faults in them.

b) Executive knowledge which is pragmatic knowledge about the mechanics of how to develop a working system. This includes things like how to use compilers, editors and similar tools, testing strategies, documentation standards, configuration management and similar project procedures.

The engineer uses this knowledge in two ways. Firstly he uses it to understand the information he recieves about the system and the way it was developed. That is he relates it to his background knowledge and identifies instances of concepts he has encountered before and also has rules for reasoning about them. Secondly he uses it to develop modifications to the system and diagnose and clear faults.

In maintenance process itself we identified four frequently occuring activities. These are:

i) Diagnosis: Locating faults which we observed require knowledge of the relationship of symptoms to faults and utilised some of the following activities.

ii) Abstraction: abstracting information about the system and building this into a model of the mechanism of the aspect of the system being investigated. These models helps the engineer reason about the system. The engineer builds a model that relates both to the system level and to the lower levels of the design so that he can reason at the system level but also relate this to the lower levels. The type of model built will depend on the aspect of the system the engineer needs to reason about. For example, if the engineer needs to reason about the way a function is calculated he will not necessarily be worried about timing considerations.

iii) Manipulation: Manipulating the model developed during abstraction to produce a modified model that reflects the revised specification. Here the relationship of the model to the system specification is important and the type of model must be such that it suitably reflects the type of change to the specification. For example, a change in the way of calculating a function would need a function model. Another need is to relate the modified model back to the design so as to develop a modified design and thence modified code.

iv) Checking: Once a modification has been formulated it needs to be checked to ensure that it does not interfer with other parts of the system. This may involve building other types of models relating to other aspects of the system using abstraction. The engineer also uses knowledge based of experience of the possible ways that system components interact to decide on the sorts of searches he needs to undertake and hence the models he needs to build.

An important idea that has come out of the application of knowledge engineering to software engineering is the idea of programming plans [7,8]. A programming plan is a procedure or strategy for realising intentions in code. It has been observed that engineers make extensive use of mental strategies based on experience rather than each time building code afresh out of the primitives constructs of the programming language. The engineer also uses programming plans to understand a section of code or part of a design by comparing what he expects as an implementation of a requirement from his programming plans and what is actually given in the design. It is feasible that programming plans can be used at higher levels of abstraction and by extension to building mechanism models. It is quite possible that there are additional programming plans for the construction of mechanism models. However, the author is not aware of any work in this direction.

EXISTING SOLUTIONS

Having looked at the sort of knowledge needed in maintenance and the way it is used we now look at the support that is currently available within maintenance projects.

Maintenance engineers are expected to join projects with sufficient background knowledge. If not then they have to rely on courses and textbooks to bridge the gap. Project specific knowledge is incorporated into project documentation. Executive knowledge is encapsulated in the project procedures manual and is usually sufficiently stlylised to make it easy to pick up. The use of individual tools can be picked up from the vendors user manuals. However, the new engineer will need to find out the style with which the project employs the tools and the places that files are held within the development system.

Information on the system design is put in the system design document. The content of such documents is defined in the project procedures such as JSP188 [9] which prescribes the content and notations to be used on the project and which the system purchaser imposes on the system builder as being the information necessary to support the maintenance of their system. From the Knowledge Engineering point of view this is like specifying a knowledge representation in which the sorts of concepts and relationships between concepts that must be identified for the system are layed down. The objective of such standards is that they aim at ensuring that in some sense the design documentation is complete and will contain all the information the maintenance engineer is likely to need.

Another aspect of the projects procedures is that they also should ensure a certain commonality of style of documentation and approach. Without such procedures the many people on the project would each produce different styles of documentation. A consistent style is important from the maintainer's point of view since it means that once he has understood one part of the documentation he can use the knowledge of the structure of this and its assumptions when he inspects in other parts.

Specific design methods will usually have one or more special notation associated with them. The advantage of such notations is that they formalise certain aspects of the design and aid reasoning about these aspects. For example, data flow diagrams formalise the data flow in a system. These notations help build mechanism models as long as the model uses the aspect related to the notation. Thus when selecting a design notation or method the engineer tries to select the one that reflects the predominent reasoning model for the type of system being developed. For example, in its simplest terms this might involve deciding between control flow or data flow notations.

The structuring of code is an important aid to understanding since it limits the number of constructs and complexity of the code, and restricts the extent of side-effects. This aids the understanding of the code since it is easier to indentify which plans are being used and also make it easier to check for interactions.

One of the more useful tools in maintenance is the code cross reference. Its immediate use is in checking interactions, for example, checking if a variable is set or read where the engineer expects it to be but it can also be of help in understanding the code as well.

FUTURE SOLUTIONS

The previous sections have shown what the maintenance process looks like from the knowledge engineering perspective. In this section we indicate where we believe tool support might be added and report on some work and how it fits our picture of the maintenance process.

One of the perenial problems in maintenance is the need for engineers to build up or refresh their knowledge of a system. One promising approach that has been investigated is the use of hypertext [2]. This is a data storeage system with a flexible retrieval and navigation user interface based on windows.

With hypertext it is possible to set up links between items in one window to items in another. By typing the links one can get a variety of information on an item. In the context of understanding the design of a system, items can be data or procedures in the code and tasks or modules in the design. One of the advantages of hypertext is that the links can form a network so that the user is free to explore in any direction he desires and is not fixed by the order of the text on a page. A study has been made of the application of hypertext to maintenance by the University of Durham [3] and we have made a study at MSWS for use in the European Fighter Aircraft [4]. So far we have not come across any reports of hypertext in use in maintenance but it is really only a question of time.

One of the areas that has received a lot of interest is the area of debugging or problem identification. Seviora [1] contains a review of a range of techniques and identifies three basic approaches.

i)   Program analysis which compares a program with its specification.

ii) I/O based which compares the actual output with the expected output.

iii) Internal trace which monitors internal events inside a running programme and compares this to a specification of the required behaviour.

The program analysis approach relies heavily on programming plans. Proust [7] is a sucessful example of this type of approach. It works from a specification of the system in terms of a number of goals and uses its knowledge base of plans to synthesis possible solutions and tries to match these to the program code. When Proust fails to match it assumes there is a program error and attempts to isolate it. Proust has only reported to have been used on small classroom examples. If it were to be used on larger problems it would need some mechanism to deal with the much larger size of knowledge base needed. One solution from existing practice would be to use a hierarchical set of levels of abstraction. This, of course, would also need a corresponding multi-level specification.

An example of an internal trace approach is the Message Trace Analyser [10]. This system relies on monitoring interprocess messages and relating these to a specification of the expected behaviour of the system as expressed in a finite state machine. This is equivalent to building a mechanism model and relating this to the monitored output from the system. The main sort of mission that the Message Trace Analyser was designed for is the analysis of large amounts of monitoring data where an actual fault is only a rare occurance, such as in telephone exchanges.

The OSIRIS system [5] developed within the SOCRATES project is an example of an I/O based system. OSIRIS captures the engineers knowledge of the way that symptoms are related to characteristics within the code. So that given a set of symptoms OSIRIS will propose a number of characteristics to be searched for in the system code. OSIRIS can then execute the search, taking into account the areas of code that would have been active when the suspected fault was observed to occur. These code searches are general purpose and thus have been found to be useful in other parts of the maintenance and development processors. OSIRIS uses the system code for searches supported by knowledge of the way the code is structured and related to system modes.

The I/O based and internal trace methods are obviously only applicable directly to the diagnosis activity. However, there are part of these systems which are more generally applicable. In the OSIRIS system the code searches have been found to be useful in identifying interactions within the code and isolating areas of code associated with a particular facility or function.

To handle system upgrades and identify the areas of design that need modifying an approach nearer to the analysis approach will need to be used. As noted above the analysis approach has only been used so far on small classroom examples. To extend it to handle larger systems it will be necessary to handle a hierarchy of levels of abstraction. Another generalisation that would be needed is in the area of mechanism modelling. An engineer will use different models depending on the aspects of the system he is considering at the time. Program documentation usually contains only a limited range of mechanism model at ony one level of abstraction so the engineer cannot rely on the documentation to supply the sort of model he needs. There is a requirement to support the building of models of a type different from that supplied in the system documentation. There is a need for futher research into the sorts of mechanism models engineers use and how they can be derived from typical system documentation.

CONCLUSIONS

We have seen by using the perspective of knowledge engineering how important the transfer of information from the development process to maintenance. This must also be matched by the ease with which the maintenance engineer can absorb the information inherited from the development. What the research into knowledge based tools should give us is a better idea of the sorts of information an engineer needs for maintaining a system and how he uses that information. This sort of knowledge should help us to improve the way we document our systems to make the task of the maintenance engineer easier and more efficient. We have pointed out several research projects in this area which have contributed to our knowlege. However, our knowledge is still incomplete and we need further research to fill in the gaps.

These research projects have also been useful in developing tools to support the maintenance process. Again there is a need to extend the coverage and several areas have been indicated in this paper. However, one problem with these systems is the size of the knowledge bases required to support them. Further research might indicate how they can be structured to get around these problems.

Overall, from our experiences of using Knowledge Engineering techniques to maintenance, we found that it has given us new and powerful insights into how engineers conceive and reason about systems. These insights are sharpened and are made more pragmatic by the need to build systems that work and can demomstrate useful functionality. We feel that there is much more to discover in this area and that knowledge engineering has a lot more to contribute in the making of these discoveries.

REFERENCES

1. Seroira, R.E., Knowledge-Based Programme Debugging Systems, IEEE Software May 1987.

2. Fidero, J., A Grand Vision, BYTE October 1988.

3. Fletton, N., Redocumenting Software Systems, Proceedings of the Second Software Maintenance Workshop 1988. University of Durham, Centre for Software Maintenance.

4. Carruthers, D., Application of Hypercode - A Hypertext Tool to EFA RDP Software Development, Internal report of Marconi Software Systems ref. MSWS/EFE/-/M/0030.

5. Williams, W., The OSIRIS Application System, SOCRATES Final Project Report GEC-Marconi Research Chelmsford.

6. The STARTS Guide. 2nd Edition National Computing Centre 1987.

7. Johnson, W.L., and Soloway, E., Proust: Knowledge-Based Program Understanding, IEEE Trans Soft Eng Vol se-11 No 3 Mar 1985

8. Williams, R.C., The Programmer's Apprentice: Knowledge-Based Program Editing, IEEE Trans Soft Eng Vol SE-8 No 1 Jan 1982.

9. JSP 188 SPECIFICATION FOR TECHNICAL PUBLICATIONS FOR THE SERVICE Documentation of Software in Military Operational Systems UK MOD.

10. Gupta, N.K. and Seviora, R.E. An Expert System Approach to Real-Time System Debugging, Proc First Conf AI Applications CS Press, Los Alamitos, Calif 1984

14

A Practical Procedure for Introducing
Data Collection
(with examples from Maintenance)

Stephen Linkman,
Lesley Pickard
and
Niall Ross

STC Technology Ltd.
Copthall House, Nelson Place,
Newcastle under Lyme,
Staffordshire, England
ST5 1EZ

Abstract

This paper describes the experience of the authors in data collection activities, both on collaborative research projects and internal to the STC corporation. On the basis of this experience, we define a procedure for the introduction of data collection schemes. Examples, based on metricating the maintenance phase, are provided.

INTRODUCTION

The ideas and methods described in this paper are the results of the involvement of the authors in major software data collection exercises in the United Kingdom and Europe, and the knowledge gained in the application of the principles established by those exercises to industrial situations within the STC corporation.

This paper descibes a mechanism and a process by which one can make a start on the introduction of measurement and control into industrial software development. As a consequence of effective and useful data collection a broader spectrum of information should be available providing a sounder basis for software engineering.

The data collection exercises were done in the Alvey sponsored SoftWare Data Library (SWDL) and the ESPRIT sponsored REQUEST (REliab ility and QUality in European Software Technology) projects. The SWDL project was wholly concerned with the collection of software data. It set up a pilot scheme which was to have been followed by a commercial, non profit service. This has not yet been created. The REQUEST project was primarily concerned with research into Quality and Reliability, with data collection as a supporting activity. This project will end in January 1990.

Our industrial experience is based on our activities within our own corporation in support of productivity and quality initiatives, and the introduction of programmes such as the IPSE and Software Factory initiatives being undertaken within STC.

When, in 1985, we began to expand our data collection activities beyond the support of Mainframe Systems within ICL (where extensive data collection has been done for many years), the steps we thought necessary to establish an effective data collection programme, were:-

1   To define metrics and a data model for structuring metrics collection formally.

2   To define customisation concepts formally (so that a general data model could be fitted to specific environments) and regularisation concepts (so that data collected to differing definitions of a metric might be compared).

3   To discover effective means of motivating software developers and line managers to collect usable data.

4   To design an integrated activity for data collection and use, supported by suitable databases, tools manuals etc.

5   To sell this completed package to client organisations.

The first set of solutions to the above was researched and implemented during 1986 and 1987 and formed the basis of the Software Data Library activities and the initial data collection activities within REQUEST. The data collected was analysed and showed major deficiencies, the correction of which required a major revision and extension of the data model and its underlying methods. In addition the formal definition of the metrics, the customisation concepts and the design of the integrated data collection and use activity had to be extensively revised. This revision was done in 1988/9, and now forms the basis of data collection exercises within STC and the REQUEST project.

In addition our experience of introducing data collection has also led us to a number of other insights into the preliminary activities that organisations must undertake if data collection and analysis is to be useful. As a result, we advocate a three stage process:-

1   Setting of the goals of the data collection

Before any data collection takes place, it is vital to identify how the information will be used and to determine how each metric contributes to each goal. Section 1 of the next chapter describes the goal-setting process and the problems in establishing these goals.

2   Creation of a process model of the software development activities.

Section 2 of the next chapter gives a brief outline of why a process model is necessary, what benefits can be gained from it, and an outline on some techniques for creating such a model. It also relates these to future issues such as the models and techniques appropriate for IPSEs

3   Creation of a customised data model relating the objects manipulated in the process model, their attributes and the roles that the people are fulfilling when they handle them.

A generic data model must be created before the development of the process model. Once the entity framework of this is clear, process modelling can proceed while simultaneously attributes of interest in the collection environment are identified, defined and placed within the data model. Once the process and generic data models are complete, they are combined (under the guidance of their intended users) to produce a specific model to structure data collection. The procedure is described in detail in section 3 of the next chapter.

The final chapter contains a justification of our choice of procedure, presented as a summary of what we thought when the data collection exercise began and what we learned during it.

A PROCEDURE FOR METRICATION

1. Setting The Goals

The first step of any metrics collection scheme is to define the overall goals, or reasons for collecting data. These goals can be in many different forms, but it is important that none of them duplicate or conflict with each other. Another important point is to ensure they do not conflict with or duplicate the goals of any existing collection process which will continue to run in parallel.

Each overall goal must be divided into clear identifiable objectives which can be quantified. The combined list should then be checked carefully to ensure that it is a true reflection of the overall goals, since the metrics will be selected on the basis of the quantifiable objectives, not the original goals which are too imprecise to quantify directly. If the mapping is incorrect then the metrics collection will not meet the overall goals.

The metrics are selected on the basis of obtaining information necessary to meet the objectives. Each metric must show a contribution before its choice can be justified. As well as showing the metric to be useful, this also identifies how the metric will be used after it is collected, and makes it easier to identify the appropriate method of analysis. Without any idea of how to analyse or use data, there is no benefit in collecting the metrics.

The most common temptation in setting up a metrics collection scheme is to start with a list of metrics and then attempt to justify each metric. This can result in two major problems which will cause the metrics collection to be less effective, or, even worse, counter productive, in terms of achieving the desired goals. The two problems are:-

1   There is no mapping between the metrics and the overall goals. This means that the goals cannot be shown to have been met by the metrics chosen. This may result in paying the costs of collection without achieving the desired benefits. In addition, the list of metrics may contain some metrics which measure the same attribute. Thus, without proper criteria for metrics selection, there is a danger of unnecessary data collection.

2   Useful, or even essential, metrics may be removed from the list due to difficulties of data collection. Without the criteria to identify important metrics the selection of metrics may be based on suboptimal criteria such as "ease of collection".

The last point does not imply that the ease of collection is not an important issue, but simply that a metric should not be dropped purely due to collection difficulties without regard to the infor mation it provides.

Different types of goals will also require different background information and resources, which may themselves impose requirements on the data collection and analysis process. For example:-

1   Goals which Enable Prediction

These require a model or an algorithm on which to base the prediction. An example would be the cost model COCOMO (cost, effort and schedule predictions) [BOEH81], which itself requires additional information so that it can be calibrated to the user's environment.

2   Goals which Enable Monitoring

These require an expected value or relationship for comparison with the actual value. This could be target number of faults per module (expected value) or a directly proportional relationship between the size of a module and the number of faults (expected relationship). In general to be effective a number of other metrics must be captured in order to explain unexpected results. Without the necessary background information the information can not be interpreted and the effort involved in the initial metrics wasted.

To be most effective metrics collection should be integrated with the development process. This will cause the least disruption to the collectors, and enable them and their colleagues to see benefit from the collection and analysis of the data. This may also help to counteract any fears of misuse of the metrics by management on the part of the workforce. Such fears must be overcome if the metrics collection is to be effective. The construction of a process model and associated data model are vital to the integration with the development process and are described in more detail in the following sections.

2.   Process Modelling

A process model provides a way of describing and modelling the processes that people and machines undertake in any activity, for example software development, and the objects that they manipulate. From such a model it is possible to understand the points at which data collection fits in and the objects to which it relates. It is then possible, by construction of the

286

Figure 1 - A simple process model of the maintenance phase

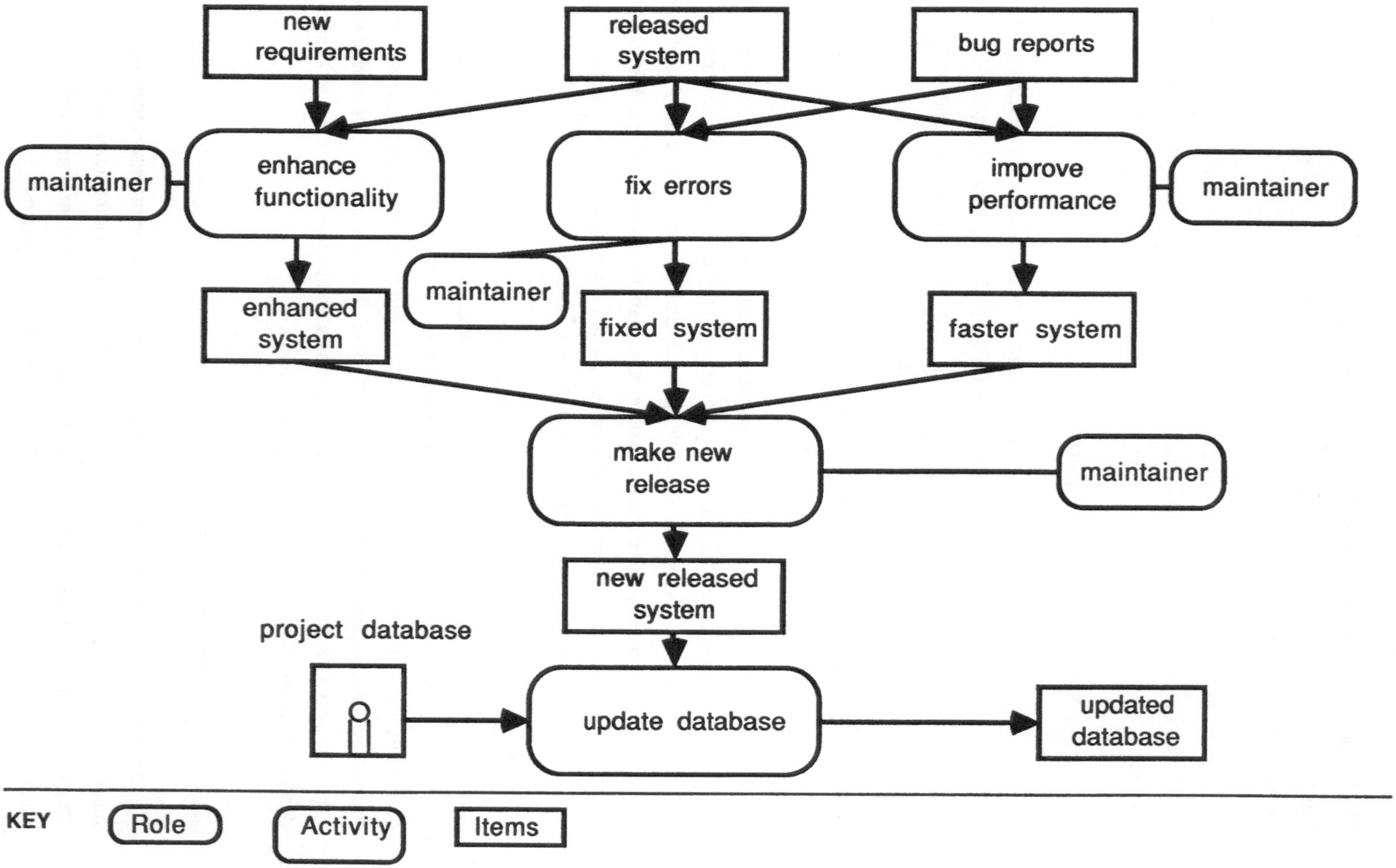

data model described in the next section, to assign to this process model the metrics associated with objects and activities and also to identify the likely sources of the information, be they machine or human.

The completeness of the mechanisms used to capture the information to construct the process and data models will affect the quality and usefulness of these models. However it is also important that the methods used be appropriate to the complexity and criticality of the process being studied.

Figure 1 shows a simple process model of the maintenance phase. This was generated using a tool called TPM which was developed by STC Technology. Used like this, TPM is acting as no more than a diagramming tool which enforces certain modelling theory conventions.

There are a number of approaches to obtaining the data to build the models:-

The modeller can, in the same manner as a knowledge engineer, sit down with the people who are part of the process, and gather information on the way in which the people work.

In an organisation which has a suitable standards or procedures manual, this can be used as a basis for creation of the model. Note, however, that this will be the view of management or of the author of the manual. This may not reflect reality and a good process engineer will, if working from such a manual, back it up with actual information from the people involved in the process.

Obtaining the information to build the process model is a very intensive operation, and often the process can be accelerated by the use of some suitable technique such as ETVX (Entry, Task, Validation eXit), which can be distributed (for example as a form like that given in Appendix A). This gathers information on the entry criteria, the tasks to be performed, the validation and the exit criteria of a step in the process. This information can be used to build an initial process model after which model refinement can proceed at much greater speed as the people involved have an object to criticise and correct.

A simple process can be captured in a single layer model. For more complex processes it is necessary to structure the model into layers, concentrating on providing the key information at the higher layers, with the internal structure of the processes of one layer being detailed as sub-processes in a lower layer.

An example of a multiple layer process model is given in figure 2, which is one of the lower layers of figure 1. A complex process may need to be described by a many-layered model.

Figure 2 - A lower level model of improved performance

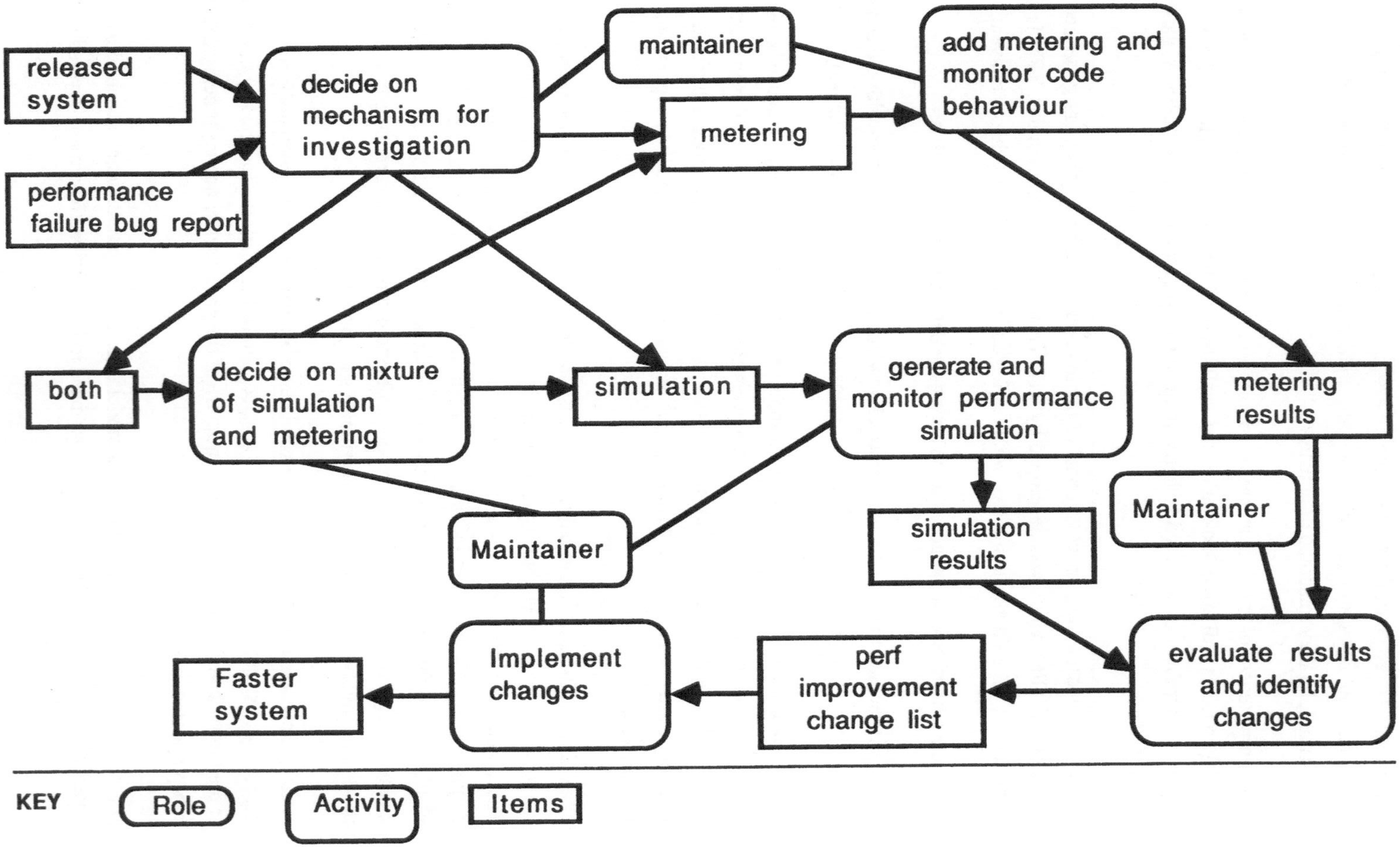

However one must always keep track of the goals and ensure that the model does not become too detailed. Any tool used to create process models should be able to handle such a hierarchy of layers.

In a complex model it is hard to validate the mass of interactions which can occur, a problem met by both the process engineer and the knowledge engineer. A knowledge engineer would validate a complex system by running trial problems and reviewing the results with the expert or experts whose knowledge is built into the system. The process model analogy is to animate the model and check the results. A model may be animated by hand or, preferably, by the tool that is used for the modelling.

A process model created in this way serves as the input to a process-based IPSE, with the advantage of the process matching reality, not some designer's view of how people will develop software. Even in the absence of an IPSE, it is possible, when the user has an animatable process model, to consider the engineering of processes. In addition if one of the goals is process improvement then one must establish a lifecycle for process engineering. Figure 3 reflects such a lifecycle that can be undertaken in process engineering. This natural step following the successful introduction of a process-based metrication scheme lies beyond the scope of this paper for discussion in detail. Figure 3 is included as a pointer to future work in this area and as an indication of some issues to be considered when undertaking fundamental process improvements.

3.   The Data Model

We use an extended semantic hierarchy modelling method to develop data models for use with the process models described in the previous chapter.

3.1   The modelling method

A modelling method intended to produce a data model describing software data requires certain features. In what follows these features are listed and briefly justified. For a full exposition of the method see [ROSS89a]. For an example of an elaborate model (with numerous primitive metrics) constructed according to these principles see [MASC89] or [ROSS89b]. For synthetic metrics related to the maintenance phase see [MELL87] and [MELL89].

290

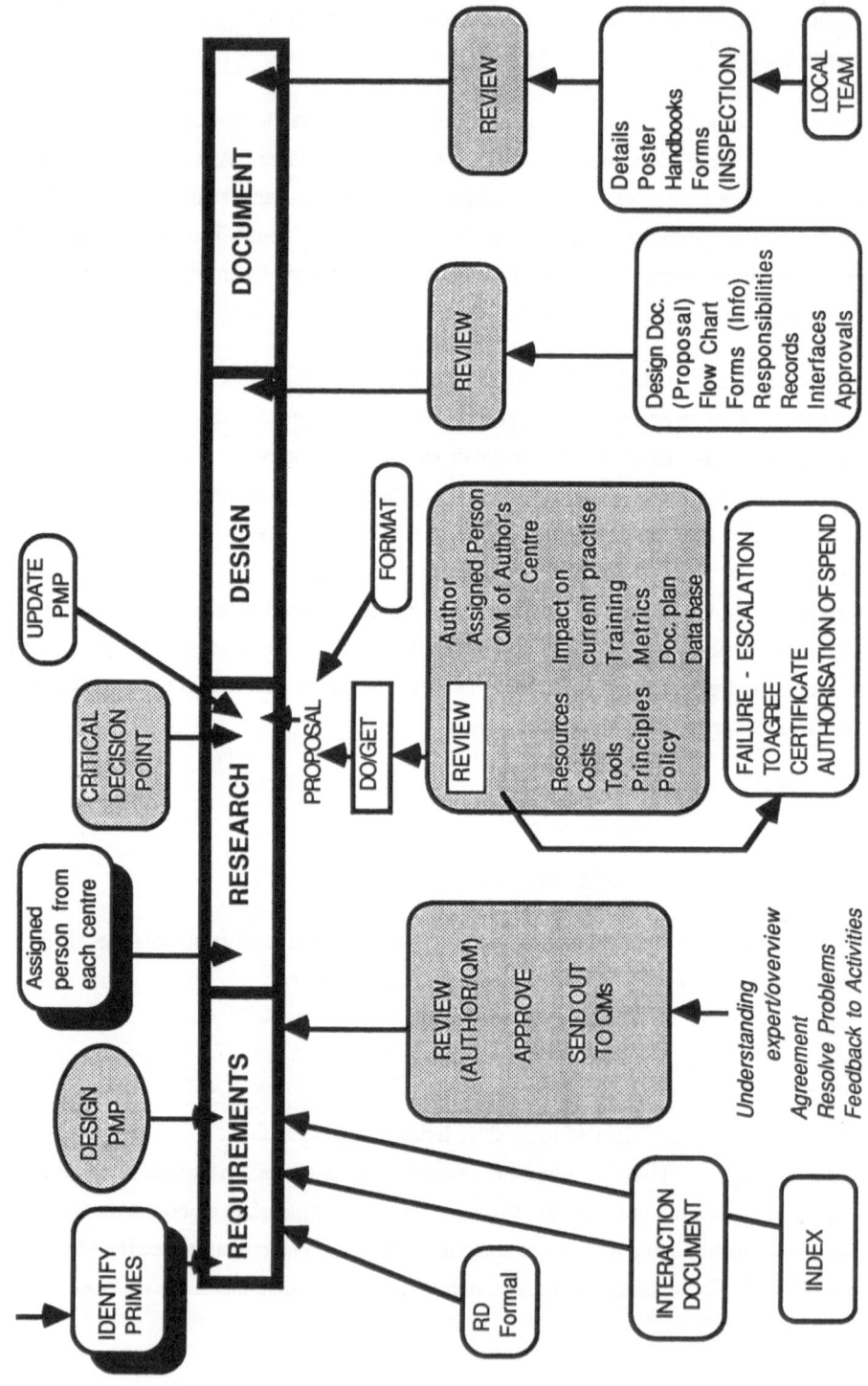

Figure 3 - A lifecycle for process changes

i)   It should be object-oriented

Data collection will occur in a series of discrete acts, in each of which a developer records data on an activity they have just finished, a module they have just coded, etc.. The objects that feature in software production will structure the collection activity and the recording of data about an object will usually be independent of recording data about other objects in respect of time, tools, etc.. In addition, basing the model on software objects makes it more intelligible to its users.

ii)   It should be hierarchic

The degree of detail that users want from the model will vary from time to time and place to place. At every time and place they will want help in navigating the model and in having complexity hidden from them. When making decisions about which metrics to collect and how, they will want all the advantages hierarchy confers of inheriting high-level decisions, so that they need only be made once.

iii)   It should underlie Entity-Attribute-Relationship modelling

Data recorders, data collection supervisors, database generators and data analysts will not always share a common view of which objects are entities, which attributes and which relationships. Data recorders think of themselves as recording values for attributes of an object they have completed. Data analysts investigating the accuracy of a predictive method may think of the predicted values as objects, of which the name of the entity they were predicting is an attribute. Customising the model to suit the data needs of differing areas often forces changes of semantic viewpoint towards an object. Because of this, the method cannot treat Entity, Attribute and Relationship as irreducible types. It must begin with more fundamental types from which they can be constructed.

iv)   It should allow the restriction of inherited properties

Since entities, attributes and relationships are each hierarchically arranged, from more general to more special objects, there are several ways of defining inheritance of the connections between them. Our definition allows some flexibility in this, so that, for example, specialisations of an attribute (to different data collection tools say) can be freely assigned to specialisations of the entity it is measuring without losing the formal control given by the modelling technique.

v)   It should support customisation

The method must provide operations for adding and deleting objects that preserve the coherence of the data. These operations must interact consistently with the operations of restriction and change of semantic viewpoint described in (iv) and (iii) above, which are also used in customisation.

3.2   Data models and Process models

The aim is to have a single integrated model of the production process and the data that is to be collected during it. In practice, the activities of data modelling and process modelling use the same modelling theory but they use it in different ways. Hence the development of the data and process parts of the model tends to progress in distinct stages and to produce a model with clear interfaces between the two areas. The sequence of development is

Generic Data Model -> Specific Process Model -> Specific Data Model -> Trial

Generic Data Model: we begin with the basic entity types Role, Process and Item (these are always present; in a very wide-ranging model other basic types might occur). We then specialise these to more detailed types (Development Role, Phase Process, Software Item) which may in turn be specialised to yet lower levels of detailed types. At each level a type inherits the attributes and relationships of its parent and has additional attributes and relationships assigned to it. (Note that these attributes and relationships are also objects in their own right and so may also be specialised.) The final result is a model containing a moderate number of hierarchically-arranged entity types almost all of which have unique sets of attributes and relationships. An example of such a model is shown in figure 4.

Specific Process Model: process modelling begins at the level where data modelling ends. The leaves of the hierarchic structure created above (specialisations of Role, Process and Item) are the basic entity types which the process modeller uses. Each of them is specialised to a large number of classes. The general relationships between the types become specific relationships between the classes (for example, " Developer Role *works in* Phase *which produces* Document" might specialise to " Designer *works in* Design Phase *which produces* Low-level Design ", among other things). The chief differences between this modelling stage and the one that precedes it are:

a) some parts of the data model will descend through several hierarchic levels.
The process model will seldom have more than a single level of specialisation

293

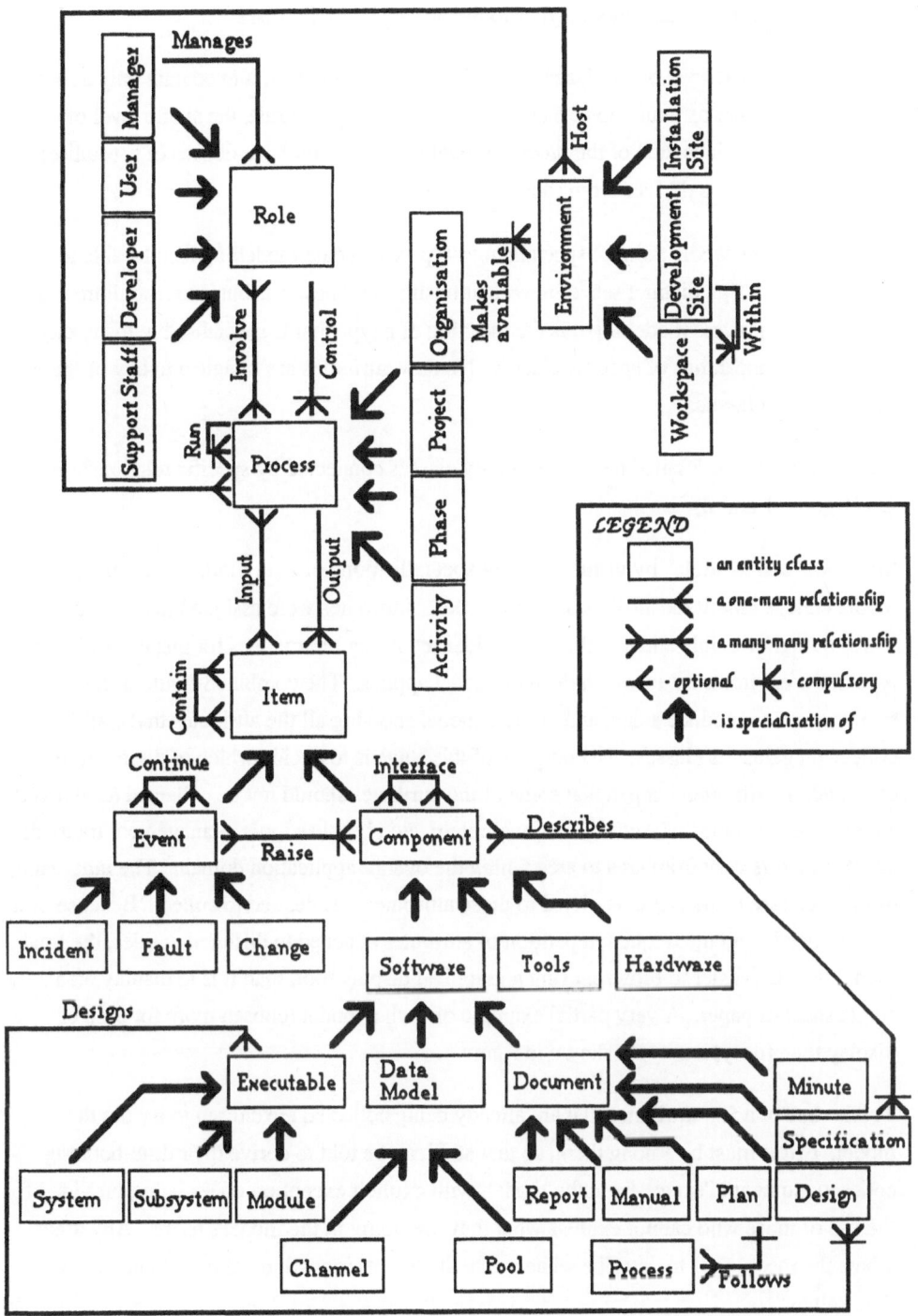

Figure 4 - data model showing kernel (Role, Process, Item) surrounded by extensive specialisations
(attributes not shown)

from the data model types to the process model classes.

b)   Each level of specialisation in the data model will tend to contain only a few times as many objects as its predecessor. By contrast, the single level of specialisation of the process model will normally have dozens of specialised classes derived from each data model type.

c)   the whole point of specialising a type when data modelling is to be able to assign distinct sets of new relationships and new attributes to its children. In process modelling it is the meaning of a type that is specialised to many distinct meanings of specific classes. No new attributes are assigned to any of these classes.

The final result is a detailed network of entity classes connected by specific relationships (c.f. figures 1 and 2).

Specific Data Model: by virtue of being specialisations of data model types, the process model classes inherit the attributes of their types. Attributes were assigned to a type because it was thought feasible and sensible to consider recording their values for instances of that type in the environment to which the data model applies. The combined result of the first two stages is to produce a data and process model showing all the attributes that could be collected against its classes. The purpose of this stage is to decide which of them will be collected. It will often happen that some of the attributes should not be collected (or not yet) against specific kinds of Activity, Software item, etc., because tools, management methods or other factors vary from area to area within the overall application domain. The inheritance of these classes is therefore restricted to those attributes it is desired to collect. Because of its level of detail, and the frequent repetition of attributes attached to different entities, the final model is much easier to browse, using a graphical display tool, than it is to display on a single sheet of paper. A very partial example of such a model (chosen more for ease of display than for typicality) is shown in figure 5.

Trial: one or a few attributes that are already being collected are chosen to try out the model. Effort must be among them, so that staff can be told to derive their time-booking codes, document id's, etc., from the model, with explicit exception codes being provided for the use of those who cannot express what they are doing in the model's terms. Any areas where the model fails to describe what is actually happening will quickly call attention to themselves.

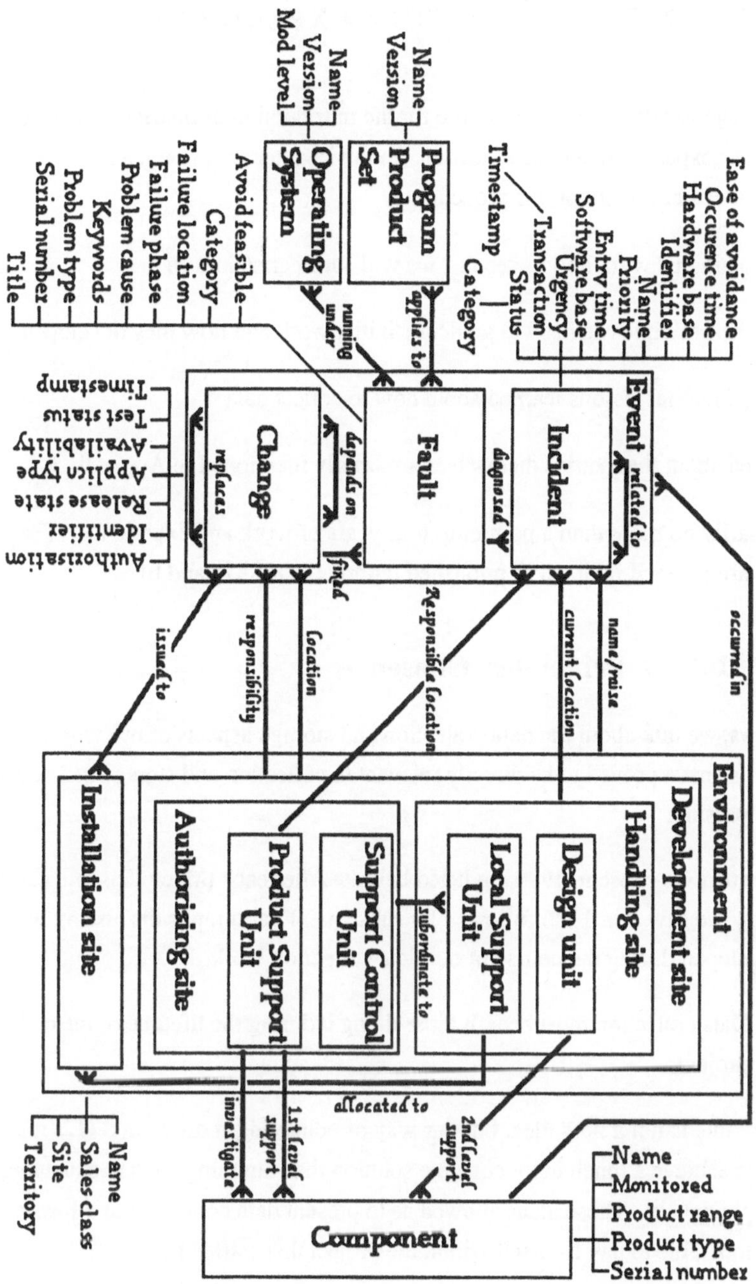

Figure 5 - part of an extensively customised data model for maintenance
(processes not shown)

LEGEND | entity class | one-many relationship | many-many relationship | are attributes of

DATA COLLECTION EXPERIENCE

The preceding chapter describes a procedure for the introduction of metrics which we have derived from our experience in data collection. In this chapter we present a resumé of the experiences that lead us to adopt this procedure.

In order to explain this work and its results, we will summarise in turn

a)   the principles devised to guide the initial work and how they developed

b)   additional lessons learned about how to collect data

Lessons learned about the metrics themselves are briefly mentioned in Appendix B.

This is necessarily no more than a pointer to four years of work and experience. The topics of (a) and (b) are covered in detail in published reports [ROSS87a and b].

a)   Initial Principles Chosen

In what follows, we talk about the data collection and storage aspects of our work. Our ideas on data use have proved to be directly relevant to collection and storage and so are mentioned in passing.

The principles that we chose in 1986 are listed below. After each principle is one paragraph describing how we saw it in 1986 followed by subsequent paragraphs discussing how our view of it developed during the course of our data collection work.

i)   Data collection must benefit those doing it during the lifetime of the collecting project.

Description: this is not a new idea, but our way of achieving it drew on STL's research into data use to achieve a much more concrete solution than anything we had encountered in the literature previously. These ideas allowed us to present data collection as a low-level management tool, able to pay for itself within the project that started it.

Experience: what we produced in '86 is best described as a specification for how projects collecting data could benefit from the process. It functioned admirably in motivating software developers to begin collecting data but was less adequate when they looked to it for help in doing data analysis and feedback. We had to develop it into a design of what data was to be fed back and how to interpret it (in effect an expert system) and a procedure for data feedback (in effect a process model for a data collection and analysis process that runs orthogonally to the software production process).

ii)   A data model, supported by a defined data modelling method, must be used simultaneously to structure data collection, define data storage and describe the data needs of analysts.

Description: this is the natural solution to a host of interrelated data definition, selection, configuration-control and storage problems. As well as solving these particular difficulties, the data model was a force for structure and coherence in every area of technical work. While principle (i) is the most important from the point of view of selling data collection, principle (ii) is the most important as regards doing it.

Experience: the degree of formality that we used in '86 was not really adequate even for a company-based collection scheme. In our multi-country project, every area where the method had been supplemented with informal text became a fertile source of misunderstandings and deviations between the database, the data collection tools, the collection manuals, etc.. This problem was compounded by a failure to enforce the method outside the site where it was devised. The method was also not good enough at hiding complexity from the end-users (the data providers).

A revised method was developed over eight months at STC Technology Ltd. This kept the strengths of the earlier one while being flexible enough to express ALL definitions formally and with sufficient structure to allow information to be compartmentalised, hiding complexity from end-users.

iii)   Data collection must be customisable.

Description: every software production environment is unique in what it collects and in how it collects it. Furthermore any given environment will change over time (especially it will wish to increase and standardise what it collects if data collection proves profitable). A collection scheme that is to cover many business units and companies must be customisable. Equally it must not loose the capacity to compare common subsets of data collected in different ways. These conflicting priorities can only be reconciled by a customisation method, acting on the data model and metric definitions, which is designed to allow the former while preserving the latter.

Experience: the 'customisation' method we devised in 1986 may be aptly compared to that of a builder who supplies a fully-furnished block of flats to all customers and invites those whose requirements were more modest to put up 'no entry' and 'don't touch' signs on all unwanted rooms and items of furniture. The navigational difficulties of the would-be purchaser of a one-room flat, whose bed, bedside table, chair, desk, bookcase and washbasin are scattered throughout this multi-storey structure, are an apt metaphor for the problems data providers had finding the measures they had agreed to collect on our cumbrous, heavily scored-out forms.

As well as revising the data definition method (see (ii) above), we revised our approach to customisation so that all data collection tools, forms, documents, etc., are fully configurable (i.e. deleting an object in the data model must cause corresponding deletion or rewriting of references in tools, manuals, ...), hiding all trace of customisation from the users.

iv)   The handling of data collection acts must be governed by a defined procedure which stresses verification through feedback.

Description: this principle is complementary to principle (i). Effective verification of collected data can only be done by its providers and must be integrated with collection.

Experience: in practice, verification took two stages, not one. Our initial ideas on how to verify data were good at detecting non-obvious errors when no gross errors were present. The addition of a preliminary stage using distinct techniques to detect and correct gross errors makes the whole process much more efficient.

v)   Setting up a data collection scheme needs a defined procedure covering motivation, definition and advice

Description: the stages of putting a scheme in place must be worked out and their effort cost known. The presentations introducing the concepts to potential data providers must answer the usual doubts and warn against the obvious pitfalls.

Experience: our ability to sell the idea was good. We learned painfully that the ability to sell the idea and the ability to do it must be kept in step. This is especially true in collaborative projects where the relative speed with which the partners complete interdependent parts of a single data collection scheme may vary greatly. Except when the data to be collected is your own, it is better to be slow in publicising a data collection project than to risk a long delay when halfway through installing a data collection scheme because the next necessary item is not yet completed to the required quality. Such delays are very demotivating to your data providers.

b) New Lessons Learned about How to Collect Data

Armed with our first version of the above guidelines, we sallied forth to persuade (mainly UK) software producers to collect data. We learned a great deal. One important lesson concerned the problems of managing collaborative projects of the kind created by the ESPRIT or Alvey initiatives. The difficulty of redistributing responsibilities once assigned and the length of time needed to get authorisation for changes to the initial plan meant that detected and solvable problems often could not be rectified. This compounded the expected initial difficulties of working in multi-company, multi-cultural projects. We will not discuss these difficulties further in this paper, but would wish the reader to bear them in mind when comparing the actual results of the REQUEST and SWDL projects with what should (and we trust will) happen in a company-based collection scheme.

Some of our technical experience has already been expressed in the later paragraphs of the items of section (a) above. Those technical points we learned that were not simply developments of our ideas but corrections or additions to them are listed below in (rough) order of importance.

1) It is useless to collect large volumes of data on paper

A data collection scheme that can rely on paper forms for data recording and on text documents for definitions of the customised data model and for guiding verification analyses is a data collection scheme that is too small and simple to justify a project for setting it up. Such a scheme can be run but it will not advance the state of the art. Tools are essential to gather data from different projects in different environments.

2) A scheme starts not by collecting data but by transcribing it

Every production unit into which we tried to import a general data collection scheme already had historical data held in a variety of databases. It also had data currently being collected on forms and data currently being generated by compilers, static analysis tools, automatic time-booking systems, etc.. A provider could only gradually be weaned off these multifarious systems and onto a single data entry system and then only if the new system could efficiently accept data from the earlier repositories. In the early stages, most data "collection" was in fact data transcription.

3)   Define the process model, then the metrics

In practice, this will be an iteration (process model -> process metrics (mainly effort) ->
process model revision -> metrics -> ...) but the process model must come first. You must
get a grip of what you are doing before trying to measure how well you are doing it.

The mistake we made was in thinking "We are a metrics activity. Therefore we must tell
people to define and collect metrics" whereas we should have told them to define their
process, with part of this definition being the attributes of the objects thus modelled (i.e. the
metrics) and the exit criteria for the processes (including the need to collect metrics on the
process and on the items it had produced). Our failure to highlight process modelling as the
essential first step meant that often the people we persuaded to join the collection scheme
began eagerly to customise our data model, halted when they discovered the lack of their
own process model and remained halted.

An important secondary discovery concerning the relationship between metrics and process
models was our realisation that the collection of process metrics could be made to drive the
refinement of a process model. When a business unit attempted to design a process model to
structure its activities, a quick initial design of a "plausible" model was always followed by a
long period of refinement, ironing out inconsistencies between teams and finding areas
where the "plausible" model did not in fact capture what was being done. This refinement
period was greatly speeded up, and its cost reduced, if effort booking codes were
constructed from the phases and activities of the current model, with an exception code for
those unable to express the work they were doing in the model's terms. This use tests the
model as no review can. Those who book time to the exception code can be interviewed and
the model revised or better explained as appropriate.

4)   Technology changes during a long-term collection scheme

The concepts devised to address a given problem will usually last the lifetime of a project
(and a lot longer) if they were correct in the first place. By contrast, the ideal delivery
platform for the tools that a project builds to implement these concepts may change between
the start of a project to define a data collection scheme and the introduction of the scheme
throughout a company several years later. If a project's tools need to be used outside the
project and if motivating such use is a major criterion of a project's success (both of which
are very much the case for metrics projects) then the developers must survey what packages,
hardware, etc. will be available in the latter half of the project and plan to build their tools
upon them. The project management must be flexible enough to allow this. We suffered

through not foreseeing this.

5)   Target and Prediction data is not the same as Actual data

The interpretation placed on the value that a metric achieves in practice often depends on what value for that metric was targetted by management or predicted by developers. However targetted or predicted values are not the same kind of data as actual values. Considerable subtlety is needed in the design of the data model to avoid the twin pitfalls of capturing this data in an unnatural way or making a cumbersome extension to the model solely to represent it. After trying several unsatisfactory solutions, we decided to treat a target or prediction as an entity in its own right. One of the attributes of this entity was the name of that attribute of which a given target or prediction was a hypothetical value, and its one relationship pointed to the entity instance whose value it predicted or targetted. This solution proved ideal both as regards collection and as regards storage.

Conclusion

The paper has presented a procedure and outlined a set of associated methods for a data collection scheme. This is based upon the experience we have gained in extensive data collection exercises, building on our failures and our successes. These ideas have been used to introduce data collection into major areas within our corporation, and have been very effective once the basic principles have been grasped.

APPENDIX A

ETVX   Process Information Capture Sheet

Development route Information

Phase

Sub Activity Area Planning/ Product Production/Quality/ Monitor

Activity Name

Entry Criteria

Tasks

Validation

Exit Criteria

APPENDIX B

The following is a list of attitudes to particular metrics that we acquired during our work. A supporting reference is listed after each remark.

i) Any size metric is useful. Any two size metrics will be highly correlated with each other but both are worth collecting because components that do not show the same relationship between size metrics as their fellows are often worthy of investigation. [ROSS87a]

ii) Simple information-flow metrics are useful both in collecting and in diagnosing anomalous items. However we have not found that the Kafura and Henry synthetic metrics based on them add any information when applied to our data. ["An Evaluation of some Design Metrics", Barbara Kitchenham, Lesley Pickard and Sue Linkman, for publication in the Software Engineering Journal]

iii) The software science claims for the Halstead metrics were wholly contradicted by our studies. Halstead primitives (operator and operand counts) were like other size metrics only harder to collect. ["M. H. Halstead's Software Science - a Critical Examination", Gillian Frewin and Peter Hamer, Proc. 6th Int. S.E. Conf., Sept. 82, pp 197 - 206]

iv) The metrics used to measure a program's control structure must be changed or extended when the complexity of a problem is encoded as data rather than as control structure (programs driven by look-up tables, etc.). A complexity metric (or group of metrics)will be useful only within a given house style of program development unless it measures data structure or data flow complexity and control flow. Data structure and data flow metrics can only practically be collected (outside research projects) by tools. [Humphries, CSR Software Reliability and Metrics Newsletter, 1987]

v) Subjective metrics (subjective complexity, quality, etc.) are unreliable for the preliminary identification of anomalies but are very useful during the diagnosis of an anomaly's cause. [Barbara Kitchenham, REQUEST Report R1.8.13]

REFERENCES

[BOEH81] Software Engineering Economics
Barry W. Boehm
Prentice-Hall, Inc.

[MASC89] Data Model Poster
R3.2.6 REQUEST/STL-bmm/112/S3/DC-RP/01
Barbara Mascetti, November 1989

[MELL87] Modelling the Support Process, Peter Mellor, September 1987 in
Measurement for Software Control and Assurance
ed Kitchenham and Littlewood, Elsevier Applied Science

[MELL89] Chapter on Maintainability in Scenario for COQUAMO-III
R1.7.7 REQUEST/TCU-pm/016/S1/QM-RP/04
Peter Mellor, June,1989

[ROSS89a] Data Model Design Principles
R3.2.9 REQUEST/STL-nfr/110/S3/DC-RP/00.5
Niall Ross, October 1989

[ROSS89b] High-level Data Model Design
R3.2.5 REQUEST/STL-nfr/111/S3/DC-RP/01.2
Niall Ross, November 1989

[ROSS87a, b] Initial Contact Presentation, Agreement Visit Presentation
Niall Ross and Elaine Burgess
SWDL Reports SWDL/COLL/ICP, SWDL/COLL/AVP
(see also references given in these two documents)

15

PROCESS SUPPORT ENVIRONMENTS
AND THEIR APPLICATION TO LARGE SCALE SYSTEMS

PETER WESTMACOTT
STC Technology Ltd
Copthall House, Nelson Place, Newcastle-under-Lyme, Staffs ST5 1EZ

ABSTRACT

Process modelling, and the execution of active process models, provides a sound basis for the exercise of control over large-scale projects. This paper describes some of the research work carried out under the Alvey IPSE 2·5 project, and the potential for exploiting this research as the basis for large scale "process support environments".

Key features are the integration of management and technical activities, the concept of a "plan" as an instantiation of a "method", and the ability for the process model to evolve over time to take account of changing requirements, both managerial and technical.

THE IPSE 2·5 PROJECT

Objectives and Scope

The IPSE 2·5 Project is being carried out under the Software Engineering Strategy of the UK Alvey Programme [1] by a consortium comprising STC Technology Ltd, International Computers Limited, the University of Manchester, Dowty Defence and Air Systems Limited, SERC Rutherford Appleton Laboratories, Plessey Research Roke Manor Limited and British Gas plc. The project lasts for four years, finishing at the end of December 1989. (More information on the project may be found in references [2], [3] and [4].) The objective of the project is

> "To produce an IPSE and evaluate its effect on the productivity and quality of systems development as measured by the costs of production and mainte-
> nance, by providing ... support for rigorously defined development processes
> which integrate management activities and development activities ..." [5]

305

The scope of the project included a number of other aspects which should contribute to this increased productivity and quality, but this paper is concerned primarily with "rigorously defined development processes."

Two concepts at the heart of IPSE 2·5 are *integration* and *process modelling*. Integration is seen as a key factor in achieving increased productivity by eliminating unnecessary and error prone transfer of information, particularly where the transfers involve human intervention. Process modelling is seen as a key factor in achieving integration in that the full potential for integration can only be realised when the total process is understood, and this requires a formalisation, or a model, of the process. (Of course we never understand the *total* process, and so we never achieve *full* integration; what matters is that the process is understood as far as is appropriate and possible at any point in time.)

The process under consideration is described using a process modelling language (PML). This model is then interpreted by a process control engine (PCE), to provide a dynamic environment for those elements, human or mechanical, participating in the actual process as described. The capabilities of the PCE include the ability to communicate with users and tools (the participating elements), the storage and retrieval of data objects (which may be process objects or product objects), and the ability to support change to the process definition itself, such change being under control of the same process model. An instance of IPSE 2·5 consists of the PCE, the PML, and a process model defined in PML.

THE PROCESS MODELLING LANGUAGE

The roots of PML are in research done in the fields of requirements modelling (specifically RML [6]) and conceptual modelling languages. The *role* is the fundamental object in the model; it represents an encapsulation of resources and behaviour—one of a number of concurrent threads of activity carried out by people or machines performing *actions* which contribute to the process. Communication and synchronisation with other roles is achieved through *interactions*, which are objects with the behaviour of communication channels. A role operates on its own set of data *entities*—the resources of the role. These resources are private to the role, although they may be made accessible to other roles by being passed through interactions. The behaviour of a role is constrained, and the correctness of the executing model is checked, by *assertions* defined over the state of a role.

This overall structure is indicated diagrammatically in Figure 1.

Whilst PML is not an object oriented language in the usual sense, it does have some of the characteristics of such languages; it has classes and inheritance (see below), and the role is an object, encapsulating its state and responding to external stimuli or messages (the interactions it has with other roles). PML is a strongly typed language, and in particular, the type of a role determines the interactions in which it can participate.

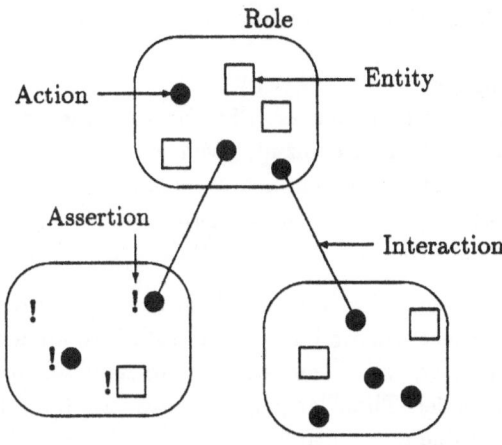

Figure 1: PML Concepts

Classes and Inheritance

PML is a class-based language with inheritance. There are four *principal classes* in PML: Role, Interaction, Action and Entity. The significance of the principal classes is that they have different semantics, which are understood, and acted on, by the PCE. Each of these classes has a (fixed) set of predefined *property categories*. Subclasses of the principal classes have *definitional properties* defined in those property categories, and instances of the classes have *factual properties* (values) associated with the definitional properties.

The class inheritance concept allows the development of generic process models, which may be specialised for particular purposes. To take a simple example, we can consider a set of Roles which together define, in general terms, the preparation and publication of a document. Some or all of these roles (and the associated Action and Entity classes) might then be expanded to define the process of producing a conference paper. There are two important points to note here; firstly, we have a form of reuse, reducing the amount of duplication required in producing similar parts of a process model. Secondly, the concept of inheritance (as defined in PML) ensures that other parts of the model which only need to know that this is a document production exercise (a library role for example) can treat it as such, while those that need to understand the specialised aspects can get the benefit of that knowledge. This provides a very powerful abstraction concept which is essential in ensuring that information can be used for different purposes without being replicated.

A class may be instantiated many times. Thus we may have a Role class defined (say Author) and have many instances of that class (one for each document which is to be produced). Similarly, there would be an appropriately defined Entity class for Document, and each instance of the Author role would produce an instance of this Entity class.

Persistence and Change

It is a pre-requisite of a system such as IPSE 2·5 that the process model should *not* be something which is invoked on demand, given some data and expected to supply a response. The model is a continuing representation of the on-going process, and does not terminate as long as the project (department, corporation, ...) is in existence; it is what we refer to as a persistent process.

Because of this continuing existence, which may span several years, it is of the utmost importance that features are built into the PML to allow the model to evolve—whether in an additive way, when new features are required, or to modify or correct existing aspects of the model. These language features have been designed to ensure that such change is both possible and controllable.

External Communication

People are as much part of the process as machines. The approach adopted is to represent a person by a "user agent", a pseudo role which is conceptually and syntactically the same as any other Role, but with its behaviour predefined rather than being described in PML. Other roles communicate with the user agent, and hence with the user, through interactions, according to a well defined protocol. For convenience these interactions are wrapped up in predefined actions which hide the protocol from the PML writer. This recognition of the user agent as a separate object allows people to be represented in the process model—the user agent "stands in for" the person. It also means that each user, through his or her user agent, may interact with (participate in) a number of roles simultaneously, and roles may be transferred from one user to another.

Tools are handled in the same way as users—so we have the concept of a role communicating through interactions with a "tool agent" which in turn understands the way in which it can communicate with the tools wherever they may be. This allows us to interface with existing external environments and the tools which they support, rather than having to demand that yet another set of tools be generated for use on the IPSE.

THE PROCESS CONTROL ENGINE

The Process Control Engine provides the environment which supports the execution of the process model. This has to include support for:

- the definition of the process model in PML (including modification of existing models, both statically, implying support for conventional reuse of components, and dynamically, while the model is active);

- storage of this process model definition, and the states of the executing roles; this includes not just the "process related information" (plans, methods, milestones, etc.), but also all the "product data" (requirements statements, designs, code, user documentation, etc.) manipulated by the model.

- interpretation of the model (including scheduling the interactions between roles, synchronising roles where necessary);

- communication with end-users (who may be playing more than one role at a time), in a location-independent and workstation-independent way;

- invocation of and communication with tools;

- general background support functions such as monitoring the progress of the models and of the PCE itself, PCE maintenance and diagnostics, installation and bootstrap, etc.

The architecture of the PCE reflects the concepts of PML; role instances (including user agents and tool agents) are mapped onto processes. The execution of a role is the execution of the process; interactions are messages passed between processes, and the agents (which are specially programmed "roles") are the access points to and from the outside world. This architecture is shown, in a simplified form, in Figure 2.

User agents are supported by a "UI Server" running on a workstation and providing a window management capability reflecting the role and action structure of PML. It is important to note the need for a good windowing system, which gives the ability for the user to select what he is to do from a number of different contexts, and to switch between activities without having to terminate each one in turn. This reflects the multiple roles with which the user may interact (via his user agent), and supports the PML concept of the influence that he may have over the behaviour of those roles by the way in which he chooses to interact with them.

Tool agents are supported by Tool servers running on the system in which the tools are to execute (which may be the same system which is hosting the PCE, a workstation supporting the IPSE UI, or any other networked machine). The tool agent provides a mapping between PML concepts and an IPSE tool protocol; a tool server understands the protocol and how to obtain the desired effects (such as initiating tools, passing information to and from tools, etc.) for its particular environment.

Since the process model does not terminate, but is continually evolving, we need to support the roles with some form of persistent processes; similarly the entities in the model are ideally stored as data objects in a typed persistent object store. The IPSE 2·5 PCE is built on a development of PISA (Persistent Information Space Architecture) [7], which is extended to give the concept of persistent processes.

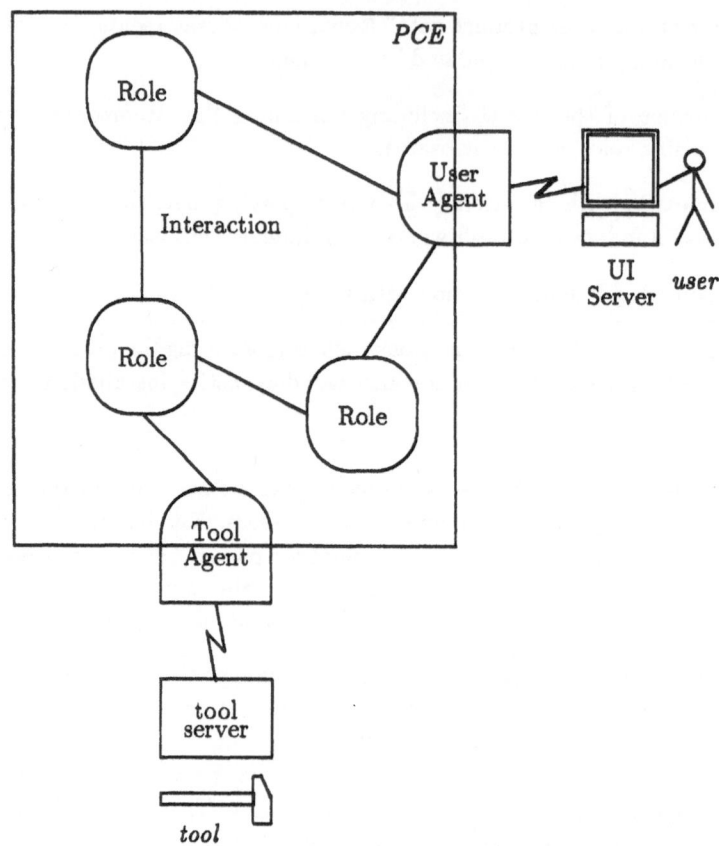

Figure 2: PCE Architecture

MANAGEMENT SUPPORT

If we exclude the personnel or "man-management" aspects, management is largely about planning, resourcing plans, monitoring progress against plans, and taking corrective action when shown to be necessary by the monitoring.

Within software projects, the type of plan, the way it is resourced, and the sort of monitoring which is possible, directly reflect the technical methods being used. For example, the plan for the development of a system using an iterative rapid prototyping approach, will be very different in form from the plan for a conventional specify-design-code-test method. Within IPSE 2·5, a technical method is a collection of interacting Role classes. A resourced plan is a collection of the corresponding role instances, allocated to people. Thus we represent a plan as an instantiation of a method, rather than as some separate object completely outside the development process; the plan is in fact the executing process model. This concept is the key to the full integration of management and engineering activities in IPSE 2·5.

In order to support this view, we need some means for representing the organisation, so that the roles may be allocated to staff in a sensible way, and to provide a context for delegation and reporting structures within the model. This is an area which is not predefined in IPSE 2·5. Rather it may be seen as just another aspect of the total process model. Significant effort within the project has however been put into developing a general, specialisable, and realistic process model for management support (PMMS), to provide a basis for evaluation of the concepts.

APPLICABILITY TO LARGE SCALE PROJECTS

There are two very different meanings of the term "large scale system" which we are interested in here. On the one hand there is the large scale *product*, and on the other, the large scale *project*.

The large scale product is characterised by size (which for a software system, could be lines of code, bytes of memory consumed, number of modules, etc.) or by capacity (number of users supported, amount of data controlled, etc.). The large scale project may be characterised by the number of people working on the development or by the time taken to develop.

For nearly twenty years now, development systems such as CADES [8],[9] have been addressing the engineering problems faced by large scale projects developing large scale products. Management support systems and tools address the problems of managing large scale projects. Process Support Environments, by emphasising integration of support for management and engineering activities, address both together, thus making the process support environment concept particularly appropriate for large scale systems.

The key areas in which the process support environment approach should benefit large systems developers are listed below.

<u>Understanding the Process.</u>   The most immediate benefit is that the act of modelling the process flushes out a lot of detail, and forces an understanding of what actually happens (and what is intended to happen, and how far these two are the same). Inconsistencies and omissions in existing procedures are exposed and can be corrected. The formality of the modelling language does not allow such problems to be glossed over lightly.

<u>Conformance to rules.</u>   Conformance to Quality Standards, Procedures Manuals etc., is achieved by embedding those rules in the process model. This eliminates the need for spot checks (which may not be enough anyway), or rigorous checks by third parties (which can be too expensive and disruptive), by ensuring that things can only be done in accordance with the rules. Of course there is always the situation of "the exception that proves the rule"—the case where it is necessary for tactical reasons to break the rules. This can be achieved by allowing an alternative approach in the process model—the point here is that the system knows that the short cut has been taken and can record the fact, and indeed bring it to the attention of somebody who should know about it. In an extreme case, the process model can be changed "on the fly" to cope with unanticipated exceptions (see "Evolution of the Process" below), but again the fact that this has been done can be made visible.

<u>Visibility to Management.</u>   Usually progress reports against plans are generated off-line from the development process, on the basis of reported achievements and predictions. In a fully integrated process support environment, preparation of progress reports is part of the process, and where factual information is available elsewhere in the process, reports can be derived automatically and accurately. Of course there is still the need for prediction and estimation, but such cases can be clearly identified and treated appropriately.

<u>Evolution of the Process.</u>   One of the problems with automated systems is that they tend to lock you in to what you thought you wanted. In the mean time the world changes, and the original ideas may be seen to be no longer appropriate. The more dependence that is placed on a support environment, the more important it is for that environment to be able to take account of change, and to evolve without having to wait for a nice inter-project gap. This is of course essential for projects with a life span of many years or even decades. Support for dynamic change has been a central theme of the IPSE 2·5 research, and features have been built in to the PML and the PCE to ensure that such change is both possible and controllable.

<u>Flexibility.</u>   A large project is likely to need to make use of various different technical methods and disparate tool systems. It is even possible (with collaborative projects in particular) to have to cope with different styles of management within the same project. A generic environment capable of supporting different but interacting specialisations at the same time is clearly a major benefit here. (It would not be easy to model a process with all of these characteristics, but it seems evident that the effort would be well worth while.)

<u>Dissemination of information.</u>   Automated communication of information means that people don't have to remember who to tell when they have done something; nor do

they need to keep looking in the library to see if there is any thing that they ought to be aware of. The system takes care of it. More importantly, with a greater degree of integration in the support environment, many forms of indirect communication become redundant—the information is made directly available within the system, as and when it is needed.

CONCLUSIONS

Process support environments of the sort prototyped in IPSE 2·5 provide a unique opportunity to combine the benefits of management support systems and of project support environments, without losing the benefits of the tools and toolsets currently in use. The integration of management and engineering activities is seen as an essential aspect of any such system if it is to realise its full potential, and the formal modelling of the process is considered to be a prerequisite for such integration.

At the time of writing, evaluations of the IPSE 2·5 approach are being carried out within the project, in a number of different contexts. These evaluations are not yet complete; however, our experience to date is that, while there is still a lot more work to be done, the concepts and architecture prototyped within the IPSE 2·5 Project are appropriate to, and should provide a major benefit in, controlling and executing large projects.

REFERENCES

1. Alvey Programme Software Engineering Strategy, 1983

2. Snowdon, R.A., An Introduction to the IPSE 2·5 Project, *ICL Technical Journal* Volume 6 Issue 3, May 1989

3. Warboys, B.C. and Veasey, P.W., Twenty Years with Support Environments, *ICL Technical Journal* Volume 6 Issue 3, May 1989

4. Snowdon, R.A., A Brief Overview of the IPSE 2·5 Project, *Ada User* Volume 9 Number 4, 1988

5. Snowdon, R.A., Scope of the IPSE 2·5 Project, IPSE Project Document number 060/00002 (available on request from STC Technology Ltd)

6. Greenspan, S.J., Requirements Modelling: A Knowledge Representation Approach to Software Requirements Definition. Technical Report CSRG-155, Computer Systems Research Group, University of Toronto, 1984.

7. Atkinson, M.P., Morrison, R. and Pratten, G.D., Designing a Persistent Information Space Architecture, *Proceedings of Information Processing 1986*, Dublin 1986, North Holland Press.

8. Pratten, G.D. and Snowdon, R.A., CADES—Support for the Development of Complex Software, EUROCOMP 1976

9. McGuffin, R.W., Elliston, A.E., Tranter, B.R., and Westmacott, P.N., CADES—Software Engineering in Practice. *Proceedings of Fourth International Conference on Software Engineering*, Munich 1979, IEEE.

16

OBJECT-ORIENTED DESIGN: A TEENAGE TECHNOLOGY

IAN SOMMERVILLE
Computing Department, Lancaster University,
Lancaster, LA1 4YR, UK

ABSTRACT

This paper examines the utility of object-oriented design paying particular attention to how effective application of the technology can reduce the costs of attaining a required level of reliability. The paper is made up of a number of sections consisting of a brief overview of the object-oriented model, a description of how the object-oriented approach may lead to more reliable software and a discussion of the immature aspects of the technology. The conclusion reflects the title of the talk; object-oriented design is a technology with potential but it is currently immature and must be handled with care.

INTRODUCTION

This paper is concerned with a relatively new approach to software design where the system is designed as a set of interacting objects. Each object maintains its own private state and operations which act on that state. The technique has derived from object-oriented programming which started with Smalltalk [1] in the computer-assisted learning community and which was developed in various artificial intelligence systems.

It was probably first brought to prominence outside these communities by the work of Booch [2, 3] who argued strongly that this was natural method of Ada program development. Jackson [4] also suggests an approach which might be called object-oriented although Cameron [5] is careful not to do so as Jackson's approach is practical and useful rather than purist.

In the last year or so, the technique has been the subject of a great deal of publicity and extreme statements have been made about how this approach reflects a paradigm shift. It is certainly true that the approach is a promising one but it is equally true that it requires a good deal more development before it supplants alternative approaches. The aim of this paper is to present an objective view, to describe object-oriented design and discuss its advantages and disadvantages.

The overall costs of large system development are dominated by the costs of system maintenance where changes to the system must be incorporated after it has gone into use. To be useful, therefore, a new approach to design must reduce the costs of system change and, in this respect, object-oriented design is likely to be of value. In an object-oriented design, the coupling between design entities is looser than in conventional approaches and there are no shared data areas. This means that changes to one part of the design are less likely to affect other design components and thus system changes are cheaper to make and to validate.

Object-oriented design, at the moment, is a technology for design-in-the-small. It is a very useful technique for the design of small to medium sized systems and, as large systems are

315

usually composed of a number of smaller systems, it is of value in large system development. However, it does not really address the problem of design-in-the-large, namely how to effectively decompose a large system into interacting subsystems. Current *ad hoc* techniques must still be used for this activity.

AN OVERVIEW OF OBJECT-ORIENTED DESIGN

Although the term 'object-oriented design' is widely used, there is a great deal of confusion as to what it actually means and how it is different from other approaches to software design. There is also confusion about the differences between object-oriented design and object-oriented programming (covered in the following section) and object-oriented design and design with abstract data types. In this section, I argue that object-oriented design is simply an alternative way of building a real-world model in a computer-based system and discuss how design with data abstraction can be viewed as a specialised form of object-oriented design.

Essentially, the role of any computer system is to model the real-world thus allowing real-world operations (such as paying invoices) to be automated, real-world predictions to be made and, in control systems, real-world events to be influenced. The activity of software design (for simplicity, I am ignoring the cases where parts of the model are implemented in hardware) therefore consists of identifying appropriate real-world abstractions and mapping these onto a computational framework which allows the system services to be implemented. At the same time, the designer must take into account non-functional requirements such as reliability, performance, user error-rate etc.

Since the concept of a writeable memory was invented by Von Neumann, the computational framework in general use for software design has been based around the notion of representing the system state in an area of writeable memory which may be accessed by functional components which reflect real-world operations. As these components execute, the system state is updated. This model is illustrated in Figure 1 and is referred to here as a function-oriented model as the basic software components model functional, real-world activities.

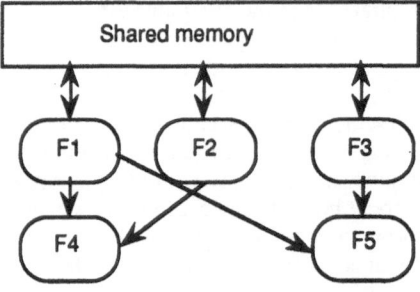

Figure 1 A function-oriented view of design

Note that function-oriented in this context does not mean the same as 'functional' as in 'functional programming'. In functional programming, the notion of a writeable memory has been discarded and the components are abstractions of mathematical expressions rather than models of real-world functions. This is an alternative form of real-world modelling which will not be discussed here.

An object-oriented approach to design is distinct from the function-oriented approach in two principal ways:

- The basic abstractions are not real-world functions such as 'sort', 'display', 'track' etc. but are real-world entities such as 'file', 'picture' or 'radar_system'.

- State information is not represented in a centralised shared memory but is distributed amongst the objects in the system. Objects communicate by message passing so that one object may discover the state information of another object by interrogating it.

Of course, somewhere or other, the real-world functions must be modelled. However, it is argued that these functions are usually associated with specific real-world entities and only require access to part of the system state information. In fact, the real-world entities are modelled by representing them as a grouping of functions and state information where the functions model allowed operations on the entities. This situation is illustrated in Figure 2.

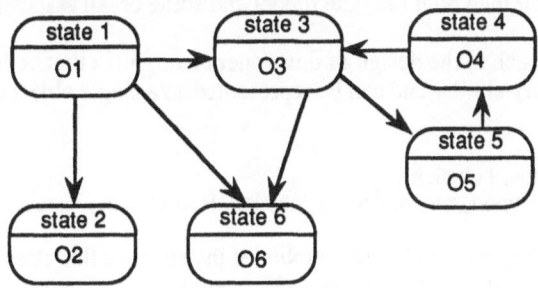

Figure 2 An object-oriented view of design

In practice, real-world entities tend to fall into classes such as 'files', 'cars', 'terminals' etc. Each class has a common set of state variables and allowed operations but individual instances of the class are distinguished by the fact that their state variables have different values. For example, the class 'cars' defines that all cars have a colour, a model name, an engine capacity etc. and individual instances of cars such as 'red Ford Fiesta', 'black Nissan Cherry', etc. can be created. Thus, in object-oriented design it is normal practice to design object classes and to provide a means of creating individual objects from these classes.

To illustrate the distinction between object-oriented and function-oriented design, consider a very simple example where it is intended to build a fire alarm system which monitors a number of smoke detectors and reports to some central console the location of a fire (as a room number) when indicated as a smoke detector. The system must also monitor a number of manually operated fire alarms and similarly report the location when one of these is activated. Assume initially that each room has a smoke detector.

In a shared-memory, function-oriented design, the system state might be represented using four arrays:

```
Smoke_detectors: array (1..Number_of_detectors) of BOOLEAN ;
Detector_locations: array (1..Number_of_detectors) of ROOM_NUMBER ;
Fire_alarms: array (1..Number_of_alarms) of BOOLEAN ;
Alarm_locations: array (1..Number_of_alarms) of ROOM_NUMBER ;
```

The values in the arrays Smoke_detectors and Fire_alarms correspond to the state of the associated hardware devices and the values in the arrays Detector_locations and Alarm_locations are constant. To discover the location of an alarm which registers in Fire-alarms (N), the corresponding element (Alarm_locations (N)) is interrogated.

The functions which operate on the system state might be:

```
Interrogate_detectors
Get_detector_location
Reset_detectors
Interrogate_alarms
Get_alarm_location
Reset_alarms
Report_fire_location
```

These functions have access to all of the state information and are tightly bound to it. If, for some reason, it is decided that detectors may cover more than one room or that large rooms may have more than 1 detector, then both the state model and some or all associated functions may have to be changed.

An object-oriented approach to the design of this system recognises that both detectors and fire alarms are actually very similar and can be represented as a single object class.

```
class Sensor
    attributes: Type, Status, Location ;
    operations: Create, Report_status, Report_location, Report_type, Reset
```

To model the real-world system, the appropriate number of instances of this class are created with their attributes initialised to the required values. For example,

```
A1 := Sensor.Create (Type -> Fire_alarm, Status -> Off, Location -> B2a)
S1 := Sensor.Create (Type -> Smoke_detector, Status -> Off, Location -> B3)
```

In this approach to design, there is a looser relationship between the modelling of the system state and the functions which operate on that state. Thus, there is no difficulty in coping with changes to the relationship between sensors and location. Each sensor knows its own location so changes to the system are localised.

The intention of this trivial example is not to demonstrate the advantages of object-oriented design but to illustrate the different underlying design models. The principal advantage of object-oriented design is the fact the designs are easier to change but this cannot be readily illustrated using small examples as all small examples are easy to change! An argument putting forward the advantages of the object-oriented approach is presented in a later section which is explicitly concerned with object-oriented design and reliability.

It has been suggested by Meyer [6] that the components of an object-oriented design are inherently more reusable than functions created during the function-oriented design process. This observation is sensible as reusability clearly depends on state information and the principal obstacle in function reuse is the need to deal with shared state. In itself, reuse should be an important contributor to reliability as components which are reused should be validated by their use in real systems.

It is often suggested that object-oriented design is a 'methodology' in the same way that MASCOT [7] and SSADM [8] are design methodologies. This is nonsense. A 'design methodology' limits the types of abstraction which may be used in a design, defines rules (usually *ad hoc*) or guidelines about how these design abstractions interact, defines required design documentation and (sometimes) suggests how one view of a design may be transformed to an alternative or more detailed view. This section of the paper has argued that object-oriented design is an approach to real-world modelling which is distinct from the approach based on shared memory and functions and certainly can't be termed a 'design methodology'. As discussed later, one of the problems with object-oriented design is the lack of an associated design methodology.

Objects and Abstract Data Types

The notion of data typing as an important abstraction in system design has been recognised for a number of years where the type of an entity governs the operations allowed on that entity. For example, it makes no sense to apply a concatenate operation to an entity of type integer nor is it sensible to multiply two objects of type string together.

An abstract data type is a type which is defined by the operations on that type and whose representation is completely concealed from other entities using that type. For example, an entity of type STACK has associated operations such as Pop, Push, Size etc. and the semantics of these operations essentially define the type. Instances of that type have a state but that state may only be changed and interrogated if appropriate operations have been specified by the definer of the type.

Obviously then, abstract data types and object classes have a great deal in common as have objects and variables of a particular abstract type. The important distinction between instances of abstract data types and objects is that the state of an object may be changed by internal operations which are private to that object whereas the state of a variable of a given abstract type may only be changed explicitly by operations defined in the abstract data type interface specification. Therefore, variables of some abstract data types are passive and sequential - they respond to external commands such as 'change state', 'deliver state' etc. By contract, objects *may* be active and include internal operations which change the state of the object without any external operation being initiated.

As an example of this distinction, say it was intended to model an aircraft's position which could be computed by cross-referencing the positions of known radio beacons. The appropriate beacons to be used are, in fact, a function of the aircraft's position. If the position is represented as an abstract data type, it must have a defined operation 'Compute_position' which takes the appropriate radio beacons as its parameters. Which beacons to use are externally determined. By contrast, if position is represented as an object, it may include a position attribute which is constantly updated by operations internal to that object which know the location of radio beacons.

Objects are autonomous and potentially active; instances of abstract data types are always passive and but obviously may be considered as a special type of object.

OBJECT-ORIENTED DESIGN AND OBJECT-ORIENTED PROGRAMMING

There is an immense amount of obfuscation about the differences between object-oriented design (OOD) and object-oriented programming (OOP). Indeed, the confusion is sometimes actively exacerbated by some proponents of particular object-oriented programming languages who themselves do not seem to understand the differences between OOD and OOP.

Object-oriented design and object-oriented programming are not the same thing. As discussed above, object-oriented design is a way of building a model of the real-world where state is hidden within objects and distributed across objects. Object-oriented programming generally means the use of an object-oriented programming language for system implementation. Obviously, object-oriented programming requires an object-oriented design but designing in an object-oriented way does not require that an object-oriented programming language be used.

In essence, object-oriented programming languages are languages which allow the direct translation of an object-oriented design into an executable program. They include constructs which allow object classes to be defined and a run-time system which supports the dynamic creation of objects of a given class. Typically, they also include support for class inheritance where one class may be said to be a sub-class of some other class and thus inherit its attributes and operations. For example, the above definition of Sensor may be a super-class and, in some circumstances, it may be sensible to define sub-classes such as Temperature_sensor which inherits the attributes and operations of Sensor but adds an additional attribute which reflects the actual temperature recorded.

It is not my intention here to discuss any specific object-oriented programming language or its facilities. Although inheritance is put forward as a key advantage of these languages, there is no standard model of inheritance so each language supports it in a different way. Furthermore, the individual models of inheritance are usually not orthogonal and are sometimes inconsistent and it is my opinion that inheritance facilities simply add complexity without providing a great deal of useful functionality.

As discussed above, object-oriented design is an approach to modelling the real-world and an object-oriented design may be implemented, in principle, in any programming language. Of course, languages such as FORTRAN, Pascal and C are explicitly oriented towards function-oriented design and attempting to implement an object-oriented design in these languages requires a good deal of discipline on the part of the programmer. It must be recognised that, however careful the programmer, mapping an object-oriented design onto a function-oriented language is likely to introduce errors which reduce the potential improvements which can result from an object-oriented approach to design.

Although languages such as FORTRAN, Pascal and C are barely adequate for implementing an object-oriented design, Ada is a more appropriate language. It is often the case that many of the object classes in a system design are passive classes and can be modelled using Ada packages to define abstract data types. Individual objects may also be modelled using packages with internal state but completely general object classes are not supported. Some generality is possible using generic packages to define object classes although this is not a completely satisfactory approach.

Although imperfect as an implementation mechanism for object-oriented designs, Ada has the advantage of inbuilt support for parallelism and exception handling, standardisation, widespread acceptance, tool support and guaranteed longevity. Thus, for the implementation of large systems which have been designed using an object-oriented approach, I would recommend Ada as the most appropriate programming language.

Apart from Smalltalk [1] which was developed in the early 1970s, most object-oriented programming languages are relatively new and have not been widely used in large-scale systems development. For reasons which are not important here, languages such as Smalltalk and Objective-C [9] involve a significant run-time overhead both in space and time and are best suited to prototyping and the development of relatively small software systems. Other languages such as C++ [10] and Eiffel [11] have explicitly attempted to avoid this run-time overhead by limiting their generality and may be more suitable for large system implementation. The use of these languages definitely simplifies the implementation of an object-oriented design but their limited availability and lack of support means that choosing such a language for a large project represents a significant management risk.

DESIGN FOR RELIABILITY

Ideally, a paper like this one would report on experiences with object-oriented design for large system construction, compare these with other systems designed using a function-oriented approach and draw some conclusions from this comparison. Unfortunately, this is not possible. There have been few large systems built using an object-oriented approach. Those object-oriented systems which have been built (such as the Smalltalk programming environment) are so specialised that they cannot serve as a general system model. Thus, we cannot rely on empirical evidence to support object-oriented design but must simply advance analytical arguments why this approach is often an improvement over function-oriented design.

It is assumed that the objective of the system designer is to produce a design which is as reliable as required. This means:

a) As far as possible, faults should not be introduced into the design.

b) The repair of detected faults should have a low probability of introducing or exposing other software faults.

c) Software components and the system in general should be resilient in the presence of software faults.

We should therefore examine object-oriented design against these three headings namely fault avoidance, fault repair and fault tolerance. The analysis suggests that the object-oriented approach to design will probably lead to more reliable systems given that all other factors are the same.

Fault avoidance

Although a precise classification of software system faults is probably impossible to achieve, it is obvious that many design faults fall into one of three classes:

1. Misunderstood abstractions. Abstractions do not accurately reflect the behaviour of the real-world entity which they are modelling.

2. Omitted functionality where some required functionality is accidentally left out by the designer.

3. Unanticipated state modifications. The system state is changed by one component in a way which is not anticipated by other components using that state. This is a particular problem in large system design where components are independently developed.

Thus, to avoid design faults we should consider an approach to design against each of these common causes and examine whether or not it is likely to reduce faults introduced into the system.

A very common fault indeed is that the designer has an incomplete or an incorrect view of the real-world operations and entities which are modelled by the computer system and this is reflected in the ensuing software design. For some classes of system, particularly those which include hardware components an object-oriented view is probably more natural than a function-oriented view in that the real-world entities being modelled are obvious physical things such as valves, sensors, thermocouples, gears, etc. It is possible to observe the real-world entity and to model it directly as a system object or object class. Because of this one-to-one relationship, it can be argued that misunderstandings are less likely so errors are less likely to be introduced.

The same argument really applies to the problem of omitted functionality. In a function-oriented design, the designer must separate state information from functions and in making the separation may leave out either essential state variables, required functions or both. Because the object-oriented approach groups the operations and their related state information, errors of omission are more obvious and more likely to be detected by the designer before the design is complete.

Finally, there is no doubt that an object-oriented approach leads to fewer inadvertent state changes. Rather than the whole state of the system being visible to all objects, each object manages its own state and all state modifications are localised. It is immediately obvious where state changes occur and the objects act as firewalls around the state protecting it from interference by other objects. Thus, this class of errors is certainly reduced by adopting an object-oriented approach.

Fault repair

It is practically impossible to demonstrate that a software system is free of faults and it must always be assumed that faults will come to light after a system has gone into use. It is important that these faults should be repaired quickly without introducing new faults into the system. Fault repair therefore relies on the system design being easy to understand and on system components being independent of other components so that changes to one component may be made without affecting other components.

Again, the grouping of relevant state and operations which is an essential part of object-oriented design leads to software which is more amenable to change. Objects may be considered as stand-alone entities without reference to other parts of the system and thus may be understood by the system maintainer. Understanding is also simplified because the operations associated with the object are likely to map directly onto real-world operations.

Changes to an object are local to that object and are unlikely to affect other objects in the system. In a function-oriented approach, changes to one function often require changing state information and this can have unanticipated side effects. Such side-effects are much less likely where all changes to a part of the state are made in one place and controlled by a known object. Thus, fault repair is unlikely to introduce new faults elsewhere in the system.

Fault tolerance

A fault tolerant system is a system which can continue to operate in the presence of faults and, again, the distribution of state information which is inherent in an object-oriented approach is of value. In a situation where all of the system state is accessible by the functions manipulating that state, an error in one of these functions can be readily propagated through the entire system state. This, of course, is likely to cause complete system failure.

However, where only part of the state is visible at any time to an object, only the state within that object may be damaged in the event of an error. Damage is not likely to be propagated throughout the system thus improving the overall probability that the system can continue to operate in the presence of an error.

The general approach to fault tolerant software involves detecting a software fault by applying predicates to the system state. If the evaluation of these predicates suggest an anomaly two alternative approaches are possible.

- The system state may be explicitly modified to same known 'safe' state ignoring the operation which caused the fault and then continuing execution in some degraded fashion.

- The system state may be restored to its state before the fault occured and some alternative operation code with comparable functionality implemented. After execution of this code, normal operation continues.

The object-oriented approach can be used to support both of these strategies. A duplicate set of 'safe' state variables may be maintained within each object and, on detection of an anomaly, copied to the 'normal' object state variables. Because each object knows which part of the state it maintains, only a limited part of the state need be restored at any one time so system overheads are limited. The rest of the system need not know that any error has occurred.

The alternative strategy can also be supported using an object-oriented approach. An object may maintain a mirror copy of its state information so, when a fault is detected, it is straightforward to restore the state to that before the call. Furthermore, the object may explicitly use private state variables to record the existence of an error and then may reactivate itself for further processing. The operation selected may depend on the error record so that alternative code may be used for processing.

RISKS OF ADOPTING OBJECT-ORIENTED DESIGN

The technical arguments put forward in the previous parts of this paper suggest than the object-oriented approach to design is, in principle at least, an improvment over the more traditional function-oriented approach. However, adopting this approach to design and system implementation does currently involve some risks and these must be taken into account before a final decision is made.

Some of the obvious risks of adopting this approach to design are as follows:

- There is a lack of industrial experience with this approach and training costs for designers may be very high. Of course, training costs for other approaches to design such as SSADM are also high but the relative immaturity of object-oriented design means that there is still a considerable lack of training material.

- Although programming languages such as Pascal and C can be used to implement object-oriented design their use is not advised. Thus, heavy investment in equipment and software may be required to support the implementation of object-oriented design.

- It has been observed by object-oriented designers that object decomposition is particularly difficult and, it may be the case that design costs with this approach may be higher than with a function-oriented approach particularly if experienced designers are not available.

- There are no object-oriented design methods or associated CASE toolsets which have been developed to the same level of maturity as MASCOT [7], Structured Design [12], SSADM [8], etc. Design methods are of little value to talented and experienced designers but they do assist inexperienced designers and they do define standard sets of design documentation which are of immense value in system maintenance. Some object-oriented design methods have been developed [13, 14] but they are mostly untried and experimental.

- Many approaches to requirements specification such as CORE [15] rely on functional decomposition and it is not obvious how a detailed requirements definition expressed in a functional style can be mapped to an object-oriented design. It is likely that the full benefits from this approach will only accrue when it is supplemented by a complementary object-oriented approach to requirements specification.

- It is not clear how the object-oriented approach can be combined with formal software specifications expressed in specification languages such as Z [16] and VDM [17]. Although it may well be possible to combine existing formal specification techniques and object-oriented design, there is a lack of experience in this area and some changes to specification notations may be required if active objects are to be effectively modeled.

Some of these risks simply reflect the immaturity of the technology and it is likely that over the next few years methods and tool support will become available as will a larger pool of experienced designers. Other difficulties such as the mismatch between function-oriented requirements and object-oriented design will take longer to resolve and will require extensive changes to company practices.

CONCLUSIONS

The title of this paper was carefully chosen. Teenagers often show promise but are clearly immature and lacking in wisdom and experience. The same is true of object-oriented design. It is very likely that it will become the preferred approach to software design sometime in the future but, in the same way as structured programming took many years to be generally accepted so too will object-oriented design.

In order to derive most benefit from this approach to design, it is important the object-oriented approach should not be confined to a single stage of the software process. Rather, object-oriented design should be supplemented by an object-oriented view of requirements and by using an object-oriented programming language (or, at least, a language with some object implementation facilities, like Ada). We can expect to see design methods mature and existing methods will be adapted to support the object-oriented approach. New developments in specification languages will also take place to provide a formal basis for this approach to design.

Teenagers have to be nurtured carefully and should not be asked to carry out tasks which are beyond their capabilities. Currently, we have so little experience with object-oriented design in large system production that its use has to be carefully controlled and it must be introduced incrementally into the software production process. In a large system, some subsystems might be designed using an object-oriented approach while others are designed using function-oriented techniques. Given that an implementation language like Ada is used, there is no reason why these techniques cannot be used in a complementary way.

REFERENCES

1. Goldberg, A. and Robson, D. (1983), Smalltalk-80. The Language and its Implementation, Reading, Mass.: Addison Wesley.

2. Booch, G. 'Object-oriented development', *IEEE Trans. on Software Engineeirng*, 1986, 12 (2), pp. 211-21.

3. Booch, G. *Software Engineering with Ada* , 2nd Edition, Benjamin Cummings, Reading, Mass., 1987.

4. Jackson, M.A. *System Development*, Prentice-Hall, London, 1983.

5. Cameron, J.R. 'An Overview of JSD', *IEEE Trans. in Software Engineering*, 1986, 12 (2), pp. 222-240.

6. Meyer, B. 'Reusability: The Case for Object-oriented Design', *IEEE Software*, 1987, 4 (2), pp. 50-64 .

7. Simpson, H. 'The MASCOT method', *BCS/IEE Software Engineering J.*, 1986, 1 (3), pp. 103-20.

8. Cutts, G. *Structured Systems Analysis and Design*, London: Paradigm, 1987.

9. Cox B.J. *Object-Oriented Programming: An Evolutionary Approach*, Addison-Wesley, Reading, Mass., 1986.

10. Stroustrup, B. *The C++ Programming Language*, Addison Wesley, Menlo Park, Ca., 1986.

11. Meyer, B. *Object-oriented Software Constructure*, Prentice-Hall, Englewood Cliffs, NJ., 1987.

12. Constantine, L.L. & Yourdon, E. *Structured Design*, Prentice-Hall, Englewood Cliffs, NJ, 1977.

13. 'HOOD Reference Manual' Issue 3, 1989, European Space Agency, The Netherlands.

14. Seidewitz, E. and Stark, M. 'Towards a General Object-Oriented Software Development Methodology', *Ada Latters*, 1987, 7 (4), pp. 54-67.

15. Looney, M. *CORE - A Debrief Report*, NCC Publications, Manchester, 1985.

16. Hayes, I. (ed), *Specification Case Studies*, Prentice-Hall, London, 1987.

17. Jones, C.B. *Systematic Software Development using VDM*, Prentice-Hall, London:, 1986.

17

SOFTWARE ARCHITECTURE MODELLING

CYDNEY MINKOWITZ
STC Technology Ltd.
Copthall House, Nelson Place, Newcastle-under-Lyme, ST5 1EZ, UK

ABSTRACT

Techniques such as formal methods and object-oriented design allow software engineers to describe the structure and design of a system at a high level of abstraction. They free software engineers from concerns about implementation details so that the engineers can concentrate on the gross organisation of the data structures and algorithms that constitute the system. This kind of software architecture modelling enables software engineers to explore the design space of a system and to clear up conceptual errors and misunderstandings about a system's basic structure. The **me too** method makes use of three techniques – formal specification, functional programming and rapid prototyping – to model software architecture. This paper discusses the use of **me too** to model the architecture of part of a large software system that is being developed for the Esprit IMSE (Integrated Modelling Support Environment) project.

INTRODUCTION

It is general practice in all branches of engineering design to adopt abstraction techniques to model complex systems. In many cases, this involves describing certain properties of a system using some general purpose design language. The design language used depends on the nature of the system and on the particular characteristics of the system that one wants to explore. For example, an electrical engineer who is interested in the physical characteristics of a circuit design will use a modelling language whose primitives are the objects of electrical networks, such as resistors, capacitors, inductors and transistors, which are characterised in terms of voltages and currents. In contrast, an electrical circuit designer who is only interested in the functionality of a device will employ a language whose primitives are signal-processing modules such as filters and amplifiers, which allows one to describe the gross organisation of the modules and their behaviour without

325

regard for their physical realisation.

Like the circuit designer, a software designer will want to call upon different languages to model the various aspects of a software system, including user requirements, functional behaviour and performance. As with circuit design, software designers wishing to model the functional behaviour of a software system will choose a language which allows them to describe the architecture of the software in an abstract way, in terms of its abstract objects and operations.

Computing scientists have found such a language in the mathematics of set theory. That language allows one to define software objects in terms of mathematical types such as sets and maps, and to define operations on the objects in terms of the mathematical constructs of those types.

A design expressed in a mathematical language is often elegant in its conciseness and simplicity. Its correctness can also be verified using the proof procedures that come with the language. Most importantly, the meaning of a correct and complete design expressed in mathematics is undisputable. It therefore serves as an excellent communication vehicle for members of a design team.

The formal design methods, VDM [1] and Z [2], borrow heavily from the language of set theory. The functional programming language, Miranda [3] includes some facility for defining set types and constructs, although it does not support as rich a mathematical language as VDM and Z. However, a design written in Miranda is also a program which can be executed just like any other program. Because of this a design specification in Miranda can also act as a prototype of the final software product.

me too [4,5] is a functional programming language designed specifically to support functional modelling. The primitives of the language are based on sets, and it contains a rich syntax for expressing operations on sets. Like Miranda, **me too** can be used for prototyping purposes.

me too was conceived by Peter Henderson, and is the product of an Alvey funded research project involving STC Technology Ltd and the Department of Computing Science at Stirling University. A tool that supports the language has been implemented in Lisp and is available from STC Technology Ltd. During the project, **me too** was used extensively for the design of software for a number of applications, including expert systems and decision support systems for business applications, and for the design of complex architectures for simulation applications and database applications. It has also been used on a number of industrial projects within ICL [6].

me too has been used by the author on the design of one of the software tools being developed under the IMSE project, which is an Esprit2 project investigating methods and tools to support performance modellers. The design of the tool will be used in this paper as an example to illustrate the use of **me too** on a substantial application. The example is appropriate to the discussion above, because it describes the design of a tool which itself embodies a method for describing the structure and performance of information systems. In this example, the **me too** description of the architecture of the tool also serves as a means of describing the method which it supports.

The **me too** model of the design is given in later sections. The reader who is unfamiliar with mathematical notation might find the specification of the design hard going. The initial concepts of the design presented in Section 3 are fairly simple, and the reader is encouraged to browse through that part of the specification in order to get a taste of high-level design languages. As this document is also intended to be a design description of the software for other members of the author's project to study, the full specification is included. For the really keen reader, an appendix has been included which contains a summary of the notation used in the paper.

First, the background to the work reported here is discussed in the next section.

STRUCTURE AND PERFORMANCE SPECIFICATION

The aim of the IMSE project is to facilitate the use of advanced systems engineering methods throughout the design cycle by the development of a support environment for performance modelling [7]. Features of the environment are: advanced graphics work-stations; extensible tool-set supporting alternative performance modelling paradigms such as queue-networks, process-interaction, petri-nets; integration of tools via a common object management system, common graphics support, and shared experimental and reporting facilities; structured system specification providing a capability for integration with external design support environments.

The IMSE project will pursue the ideas originated in the SIMMER project under the Alvey Software Engineering programme. The SIMMER project adopted a method called *sp*, standing for Structure and Performance specification, which was originated by Peter Hughes at the University of Trondheim in Norway. The *sp* method supports information capture and complexity analysis about information systems. The method can be used for sizing systems, but its emphasis is on support for the evolution of large product families during design and development. The IMSE project is investigating the use of *sp* further and is developing a companion software tool .

The SIMMER project produced a prototype tool for *sp* [8], which helped to explore the fundamental principles. Since then, the ideas behind *sp* have been refined for use in a wider range of applications, and the time was ripe for a more formal approach to the specification of *sp*. A high level description of *sp* was given using entity-relationship diagrams. Although this exercise helped communicate some of the ideas, it left many questions unanswered, and so a mathematically-based specification was sought. **me too** was the choice of specification language, because of the wish to test out the functions defining complexity analysis by executing them on known examples.

So far, a **me too** model has been produced that clarifies the established notions of *sp* . It will now serve as a basis on which to explore other notions. It has also been used as a design document for another prototype tool.

The **me too** model of *sp* is presented in the following
sections. The specification serves two purposes. It is a
specification of the concepts underlying *sp*. It is also a model
of the objects and operations contained in the accompanying
software tool. The rationale of the concepts specified are not
covered here. A thorough discussion of the principles of *sp* can
be found in [9].

As the name suggests, there are two sides to *sp*. The first
side concerns the specification of structural attributes of a
system. This involves giving an abstract description of a
system in terms of the properties of the basic building blocks,
or modules, from which it is constructed. These properties
include the set of operations supported by a module, and the set
of lower-level modules on which a given module depends. The
second side involves specifying the performance attributes of an
implementation of a module, which include the work and space
complexity functions which describe its efficiency with respect
to the lower-level modules, and the extent/capacity of the
physical data/storage structures of a system, so that sizing can
be performed. The structural side of *sp* is covered first.

STRUCTURAL ANALYSIS

A simple way of describing an information system is as a
collection of *nodes* linked together in a hierarchy. Figure 2
shows such a hierarchy for an order registration system, which
is represented as the Bachman diagram in Figure 1. Each node in
the system is an instance of a component of some type, such as a
CPU or a database manager, and has a data structure, such as a
workspace for the CPU, or records C, OI, OL and A for the
database manager.

In the **me too** model, a system is represented as follows:

```
System ::
    nodes : map(NodeName,Node)
    links : rel(NodeName,NodeName)
```

This says that a system is composed of a collection of nodes
indexed by name, and links which describe how the nodes relate
to one another in a hierarchy.

A node is described thus:

```
Node ::
    module : ModuleName
    data_structure : rel(DataClass,DataElement)
```

It has a data structure, which is a collection of data elements
of a given data class, for example records C, A, OI and OL. It
is also associated with a *module*, which determines what type of
component it is an instance of.

customers
C
file 1
articles
A
file 4
order
inventory
OI
file 2
index
file 5
order-line
OL
file 3

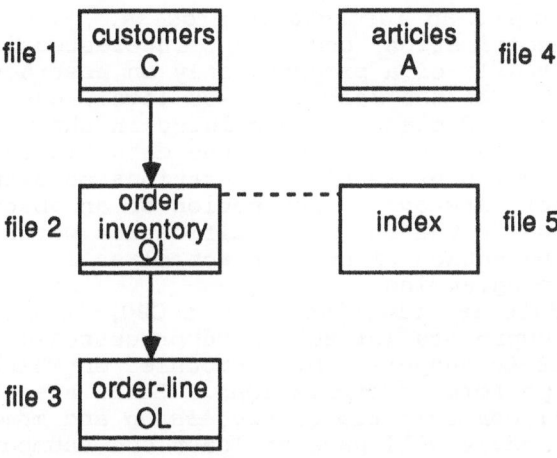

Figure 1. Database design for order registration system.

an Application
db view
picture
workspace
records C, OI, OL, A
a ScreenHandler
a HighLevelLanguage
a DatabaseManager
terminal
files 1-5
a CommsHandler
a FileHandler
lline
workspace
unit
a Comms
a CPU
a Disc

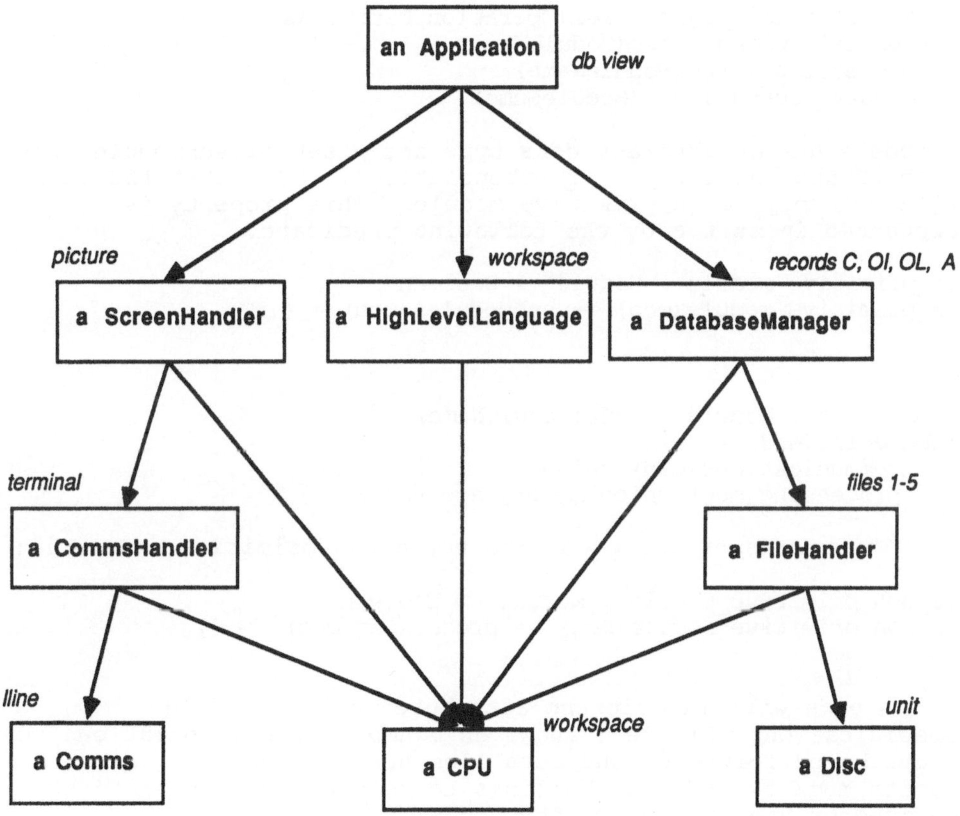

Figure 2. An order registration system.

A module supports an *information process*. For the purposes
of structural specification, one is not interested in the
implementation details of a process, only an abstract
description of it. At the most abstract level, one only needs
to know about the data classes manipulated in the process, and
the operations that are performed on the data classes during the
process. A collection of abstract operations on data classes is
called an *abstract data type*. The notion of an abstract data
type is well known in the formal specification world, and
corresponds to the notion of an abstract class in
object-oriented programming.

Unless a module is primitive, e.g. a CPU, it must itself
call upon some subprocess (or set of subprocesses). That
subprocess itself is supported by *submodules* on which the
calling process performs *suboperations*. There are three types
of suboperations: *communications*, *processing* and *memory access*.
A non-primitive module will have at least one submodule on which
it does its processing.

In the **me too** specification a module is represented by the
following:

```
Module ::
    abstract_data_type : rel(Operation,DataClass)
    communications : set(ModuleName)
    processing : set(ModuleName)
    memory_access : set(ModuleName)
```

A module has an abstract data type and a set of submodules for
each of the three types of suboperations. Note that the sets
will be empty for a primitive module. This property is
expressed in **me too** by the following predicate.

```
is_primitive_module : Module -> Boolean
is_primitive_module(mod) == submodules(mod) = {}
```

where

```
submodules : Module -> set(ModuleName)
submodules(mod) ==
    communications(mod) union
  ( processing(mod) union memory_access(mod) )
```

The corresponding predicate for a non-primitive module is:

```
is_non_primitive_module : Module -> Boolean
is_non_primitive_module(mod) == processing(mod) /= {}
```

A node will inherit the attributes of its module
specification. Figure 3 shows an example of the operations that
might be performed on the data elements of each node, as defined
by its module, and how the links correspond to suboperations
defined by the modules of the nodes.

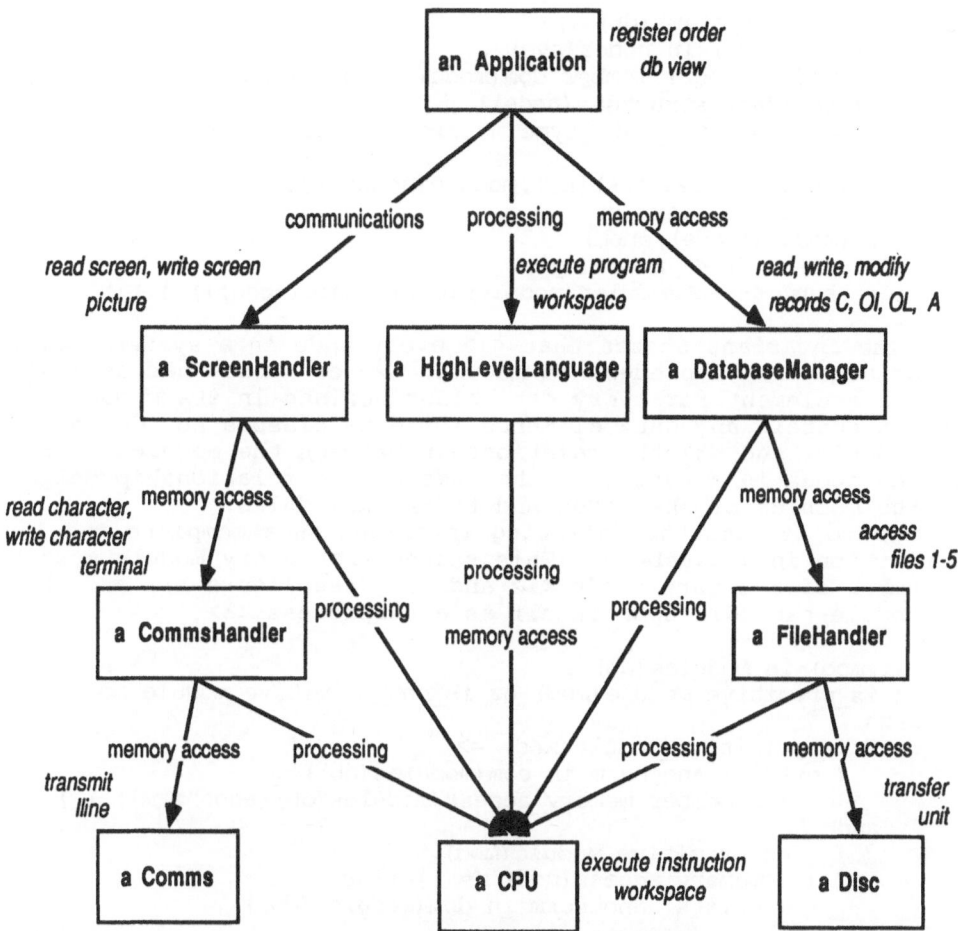

Figure 3. Operations and suboperations of order registration
system.

In a design and development environment, a system specifier
should be able to choose from a number of module specifications.
These specifications, and also the specifications of systems,
will be held in a central database, which is represented as:

```
Db ::
   modules : map(ModuleName,Module)
   systems : map(SystemName,System)
```

A system in the database that is deemed complete must have
certain properties. We define these properties as an *invariant*
on systems. For a given database *db*, that invariant is
expressed as follows:

```
all (s,sys) in systems(db) .
  ( ( all (n,node) in nodes(sys) .
         ( module(node) member dom(modules(db)) ) and              <1>
         ( dom(data_structure(node)) =                             <2>
           dom(abstract_data_type(modules(db)[module(node)])) ) )
    and
    ( { (module(nodes(sys)[h]),module(nodes(sys)[l]))              <3>
      | (h,l) <- links(sys) } =
      { (module(node),subm)
      | (n,node) <- nodes(sys) ,
        subm <- submodules(modules(db)[module(node)]) } ) )
```

The invariant states that <1> every node in a system must be associated with a predefined module, <2> each node has at least one data element for every data class defined in its module and cannot contain any data elements for data classes not defined in its module, and <3> the relationship between the modules of the linked nodes in a system is the same as the relationship defined by the modules of the nodes and their submodules.

There is also the following invariant on a complete module definition in a database. This states that every module must be a member of a *memory chain* <1> and <2> (see Figure 3), and that no module can call upon itself as a subprocess <3>.

```
all (m,mod) in modules(db) .
  ( ( is_primitive_module(mod) or is_non_primitive_module(mod) )
    and
    ( ( is_primitive_module(mod) =>                               <1>
        ( exists1 anotherm in dom(modules(db)) .
            ( m member memory_access(modules(db)[anotherm]) ) ) )
      and
      ( is_non_primitive_module(mod) =>                           <2>
        ( ( ( memory_access(mod) /= {} ) or
            ( exists1 anotherm in dom(modules(db)) .
                ( m member
                  memory_access(modules(db)[anotherm]) ) ) )
          and
          all subm in submodules(mod) .                          <3>
            ( ( subm member dom(modules(db)) ) and
              inv_submodule(db,m,subm) ) ) ) ) )
```

where

```
inv_submodule : Db x ModuleName x ModuleName -> Boolean
inv_submodule(db,m,subm) ==
  ( subm /= m ) and
  ( all othersubm in submodules(modules(db)[subm]) .
      inv_submodule(db,m,othersubm) )
```

This completes the **me too** model of structural specification in *sp*. The mathematical notation has enabled a simple yet precise description of both the concepts of system specification and the objects and operations of the prototype tool that supports it. A similar description could have been given using other specification languages. The advantage of using **me too**

333

was that the invariants could be tested by executing the
specification on sample systems and modules expressed as **me too**
objects.
 The model of the performance analysis side of *sp* is given
next.

PERFORMANCE ANALYSIS

The activity of selecting components and deciding how they
should fit together in a system is known as *configuration*. The
activity of designing a configuration with sufficient data
storage and processing power for the intended workload is known
as *sizing*. The method described above supports the configurer
in specifying the structure of a system in terms of its parts.
sp also provides support for defining the implementation details
used to determine a system's resource usage and workload, and a
calculator for sizing exercises.

Components
The physical properties of a node are determined by how its
module is implemented. The term *component* is used in *sp* to
describe an implementation of a module. (Recall that nodes are
instances of components.) A module can be implemented by a
number of components. The components may differ in the way in
which they represent the data classes of a module or the
algorithms they employ to carry out its operations. For
example, a file handler module can be implemented by a component
that uses direct-accessing to update its files, or one that uses
sequential-accessing.

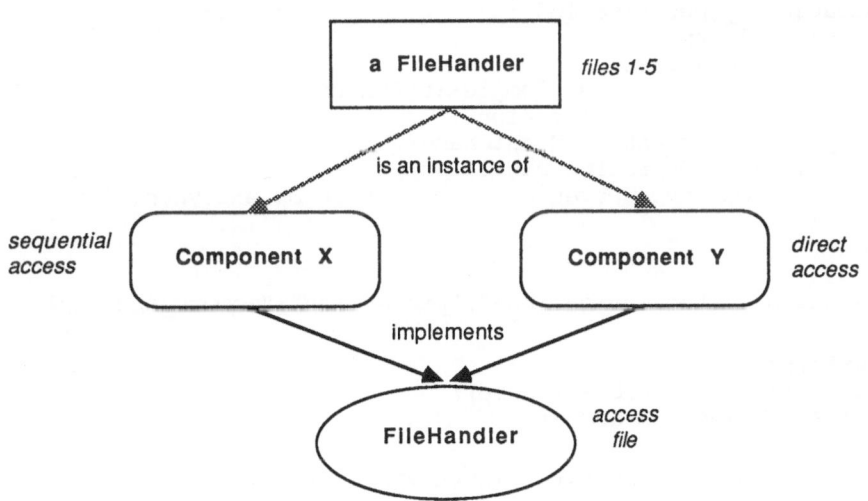

Figure 4.   Example components.

With a component, one specifies physical attributes
concerning the implementation. These attributes are called
structure parameters because they define properties which the
data structures of their instances possess, such as the number
of fields in a record. Different implementations of a module
may have different structure parameters. A particular structure
parameter, *extent*, defines the capacity of a data structure.
The other information specified with a component is closely
related to algorithmic complexity and is termed a *complexity
specification*. A complexity specification is a collection of
mapping functions representing two kinds of property which
determine the efficiency of an implementation:

- *compactness* determines how many data elements at the level
  of a calling process can be mapped to a unit of storage
  structure in each of the submodules which it uses for
  memory access (e.g. records to blocks)

- *work complexity* determines for each operation at the level
  of the calling process, how many invocations there will be
  of each operation in each of its submodules

In many cases complexity functions must be highly
parameterised, since the mapping can vary both with the values
of an operation's arguments and with the properties of the data
structure to which it is applied.
The definition of a component in the **me too** model is as
follows:

```
Component ::
    module : ModuleName
    structure_parameters : map(DataClass,map(Name,Parameter))
    extent_parameters : map(DataClass,NumberParameter)
    compactness_specification :
      map(ModuleName,
          map(DataClass,
              map(DataClass,ComplexityFunction)))
    work_complexity_specification :
      map(tup(Suboperation,ModuleName),
          map(tup(Operation,DataClass),
              map(tup(Operation,DataClass),ComplexityFunction)))

where

Suboperation = {"communications","processing","memory_access"}

ComplexityFunction ::
    pars : seq(tup(DataClass,Name))
    fn : seq(Value) -> Number

Parameter = NumberParameter | IntegerParameter | ...
NumberParameter ::
    range : set(Number)
    default_value : Number
(similarly for IntegerParameter etc.)
```

```
Name = String \ {"extent","capacity"}
Value = Number | Integer | ...
```

The designer and developer now has the ability to catalogue components for use (or re-use) when configurating systems. The central database of objects that the *sp* tool manipulates now has this representation:

```
Db ::
  modules : map(ModuleName,Module)
  systems : map(SystemName,System)
  components : map(ComponentName,Component)
```

Once a component has been selected for a node's module, implementation details specific to a node can be given. By default, a node will inherit the properties of its component. So, for example, the capacities of its data elements will inherit the default values specified with the extent parameters of its components. Specific values for the structure parameters can be given to override the default values. Specific numbers can also be entered for the memory mappings of its data structure to the data structure of its lower-level node, and the calls its operations make on those of the lower-level nodes.
This leads to a new definition for a node:

```
Node ::
  module : ModuleName
  component : ComponentName
  data_structure : rel(DataClass,DataElement)
  structure_values : map(tup(Name,DataClass,DataElement),Value)
  capacities : ExtentVector
  extents : ExtentVector
  memory_mappings : map(NodeName,MemoryMapping)
  work_matrices : map(tup(Suboperation,NodeName),WorkMatrix)
```

where

```
MemoryMapping = map(tup(DataClass,DataElement),ExtentVector)
ExtentVector = map(tup(DataClass,DataElement),Number)
WorkMatrix = map(tup(Operation,DataClass,DataElement),WorkVector)
WorkVector = map(tup(Operation,DataClass,DataElement),Number)
```

Resource usage
sp performs two kinds of static performance analysis - *resource usage analysis* and *workload analysis*. Resource usage analysis determines how much storage space is required at a lower-level node in a system to service the demands of a higher-level node.
The data structures of successive nodes in a memory chain have a special relationship. The data structure of the lower-level node becomes the storage structure of the *user* node (i.e. the higher-level node that uses the storage structure of the lower-level node). The extent of a data structure of a node defines the amount of space it uses. The capacity of the data structure defines how much space it has. At a top-level node,

the extent is limitied in range by the extent parameters of the
node's component. At a lower-level node the extent parameters
limit the range of the capacity of the storage structure. The
extent of a lower-level node is devolved from the extent of the
data structure of its user and the specified memory mappings.
In a sizing exercise, a configurer must ensure that the capacity
of a storage structure is not exceeded by the devolved extent.

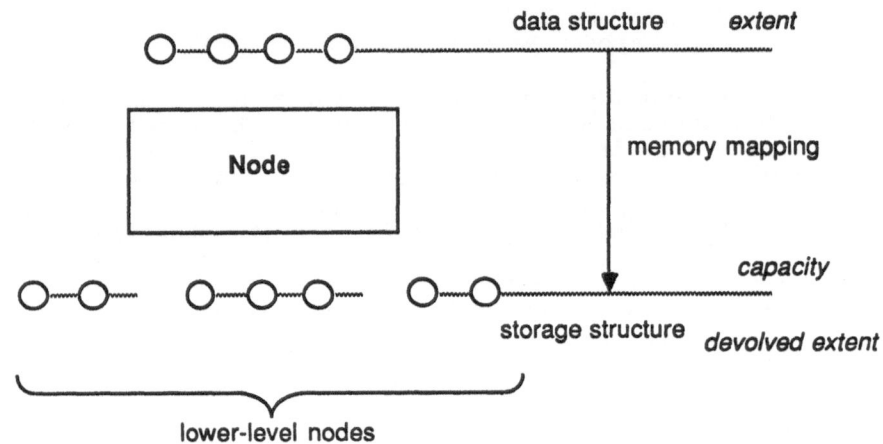

Figure 5. Memory mappings.

The properties of extents and capacities can be expressed by
the invariant below.

```
all (n,node) in nodes(sys) .
  ( ( ( all ((cl,el),extent) in extents(node) .
      ( (cl,el) member data_structure(node) ) )
    and
      ( ( ( not(n member rng(links(sys))) ) =>
          ( all ((cl,el),extent) in extents(node) .
            ( extent member
              range(extent_parameters(components(db)
                                        [component(node)])
                  [cl,default_extent_parameter()]) ) ) )
      or
        ( extents(node) =
          devolved_extent(db,sys,user(db,sys,n),n) ) ) )
    and
    ( ( capacities(node) /= {} ) =>
      ( ( n member rng(links(sys)) ) and
        ( all ((cl,el),capacity) in capacities(node) .
          ( ( (cl,el) member data_structure(node) ) and
            ( capacity member
              range(extent_parameters(components(db)
                                        [component(node)])
                  [cl,default_extent_parameter()]) ) ) ) ) )
  ) )
```

```
where

default_extent_parameter : -> NumberParameter
default_extent_parameter() ==
  mk_NumberParameter({0,...,infinity},0)
```

The devolved extent of a data structure at a lower level in a system hierarchy is a function of the extent of the data structure of its user. The user of a node is specified by the following function.

```
user : Db x System x NodeName -> NodeName
user(db,sys,n) ==
  the({ h | (h,l) <- links(sys) ;
       ( l = n ) and
       ( module(nodes(sys)[l]) member
         memory_access(modules(db)[module(nodes(sys)[h])]) ) })
```

The following function calculates the devolved extent of a node as the product of the extent vector of the user and the memory mapping defined between the user and the node.

```
devolved_extent : Db x System x NodeName x NodeName -> ExtentVector
devolved_extent(db,sys,u,n) ==
  Mprod(extent_vector(db,nodes(sys)[u]),memory_mapping(db,sys,u,n))
```

The following function determines the extent vector of the user. For a user which is also a lower-level node, that vector will be devolved from its user. For a top-level user, it will be determined by the extent defined for its component overriden by any specific extents defined for the data elements of the node.

```
extent_vector : Db x Node -> ExtentVector
extent_vector(db,node) ==
  { (cl,el) : data_structure(node) ->
     extents(node)
      [(cl,el),
       default_value(extent_parameters(components(db)
                                       [component(node)])
                    [cl,default_extent_parameter()])] }
```

The following function determines how the data structure of the user is mapped to the storage structure of the node. If specific memory mappings between data elements in the data structure to the data elements of the storage structure have been specified, then they are used in the calculation. Otherwise, the user's component's compactness functions will be applied to the properties of the user's data structure.

```
memory_mapping : Db x System x NodeName x NodeName -> ExtentVector
memory_mapping(db,sys,u,n) ==
  let unode == nodes(sys)[u],
      nnode == nodes(sys)[n]
  in
    { (ucl,uel) : data_structure(unode) ->
      { (ncl,nel) : data_structure(nnode) ->
        memory_mappings(unode)
          [n,{}]
           [(ucl,uel),{}]
            [(ncl,nel),
             let complexity_function ==
                   compactness_function(db,component(unode),
                                           module(nnode),ucl,ncl)
             in
               apply(fn(complexity_function),
                      bind(db,unode,uel,pars(complexity_function)))
            ] } }
```

The following functions are used to retrieve a compactness
function defined in a component for a given data class and the
data class of a given submodule, and bind the formal parameters
of the compactness function to the values of the node's
structure parameters.

```
compactness_function :
  Db x ComponentName x ModuleName x DataClass x DataClass
                      -> ComplexityFunction
compactness_function(db,c,m,ucl,ncl) ==
  compactness_specification(components(db)[c])
    [m,{}]
     [ucl,{}]
      [ncl,mk_ComplexityFunction([],lambda().0)]


bind :
  Db x Node x DataElement x seq(tup(DataClass,Name)) -> seq(Value)
bind(db,node,el,formal_pars) ==
  [ if name = "extent"
     then
       extents(node)
         [(cl,el),
          default_value(extent_parameters(components(db)
                                            [component(node)])
                        [cl,default_extent_parameter()])]
     else
       structure_values(node)
         [(name,cl,el),
          default_value(structure_parameters(components(db)
                                               [component(node)])
                        [cl][name])]
  | (name,cl) <- formal_pars ]
```

After a successful sizing exercise, the following invariant
on a system *sys* will be true.

```
all (n,node) in nodes(sys) .
  all ((cl0,el0),extent) in extents(node) .
    all ((cl1,el1),capacity) in capacities(node) .
      ( ( ( cl0 = cl1 ) and ( el0 = el1 ) ) =>
        ( extent <= capacity ) )
```

Workload analysis
Workload describes the amount of work offered to a system over
some time period. Given a unit of work for each node at the
top of a system hierarchy, expressed in terms of its operations,
and a complete set of work complexity specifications, the total
static work devolved by a system is the aggregated devolved
workload of the nodes at the bottom of the hierarchy. The
devolved work for a bottom-level node can be calculated as the
product of the work-unit of the top-level node and the sum of
the products of the work-matrices along each path from the
top-level node to the bottom-level node. For a more detailed
explanation of workload analysis see [9]. For the sake of
completeness, the full set of functions that calculate workload
are given below. No further explanation of the model is given,
and it is left for the reader to digest if so desired.

```
Path = set(seq(tup(NodeName,Suboperation,NodeName)))


total_devolved_work : Db x System -> map(NodeName,WorkVector)
total_devolved_work(db,sys) ==
  { b : bottom_level_nodes(sys) ->
      MSigma({ t : top_level_nodes(sys) ->
                 devolved_work(db,sys,t,b) }) }


devolved_work : Db x System x NodeName x NodeName -> WorkVector
devolved_work(db,sys,t,b) ==
  MProd(work_unit(db,nodes(sys)[t]),
        MSigma({ p : paths(db,sys,t,b) ->
                   work_multiplier(db,sys,p) }))


work_multiplier : Db x System x Path -> WorkMatrix
work_multipler(db,sys,p) ==
  MPi([ work_matrix(db,sys,h,subop,l) | (h,subop,l) <- p ])
```

```
work_matrix :
 Db x System x NodeName x Suboperation x NodeName -> WorkMatrix
work_matrix(db,sys,h,subop,l) ==
   let hnode == nodes(sys)[h],
       lnode == nodes(sys)[l]
   in
     { (hop,hcl,hel) : operations(db,hnode) ->
         { (lop,lcl,lel) : operations(db,lnode) ->
             work_matrices(hnode)
               [(subop,l),{}]
                [(hop,hcl,hel),{}]
                 [(lop,lcl,lel),
                   let complexity_function ==
                         work_complexity_function(db,component(hnode),
                                                   subop,module(lnode),
                                                   hop,hcl,lop,lcl)
                   in
                     apply(fn(complexity_function),
                            bind(db,hnode,hel,pars(complexity_function)))
                 ] } }


work_complexity_function :
 Db x ComponentName x Suboperation x ModuleName x
 Operation x DataClass x Operation x DataClass -> ComplexityFunction
work_complexity_function(db,c,subop,m,hop,hcl,lop,lcl) ==
   work_complexity_specification(components(db)[c])
    [(subop,m),{}]
     [(hop,hcl),{}]
      [(lop,lcl),mk_ComplexityFunction([],lambda().0)]


work_unit : Db x Node -> WorkVector
work_unit(db,node) == { (op,cl,el) : operations(db,node) -> 1 }


operations : Db x Node -> set(tup(Operation,DataClass,DataElement))
operations(db,node) ==
   { (op,cl,el)
     | (op,cl) <- abstract_data_type(modules(db)[module(node)]) ,
       (cl0,el) <- data_structure(node) ; cl0 = cl }


top_level_nodes : System -> set(NodeName)
top_level_nodes(sys) == dom(links(sys)) diff rng(links(sys))


bottom_level_nodes : System -> set(NodeName)
bottom_level_nodes(sys) == rng(links(sys)) diff dom(links(sys))
```

```
paths : Db x System x NodeName x NodeName -> Path
paths(db,sys,t,b) ==
  if t = b then {[]}
  else
   { [(t,subop,l)] conc p
    | l <- rng(links(sys) dr {t}) ,
      subop <- suboperations(db,module(nodes(sys)[t]),
                             module(nodes(sys)[l])) ,
      p <- paths(db,sys,l,b) }


suboperations : Db x ModuleName x ModuleName -> set(Suboperation)
suboperations(db,m,subm) ==
    ( if ( subm member communications(modules(db)[m]) )
        then {"communications"} else {} ) union
  ( ( if ( subm member processing(modules(db)[m]) )
        then {"processing"} else {} ) union
    ( if ( subm member memory_access(modules(db)[m]) )
        then {"memory access"} else {} ) )
```

CONCLUSIONS

Promoters of formal methods and prototyping argue that the way
to reduce software development costs and to improve product
quality is to invest more in the early stages of development,
thereby reducing the risk of discovering errors late in
development when they are more costly to repair, and improving
the likelihood of product acceptability. This argument is
strengthened by observing how much emphasis is placed on early
experimentation and design validation in other, more mature
fields of engineering.

In other engineering disciplines, mathematical analysis and
simulation techniques are used to model various aspects of a
system design, including functional behaviour and performance.
Computer scientists are adopting similar techniques to model the
different aspects of designs of software systems.

This paper has demonstrated the use of a functional
programming language based on set theory, called **me too**, to
specify and validate the functional behaviour of software
systems. There are other executable specification languages
that can be used in the same way, for instance Prolog, which is
based on first-order predicate logic [10], and OBJ, which is
based on algebraic specification [11].

Apart from helping to validate a design, functional
modelling improves one's understanding of a design. The
formalism of the modelling techniques also helps to simplify a
design, while communication is enhanced by the concise and
unambiguous nature of mathematical specification.

The modelling exercise presented in this paper improved the
author's understanding of the basic concepts of a tool to
support structure and performance analysis of information
systems. The model is now being used to explore new ideas, and
to specify further functional requirements on the tool.

342

There are no hard and fast rules about applying functional
modelling methods. They can be applied to high-level
architectural aspects of a system, or they can be applied to
low-level details, such as algorithms. The example in this
paper demonstrates both modes of use.

In a large system development, it may be inappropriate to
model all parts of the system, especially if there are tight
budget constraints. In that case, it would be wise to
concentrate on those parts which are the most complex, and/or
the most critical, as was the case in the example reported here,
where a model was made of a key component of a large system.

REFERENCES

1. Jones, C.B., _Systematic Software Development using VDM_,
   Series in Computing Science, ed. C.A. R. Hoare, Prentice
   Hall International, 1986.

2. Hayes, I., _Specification case studies_, Series in Computing
   Science, ed. C.A.R. Hoare, Prentice Hall International, 1987.

3. Turner, D., Functional Programs as executable specifications.
   In _Mathematical Logic and Programming Languages_, eds. C.A.R.
   Hoare and J.C. Shepherdson, Prentice Hall International,
   1985.

4. Henderson, P. and Minkowitz, C., The **me too** method of
   software design. _ICL Technical Journal_, Vol. 5, No. 1, 1986.

5. Henderson, P., Functional Programming, Formal Specification
   and Rapid Prototyping. _IEEE Transactions on Software
   Engineering_, Vol. 12, No. 2, 1986.

6. Alexander, H. and Jones V., _Software Design and Prototyping
   using **me too**_, Prentice Hall International, 1989.

7. Hughes, P.H., Barber E., Pooley R., Titterington G.C. and
   Uppal C., The Integrated Modelling Support Environment Design
   Study. STC Technology Ltd. Technical Report 059/ICL229/1,
   July 1988.

8. Barber, E., _sp_ Users' Guide. STC Technology Ltd. Technical
   Report 059/ICL218/4, April 1988.

9. Hughes P.H., _sp_ Principles. STC Technology Ltd. Technical
   Report 059/ICL226/0, July 1988.

10.Kowalski R., The relation betweem logic programming and
   logic specification. In _Mathematical Logic and Programming
   Languages_, eds. C.A.R. Hoare and J.C. Shepherdson, Prentice
   Hall International, 1985.

11.Gougen J.A. and Winkler T., Introducing OBJ3. SRI
   International Technical Report, SRI-CSL-88-9, August 1988.

APPENDIX

Summary of **me too** operations and types used in the paper.

Boolean expressions

b1 and b2	logical and
b1 or b2	logical or
not(b)	logical negation
b1 => b2	logical implication
x = y	equality
x /= y	inequality
x <= y	less than or equal to

Functions

f(arg1,..., argn) == e	function definition
f(a1,...,an)	function invocation
apply(f,[a1,...,an])	function application

Conditional expressions

if b then e1 else e2

Local expressions

let x1 == e1,...,xk == ek in e   declaration of local object

Sets

{e1,...,ek}	enumerated set
{}	the empty set
s1 union s2	set union
s1 diff s2	set difference
x member s	set membership
the(s)	the element of a singleton set *s*
{ e | x <- s }	the set of all *e*, where *e* is an expression which may involve *x*, where *x* is taken from the set *s*
{ e | x <- s ; b }	same as above except the set is restricted to those expressions on *x*, where the predicate *b* is true for *x*
{ e | x <- s1 , y <- s2 ; b }	same as above, where *e* is an expression which may involve *x* and *y*, where *x* is taken from *s1* and *y* is taken from *s2*, and the predicate *b* is true for *x* and *y* - generalises to any number of generators
all x in s . b	every element *x* in a set *s* satisfies the predicate *b*
exists1 x in s . b	there exists one and only one element *x* in a set *s* which satisfies the predicate *b*

Binary relations

dom(r)	the domain of a relation *r*
rng(r)	the range of a relation *r*
r dr s	domain restriction

Tuples
(e1,e2)   pair
(e1,e2,e3)   triple

Maps
{ x : s -> e }   constructing a map from every
                                       element *x* of a set *s* to an
                                       expression e

m[index]   indexing a map *m*
m[index,default]   specifying a default if the map
                                       does not contain the index in
                                       its domain
m   indexing a triply-nested map
  [index1,default1]
   [index2,default2]
     [index3,default3]

Sequences
[e]   a sequence with one element
[]   the empty sequence
q1 conc q2   *q1* concatenated with *q2*
[e | x <- q]   sequence generation

Records
fld(r)   selects field fld of record *r*
mk-<record-name>(e1,...,ek)   make a record of type *record-name*
                                       with fields *e1,...,ek*

Type specification
T = T1   *T* is of type *T1*
T = {x1,...,xk}   enumerated set
T = T1 | T2   the union of types *T1* and *T2*
T = T1 \ T2   the difference of types *T1* and *T2*
T = set(T1)   set whose elements are of type *T1*
T = rel(T1,T2)   binary relation with domain
                                       elements of type *T1* and range
                                       elements of type *T2*
T = map(T1,T2)   map from elements of type *T1* to
                                       elements of type *T2*
T = tup(T1,...,Tk)   k-tuple, ith element is of type
                                       Ti
T = seq(T1)   sequence whose elements are of
                                       type *T1*
f : T1 x ... x Tk -> T   function on objects of types
                                       T1,...,Tk which returns an
                                       object of type *T*
T :: fld1 : T1 ... fldk : Tk   record with *k* fields, kth field
                                       is of type *Tk*

Auxiliary functions on matrices
Mprod(M1,M2)   matrix product
MSigma(s)   the sum of a set of matrices
MPi(q)   the product of a sequence of
                                       matrices

18

Mathematics as a Management Tool: Proof Rules for Promotion*

J.C.P. Woodcock[†]

Abstract

We consider how the Z notation is used to produce structured specifications. In particular, we consider the technique known as *promotion,* and give an example of its use in the structured specification of a file system. We then consider how the proof of this system's correctness can follow the structure of its specification. Promotion has traditionally been treated rather informally, and proofs of correctness have relied on the expansion of definitions and the subsequent loss of structure. We formalise the notion of promotion, and observe that it is a kind of data refinement calculation. We prove that promotion is monotonic, and that it distributes through the major specification combinators: disjunction, conjunction, and the precondition calculator. Finally, we apply our results to the proof of the file system.

1   Introduction

It has long been recognised that in the development of large, important software systems, improved management techniques can have only a limited effect. This is because they do not get to the heart of the matter: they do

---

†Joint Rutherford-Pembroke College Atlas Research Fellow in Computation, Oxford University Computing Laboratory, Programming Research Group, 8-11 Keble Road, Oxford OX1 3QD

not tackle complexity. They may be likened to rearranging the deck chairs on the promenade deck of a Titanic software development. They may make the ship look more appealing, but they do nothing to change the inevitability of the looming iceberg ahead. Rather, the only hope is the application of mathematics to provide some leverage in the fight against the complexities of size.

In this paper we consider how the devices of the schema calculus in Z [Spivey, 1988, 1989] are used to address the problem of large-scale software development. Like other mathematical techniques, Z offers the manager of such a development the opportunity to use the power of abstraction, enforced through the use of modularity and data refinement. For examples, see [Hayes, 1987; Morgan, 1990; Woodcock, 1989].

Conventional managerial wisdom states that proof in the development process should be used only *in extremis:* it is simply too expensive. Some hope is held out—as usual— that the future development of tools may somehow improve matters. We shall argue that proofs may be structured in such a way that the burden of carrying them out is dramatically reduced. By considering the theory of proofs in Z, we shall propose some techniques that make the prospect of *routine* proofs a reality.

2   Compositionality

The Holy Grail for those interested in proof is a compositional proof system: that is, one where proofs about composite objects may be built from proofs about constituent parts. A composite object that occurs often in Z specifications is an operation defined as the disjunction of several partial behaviours. For example, Op may behave either as described by Op_1, or as described by Op_2

$$Op \mathrel{\widehat{=}} Op_1 \vee Op_2$$

In order to calculate the precondition of Op, we need only calculate the preconditions of Op_1 and of Op_2 and disjoin them, since pre is a disjunctive operator

$$\mathrm{pre}\,Op \equiv \mathrm{pre}\,Op_1 \vee \mathrm{pre}\,Op_2$$

The proof technique here is certainly compositional, and this is because calculating the precondition is simply existentially quantifying after-variables, and existential quantification distributes through disjunction.

The situation is obviously not so satisfactory if we have

$$Op \ \widehat{=} \ Op_1 \wedge Op_2$$

since pre does not, in general, distribute through conjunction. This does not matter if our specifications of operations never contain conjunction, but this is not our experience. In Z there is an elegant device known as *promotion* or *framing* which is used to produce layered descriptions of systems; it was first worked out by Carroll Morgan and Bernard Sufrin to simplify their description of the UNIX filing system [Morgan & Sufrin, 1984]. It is an important device for reducing the complexity of a specification, so it would be a pity if it did not yield some technique for reducing the complexity of a proof. As we shall see, promotion uses conjunction, so if we are to manage our proofs, we shall have to find a proof rule that is compositional for this particular use of conjunction.

The next section presents as an example of promotion, the specification of an indexed file system.[1]

3   An Indexed File System

3.1   The System State

An indexed file stores records which are indexed by keys. We introduce the set of records and the set of keys as given sets: for the purposes of this specification we need to know no more about them

[*Record, Key*]

We can model a file as a partial function, since each key in a file must identify a record uniquely

---

[1]A complete account of this specification may be found in [Woodcock, 1989], although it has a longer history: it was first created by Jean-Raymond Abrial, and used in lectures by Ib Holm Sørensen, Ian Hayes, and Jim Woodcock.

```
┌─ File ──────────────────────────────────────────────
│ f : Key ↦ Record
└──────────────────────────────────────────────────────
```

A file is empty initially

```
┌─ FileInit ──────────────────────────────────────────
│ File'
├──────────────────────────────────────────────────────
│ f' = {}
└──────────────────────────────────────────────────────
```

Operations on a file must preserve the functionality of f

```
┌─ ΔFile ─────────────────────────────────────────────
│ File
│ File'
└──────────────────────────────────────────────────────
```

Interrogations of the state will have no side-effects

```
┌─ ΞFile ─────────────────────────────────────────────
│ ΔFile
├──────────────────────────────────────────────────────
│ θFile' = θFile
└──────────────────────────────────────────────────────
```

A record that is in a file may be read or written, providing that the key is given. Reading has no side-effects

```
┌─ Read₀ ─────────────────────────────────────────────
│ ΞFile
│ k? : Key
│ r! : Record
├──────────────────────────────────────────────────────
│ k? ∈ dom f
│ r! = f k?
└──────────────────────────────────────────────────────
```

Writing merely replaces the existing record stored under the key

$$
\begin{array}{|l}
\hline\ \_Write_0_____ \\
\Delta File \\
k? : Key \\
r? : Record \\
\hline
k? \in dom\ f \\
f' = f \oplus \{k? \mapsto r?\} \\
\hline
\end{array}
$$

A record may be added under a *new* key

$$
\begin{array}{|l}
\hline\ \_Add_0_____ \\
\Delta File \\
k? : Key \\
r? : Record \\
\hline
k? \notin dom\ f \\
f' = f \cup \{k? \mapsto r?\} \\
\hline
\end{array}
$$

Finally, a record stored under an existing key may be deleted

$$
\begin{array}{|l}
\hline\ \_Delete_0_____ \\
\Delta File \\
k? : Key \\
\hline
k? \in dom\ f \\
f' = \{k?\} \lhd f \\
\hline
\end{array}
$$

3.2 Errors for Individual Files

So far we have described only partial operations on particular files: we have specified what happens in successful operations. We must continue our descriptions to cover every eventuality, if we are to present a robust interface to our users. To do this we must carry out some investigation into the preconditions of our operations; that is, to which starting states do our descriptions apply? For example, the *Add* operation will add a new record under a new key in an existing file. If *Add* is unsuccessful, then an error report will be given. The possible reports are described by the following free data type

$Report ::= Ok \mid KeyAlreadyInFile \mid KeyNotInFile$

The errors on named files always involve a key and a report

```
┌─ Error ─────────────────────────────────────────
│ ΞFile
│ k? : Key
│ reply! : Report
└──────────────────────────────────────────────────
```

There are two sorts of errors that can arise on operations on individual files: the key might not exist when it should; and the key already exists when it shouldn't

```
┌─ KeyDoesntExist ────────────────────────────────
│ Error
│ ───────────────────────────────────────────────
│ k? ∉ dom f
│ reply! = KeyNotInFile
└──────────────────────────────────────────────────
```

```
┌─ KeyExists ─────────────────────────────────────
│ Error
│ ───────────────────────────────────────────────
│ k? ∈ dom f
│ reply! = KeyAlreadyInFile
└──────────────────────────────────────────────────
```

Successful operations always reply in the same way

```
┌─ Success ───────────────────────────────────────
│ reply! : Report
│ ───────────────────────────────────────────────
│ reply! = Ok
└──────────────────────────────────────────────────
```

Now we can describe the total interface for individual file operations

$$
\begin{aligned}
Read &\;\widehat{=}\; (Read_0 \wedge Success) \vee KeyDoesntExist \\
Write &\;\widehat{=}\; (Write_0 \wedge Success) \vee KeyDoesntExist \\
Add &\;\widehat{=}\; (Add_0 \wedge Success) \vee KeyExists \\
Delete &\;\widehat{=}\; (Delete_0 \wedge Success) \vee KeyDoesntExist
\end{aligned}
$$

These descriptions have been built up in a structured fashion from small components.

3.3 Named Files

Now we consider named files; names are drawn from the set

[Name]

The file system contains a number of named files, with each name referring to at most just a single file, and a set of *open* files, all of which must be known to the file system

$$\begin{array}{|l}
\_\_FSys_____ \\
fs : Name \nrightarrow File \\
open : \mathbf{P}\ Name \\
\hline
open \subseteq dom\ fs \\
\end{array}$$

Initially, the file system is empty

$$FSysInit \;\hat{=}\; [FSys' \mid fs' = \{\}]$$

Operation on the the file system's state include the schema

$$\Delta FSys \;\hat{=}\; FSys \wedge FSys'$$

The operations on individual files may be *promoted* to operate on an open file within the file system by

$$\begin{array}{|l}
\_\_FSysPromote_____ \\
\Delta FSys \\
fn? : Name \\
\Delta File \\
\hline
fn? \in open \\
\theta File = fs\ fn? \\
fs' = fs \oplus \{fn? \mapsto \theta File'\} \\
open' = open \\
\end{array}$$

The appropriate file, which must be open, is selected and updated by one of the operations on records in a file. The set of open files does not change.

The promoted operations are

$$FRead_0 \triangleq (Read \wedge FSysPromote) \setminus \Delta File$$
$$FWrite_0 \triangleq (Write \wedge FSysPromote) \setminus \Delta File$$
$$FAdd_0 \triangleq (Add \wedge FSysPromote) \setminus \Delta File$$
$$FDelete_0 \triangleq (Delete \wedge FSysPromote) \setminus \Delta File$$

4 Promotion and Abstraction

Promotion, as we have seen, is a way of taking the definitions of operations defined in a local context, and putting them into a larger, global context. In our example, the local context was simply an anonymous file; the global context was a named file within the file system. The details of reading, writing, adding, and deleting were all most conveniently described locally, without reference to other files in the system.

Promotion must satisfy an intuitive definition: a promotion is simply the translation of a local description into a wider context, *without changing the local description*. This local description is an abstraction, providing an abstract data type with its attendant operations. It provides a layer of the system description upon which we can build a more elaborate specification which captures more system properties. We can picture these layers in Figure 1. The outermost layer is the interface that we present to the user. We can enrich the system interface with new operations, such as *Create*, *Destroy*, *Open* and *Close*, all of which are operations on the file system, and none of which could therefore have been described at the inner layer.

The important thing about promotion is that it doesn't add any further constraints to the local state invariant. Recall that we specified how the *Read* operation behaves for an anonymous file. The next layer can use this description, *but must not change it;* if it did, then we would be violating the abstraction that we have created by layering the system. In summary, promotion must be monotonic with respect to data refinement.

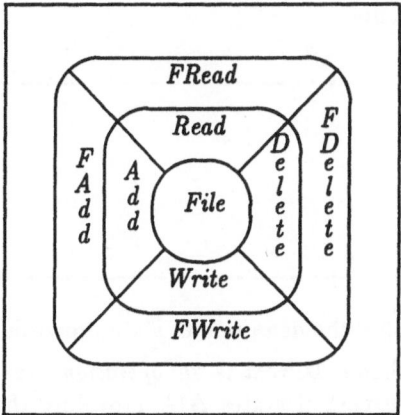

Figure 1: The onion skins of system development.

5 Proof Rules for Promotion

In order that we may understand promotion better, we must formalise it and find some of its general properties.

In the file system we saw an example of promoting an operation; we can also promote a state.

Definition 1 A schema *SProm* is a *state promotion* from state *L* to state *G*, providing that *SProm* includes both *L* and *G*, and that it has a functional inverse. For such a state promotion, we can find some function *f* of *G* such that

$$SProm \vdash \theta L = f(\theta G)$$

□

The definition of state promotion ensures that the local state is embedded in the global state in such a way that it can be extracted uniquely: local states don't become confused upon promotion. It also means that the promoted system can be thought of as a data refinement of the local system in the sense of [Jones, 1986]. In the definition of state promotion, *f* is the *retrieve function*.

For example, define

```
┌─ FSysSProm ──────────────────────────────
│ FSys
│ fn? : Name
│ File
├──────────────────────────────────────────
│ fn? ∈ open
│ θ File = fs fn?
└──────────────────────────────────────────
```

This obviously satisfies the definition of state promotion.

Definition 2 A schema *DProm* is an *operation promotion* from the pair of states ΔL to the pair of states ΔG, providing that *DProm* is a state promotion from L to G and L' to G', and that it is *total* with respect to L

$$DProm \setminus G' \equiv (\text{pre } DProm) \wedge L'$$

□

For example, define

```
┌─ FSysDProm ──────────────────────────────
│ FSysSProm
│ FSysSProm'[fn?/fn?']
├──────────────────────────────────────────
│ {fn?} ◁ fs' = {fn?} ◁ fs
│ open' = open
└──────────────────────────────────────────
```

Clearly we have that

$$FSysDProm \equiv FSysPromote$$

As we shall see later in Theorem 9, *FSysPromote* is an operation promotion.

In general, we talk about promoting a schema, and it will be clear in specific applications whether it is state or operation promotion.

We shall now prove four useful theorems about promotion: it is monotonic, and it distributes through disjunction, conjunction, and pre.

Theorem 1 Promotion is monotonic

$$\frac{\forall L \bullet P \Rightarrow Q}{\forall G \bullet (P \wedge Prom) \setminus L \Rightarrow (Q \wedge Prom) \setminus L}$$

Proof:

1	$\forall L \bullet P \Rightarrow Q$	[hypothesis]
2	$P \Rightarrow Q$	[1 $\forall$ Elim]
3	$P \wedge Prom$	[assumption]
4	P	[3 $\wedge$ Elim1]
5	Q	[2,4 $\Rightarrow$ Elim]
6	$Prom$	[3 $\wedge$ Elim2]
7	$Q \wedge Prom$	[5,6 $\wedge$ Intro]
8	$(Q \wedge Prom) \setminus L$	[7 $\exists$ Intro]
9	$(P \wedge Prom) \Rightarrow (Q \wedge Prom) \setminus L$	[3–8 $\Rightarrow$ Intro]
10	$\forall L \bullet (P \wedge Prom) \Rightarrow (Q \wedge Prom) \setminus L$	[9 $\forall$ Intro]
11	$(P \wedge Prom) \setminus L$	[assumption]
12	$(Q \wedge Prom) \setminus L$	[10,11 $\exists$ Elim]
13	$(P \wedge Prom) \setminus L \Rightarrow (Q \wedge Prom) \setminus L$	[11–12 $\Rightarrow$ Intro]
14	$\forall G \bullet (P \wedge Prom) \setminus L \Rightarrow (Q \wedge Prom) \setminus L$	[13 $\forall$ Intro]

QED

$\square$

This is an important theorem: it says that, for any property of a system, there is a promoted property of the promoted system.

Theorem 2 Promotion distributes through disjunction

$$((P \vee Q) \wedge Prom) \setminus L \equiv ((P \wedge Prom) \setminus L \vee (Q \wedge Prom) \setminus L)$$

Proof:

$$((P \vee Q) \wedge Prom) \setminus L$$
$$\equiv ((P \wedge Prom) \vee (Q \wedge Prom)) \setminus L \qquad [\wedge \text{ disjunctive}]$$
$$\equiv (P \wedge Prom) \setminus L \vee (Q \wedge Prom) \setminus L \qquad [\exists \text{ disjunctive}]$$

QED

□

Theorem 3 Promotion distributes through conjunction

$$(P \wedge Q \wedge Prom) \setminus L \equiv ((P \wedge Prom) \setminus L \wedge (Q \wedge Prom) \setminus L)$$

Proof:

$$
\begin{aligned}
&(P \wedge Q \wedge Prom) \setminus L \\
&\equiv (P \wedge Q \wedge Prom \wedge \theta L = f(\theta G)) \setminus L && \text{[by definition]} \\
&\equiv (P \wedge Q \wedge Prom)[f(\theta G)/\theta L] && \text{[one-point rule]} \\
&\equiv ((P \wedge Prom) \wedge (Q \wedge Prom))[f(\theta G)/\theta L] && \text{[properties of } \wedge] \\
&\equiv (P \wedge Prom)[f(\theta G)/\theta L] \wedge \\
&\quad (Q \wedge Prom)[f(\theta G)/\theta L] && \text{[distributivity of subst]} \\
&\equiv (P \wedge Prom \wedge \theta L = f(\theta G)) \setminus L \wedge \\
&\quad (Q \wedge Prom \wedge \theta L = f(\theta G)) \setminus L && \text{[one-point rule]} \\
&\equiv (P \wedge Prom) \setminus L \wedge (Q \wedge Prom) \setminus L && \text{[by definition]}
\end{aligned}
$$

QED

□

Theorem 4 Promotion distributes through pre

$$\text{pre } Op \equiv (\text{pre } LOp \wedge \text{pre } Promote) \setminus L$$

Proof:

$$
\begin{aligned}
&\text{pre } Op \\
&\equiv \text{pre}((LOp \wedge Promote) \setminus \Delta L) && \text{[by definition of } Op] \\
&\equiv (LOp \wedge Promote) \setminus G' \setminus \Delta L && \text{[by definition of pre]} \\
&\equiv (LOp \wedge (Promote \setminus G')) \setminus \Delta L && \text{[since } G' \text{ not free in } LOp] \\
&\equiv (LOp \wedge ((\text{pre } Promote) \wedge L')) \setminus \Delta L && \text{[by hypothesis]} \\
&\equiv (LOp \wedge \text{pre } Promote) \setminus \Delta L && \text{[since } LOp \text{ includes } L'] \\
&\equiv (LOp \wedge \text{pre } Promote) \setminus L' \setminus L && \text{[by definition of } \Delta L] \\
&\equiv ((LOp \setminus L') \wedge \text{pre } Promote) \setminus L && \text{[} L' \text{ not free in pre } Promote] \\
&\equiv (\text{pre } LOp \wedge \text{pre } Promote) \setminus L && \text{[by definition of pre]}
\end{aligned}
$$

QED

□

   This theorem really does describe distribution, since we could use the
equality that $\mathrm{pre}(\Delta L) \equiv L$ to rewrite it as

$$\mathrm{pre}\, Op \equiv (\mathrm{pre}\, LOp \wedge \mathrm{pre}\, Promote) \setminus \mathrm{pre}(\Delta L)$$

which is less usable, but has a very pleasant look to it.[2]

Corollary 1 The precondition of a promoted total operation is simply the
precondition of the promotion schema, projected onto the global state

$$\mathrm{pre}\, Op \equiv (\mathrm{pre}\, Promote)[f(\theta G)/\theta L]$$

Proof:

   $\mathrm{pre}\, Op$

$\equiv (\mathrm{pre}\, LOp \wedge \mathrm{pre}\, Promote) \setminus L$	[Theorem 4]
$\equiv (L \wedge \mathrm{pre}\, Promote) \setminus L$	[by hypothesis, LOp is total]
$\equiv (\mathrm{pre}\, Promote) \setminus L$	[idempotence of $\wedge$]
$\equiv (\mathrm{pre}\, Promote)[f(\theta G)/\theta L]$	[one point rule]

QED

□

6 The Correctness of the File System

We shall now apply our theory to the proof of correctness of the $FRead_0$
operation in the file system. First we shall calculate the preconditions of our
basic components: $Read_0, Success, KeyDoesntExist$.

Theorem 5 The precondition of $Read_0$ is that the state invariant holds, and
that the required key is in the file

$$\mathrm{pre}\, Read_0 \equiv [File; k? : Key \mid k? \in (dom\, f)]$$

---

[2]This observation—for which I am grateful—was made by Jeremy Jacob.

Proof:

pre $Read_0$
$\equiv$ [by definition]

$File$
$k? : Key$

$\exists\, File';\; r! : Record\; \bullet$
    $\theta File' = \theta File$
    $k? \in (dom\; f)$
    $r! = (f\; k?)$

Continuing with the predicate part of this

$\exists\, File';\; r! : Record\; \bullet$
    $\theta File' = \theta File \land k? \in (dom\; f) \land r! = (f\; k?)$
$\equiv$ [by definition of $File$]
    $\exists\, f' : Key \nrightarrow Record;\; r! : Record\; \bullet$
        $f' = f \land k? \in (dom\; f) \land r! = (f\; k?)$
$\equiv$ [by the 1-pt rule]
    $f \in Key \nrightarrow Record$
    $\exists\, r! : Record\; \bullet\; k? \in (dom\; f) \land r! = (f\; k?)$
$\equiv$ [by the 1-pt rule]
    $f \in Key \nrightarrow Record \land (f\; k?) \in Record \land k? \in (dom\; f)$
$\equiv$ [since $f \in X \nrightarrow Y \land x \in (dom\; f) \Rightarrow (f\; x) \in Y$]
    $f \in Key \nrightarrow Record \land k? \in (dom\; f)$
$\equiv$ [by the invariant on $File$]
    $k? \in (dom\; f)$

QED

$\square$

Theorem 6 The precondition of $Success$ is simply $true$

pre $Success \equiv [true]$

Proof:

    pre *Success*

$$\equiv [\exists \, reply! : Report \bullet reply! = Ok] \qquad \text{[by definition]}$$
$$\equiv [Ok \in Report] \qquad \text{[one point rule]}$$
$$\equiv [true] \qquad \text{[by definition]}$$

QED

□

Theorem 7 The precondition of *KeyDoesntExist* is that the state invariant holds, and that the required key is not to be found in the file

$$\text{pre } KeyDoesntExist \equiv [File;\ k? : Key \mid k? \notin (dom\ f)]$$

Proof:

    pre *KeyDoesntExist*

$\equiv$ [by definition and expansion]

File
k? : Key

$\exists f' : Key \rightarrowtail Record;\ reply! : Report \bullet$
    $f' = f$
    $k? \notin (dom\ f)$
    $reply! = KeyNotInFile$

Consider the predicate part

    $\exists f' : Key \rightarrowtail Record;\ reply! : Report \bullet$
        $f' = f \land k? \notin (dom\ f) \land reply! = KeyNotInFile$
    $\equiv$ [by two applications of the 1-pt rule]
        $f \in Key \rightarrowtail Record \land KeyNotInFile \in Report \land k? \notin (dom\ f)$
    $\equiv$ [by definition of *Report*]
        $f \in Key \rightarrowtail Record \land k? \notin (dom\ f)$
    $\equiv$ [by appeal to the state invariant]
        $k? \notin (dom\ f)$

Operation	Precondition
$Read_0$	$[File;\ k? : Key \mid k? \in dom\ f]$
$Success$	$[true]$
$KeyDoesntExist$	$[File;\ k? : Key \mid k? \notin dom\ f]$

Figure 2: Summary of Preconditions.

QED

□

Figure 2 summarises the results so far.

Now we shall present a simple, but nevertheless useful, result about *Success*, and then show that *FSysPromote* is a promotion, generating as we do so the precondition of *FSysPromote*.

Theorem 8 *Success* is promoted by any other operation. For any operation *AOp* on any state S, we have that

$$\mathrm{pre}(Success \wedge AOp) \equiv \mathrm{pre}\,AOp$$

Proof: First, AOp is a promotion with respect to the empty state $[true]$:

$AOp \setminus S$
$\qquad \equiv \mathrm{pre}\,AOp$ $\hfill$ [by definition]
$\qquad \equiv (\mathrm{pre}\,AOp) \wedge [true]$ $\hfill$ [property of schema $\wedge$]

Thus

$\mathrm{pre}(Success \wedge AOp)$
$\qquad \equiv \mathrm{pre}((Success \wedge AOp) \setminus [true])$ $\hfill$ [property of schema $\setminus$]
$\qquad \equiv (\mathrm{pre}\,AOp) \setminus [true]$ $\hfill$ [Corollary 1]
$\qquad \equiv \mathrm{pre}\,AOp$ $\hfill$ [property of schema $\setminus$]

QED

□

Theorem 9 *FSysPromote* is a promotion

$$FSysPromote \setminus FSys' \equiv (\text{pre } FSysPromote) \wedge File'$$

Proof:

$$FSysPromote \setminus FSys' \equiv$$

FSys
fn? : *Name*
$\Delta File$

$\exists FSys' \bullet$
      fn? $\in$ *open*
      $\theta File = fs\ fn?$
      $fs' = fs \oplus \{fn? \mapsto \theta File'\}$
      $open' = open$

Continuing with the predicate part of this

$\exists FSys' \bullet fn? \in open \wedge \theta File = fs\ fn? \wedge$
      $fs' = fs \oplus \{fn? \mapsto \theta File'\} \wedge open' = open$
      $\equiv$ [by definition]
      $\exists fs' : Name \nrightarrow File;\ open' : \mathbb{P}\ Name \bullet$
          $open' \subseteq dom\ fs' \wedge fn? \in open \wedge \theta File = fs\ fn? \wedge$
          $fs' = fs \oplus \{fn? \mapsto \theta File'\} \wedge open' = open$
      $\equiv$ [by the one point rule]
      $fs \oplus \{fn? \mapsto \theta File'\} \in Name \nrightarrow File \wedge open \in \mathbb{P}\ Name \wedge$
      $open \subseteq dom\ (fs \oplus \{fn? \mapsto \theta File'\}) \wedge fn? \in open \wedge \theta File = fs\ fn?$

By the state invariant on *FSys*, we have that $fs \in Name \nrightarrow File$, and from the declaration of *fn?* and the state invariant on *File'*, we have that $\{fn? \mapsto \theta File'\} \in Name \nrightarrow File$. Therefore $fs \oplus \{fn? \mapsto \theta File'\} \in Name \nrightarrow File$. From the declaration of *open*, we have that $open \in \mathbb{P}\ Name$. Thus our predicate is reduced to

$$open \subseteq dom\ (fs \oplus \{fn? \mapsto \theta File'\}) \wedge fn? \in open \wedge \theta File = fs\ fn?$$
      $\equiv$ [since $open \subseteq dom\ fs$]
      $fn? \in open \wedge \theta File = fs\ fn?$

Thus we have

(pre $FSysPromote$) $\wedge$ $File'$

$\equiv (FSysPromote \setminus FSys' \setminus File') \wedge File'$

$\equiv [FSys; fn? : Name; \Delta File \mid$
  $fn? \in open \wedge \theta File = fs\ fn?] \setminus File' \wedge File'$

$\equiv [FSys; fn? : Name; File \mid fn? \in open \wedge \theta File = fs\ fn?] \wedge File'$

$\equiv [FSys; fn? : Name; \Delta File \mid fn? \in open \wedge \theta File = fs\ fn?]$

$\equiv FSysPromote \setminus FSys'$

QED

$\square$

Corollary 2 The precondition for the promotion schema is

pre $FSysPromote$
  $\equiv [FSys; fn? : Name; File \mid fn? \in open \wedge \theta File = fs\ fn?]$

Proof: Derived from Theorem 9. $\square$

Finally, we are in a position where we can calculate the preconditions of $Read$ and $FRead_0$.

Theorem 10 $Read$ is a total operation

pre $Read \equiv [File; k? : Key]$

Proof:

pre $Read$

$\equiv \text{pre}((Read_0 \wedge Success) \vee KeyDoesntExist)$ [def of $Read$]

$\equiv \text{pre}(Read_0 \wedge Success) \vee$ [pre disjunctive]
  pre $KeyDoesntExist$

$\equiv \text{pre}\ Read_0 \vee \text{pre}\ KeyDoesntExist$ [Theorem 8]

$\equiv [File; k? : Key \mid k? \in (dom\ f)] \vee$ [from above]
  $[File; k? : Key \mid k? \notin (dom\ f)]$

$\equiv [File; k? : Key \mid$ [schema disjunction]
  $k? \in (dom\ f) \vee k? \notin (dom\ f)]$

$\equiv [File; k? : Key \mid true]$ [Law of the excluded middle]

QED

□

Since *Read* is a total operation, and *FSysPromote* is a promotion, we need only the precondition of *FSysPromote*, with *File* hidden, to calculate the precondition of $FRead_0$.

Theorem 11 The precondition of $FRead_0$ is that the state invariant holds, and that the chosen file is open

$$\text{pre } FRead_0 \equiv [FSys; \ k? : Key; \ fn? : Name \mid fn? \in open]$$

Proof:

$\text{pre } FRead_0$

$\equiv \text{pre}((Read \wedge FSysPromote) \setminus (\Delta File))$ [by definition]

$\equiv (\text{pre } FSysPromote) \setminus File$ [Theorems 9, 10, Corollary 1]

$\equiv [FSys; \ fn? : Name; \ File \mid$
      $fn? \in open \wedge \theta File = fs \ fn?] \setminus File$ [Corollary 2]

$\equiv [FSys; \ fn? : Name \mid fn? \in open \wedge fs \ fn? \in File]$ [one point rule]

$\equiv [FSys; \ fn? : Name \mid fn? \in open]$

since $fs : Name \nrightarrow File$, and $fn? \in open \subseteq dom \ fs$.

QED

□

7 Discussion

In the last section we calculated the precondition of $FRead_0$, using a number of small proofs. The only part of the calculation that is not reusable in the rest of the proofs is the calculation of the precondition of $Read_0$. In order to calculate the preconditions of $FWrite_0$, $FAdd_0$, and $FDelete_0$, we need first to calculate the preconditions of $Write_0$, Add_0, $Delete_0$, and $KeyExists$. These calculations are all of the same size as Theorem 5. Next, we need to combine these results in the manner of Theorem 11, using the results about *Success* and *FSysPromote*. It is clear that a great economy has been achieved using the laws of promotion and the schema operators. It is hoped that they will help to make proofs, and therefore software development, more manageable.

The technique of promotion has been known in the Z community for at least eight years; however, this paper contains the first formal analysis of the technique. The observation of the connection between promotion and data refinement is new, and promises much in the way of future research. It offers a way of calculating data refinements, and calculation is always better than proof. The notion of data refinement here is similar to that in [Jones, 1986], in the sense that it is functional from the concrete (promoted) state to the abstract one. Perhaps the VDM community can also find something useful in these ideas.

The form of promotion $((P \wedge Prom) \setminus S)$ is identical to the form of the representation transformer in [Gardiner & Morgan, 1988]. They prove there that data refinement distributes through the program combinators; in this paper, we have shown that data refinement (promotion) distributes through the *specification* combinators, and these results are new.

Acknowledgments

I thank Paul Gardiner, Ian Hayes, Jeremy Jacob, Steve King, Jock McDoowi, and Carroll Morgan for their comments on an earlier draft.

This paper has been produced as a contribution to the joint IBM-Oxford collaboration, which is applying Z to the development of CICS, and IBM's support is gratefully acknowledged. The technical ideas in this paper came about during the author's time as Gastprofessor at the University of Klagenfurt in Austria, supported by the Austrian Ministry of Science and the British Council. I thank the Rutherford-Appleton Laboratory for providing me with an Atlas Research Fellowship.

8   References

1. P. Gardiner & C. Morgan, "Data Refinement of Predicate Transformers", *in* C. Morgan, K. Robinson & P. Gardiner, *On the Refinement Calculus,* Technical Monograph PRG-70, Programming Research Group, (1988).

2. I. Hayes (editor), *Specification Case Studies*, Prentice-Hall International, (1987).

3. C.B. Jones, *Systematic Software Development Using VDM*, Prentice-Hall International, (1986).

4. C.C. Morgan, *Programming from Specifications*, Prentice-Hall International, (1990). *in press*

5. C.C. Morgan & B.A. Sufrin, "Specification of the UNIX filing system", *IEEE Transactions of Software Engineering*, 1984, **SE-10**(2), 128–142.

6. J.M. Spivey, *Understanding Z: A Specification Language and its Formal Semantics*, Cambridge Tracts in Theoretical Computer Science, **3**, (1988).

7. J.M. Spivey, *The Z Notation: A Reference Manual*, Prentice-Hall International, (1989).

8. J.C.P. Woodcock, *Using Z: Specification, Refinement & Proof*, draft book, Programming Research Group, 1989.